From Baudelaire to Surrealism

Peint et Gravé par Manet 1862.

Imp. A. Salmon.

Baudelaire by M

Marcel Raymond/FROM BAUDELAIRE
TO SURREALISM/*translated from the French*

METHUEN & CO LTD
11 New Fetter Lane · London EC4

First published as De Baudelaire au Surrealisme *1933*
First English translation 1950
First published as a University Paperback 1970
Bibliography © 1970 S. I. Lockerbie
Filmset by St Paul's Press Ltd, Malta
Printed in Great Britain
by Cox & Wyman Ltd, Fakenham, Norfolk

SBN 416 27950 3

Distributed in USA
by Barnes & Noble Inc.

Contents

Book III: Adventure and Revolt

Foreword

It seems to me that since Romanticism, poetry has followed a very definite line of development which I hope will be apparent throughout this study. The chapters of this book are organized in terms of the principal aim of the moderns: to grasp poetry in its essence. The reader will not find in it a complete treatment of the poetry written in our century nor anything like a gallery of portraits; I apologize for this to so many poets whom I hold in high esteem and would have liked to quote in these pages.

If I am accused of partiality in my judgments, I will say in my defense that I have always endeavored to take the side of poetry.

Marcel Raymond

1933

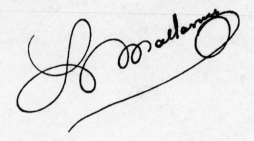

1862.

Stéphane Mallarmé

exprimez tous mes Compliments.

Stéphane Mallarmé

Mardi 30 Août 1887

Mallarmé's Signature

Introduction

1.

Les Fleurs du Mal is generally considered one of the well-springs of modern poetry. One stream, which flowed out of it, that of the "artists," is said to lead from Baudelaire to Mallarmé, and then to Valéry; another stream, that of the "seers," from Baudelaire to Rimbaud, and thence to the latest comers among the seekers for adventure. Approximate though it may be, this view seems acceptable. By the almost desperate boldness of their ambitions, by the radiant beauty of some of their poems—not to mention the magnetism of their personalities—the great lyric poets of the latter half of the nineteenth century still hold us under an almost irresistible spell. But to find the origins of contemporary poetry and to understand its profound significance one must go farther back than Baudelaire, Hugo and Lamartine, one must go back to the pre-romantic period.

An explosion of the irrational elements in the human personality had occurred in the era of the Counter-Reformation and Baroque art, but at that time the Church had determined the course of the mystical upsurge without much difficulty. Two centuries later, after the critique of the "philosophers," she was no longer in the same commanding position. It was the task of art (but not of art alone) to gratify some of the human demands that religion had thus far been able to exorcise.

From then on poetry tended to become an ethic or some sort of irregular instrument of metaphysical knowledge. Poets were obsessed by the need to "change life," as Rimbaud puts it, to change man and to bring him into direct contact with existence. The novelty lies less in the fact than in the intention, which gradually emerges from the realm of the unconscious, of reconquering man's irrational powers and of transcending the dualism of the self and the universe. To find out why this conscious aim awakened at a particular moment of history, the end of the eighteenth century, we would have to examine the situation of the writer and the poet in modern civilization. Is it an accident that modern civilization—which in many respects embodies the doctrines that were popularized for the first time in the *Encyclopédie*—should have crystallized at exactly the same time as Romanticism? Since then it has become increasingly identified with a rational and positivistic view of the world and of life, and its constraint on the human mind—a kind of demurrer against the unconscious—has been increasingly more violent. Because it separated man from the universe and from a part of himself, that is, from his nonrational powers (and this at the very moment when Christianity was losing its sway over men's souls and no longer offered them the path of personal salvation), it aggravated to an almost intolerable degree the natural discordance between the total exigencies of the mind and the limited existence that is the lot of man.

From that time on then, the poets, in so far as they conceived of the poetic act as a vital operation, have performed a compensatory function in our society. Though poetry is one of the available means of securing communication with what Goethe called "The Mothers," it is also the manifestation of a permanent human aspiration. But in a period when only the "real" is looked upon as knowable, and when this aspiration is constantly being frustrated, the transitions from the unconscious to the conscious are effected in unaccustomed ways, and the need for a complete existence assumes a metaphysical form.

It is in Germany that these movements first rose up to oppose the rationalism of the Englightenment, and that a number of individual experiences, distinct from one another but of identical meaning, produced the extraordinary and admirable works that bear the names of Novalis, Jean-Paul, Hoffmann, Arnim, and others, thus tracing on the sky of Europe the legendary constellation of German Romanticism. In France, Albert Béguin's great work has made the whole world of letters familiar with the origins and scope of this important movement. We may also mention the parallel effort of the British poets from the visionary Blake to Coleridge and Shelley, and of the American Poe.

But our purpose here is not to write history. It is not our task to determine causal relationships or to define filiations and influences. Our task is to discern the essential features of an adventure or drama in which a number of privileged beings have taken part, to record the premises of a dialectic that has developed and fulfilled itself in the course of human history, tracing on the spiritual plane an ideal cycle of acts and aspirations that reveal a mysterious coherence.

If we now turn to France and Rousseau, it is not to designate Rousseau as the forerunner and preceptor of the poets of our time. Surely, Jean-Jacques has nothing of the magician or the conquering metaphysician; however, it is in him that there first appears a very special moral and mystical climate, the very climate that was to encourage the effort of the spirit to break its fetters and to make poetry a *vital* action.

The powerful sense of nature, almost divested of the picturesque, that appears in the Fifth Promenade of *Rêveries*, seems to have been born of a progressive fusion of spirit and nature—the self has come into possession of its unconscious forces and assimilated the inanimate, while inanimate things have "fixated the senses" of the dreamer. The borderline between the subjective and the objective is effaced; the universe is again subjected to the control of spirit; the mind "participates" (in Lévy-Bruhl's sense) in all forms and beings; the life of the landscape is perceived, or more accurately, felt from the inside: "the sound of the waves and the agitation of the water," the tide and ebb, produce a rhythm that is no longer distinguished from that of the heart, of the blood. But soon Narcissus, withdrawn into himself, no longer even desires to see himself; only the confused and delicious sense of existence survives in his ecstasy. "What does one enjoy in such a situation? Nothing outside oneself, nothing except oneself and one's own existence; so long as this state endures, one is self-sufficient like God." For opposition to the world has been renounced, and the self can no longer be distinguished from the cosmos. It is a natural mystical experience; the "great Being" that Rousseau continues to call God, is the universal immanent life which he feels in himself as a rising tide. (It is true that if he agrees to be absorbed in this being, it is because all the veins of this infinity seem to end in his heart.)

This state of happiness, "perfect and complete," ineffable as such, is also ephemeral. When it is gone, man is left with an even more acute awareness of his limitations and of the precariousness of his life. He will not rest until he has again forced the gates of Paradise, or if this is impossible, until he has profited from these revelations. While experiencing ecstasy, he cannot find words to express it; but the memory of it brings fitting words to his mind; images sparkle like foam on a wave. The soul engages in a kind of game, but aspires to an activity that is more elevated than any game, however noble—aspires to re-create its lost happiness by means of the *word*. And the function of these images, whose elements are borrowed from the dust of sensation, is not to describe external objects, but to prolong or to revive the original ecstasy. "In this state of illusion," says Novalis, "it is less the subject who perceives the object than conversely, the objects which come to perceive themselves in the subject." Every image secretly organizes itself into a symbol. Words are no longer signs; they participate in the objects, in the psychic realities they evoke.

While the classical writer, bent upon self-knowledge, relied on introspection and transposed the results of his observations to the plane of discursive intelligence, the romantic poet renounced all insights that did not convey a sense and an enjoyment of himself—and a sense of the universe experienced as a presence—and expected his imagination to compose a metaphorical, symbolic portrait of himself in his metamorphoses. That is the core of the new mode of expression inaugurated by Rousseau and Chateaubriand—a mode of expression which is natural, and even direct, despite appearances to the contrary, and which is superior to the analytical mode of expression in that it restores some of the most ancient prerogatives of language, the very prerogatives that Baudelaire attempted to exploit in order to make poetry a "suggestive magic."

"To release one's soul," to rediscover "the state of nature"— what ultimately was this hope, if not the consequence of an age-old dream, half-submerged in the unconscious, the dream of a *magical* universe in which man would not feel himself distinct from things, in which the spirit would rule directly over phenomena, without rational mediation.

It is well known that the romanticism of the poets of the 1820's and 1830's was born of a compromise between the inherited classical modes of thinking and writing, and the summons from the depths to which Rousseau had responded. Moreover, in the bour-geois, industrial world of Louis-Philippe, those who were unwilling to "serve" were an object of distrust. The greatest men of this epoch wanted to be useful to mankind. At the same time, another transformation of primitive romanticism was paving the way for the descriptive literature of the Parnassian school. It was a far cry from the poetry inaugurated by Rousseau and Chateaubriand, and grounded in a sense of the reciprocal penetration of spirit and nature, to the art of poetic painting, as it was later practiced by Gautier who tried to achieve objectivity. But these two deviations from romanticism are similar in some respects: the Parnassian of the Second Empire, like the social-minded poet of 1840, turned away from the "inner abyss" to which Olympio refers; both looked toward the illumined zones of consciousness, the social-minded poet wrote of general feelings, communicable to the masses, while the Parnassian set himself in opposition to the external world in order to obtain a better and more impassive view of its forms and colors. Finally, since their intention was to describe objects or communicate insights both contented themselves with the didactic tone and patterns of rational speech. Nerval alone advanced as far as the land from which there is no return and he did so with an ever-increasing boldness that reminds one of Novalis. His will to go on to the end, to force the ivory gates, to entrust his destiny to poetry—all this to the point of insanity—was unprecedented, a transcending of frontiers in the very heart of France. Between dream and life, the poet seeks his path, and a kind of new equilib-rium that would be natural and normal; night and day, the invisible and the visible have equal claim to his interest and form two complementary worlds, two harmonized modes of essential reality. "I believe that the human imagination has invented nothing that is not true" is a fine statement; but for Nerval, the visible world is true also, by a second truth, which is that of the dream. I am pleased to see that André Breton, in these recent years, has more urgently explored this twofold picture of dream and life which have mutually corresponding symbols, and that he has lingered in that region of the mind where Nerval had preceded him.

As for Hugo, he was still generally misunderstood in 1860 despite all his fame. The picturesque Hugo, the sentimental Hugo had won acclaim; the public cherished the poet of freedom, of humanity, the "epic National Guard." But the visionary, the prophet, the primitive found no following whatever, and was instinctively shunned— even today, the majority of his admirers are unaware of this aspect of Hugo. True, Baudelaire discerned in him "the man most gifted, most obviously chosen to express the *mystery of life*," and Rimbaud admitted that Hugo "in his last volumes did actually *see*," but countless critics refused to admit that the author of *Bouche d'Ombre* could even for a moment *believe* in his metaphors and that his frantic plunges into the realm of the imaginary were for him anything more than a marvelous game. Following the *Contemplations* and the *Légende*, the posthumous publication of the great mystical poems, *La Fin de Satan* and *Dieu*, cast a belated light on the fissure that had opened long years before in the very center of this laurel-crowned, then banished, poet's personality, and later deepened to an abyss, in the depths of which the dreamer carried on his "eternal adventure," and his unwearying eye discovered many things in "the shadow formed by the absence of God," to use the words of Claudel. To-day we interpret all of Hugo's life in terms of these ultimate revelations. He holds greater interest for us than ever since we know that for many years he was only waiting to yield to the spirits! And his genius bears witness to his calling which was to lend the forces of nature a voice, the "august voice" (that of the possessed, self-alienated poet) of Paul Valéry's "Pythian priestess,"

> *Qui se connaît quand elle sonne*
> *N'être plus la voix de personne*
> *Tant que des ondes et des bois!*

> Which knows when it speaks
> That it is not the voice of any man
> But of the waves and woods!

But this Hugo, I repeat, was barely emerging from the mist. At the end of the last century, the sophisticates, as they glanced through his poems, were overwhelmed by the rhetoric which he claimed to have done away with, but which had avenged itself by afflicting him with a monstrous verbal incontinence; cultivated opinion was sure that it had a thorough knowledge of this highly overrated poet and was turning away from him, and official critics (Faguet, among others), without understanding of the very essence of poetry, naïvely accused him of having commonplace ideas, if any.*

It is the extraordinary complexity of the "human soul" in Baudelaire, and his success in voicing some of the most violent postulates of romanticism, that primarily account for his influence. Divided between the desire to rise to the contemplation of the "thrones and dominations" and the need to taste the heady liquors of sin; alternately, and sometimes simultaneously, attracted and repelled by opposite extremes—love calling forth hate and feeding upon it—the poet tormented by this cruel affective ambivalence, ended by becoming immobilized at the center of himself, and surrendered to a kind of ecstatic horror. "Absolute frankness, an instrument of originality"—true enough, but before becoming an artistic instrument, this "frankness" answered an imperious need in Baudelaire, the need to go to the very end of the potentialities of his being and to cultivate exceptional states of mind. "All the elegiacs are scoundrels," he said, refusing to see in them anything other than men engaged in fooling themselves. He was spiritualist and materialist all in one, a slave of his body and of his "obscure perceptions." Moreover, breaking with conventional morality and psychology, he accepted the close interrelation between the physical and the spiritual as an evident fact, and in his poetry he exploited the consequences of this fact. A perfume "charged with apathy" had power to fetter all his powers and "change his soul." This deep feeling for the long unsuspected kinship between the highest and the lowest regions of the mind, between the demands of the unconscious and man's superior aspirations, in brief, this awareness of the unity of psychic life, is one of the most important revelations of Baudelaire's poetry.

However—and this is a symptom of the affective ambivalence we have mentioned—the poet conceived a strong aversion from this "body and this heart" to which he nevertheless was almost lovingly attached; "horror of life, ecstasy of life," he writes with terrible lucidity. Thus he is condemned to perpetual dissatisfaction, forced to overburden his tired constitution, and endlessly to seek new means of forgetting "the horrible burden of time." The normal

*An exception to this judgement is to be found in G. Saintsbury's *Short History of French Literature*, Oxford, 1884, p. 521–527. (Publisher's note.)

conditions of earthly life could bring him no pleasure that was not soon changed into pain, and only by forgetting a deplorably relative world could he raise himself for a moment above the gray lands of boredom. His story is told in the first lines of *The Voyage* and the motto at its end: "To the depths of the unknown to find the new!"

But this drama involves more than a sick and strange personality; through his mad desire to touch land "anywhere outside the world," Baudelaire raised the romantic theme of revolt and evasion to a tragic level. The secret of the crucial influence of his work on modern sensibility must be sought in the fundamental harmony, so long unperceived, between the feelings and aspirations to which he gave form, and the obscure, yearning soul of his century.* "Romanticism of the lower depths," someone has said of him; we shall retain this epithet, but with the emphasis on "depths," on that which relates to the very marrow of existence. Consequently, *Les Fleurs du Mal* must not be regarded as merely a conscious illustration of the poetics of art for art's sake,† nor can it be explained by a deliberate intention to something different from Lamartine, Musset, Vigny, and Hugo, as has recently been claimed by Paul

---

*I cannot refrain from quoting in this context the following lines by Robert Vivier *L'Originalité de Ch. Baudelaire*, Paris, 1926, p. 314: *From the abortive currents of romanticism [Baudelaire] took over elements which had not yet achieved full literary expression. These were, to begin with, a certain exotic dream, charged with indolent voluptuousness, that was anticipated in the eighteenth century by Parny and Bertin; the "spleen" foreshadowed by Gautier, Sainte-Beuve, O'Neddy; the rebellious sarcasm in which Baudelaire froze and hardened the over-simple revolt of a Borel; the atmosphere, both commonplace and profound, in which the humblest objects reveal the eternal tragedy, the atmosphere of* Les Tableaux parisiens, *anticipated in some cases in* Les Poésies de Joseph Delorme. *Finally we must speak of that furious and desperate appetite for death which, beginning in the gloomy early outpourings of English romanticism and maturing with the majestic orchestration of melancholy by Chateaubriand and Lamartine, gained such currency between 1830 and 1840. Baudelaire incorporated all these elements in his work and gave them the place and prominence determined by the needs of his inspiration.*

For my part, I believe that Baudelaire found these dreams, this "spleen," these "elements," primarily in himself.

†Once again it seems necessary to quote this irrefutable passage: *In this atrocious book, I have put all my heart, all my tenderness, all my religion (travestied), all my hate. True, I shall write the opposite, I shall swear by all that is sacred that it is a book of pure art . . .*

Valéry who is always inclined to see premeditation and calculation in his fellow man. Their moral and philosophical (in the broad sense) content must not be neglected. If there is an element of play in Baudelaire, it is no innocent game he is playing.

But the moralist in Baudelaire was able to free himself—temporarily—from his anxieties only with the help of the artist, who was half of his soul. "Passionately in love with passion and coldly determined to find the means of expressing it," thus Baudelaire defined Delacroix, and defined himself at the same time; this accounts for his frequent insistence, inspired or not by Edgar Allan Poe, that lucid workmanship is the chief element in the creation of a poem. Thus it came about that we have today an aesthetic tradition founded by *Les Fleurs du Mal* (a tradition later developed by Mallarmé) which includes poets for whom the human adventure lived by Baudelaire probably remains nothing but a "curio."

2.

Let us recall some of the current problems arising from this artistic tradition that Baudelaire originated.

In the first place, there is the idea that it is essential to purify poetry, to eliminate the dross, the *impedimenta* which tarnish its brilliance or encumber its movement in most works of the past, so as to preserve only the spiritual fluid or high tension current that will convey the suggestive powers inherent in poetry with the highest chance of success. In a famous passage in *l'Art romantique* (article on Th. Gautier), Baudelaire, following in Poe's footsteps, distinguishes the poetry of passion, "which is the drunkenness of the heart" from that of truth, "which is the food of reason," and attacks the "heresy of didacticism," which chains poetry to the earth, to prose, captures our *intellectual* attention and thwarts the "rapture of the soul," the "human aspiration to a superior beauty," which remains the goal and principle of poetry. He admits that concepts and feelings can enter into the work as indispensable raw material, but maintains that they can become effective conductors of the poetic fluid only after undergoing a real transsubstantiation, after being penetrated by a psychic "influx" that changes their nature.

Recently, this theory, which ascribes to art the power of achieving a mysterious catharsis, has been eloquently expounded by Abbé

Brémond, who adduces a good deal of evidence in its favor, mostly from Anglo-Saxon poetry. According to André Ferran, Baudelaire the aesthetician, the disciple of Poe, also learned from Coleridge and from the early English romantics. This is true; but one must distinguish between theory and practice; Poe, like many of his compatriots, is a Platonic and seraphic poet, whereas the author of *Les Fleurs du Mal* (whose original title was *Les Limbes*) creates a more human beauty not always free from passion, and sometimes plunges into an atmosphere that is more infernal than paradisiac. The moral complexes that constituted the core of his nature would doubtless have prevented him from developing into a completely "pure" poet. But whether the spiritualist explanation of Brémond is accepted or not, Baudelaire's poetry appears to be much less sentimental and much more clearly "psychic" than that of the early romantics; addressed less to the "heart" than to the "soul," it aims at stirring the darker regions of the mind, the regions beyond our sensibility.

On the other hand, Baudelaire assumes an extremely significant attitude toward outward nature. He regards it not as a reality existing in itself and for itself, but as an immense reservoir of analogies and as a kind of stimulant for the imagination. "The whole visible universe," he writes, "is only a store of images and signs to which the imagination accords a relative place and value; it is a kind of fodder that the imagination must digest and transform" (*Art romantique*, study on Delacroix). It follows that we must regard Creation as an ensemble of figures to be deciphered just as Lavater looked on man's features as a sign from which his character could be read, or as a mystical allegory (Baudelaire says: "a forest of symbols") whose hidden meaning must be discovered. The knowledge of this true, real meaning of things, which are only a part of what they signify, enables some privileged men—specifically, the predestined poets—to penetrate the spiritual beyond that envelops the visible universe, and move about in it with ease. "For all that is visible," says Novalis, "rests on an invisible foundation, all that is audible, on an inaudible foundation, and all that is tangible on an impalpable foundation." The important thing about perceptions is that they can, in some cases, help us to communicate with the occult. Baudelaire is referring here to the tradition of occultism, rejuvenated by Swedenborg, to which Hoffmann, Lavater, Nerval,

Balzac, Fourier also belonged. All of them guided him in the elaboration of that mystical philosophy, that strange syncretism which he seems to have professed, though without sacrificing his poetic freedom.

What form does this freedom take? It is the function of the imagination, Baudelaire tells us, to give images and symbols "a relative place and value"—relative to the human mind, to the work that he decides to accomplish. With the help of the disordered material supplied by his perception or memory, the poet creates an order that is the *infallible* expression of his soul* in relation to a specific moment or condition, to "the actual circumstance" (if such an ideal can ever be attained). And this expression—although the elements forming it seem to relate to natural things—will none the less be essentially supernatural. For the soul, by virtue of its origin and destiny, finds its true homeland only in the spiritual beyond in which nature is rooted. The mission of poetry is to open a window on this other world, which is actually our world, to enable the self to escape from its limitations and to expand to the infinite. This expansion prepares or effects a return to the unity of the spirit.

To understand how Baudelaire proceeds to cut himself a path in the world of analogies and to arrange and order the material supplied him by nature, let us reread the sonnet *Correspondances*:

> La Nature est un temple où de vivants piliers
> Laissent parfois sortir de confuses paroles;
> L'homme y passe à travers des forêts de symboles
> Qui l'observent avec des regards familiers.
>
> Comme de longs échos qui de loin se confondent
> Dans une ténébreuse et profonde unité,
> Vaste comme la nuit et comme la clarté,
> Les parfums, les couleurs et les sons se répondent.
>
> Il est des parfums frais comme des chairs d'enfants,
> Doux comme les hautbois, verts comme les prairies,
> —Et d'autres, corrompus, riches et triomphants,

---

*In the best poets there is no metaphor, no comparison or epithet that is not a mathematically exact adaptation to the actual circumstance, because these comparisons, metaphors, and epithets are drawn from the inexhaustible store of universal analogy, and because they cannot be drawn from elsewhere (Art romantique, article on Victor Hugo).

Ayant l'expansion des choses infinies,
Comme l'ambre, le music, le benjoin et l'encens,
Qui chantent les transports de l'esprit et des sens.

Nature is a temple whose living pillars
Sometimes give forth indistinct words;
In it man passes through forests of symbols
Which watch him with familiar glances.

Like long echoes which from a distance fuse
In a dark and profound unity,
Vast as the night and as the radiance of day,
Perfumes, colors, and sounds respond to one another.

There are perfumes fresh as a child's skin,
Sweet as oboes, green as meadows,
And others, corrupt, rich, triumphant,

Having the expansion of infinite things,
Like amber, musk, balsam, and frankincense,
Which sing the raptures of the spirit and the senses.*

Consequently, the poet's task is to follow an intuitive sense with which he is endowed and to perceive analogies, correspondences, which assume the literary aspect of the metaphor, the symbol, the comparison, or the allegory. On the basis of the sonnet quoted here, these correspondences seem to develop on three planes:

(1) There are equivalences between the data of the various senses—scents, colors, sounds, etc. Baudelaire alludes here to the phenomena of synesthesia, the best known of which are perhaps those of "colored audition." Association of this kind can occur spontaneously between sensations that do not belong to the same range, and this probably because they have a common affective tonality that logic in most cases cannot account for. A vast field is thus opened to the poet who will no longer feel bound to identify one form with another form and one sound with another sound, but will boldly use metaphors the terms of which evoke sensations of different orders. One may also anticipate another

*Among other passages relating to the *theory of correspondences*, we may mention the following lines: *Moreover Swedenborg ... has already taught us ... that everything, form, motion, number, color, scents, in the spiritual as well as in the natural realm, is significant, reciprocal, converse, corresponding ...* (*Art romantique*, article on Victor Hugo).

consequence that has often been illustrated in practice and that Baudelaire himself formulates as follows: "The arts aspire, if not to complement one another, at least to lend one another new energies."

(2) Since sensuous data can have "the expansion of infinite things," it follows that a desire, a regret, a thought—things of the mind—can awaken a corresponding symbol in the world of images (and vice versa). In *L'Invitation au voyage* (in prose), the poet, after describing an enchanted landscape, inquires of his companion: "Are you not framed in your analogy, and could you not contemplate yourself, as the mystics would say, in your own *correspondence*?" A little further, even more clearly: "These treasures, this furniture, this luxury; this order, these perfumes, these miraculous flowers, are you." The composition of such a "mental landscape" implies above all that "sense of nature" which we have mentioned before. From the world of the senses the poet takes the material in which to forge a symbolic vision of himself or of his dream; what he asks of the world of the senses is that it give him the means of expressing his soul.

(One of Baudelaire's great distinctions is to have made the urban landscape, houses, rooms, "interiors," objects of his contemplation, and to have perceived even in their shabbiness and incongruities, secret analogies with the contradiction in his own soul. In the crowd, "this vast wilderness of men," in the streets of the great city with its faces of stone and brick, the "solitary walker"* lost in a transformed, fabricated, unrecognizable nature, was no doubt the first man ever to abandon himself to what he calls a "sacred prostitution of the soul," and raise himself to that state of "universal communion" in which subject and object absorb one another.)

(3) Finally, what we see clearly is only the reverse side of people and things—this is asserted in the sonnet's first quatrain. Only a mind endowed with a kind of second sight can read appearances as signs and symbols and discern the reflections of the supra-sensible universe behind them. But if what we have said above is true, it must be noted at once that this third plane of correspondences comes so close to the second plane as almost to merge with it. For the soul

---

*Cf. *Les Foules*, in the prose poems. It is known that Baudelaire first intended to call his book *Le Promeneur solitaire*.

has a means of communicating with this occult beyond; there exists an intermediate common language which makes it possible for the macrocosm and microcosm, both spiritual in their essence, to reveal themselves and to recognize each other—this is the language of symbols, metaphors, analogies. What can be the purpose of nature but to give the soul an opportunity to see itself, and the supernatural an opportunity to manifest itself? At the end of the poet's meditation, the "dark and profound unity" is revealed to him; he is filled with the obscure foreboding that all things participate in, correspond with, one another, and are fundamentally in accord. The analogies, sometimes so strange, that force themselves upon him with the accent of indisputable evidence, are for him proofs of this primal unity. He fancies that he perceives in all beings a sign that bears witness to their kinship and to the secret imprint, as it were, of the primordial word.

"You are a lovely autumn sky, rose-colored, clear . . ." Let there be no mistake about it; this is, without doubt, more than a mere comparison, more than a mere literary identification. How can one assert that the poet did not, for only a second perhaps, have the revelation of a common essence, of a kind of magical identity? If he looks into his mind as into a mirror, if he tries to increase at any cost—and even by artifices—its plasticity, its "agility," its transparence, it is because something in him obscurely hopes one day to discover in it, and to decipher, the image of the whole universe.

Thus, Baudelaire seems to be illumined by a light from the fire of the most ancient mysticism. One might say that he intended to restore the ancient covenant. It would be easy at this point to evoke Neo-Platonism and to lose oneself in the maze of the various occult traditions. The point to be emphasized is that, from the beginning, man held in his soul this subterranean river, this mass of beliefs, dreams, unsatisfied aspirations which romanticism has released, which flows in us, deeper than our thoughts and our feelings, and in which so many poetic works of our time, without always being aware of it, have sought blood and nourishment.

This approach (even allowing for the fact that its significance was realized only gradually) was in practice a call to despise perceptible appearances and the principle of imitation of nature; it was a call to use words and images freely, and to associate them not according to their usage and pure logic, but their psychological resonance and the mysterious law of universal analogy. It contributed to a considerable strengthening of the mystical and metaphysical tendencies in French poetry—more so than did the *Contemplations* and the first *Légende des Siècles* at the same period, and by other means. Ceasing to be a "game of chance," the poet's art was becoming an "evocative magic," a sacred function.

But this Baudelairian art, which contains an element of delirium, is also a method. Though naturally inclined to the irrational and the occult, Baudelaire was far from letting himself be guided by instinct alone. He saluted inspiration as "the reward of daily effort." He looked upon the completed work as a perfect synthesis, all of whose psychic and musical elements have been integrated into an infinitely complex and coherent system of reciprocal relations; at that moment it is like a symphony which strikes the listener as being of one piece, a musical organism uttered by a single voice, but which is none the less the result of patient elaboration. In this respect, Baudelaire's immediate precursor was de Vigny, and he is the heir of the classic poets more than of the romantics who were swayed by every wind; he is also the disciple of Edgar Allan Poe. He is at the head of a line of artists (Mallarmé, Valéry, and others) who may wish to find "the premises of their song in the sensory forest" (like the author of *Charmes*) or in the night of the unconscious, but who strive in their works to manifest the order and unity that mark the triumph of the mind over incoherent nature. Baudelaire classed himself among the artists who aspire to "discover the obscure laws by virtue of which they have created, and to draw from this study a number of precepts whose divine goal is the infallibility of poetic production" (*Art romantique*, article on Richard Wagner). It is known that Mallarmé devoted—one might almost say "sacrificed"—his life to the quest of this *infallibility*, to the conquest of this domination over "chance." It is a dangerous temptation, which can lead into a blind alley. For it is difficult to harmonize in one mind the deliberate effort of critical intelligence, and the mystical activities that the practice of poetry, according to Baudelaire, requires of the poet, the necessary intimacy with the supernatural, the feeling that things and people are related by bonds invisible to any positive science—in brief, the return to states of mind that the psychologist would call prelogical or primitive, which is another temptation, and which can lead who knows where? It is easy to foresee the possibility of irreconcilable conflicts between these two requirements.

As for Baudelaire, who succeeded, not without difficulty, in harmonizing to some extent these two tendencies of his nature, and whose work for this very reason has exemplary value, behold him, in the depths of an earthly hell, in which he was crushed by boredom, invoking heaven as witness that he had fulfilled his duty "like a perfect chemist and a saintly soul!"

3.

Verlaine is entirely a natural poet, to be sure a very refined and complex one, knowing how to profit by influences, but spontaneous and immediate, profoundly original, and drawing his force from life itself. No one was less of a theoretician than he, less concerned with the aesthetic and philosophical ambitions of his contemporaries, less of an alchemist (like Mallarmé), less of a visionary and prophet (like Rimbaud). He was born to bring to its perfection the intimate and sentimental lyricism founded by Marceline Desbordes-Valmore and Lamartine, and to discover that tone of spoken poetry which belongs exclusively to him, suitable both for the unaffected prayer and for the whispered confidence, for the expression of harsh desire or tender effusion, a tone in which a certain "outline of subtle voice" always dies down in the end like a fleeting arabesque in a sonorous halo. With unequalled intensity this poetry evokes the music of everyday joys and sorrows, the sense of life, naked physiological life, in which thought is only a dream of the blood that sustains the flesh.

But it is not easy to draw a lesson from Verlaine, to cite him in support of an artistic doctrine or a moral attitude. In the quest for an absolute, which the development of poetry for almost three-quarters of a century resembles in various respects, the name of Verlaine is not the symbol of an advance, a victory or a failure. The very "novelties" of *Romances sans paroles* lost prestige when Rimbaud began to be better known. Verlaine's reputation, considerable until about 1900, was on the downgrade from then until about 1930.

This is partly accounted for by the general intellectual and emotional climate of his time, and by the fact that many poets now sought their inspiration outside the all-too-human world of feelings, of the pleasures and sorrows of the heart. But how unjust it is to assert, like the editor of an *Anthologie de la nouvelle poésie française* which appeared a few years ago, that "Verlaine represents the end of something. . . ." Let us recall how much is owed him by poets as far apart as Francis Carco, Georges Chenneviére, Guillaume Apollinaire. A slight change in the present orientation of poetry—are we not witnessing such a change?—might suffice to revive Verlaine's influence. A naturalness that owes nothing to automatism is worthy of great esteem; the next generation will surely be better able to appreciate the ease and freedom which result from a certain in-genuousness; the balance which, on the whole (until *Sagesse*), Verlaine that "unbalanced" poet, maintains between the summons of his almost inconceivably rich unconscious, and his sensuous intelligence; and finally, his ability to bestow existence upon the most evanescent inner states.

For approximately twenty-five years—after the period of relative oblivion, of purgatory, which usually begins on the morrow of a great artist's death and precedes his entry into immortality—Mallarmé's star has been on the ascendant. The destiny of this pure poet, this thinker "who willingly exhibited his incompetence in everything except the absolute," his heroism tempered with irony, have enchanted the imagination of the younger generation, and his work that was said to be sterile has borne fruit.

At first glance, his poems reveal his exceptional mastery over his material. "His marvelously finished little compositions compelled recognition as types of perfection," writes Paul Valéry, "so sure were the links between words and words, lines and lines, movements and rhythms; so completely did each one of them give the idea of an object in a certain sense absolute, an object produced by a balance of intrinsic forces, and preserved by a miracle of reciprocal combina-tions from those vague impulses to make improvements and changes that one unconsciously conceives when reading most texts." But Valéry's words, his reference to an "absolute," for example, suggest that, for Mallarmé, a finished work was more than a mere technical success, the labor of a good Parnassian. To draw from oneself, in full consciousness, an intangible object, is to dream that one has escaped from "the fatalities that misfortune metes out to one's existence," from the baseness and imperfection of the world and from *chance*; to dream that one has created an absolute.

Mallarmé's poems, the recently published sketches of *Igitur* ("fragments of some grandiose game," as Valéry said of Leonardo da Vinci), a few letters that have been preserved, a few *"mots,"* enable us to divine the meaning of his drama, to imagine the icy solitude into which he withdrew, and to evoke the hyperbolical image of the pure poet, the Magician who cannot accept his limitations, and wishes to extend the field of his consciousness forever farther. It is life that is the great enemy:

> *Je fuis et je m'accroche à toutes les croisées*
> *D'où l'on tourne l'épaule à la vie et, béni,*
> *Dans leur verre, lavé d'éternelles rosées,*
> *Que dore le matin chaste de l'Infini*
> *Je me mire et me vois Ange! . . .*

> I flee, and cling to every casement window,
> Turning my back on life and, blessed,
> In their panes washed by eternal dews
> And gilded by the chaste morning of the infinite
> I look upon myself and see myself an Angel!

(From *Les Fenêtres*)

Here a Catholic would find the sin of "angelism"—the sin of a man who rejects human existence and wants to be like God. According to Mallarmé, the poet's supreme triumph would be to conquer the fatalities and laws of the world, chance and everything that thought cannot subject to its rule, and thus compose the Work, the Book—the only Book. And this book, of which Mallarmé always dreamed, would be (as he wrote to Verlaine in 1885) no less than "the Orphic explanation of the Earth, which is the only duty of the poet and the literary game par excellence." To explain a thing is to know it, to reduce it to oneself. But the term of "Orphism" reminds us that though the poet's task may run parallel to the scientist's the two are not identical; the analogies that each of them tries to discover are not of the same order, and the worlds they construct rest on different foundations. Moreover, Mallarmé's Orphism may be a matter for discussion; according to Charles du Bos, the true Orphic attitude implies a belief in and submission to the mysteries, even a certain passivity devoid of all pride with regard to "illuminations," and all this is incompatible with Mallarmé's striving for hyperconsciousness. Be that as it may, no French writer before him would seem to have conceived such lofty ambitions, to have endowed Art with this ultimate mission of summing up Creation, as it were, and by the same token of justifying it to the human spirit.

Mallarmé's obscure, but pathetic admission of failure is contained in the poem entitled *Un coup de dé jamais n'abolira le Hasard*. One may well call it a Promethean failure; in their own way, the "little compositions" (mere experiments, approximations, in the eyes of their author) which charmed Valéry and include so many verses of extraordinary beauty, also bear witness to it.

A venture so singular—which aimed at nothing less than at absolutizing arrangements of words borrowed from that worn-out, soiled material that is language—can be understood only if one recalls that the poet intended "to separate, on the basis of different attributes, as it were, the twofold condition of words, crude and immediate on the one hand, essential on the other . . ." (*Divagations*). The "immediate" word can serve only as a generally accessible means of exchange—"as though one were to take a coin and silently put it into another man's hand"; useful for inter-human communication, for the transmission of concepts and ideas, it dies as soon as it is understood, and properly speaking, has no *real* existence. By contrast, the "essential" word is something other than an intermediary between two minds; it is an instrument of power. Its aim is to move, in the most emphatic sense of the word, to shake the soul to its ultimate depths, to promote the birth and metamorphosis of "open" reveries, capable of operating freely and indefinitely. "It enjoins upon us to come into being much more than it stimulates us to understand," (says Valéry). It is an entity whose meaning has less effect upon us than the form, color, resonance, the secret affinities and the halo of psychic suggestions that it diffuses like a perfume. "I say: a flower! and, outside the oblivion to which my voice relegates all outlines—musically the idea itself arises, the sweet idea that is absent in any bouquet . . ." The mystical element in such a conception of language is evident. We have, in short, an attempt to restore it to its full *efficacy* on the presumption that the uttered word has power to create a void around itself, to reject all vision coming from the world of the senses and then to evoke—as music does, according to Schopenhauer—the idea itself, pure as on the first day of the Creation, solitary, divinely useless.

The sonorous envelope of the word thus contains a real essence; Mallarmé says: "Approaching the organism that is the repository of life, the word with its vowels and diphthongs represents a kind of flesh" (*Les mots anglais*). But the spirit that animates it partakes not of the sullied derelict world of our senses, but of the ideal world, of the lost beauty that our dream anticipates "under an anterior sky." It is no exaggeration to maintain that Mallarmé here seeks to assume some of the prerogatives of the divine word; if he does not create *ex nihilo*, he strives at least, by means of "incantatory" words, to restore the integrity and primordial innocence of things that have been bastardized and disfigured. He himself assures us that "between the old methods of magic and the sorcery which poetry will remain, there exists a secret parity." Thus he continues that work of suggestive magic to which Baudelaire devoted himself and which is made possible only by a veritable *linguistic art*—and by a clear separation, at least in theory, between the expressive and creative functions of words. This linguistic art is an experimental and intuitive science of the poetic value and meaning of words, of their reciprocal relations and reactions, a method of reviving the original images and mythical residues that subsist in them, and of bringing back, for the span of a second, the day when words poured forth from the mouths of men to worship the gods or to exorcise their hatred.

Needless to say, we cannot call this a complete innovation; Mallarmé's discovery consists primarily in bringing the light of consciousness to bear upon an instinct to which most of the great poets before him yielded spontaneously. As has often been noted, the old-time euphuists like Scève or Tristan (to mention only Frenchmen) offer numerous examples of this poetry which keeps carefully away from sensory reality and external things, and is brewed in a retort like a quintessence.

As for obscurity, even if one is prone to condemn it *a priori*, one must admit that it represents an indispensable element in a poetics of this sort. The poet must avoid imposing a single, indisputably certain meaning at the outset; he needs "elbow room" in his expression, a "blank space" around his words, which will enable them to radiate fully; it is when their meaning is at first uncertain that they assume that strange, unfamiliar and miraculous quality. But

it is also important that the poem—and in this respect Mallarmé
(and how many others among the moderns!) no doubt sinned more
than once—should be sufficiently attractive to hold all the reader's
attention, to fulfill its "narcotic" function (according to Valéry),
suspending the normal activity of the self, bewitching it like an
incantation.

Moreover, Mallarmé's poetics logically implies the continuous
disregard of facts and objects, in favor of the allusion, the foam,
star, and smoke, that symbolize that astral body which the "pure"
poem must be. Such a poem will progress in a discontinuous movement, abandoning oratorical rhythms; the images will slip in
obliquely, they will remain undeveloped, implied in one another,
they will suddenly flutter by, flashing a bit of color, a spark, vanish-
ing in a rosy cloud. A complex syntax will trace almost invisible
relations between the words, and these relations will remain in a
sense virtual, up to the moment when the reader perceives them.
The poem will stand by a miracle, "sustained by the internal force
of its style" (Flaubert), like a house of cards,—in short it will be a
gratuitous game, which need not mean anything whatsoever, but
must bear witness to its own existence and transfigure Life:

> *O rêveuse, pour que je plonge*
> *Au pur délice sans chemin,*
> *Sache, par un subtil mensonge,*
> *Garder mon aile dans ta main.*

> *Une fraîcheur de crépuscule*
> *Te vient a chaque battement*
> *Dont le coup prisonnier recule*
> *L'horizon délicatement.*

> *Vertige! voici que frissonne*
> *L'espace comme un grand baiser*
> *Qui, fou de naître pour personne,*
> *Ne peut jaillir ni s'apaiser.*

> *Sens-tu le paradis farouche*
> *Ainsi qu'un rire enseveli*
> *Se couler du coin de la bouche*
> *Au fond de l'unanime pli!*

Le sceptre des rivages roses
Stagnants sur les soirs d'or, ce l'est,
Ce blanc vol fermé que tu poses
Contre le feu du bracelet.

O dreamer, to plunge me
Into pure pathless delight,
You need only, by means of a subtle lie,
Hold my wing in your hand.

A freshness of dusk comes
To you with each wing-beat
Whose imprisoned stroke delicately
Thrusts back the horizon.

O intoxication! Space quivers
Like a great kiss
Which, frantic at being born for no one,
Can neither spring forth nor be appeased.

Do you feel the diffident paradise
Like entombed laughter
Flowing from the corner of your mouth
Into the universal wrinkle?

The scepter of pink shores
Stagnant on the golden evenings this is it
This closed white flight that you set
Against the fire of the bracelet.

That is surely the kind of poetry that would have charmed Edgar
Allan Poe, a poetry pure of all passion, matter having been almost
completely eliminated. A fan, a head of hair, a painted piece of
procelain, a trinket, a console table—the subject is reduced virtually
to nothing, the poem's starting point is infinitely transcended, but a
great dreamlike effervescence is born of this whisper that is so
close to silence.

As Mallarmé progressively masters his aesthetic, his poems become less personal, or lyrical in the ordinary meaning of this term;
his attempted "divine transposition of the fact into the ideal"
diminishes more and more the importance of circumstances, the
particular, the individual, that is to say, of Chance, and in placing
general elements in the foreground, if not in full light. We may also
recall that this poet, although individualistic and impressionistic,
in many respects, had the curious intention of producing an im-

personal work, of composing a book that would be The Book, a poetry that would be The Poetry, as though the structure of our minds were marked with the imprint of the whole universe and as though, in the words of Valéry, "the poetic instinct were to lead us blindly to truth."

It is a fact that the sublimation of matter achieved by Mallarmé and his desperate quest of essence ends up in a kind of supra-lyricism; the general and the universal are rediscovered at the very roots of subjectivity. The poem then acquires the elegance of a blue-print, of a mathematical function, and in some instances several inter-pretations of it are justified—I am referring particularly to the famous sonnet *Le Cygne* which perhaps, if we disregard its various applica-tions, expresses the drama of man caught between the urge to live and the will to protect himself against life. The symbol is here synthesis, and the poetry of the self is transformed into a poetry of the mind.

So many demands make poetry a hyperbole—the first word of *Prose pour des Esseintes* recalls this. For absolute purity is conceivable only outside the world. It can be only a nonbeing. In the absence of fruit Mallarmé finds an "equal savor" that satisfies him. In the last years of his life, haunted by this nonbeing, by silence, by absence, he strove to confer a positive value upon them. How could this be done, unless the reader were forced to supplement everything that the work contained only potentially, unless all its charms were kept in a virtual state, unless it was not realized? This temptation of nonexistence is a terrible danger for poetry, but it is a danger consciously sought out and consciously confronted, and Mallarmé would doubtless have liked it to be even greater. Does he not ultimately aim at charting the transition from the relative to the absolute, from the finite to the infinite? To instruct or divert respect-able people is of little account when the poet's fate, his "salvation," is at stake. It is not surprising that his successors required more than a few years to profit from his experiments—whether they strove in vain to repeat them, or modified their conditions, or resolutely took the opposite course in the conviction that whatever poetry gains in angelic purity, it loses in humanity or effectiveness.

But authentic greatness moves us as a presence, long before it can be measured. In the gray years of the closing nineteenth century, there is no nobler figure than Mallarmé, "a sign of contradiction" for all, a hero even then in the eyes of some; through him, spirit, rarity triumphed over number, habit, laziness. "And I saw in us," wrote Valéry, his most fervent disciple, "welling up and going toward him, true glory, which is a hidden, not a shining thing."

4.

To the problem of Rimbaud, the best studies published in the course of recent years have succeeded in giving only approximate solutions. In the face of an almost mythical man engaged in an unprecedented "spiritual chase," it is possible only to indulge in the fascinating and deceptive game of hypotheses and attempt to imagine the course he followed, apart from all beaten tracks. Rimbaud was not the man to suppose that a Book could ever justify the existence of the world. Poetry—"one of my follies"—is in his eyes primarily a method of exalting life and transcending man. A demon drove this bad boy who slept in ditches and shared the soup of farm laborers. The September dew quenched his thirst; he spoke of "my stars," and saw a path of light descending from them to him; he would press forward "to the birds and the springs," to "the end of the world." "A man with feet of wind," Verlaine called him, a nomad and a conqueror, for whom the absolute was something to be seized at the end of his journey.

Rimbaud's demon was the demon of revolt and destruction. "The era of the assassins" had begun. He dreamed of springing like a beast of prey upon "civilization" and Western man. He negated and jeered at the State, public order and its restrictions, "established happiness," the conventional routine of love and the family, Christianity, morality, in short, all the products of the human mind. What then remains to be extirpated is the root of the evil, the human mind itself, such as it has been slowly formed in the course of centuries. Can one see in it anything but a channelized, imprisoned spring? For the sake of utility, this mind has consented to accept frames, constraints, boundaries—a form, a logic—to break the bonds that linked it to universal life, to live *separate*, to waste away. But to make up for its losses, is it not at least attuned to this world that is conventionally called "real"? It is a precarious reality, this reality of the so well named "external" world! It has been projected, constructed at the same time as ourselves, by ourselves, by our fault.

Before our eyes things have become petrified, they have ceased to be present in us, they have become remote, fragmented, effaced, yielding finally to the multiple properties that science discovered in them. We no longer know how to see them, to take them, except to make use of them."Our pale reason hides the infinite from us." And Rimbaud has only sarcasm for this reason, "an angels' ladder of common sense," for this trickery practiced by man who "proves to himself the obvious, swells with pleasure at repeating his proofs, and lives only for this."

"No doubt, even certainly, this is not true," Plato said about his myths, "but there is something more or less like it that is true." It is thus that we may ascribe such ideas to Rimbaud. But did he ever have an idea—a frozen thing? Nothing impedes the dynamism of his thought, and he is not the man to repeat his proofs.

This attitude foreshadows certain "anti-intellectualist" theses of today, as well as the explorations and hypotheses of para-psychology, this in itself would make it worth mentioning; but what is more significant for us is that it is rooted in esoteric tradition. Once again we must look in that direction. Does this mean that Rimbaud, having gone back to the pythagorean and Hindu sources, succeeded in identifying his fate with that of the yogi, in renewing their mystical experience, in adopting the beliefs and mythologies of the sages of the East? Such is the thesis of Rolland de Renéville in his remarkable work. For my part, I would not go so far; it seems to me that Rimbaud remained until the end the absolute non-conformist, who breaks all systems or disregards them. Beyond all the doctrinal systems, beyond all formulas, an irrepressible élan carried him toward the conquest of a primitive condition in which the personal soul escapes from its limitations and in mystical intoxication yields its forces up to the universal. "A son of the sun, a golden spark of that light, nature," borne on the rhythms of music, he lived for the sake of those exceptional adventures in which the universe, finally given back to itself, is experienced from the inside like an imponderable blazing mass whence flaming forms gush forth, to fall endlessly. It is a Dionysiac dance in which joy is born of the immediate possession of the Totality absorbed like a sacred essence.

Is this the road to omnipotence, to the omniscience pursued by the magician, or the road to nothingness, through the loss of all consciousness? These states are opposite, but complementary.

Rimbaud seems to have known them, to have desired both, passing from the folly of heroism and demiurgic activity to the voluptuousness of nirvana in a paradise of innocence. But there is no doubt that he believed in his prophetic calling. "O, I am he who will be God," exclaims the demon whom Verlaine endowed with the features of his companion in exile in *Crimen amoris*. He wanted to be a wonder-worker, and this may be ascribed to his pride, but also to his unquenched, desperate need to be at last recognized by men to be loved for his own sake, as a god is worshipped who in return loves infinitely.

Indeed, so much violence does not go without a respite, without oblivion. Rimbaud had strange charitable impulses that impelled him toward something that would not be unworthy and sullied, that would pertain truly to "the world," and be forever saved from the earthly hell. And then one discerns in him, pushed to the point of the most unrestrained savagery, the intolerance and idealism of an adolescent who suddenly discovers what by common consent, *is*, what mankind has made of itself, and of the world; who is seized with horror at his discovery, and henceforth strives to reject everything rather than to be like the others, rather than to live in the world of the others, and to renounce himself, his beliefs and his dreams, which are *the truth*.

Rimbaud thus assigned to the poet the task of "making himself a seer," that is, the task of awakening the slumbering faculties of his mind, which will bring him in contact with authentic reality. The "long, immense, and deliberate *derangement of all the senses*" that he advocates in his famous letter of May 15, 1871, the duty of the poet to exhaust "all forms of love, suffering, insanity," are expected to provide him with the means of attaining to *the unknown*. He and those who listened to him were above all determined to go beyond man's accepted possibilities, which in reality are merely the wretched fruit of his habits and his laziness. For them the essential was for man to "cultivate his soul," but this action of the self upon the self necessarily requires freedom from what is called "culture." Thus the poem that is "speech accessible to all the senses," speech "of the soul to the soul, summing up everything, perfumes, colors, sounds, thought catching thought and tugging at it," will have all the marks of a revelation. It is superfluous to recall that such ambitions partly stem from Baudelaire who ("the first of the seers, a real god") engaged in "gymnastics" of the same kind for the purpose of infinitely extending the range of his sensations and the network of their correspondence, of removing the walls of his prison.

As for the deliberate, or if you will, artificial, character of this method, of this "training of the soul," that reminds one of the spiritual exercises of the mystics, I do not think it implies *ipso facto* that the words and images in the poems of *Illuminations* were deliberately arranged. It would be wrong to adduce, as a decisive argument proving the existence of the poet's deliberate intention, the organic and plastic character of his visions; for a hallucination often takes on a distinctness and relief that one would seek in vain in a landscape normally perceived. Even dream fancies, occurring when consciousness is very weak, are not always amorphous and inorganic. The most reasoned method in such cases seems to aim at giving the mind access to a state of "clairvoyance" which is anything but reasonable; the poems may be contemporaneous with these exceptional states and arise spontaneously from the depths of our being, or else they may transmit to us the memory of such experiences.

Be that as it may, we discern here a new conception of literature—a conception that has been clearly recognized only in our day. The poetic sense becomes closely akin to the mystical and prophetic sense, a means no longer of expression but of discovery, an instrument as subtle as the finest point of the mind and capable of projecting its antennae into the very heart of the unconscious. However, the true mystic refuses to admit in himself any powers other than those which God exercises at will through his person. On the contrary, Rimbaud, the demoniacal thaumaturge, abandons himself only to recover himself, to enjoy his will to power and attempt to capture supernatural forces for his own profit. He is a sorcerer rather than a mystic, and it is only intermittently that he can forget his transcendent egoism.

Setting aside the poems that are directly linked to his idea of a prophetic calling (allegorical stories, parables, symbols), we can group together a fairly large number of pieces in *Illuminations* which are, strictly speaking, visions of the *seer* and which bring us the reflections and echoes of Rimbaud's universe. Now, though it is possible, as Jacques Rivière showed so well in his *Rimbaud*, to discern familiar sensations and objects in these pieces—a flower, a water-fall, the taste of ashes, the smell of wood in the fireplace—though it is true that these objects are presented with the index of reality that characterizes the world of the senses, the relations into which they enter, the rhythms that carry them along, and above all the architecture of the whole, strike us at once by their aspect of irremediable strangeness. Resting on precarious foundations and always uncertain of their own identity, things escape from themselves and burst the framework in which we enclose them; despite their relief, their density in each of the situations in which the poet places them, they glide from one form to another like the ephemeral images in a kaleidoscope. Sometimes threats are heaped up in an atmosphere of great cosmic death, and the objects as though panic stricken yield to a kind of incoherent gravitation; sometimes an enchanted realm of superhuman freshness opens before our eyes.

> *La douceur fleurie des étoiles et du ciel, et du reste descend en face du talus, comme un panier, contre notre face et fait l'abîme fleurant et bleue lá-dessous.*

> Across from the hillside, the flowery sweetness of the stars, and of the sky, and of the rest descends upon our face like a basket, and creates the blossoming, blue abyss below. (From *Mystique*)

In every instance, one enters a world which contradicts the laws of equilibrium but which emanates from a thought endowed with extraordinary plasticity, which seems freed from the logic and the "categories" of the sensory world. We also witness the triumph of the principle that was implicit in Baudelaire's lesson: that the artist, instead of imitating nature, should assimilate it and embody his *self* in it. When Rimbaud alludes to his "atrocious skepticism," he is referring no doubt to his total questioning of the validity of the world's appearances and of the fixed feelings and beliefs that constitute the normal *habitus* of modern man; he intends to give notice that everything that exists is absolutely arbitrary and depends on an initial fact which might not have been, on an error that was committed on the day when we consented to be only what we are, not gods.

The first romantic, like the classic writers, believed for the most part in the corruption of man; but they protested that the punishment of Adam was unjust, and the Fall undeserved. Rimbaud, on the other hand, is dazzled by "the extent of his innocence"; pure in a derelict world, he remains here "without heart"; nothing counts for him. "We are not in the world!" This cry of *Une Saison en Enfer* resounds like an immense *sauve-qui-peut*. And the poet, taking the dice back in his hands, attempts to repeat on his own the act of creation, to bring forth the world anew, like a demiurge. Is this pure madness, insane subjectivity? But, on the other hand, would not "submission to the object" be a dupery? Something in the modern artist, who is drunk with the wine poured out by Rimbaud, will answer that these data that he tries to grasp, these calls that he vaguely feels in himself, like the elements of an alphabet the key to which is lost, cannot lead him entirely astray, and that by heeding them he will have a chance of coming closer to the source of Being.

   The problem cannot be solved rationally. How can the objective value of a revelation be measured? However, we have merely tried to draw a few features of Rimbaud's physiognomy because most of the motifs of exaltation, the poetic and metaphysical themes that have obsessed the poets of the last generation, were proclaimed with disconcerting boldness by the author of *Illuminations*. He died without revealing his secret, and there is more than one man alive who would say that art, life and more than life depended on that very secret. The "total freedom of the mind" which appeared as the sovereign good on the morrow of the first world war, the revolt against the facts and the very conditions of existence, the negation of the sensory appearance that led some to the belief in a divine supernatural and others to the conception of a super-reality, and on the other hand the development of prose-poetry which answers a need for fidelity to emotion, to inspiration—these are some of the paths along which revolutionary poetry has progressed. At the beginning of these paths the figure of Rimbaud stands in the half-light. Even his renunciation of writing, of "changing life"— for which there have been different explanations—adds something to the problematic quality of his destiny.

5.

A certain kinship is revealed between these various spiritual adventures if one forgets for a moment their irreducible elements and their historical contexts. In each case, a mind strives to free itself from things and to return to an infinitely remote homeland. That is the hope that guides all mystics. But the poet cannot rid himself of things. He must not, if he wants to remain a poet.... Only the taste of flesh and a voluptuous attachment to his sensations will enable him to fertilize his memory and to prepare in silence the harvest of images that are to populate his work, while the true mystic strives to die to the world of the senses, to die to himself, and to arouse illuminations in an inner and closed kingdom.

This perhaps is the major reason for the failure of the poets in the realm of mysticism, especially the failure of Rimbaud. The mind can cross the threshold of a new life and know purity only through genuine asceticism, by wresting itself free from the body and from matter. But the ecstasy is ineffable. "How can one give a form to what has no form?" says Suso, the medieval German mystic (quoted by Jean Baruzi). "No comparison can help us. However, in order to dispel images with images, I shall attempt to show here, through the figure of a given language, at least to the extent that this is possible, this meaning which is itself devoid of images." the difficulty is obvious; it is quite likely that, with some exceptions, the "success" of the poet and that of the mystic are incompatible in the same man. And yet the poet can raise himself only by following the "inner paths"; there he will enrich that feeling of the universe which will carry him like a river sown with mysterious spawn.

Moreover, the modern poet does not believe that he deserves his exile. "The records of the great trial have been burned," de Vigny had said. He would rather accept the dogma of his own immaculate conception, he would rather accuse God, or man who has isolated himself in the universe and feeds on sterile thoughts "for not having known how to sing of a region in which to live." It might be pertinent to evoke here the theme of the *Novices of Sais*, by Novalis. Who, then, will lift the veil and contemplate Isis in her snowy whiteness? These poets are forever concerned with the golden age, even when they do not mention it, and with the paradise that has been lost, and found again. "The contribution of nineteenth-century poetry," said G. Ungaretti, "is an unquenched hope for innocence." From Baudelaire's "innocent paradise of childhood loves" to the "rational song of the angels" heard by Rimbaud, to Mallarmé's swan, everything is animated by the same breath that had swelled, *mutatis mutandis*, the breast of Rousseau.

But this innocence goes hand in hand with power, and mystical exigencies assume a demoniacal character. What man needs is the integrity and fulness of himself and of Nature. By means of science he has forged an Antiphysis which weighs on him with its automatic weight, he has made his consciousness into an island, in which he perceives only weakened echoes, colorless images of a life no longer accessible. But the hope subsists. Paul Claudel tells us that Mallarmé, in the presence of any "thing," asked himself only one question: "What does it mean?" The poet must always favor the birth of images, he must follow analogies back to their remote and obscure source, as though, in these mysteries, the universe might be revealed to itself in its true face.

Such a design is at bottom metaphysical. But no one expects here to find reality, the absolute, if you will, at the end of a system of concepts or of a dialectic; the intention is to discover it in psychic concreteness. A new sensibility, infinitely delicate, oriented toward the phenomena of "metapsychology"—that is, strictly speaking, the faculty of the modern poet. It may help him to rediscover the universe in the self, and to imagine the meaning of this universe.

Baudelaire, Mallarmé and Rimbaud—the last two particularly—dreamed of "transcending man." (At the same time Nietzsche was wearing himself down to madness in the same endeavor.) All of them failed, and we may liken them to Icarus or Prometheus. This is not the place to inquire into the circumstances which, after a century of romanticism, caused the eternal restlessness, the eternal metaphysical ambition to become so exacerbated—at the very time when philosophers were bowing so low to positive science—and why it was that man decided to ask poetry for a solution of the problem of his fate.

I have placed these three poets side by side because today they are like three beacons in the Baudelairian sense of the word, illumining the virgin lands into which others have ventured after them. If our purpose had been to study the symbolist movement proper, we should have chosen another perspective, we should have placed Verlaine in full light and emphasized certain aspects of Baudelaire which today are left in the shadow. But complex and truly new works can supply nourishment to more than one generation. It is only gradually that Baudelaire, Mallarmé, and Rimbaud have been discovered.

BOOK I

Ebb Tide

Verlaine and Friends

CHAPTER ONE

Considerations on Symbolism

M. G. Bonneau, author of a book on French symbolism, has drawn an amusing comparison between the symbolist movement and the dragon of Alca in the second book of *Ile des Pingouins*, which none of those who had allegedly seen him could describe. Symbolism embraces a number of diverse trends and individual efforts; what they all have in common would seem to be, essentially, their protest against modern society and positivistic philosophy. A sense of the deep life of the spirit, a certain intuition of mystery and of a reality transcending the phenomenal world, a new will—at least in France—to grasp the essence of poetry and to free it from didacticism and sentimentalism: such are the elements generally underlying the activity of the poetic generation of 1885.

In connection with the term "symbol"—one of those fetishist words that are all the more suggestive because they are charged with complex meanings difficult to define—it is very important to avoid misunderstandings on a capital point which concerns the poetry of today as much as that of yesterday; for the symbolist mode of thought and expression does not characterize any specific historical period.

It seems that the human mind, in dreams, daydreams, or even in waking hours, is endowed with the faculty of autonomous creation, and that it freely imagines fables, figures, images in which the deep emotional life of the self is projected. This spontaneous symbolism is restrained among civilized men by the various organs of censorship, but it functions almost uninhibited among so-called primitive peoples, or in the dreams of the sophisticated. Thus arise the myths and other fabulous constructions which common-sense denounces as unreal, but which are true psychologically (and can also be true otherwise) because on the level of the imagination they correspond to the feelings and thoughts which engendered them. As a result of this correspondence, the subject comes to feel that the image mystically partakes of the psychic reality it symbolizes.

We are familiar with this notion of correspondence or equivalence. It is applicable to the poet who entrusts images with the mission of expressing or embodying a state of mind. The work of elaboration in which he engages and the elementary, direct process that we have just defined are naturally related; the two coincide when the poet eschews thought and construction and passively yields to dreaming. This activity of the mind reduced to its own forces, which builds up a story that is the mind's own history, enables us to perceive the phenomenon of creative imagination in the raw, prior to any kind of aesthetic arrangement or intention.

However, if we may say that any fable, any association of images emerging into consciousness tends to organize itself into a symbol, there is no question here of a two-term relation between a clearly perceived feeling or thought and the images into which it is projected. For the genuine symbol results from a direct adherence of the mind to a *naturally* figurative form of thought; and, as Jean Baruzi says, "since it is never a translation, it can never be translated." This is an essential fact, often ignored; it follows that the symbols of dreams and of nondirected daydreams are "polyvalent" as the psychologists say, that is, they represent a complex state, which is, moreover, in process of transformation. Consequently, such symbols will as a rule have several "values"; furthermore, these are interconnected by affective links, and none of them can be reduced to a simple formula. This fact is overlooked by many readers and commentators who, when confronted by a modern poem cannot rest until they have ascribed to its symbols a logical *meaning* that precludes any other interpretation. There is no doubt that many works produced in the course of the last fifty years, whose elements took shape in an obscure area of consciousness, are polyvalent.*

If anyone argues that this conception of the symbol also applies to poets who are quite unlike the symbolists of the late nineteenth century, we shall readily agree; if anyone declares that it does

*As early as 1901, M. G. Pelissier voices similar views in *Revue des Revues* (March issue).

not apply to the symbolists because most of them deliberately resorted to an indirect method of expression and grouped images which they invested with a quite precise meaning (at least for them), we shall answer that we have no intention of denying that the intellect is capable of becoming aware of the spontaneous process we have described, and of associating a representation with a psychic reality, state of mind, feeling, or idea. It is quite true that the symbolists often did proceed in that way. One might conclude that it is for the very reason that they were for the most part intellectuals and artists devoid of innocence and extremely civilized, that they came to substitute an effort of auscultation, analysis, and synthesis, for the natural movement of alogical thought. (It has often been observed that the more a man knows himself, the less active he is, that he has greater difficulty in performing a psychological function once he has understood its mechanism.) The deliberate effort to express oneself symbolically may considerably decrease the authenticity of the symbol, which then becomes something it is not when the mind is left to itself: an indirect mode of expression, in which, through choice, the signifying object supplants the signified object.

It must be noted that the foregoing remarks rather simplify the actual state of affairs. Actually, there are a host of intermediary positions between the unconscious and the conscious, a number of relations between thought and symbol. Originally, we are confronted with the free activity of the mind, accompanied by the mystical presence of reality in the image; in the end we obtain, on the level of the intellect, the symbol as it has been defined by Jules Lemaître: "an extended comparison, of which we are given only the second term, a sysetm of consistent metaphors."

According to Paul Valéry, "what was baptized symbolism may be summed up very simply in the intention, common to several families of poets (incidentally hostile to one another), to recover their property from Music." (Foreword to *Connaissance de la Déesse*, by Lucien Fabre.) It is unlikely that the situation is as simple as all that, that the poets—from Ronsard to Racine, Chénier, Hugo— had ever allowed themselves to be expropriated, and that the music of musicians can be assimilated to that of poets. Nevertheless, it is true that one of the capital articles of symbolist aesthetics was to put the musical resources of language to deliberate use.

But the musicality—in the full sense of the term—of poetry,

like that of prose, is not measured in quasi-mathematical terms by more or less sonorous combinations of words considered as a pure system of sounds. Many verses are harmonious to the ear, but their resonance ends with the last syllable and they fail to leave a musical impression on the mind. This elementary observation suffices to invalidate the thesis of the aestheticians who attempted to explain the secret of a musical verse by simple sound relations, overlooking the possible power of psychological suggestion in words. In reality this phenomenon is much subtler, and the "musical" poet must be capable of feeling the affinities existing between the world of sound and the world of thought. Here again, the problem is to bring out mysterious "correspondences"; certain syllables, thanks to an infinitely subtle accord with the meaning of the word which they compose, by virtue of the confused memories evoked by this word even more than by its sonorous charm, actually "move" the mind, magnetize it in a specific direction. But in no case can the psychological value of the word and its virtual treasury of images and associations be considered independently of its sonorous qualities. Consequently, the "music" of words can be distinguished only arbitrarily from their meaning—in the broadest sense—and a certain "inner music" must always be placed above a quasi-material harmony, which is pleasing only to the ear.

One of the symbolists' greatest merits was their awareness of the complexity of these phenomena. "In my writing I arrange the great flow of words musically, placing them on the orchestral staves: here are the strings and the woods, there the brasses and the percussion instruments . . ." These graphic words of Saint-Pol Roux show us that a virtue carried to the extreme can defeat itself. The systematic application of the principle resulted, it would seem, in a new servitude and in two errors of capital importance. First of all, the symbolists often sacrificed inner musicality to the mere juggling of sonorities—hence their abuse of "strings" and "brasses." Then, although they were rightly concerned with the relations between sound and thought, they—at least some of them, and particularly René Ghil—made the mistake of neglecting individual divergencies for the pleasure of formulating laws, principles, prescriptions that are largely fanciful. These errors were patent enough, and they served as a warning to the successors of the symbolists. For the last thirty years the dream of the "merger of the arts" has ceased to haunt the imagination of our poets. And the representatives of the young schools have sought to ally themselves with painters rather than with musicians.

As for free verse, which was born partly, it would seem, of a desire to express one's thought "without deforming it" (this was the intention of Laforgue who rather embodies the "decadent" spirit), and partly from musical preoccupations (G. Kahn and the symbolists), it originated in the nineteenth century, and the poets of today have only inherited an instrument forged by their predecessors, sometimes transforming and abusing it. The passions that it aroused have long since calmed down, and many an illusion has perhaps been dispelled; free verse has not succeeded in killing regular verse for in *radically* differentiating itself from rhythmic prose. So many automatisms of so many kinds lurk in wait for the writer, that deliberately accepted restrictions have in some quarters come to be regarded as a favorable condition for the exercise of poetic thought.

On the other hand, it has been realized that the French language is not devoid of accentuation, and that every text in prose, and above all, any spoken utterance, is naturally articulated in rhythmic feet, with several atonal syllables preceding each accented syllable. Ultimately, free verse is characterized only by the small number of syllables in each rhythmic foot and the intensification of the cadence, which, it is true, considerably modifies the *tone* of the discourse. Moreover, we shall see that in the eyes of many modern poets verbal rhythm tends to merge with psychological rhythm, and that a weakly accented "verse" is nothing but a proposition, an ideological unit. Gradually, an absolute individualism, partly reflecting the general trend of the century, achieved dominance in the domain of prosody. The "emancipated" verse, blank verse, the symbolist free verse (of which several styles should be distinguished), the verset, prose arranged in lines, "consecutive" prose—all these "forms" do not deter the strictest regular verse from continuing its course of development. Such variety borders on anarchy, and one need hardly emphasize its dangers, but to those who keep in mind the diversity of the poets' intentions, it will be apparent that this great diversity could not have been avoided.

"The symbolist school," writes Bernard Fay, "was a misunderstanding. These young men seduced by Verlaine, enthusiastic admirers of Rimbaud and Mallarmé, did not see that in reality their masters wished them to engage in a crusade, a 'spiritual' hunt. These young men engaged in literature and sought to found groups, when they should have worked on themselves ..." This judgement is severe, and in its bald form, even unjust; the symbolists of 1885 and 1890 were, on the whole, anything but careerists. Nevertheless it is true—and this is essential—that Baudelaire, Mallarmé, and Rimbaud had boldly raised poetry to a vital plane; they had made it a transcendent activity; while the majority of their disciples— unwittingly in many cases—brought it back to the literary plane. I am quite aware that there was a certain wisdom in asking of literature only what it can give, and in keeping away from insoluble problems. Yet how is it that these problems are the only ones that still deserve to be raised, in the eyes of certain men, among them those poets whom Nietzsche calls "the expiators of the spirit"?

As men of letters and artists, the symbolists came to consider questions of form *for their own sake*. That is why they searched for a suggestive imagery, resorted to mythology, legend and folklore, and tended to conceive of the symbol as an idea that is subsequently clothed in what Moréas described as "the sumptuous simars of external analogies," that is, as a two-term relation similar to the allegory or emblem. To be sure, the images of fauns, sirens, swans, and dream-women are so full of human and aesthetic meaning that they easily lend themselves to the play of the imagination; still, one must go deep down into oneself if one is to come close enough to the source of these dreams to embody in them something of one's own life. This also explains the need (another heritage of the Parnassus) to dwell upon "beauties of detail," which sometimes resulted in the so-called "coruscating" style, brilliant with ornaments and gems, heavy and over-refined, and terribly outmoded today.

The cult of the Beautiful ends in aestheticism. In his article *"L'Ecole paienne"* Baudelaire had already declared that "the exclusive passion of art is a canker which devours everything else." Often art safeguards itself only by renouncing itself. As for culture, it is well known that it can become a means of escaping from life, of protecting oneself against ideas and feelings, a means of self-betrayal. And the religion of the Beautiful, grafted on an extensive culture, was a prominent characteristic of most of the symbolists. If we also recall that they possessed an extremely flexible and lucid

intelligence, we shall be able to grasp the truth paradoxically formulated by Jacques Rivière who ventured an abstract definition of
the spirit of the symbolist poet: "An intellect that goes straight to
the end, that finds no resistance in the things it invents, but flows
right through them, and is so fluid, keen, and penetrating that it
reaches the extremity of its subject at one stroke. Everything in the
work of the symbolists bears the mark of an ultra-conscious creator."

All this leads us to conclude that in a number of cases a kind of
discordance prevailed between the goal that the poets set for themselves and the education they had received, between their refined
sensibility, their discernment, and the artistic resources they brought
into play. Symbolism offered the spectacle of a poetry which attempted to express the "soul" of things and the profound stirrings
of life, yet resulted from a painstaking effort of analysis; of poets
who wished to "suggest mystery," yet, out of dilettantism or a taste
for the precious and the enigmatic, turned their back on the real
mysteries in order to invent others. On the other hand, there is
Laforgue who had studied Hartmann's work on the *Unconscious* and
sought to silence his reason: "Create living life in the raw, and drop
the rest," he exclaimed. In reality, nothing is more deliberate than
the "lifelike" incoherence of his *Complaintes*, while the "incongruous
marriages" of his verbal associations strike one rather as laboratory
products. The real Laforgue, the Laforgue who is so moving, must be
sought elsewhere. In passages of this kind we seem to perceive an
over-subtle intellect vainly spending itself in attempts to mimic
the movements of the unconscious.

The foregoing remarks on symbolism are by no means intended
as an appreciation of the postive contribution of the School of
1885. We have merely indicated why it did not live up to the
example and ambitions of its masters, in order to make possible a
better understanding of what took place around 1900. At that time
French poetry tried to renew itself by going back to older (romantic)
sources and models, and proceeded to draw sustenance from the
works of Baudelaire, Mallarmé and Rimbaud, and from a closer
contact with the spirit of the times, a spirit of revolt and adventure.

CHAPTER TWO

Romanism and Naturism

1.

It is important to determine the significance of the two principal
protests against symbolism, less for the interest they carry in themselves than for the light they cast upon the deep subterranean work
accomplished in men's minds during the transition from the nineteenth to the twentieth century. The Romanic school and the Naturist
movement were both ephemeral, but their effects by far transcend
the effects of the poetic works written under their aegis at that time
and during the years that followed.

The about-face of Moréas who published his charter of the
"Romanic" poets on September 14, 1891, only six months after he
had been saluted as the spokesman for triumphant symbolism at a
banquet organized by *La Plume* on February 12th of the same year,
must indeed have come as a shock to the admirers of Verlaine and
Mallarmé. In this charter, Moréas wrote: "The French Romanic
School affirms the Greco-Latin principle, the fundamental principle
of French letters, which flourished in the eleventh, twelfth, and
thirteenth centuries with our troubadours, in the sixteenth century
with Ronsard and his school, and in the seventeenth century with
Racine and La Fontaine. In the fourteenth and fifteenth centuries
as well as the eighteenth century, the Greco-Latin principle ceased
to be a living source of inspiration and manifested itself only
through the voices of some excellent poets, such as Guillaume de
Machaut, Villon, and André Chénier. Romanticism was responsible
for the corruption of this principle both in its conception and in its
style, thus depriving the French muses of their legitimate heritage.
The French Romanic school restores the continuity of the Gallic
chain, which was broken by romanticism and its Parnassian,
naturalist, and symbolist descendants . . ."

It is hard to imagine a more radical break with contemporary trends. Moréas' statement of principles was based on a repudiation of the entire nineteenth century tradition in favor of the Greece of Homer and Pindar, of Rome ("whose literature reached its climax with Virgil"), of medieval, Renaissance, and classical France, in which, disregarding necessary distinctions, he saw the direct descendant of ancient humanism. Thus, in his view the real domain of this "Romanism" extended approximately from the *Chanson de Roland* to Chénier.

And actually, the four Romanic poets—du Plessys, de la Tailhède, Ernest Raynaud and Moréas, after going as far back as Eustache Deschamps in their franzy to unearth archaic words, reveled for some time in imitating Ronsard. Listen, for example, to Raymond de la Tailhède blowing the trumpet of Pindarism to invoke the Tyndarides, guides of the Argus, and vowing to restore, with the help of Virgil and Ronsard,

> *Athènes éternelle et l'antique renom*
> *Latin des Gaules . . .*

> Eternal Athens and the ancient
> Latin glory of the Gauls. (In *La Plume*, Feb. 1, 1892.)

Is this not a resurrection of the heroic times when Ronsard and his followers were pillaging "Thebes and Apulia"? Thibaudet called them a *Pléiade d'étagère*. Obviously such erudite affectation could not lead them far. Their pedantry reflected the modern need to distinguish oneself from a world irretrievably abandoned to the Common Herd. In thus trying to "cheat the centuries" these poets were seeking an alibi, as Mallarmé said, an alibi not very different from that found by the Parnassians in their belief in a Hellenic golden age, and quite close to the "havens" which the symbolists provided for themselves in the mysterious sites of the Wagnerian legend.

More important in the domain of aesthetics than the few charming pastiches which constituted almost all the positive contribution of the Romanic school up to 1895, is the personal influence of Charles Maurras, who at once became the critic and philosophical leader of the group, expressing his ideas in *La Plume* and the *La Revue Encyclopédique*. His first articles, so polemical in tone as to constitute almost an indictment, were based on principles so remote from the world of ideas and feelings within which the symbolists moved, that it seemed as if no agreement could ever be possible between the demands they formulated and the teachings of Baudelaire or Mallarmé.

Maurras, as is well known, charges the writers of the nineteenth century with having corrupted the language, degraded poetic style, and wrecked traditional verse. Bent upon tracing the contours of every tiny sensation, and pursuing the phantoms of their thought even unto nothingness, they forged a bastard vocabulary, and resorted to a loose or over-complicated syntax. All of them, he says, renounced style, which consists not in investing words with color and music, in combining them according to the dictates of a more or less evanescent "state of mind," but, as Buffon recommended, in imposing order and movement on one's ideas, in subjecting them to a superior rationality. This insures the intimate subordination of the parts to the whole, of the word to the sentence, the sentence to the page, and the page to the book, which is the prerequisite of all beauty. By the same token, the physical data of the self, purified and chemically transformed by the fire of the mind, are represented only by a regulated play of rhythms and relations contrived to seduce intellectual sensibility. For beauty can only be the result of harmony, form, style. The romanticists and the symbolists are content with expressing themselves, but they do not know how to compose works, they misunderstand the nature of art. The true poet, on the contrary, is "the one who does something with what he feels. . . ."

This clearly represents a return to an entirely classical and ancient concept of the Beautiful, and the least that can be said of it is that it goes counter to almost all the ideas of the nineteenth century, which identified the Beautiful with the characteristically original, or, after Chateaubriand, with the poetical. However, the search for the original makes it inevitable that the emphasis be laid on differences at the expense of harmony; and the poetical, whether, in the words of Chateaubriand, it be "sad, vague, sublime," or not, is essentially moral; it encourages revery, opens paths for the imagination, unveils mysteries. In sum, for Maurras the elements of the self have no value as such, and a psychological experience, however far it is pushed, cannot contain the germ of any revelation about life—

an opinion that hardly conceals a very profound skepticism. All value resides in the human act, in the act illumined and determined by reason. It is delusive to regard an aggregate of sensations or vague "states of mind" as a kind of absolute. For "there is a perfect man," and that man is "an animal who reasons. . . . It is reason that distinguishes man, without separating him, from the rest of nature."*

As for the "barbarian," Maurras grants that he sometimes has his usefulness: "He has strong, violent sensations. . . . But he is incapable of disposing elements into a harmony." And perfection alone is important. After Adolphe Retté had written his "Thule of the Mists," Maurras said to him: "You have seen the primal being. . . . But you have stopped there. You have not seen the order of the earth and the heavens blossom from the mixtures of this universal mud. And you have done nothing to hasten the birth of lights and harmonies. . . . No origin is beautiful, true beauty is at the end of things."

This is a fierce anti-romantic declaration, and it is illuminating because it makes explicit Maurras' opposition to the lyricists of the end of the nineteenth century, whose natural impulse was to return to a lost happiness, to try to go back to the mother deities, and to overhear a first echo of their secret. To give a full account of the debate it would no doubt be necessary to show a poetry and philosophy of the finite confronting a poetry and philosophy of the infinite, the former Hellenic in origin and rationalistic, the latter modern and "spiritualistic."†As early as the beginning of the nineteenth century the question of classicism and romanticism had been formulated in the same terms. René thinks only of "an unknown good," of which he can say nothing; for Chateaubriand, "there is nothing beautiful, sweet, great in life except the mysterious

*It is amusing to find that in 1656 the following lines were written by Pelisson [in his *Discours sur Sarrasin*]: *Just as man has, for the things of the body, a universal instrument which is the hand . . . he also has for the things of the spirit a universal instrument which is reason.* And: those who fail to submit completely to reason *act by virtue of a blind faculty and the mere imagination, which is the part that we have in common with the beasts.*

†I shall quote the following sentence from *Défense du Système des Poètes romans* [in *La Plume*, July 1, 1895]: *I am calling attention to a fact that is worth noting. There is in Paris a literary group of six writers. . . . They are philosophically minded*; yet not one has used the term: the infinite.

things"; and Madame de Staël adds that "man owes his greatest exploits to the painful and incomplete sense of his destiny." Indeed, Maurras gave a new twist to the thesis of *De la Littérature*, which distinguishes more or less confusedly between the poetry of the North and the poetry of the South; as early as July 1891, in a special issue of *La Plume* devoted to the Félibriges,* he clearly defined the distance separating the Hyperborean barbarians from the meridional Romans, and the latter's kinship with the poets of the Provençal Renaissance. "One cannot conceive an idea or a dream that was not created by the Mediterranean," he maintained; and a few years later he specified his concept of barbarism: "It is proper to call barbarian that which is alien to these classical letters, not only because it is outside the common Helleno-Latin treasure, but also because it is foreign to higher humanity.† Thus a bridge was spanned between Athens and Paris, and that bridge led to Maurras' idea of Atticism, which he found reincarnated in the France of Louis XIV. "We found that the taste of Paris was the same as that of Athens," Racine declared after the first performance of his *Iphigénie*, "the spectators were moved by the same things as once brought tears to the eyes of the most sophisticated nation of Greece." Maurras also pilloried the Belgians who wanted "to conquer the French race"—Verhaeren, Maeterlinck, Rodenbach, Fontainas, Mockel, etc.

In a few years the propositions of Maurras resulted in strongly establishing the idea of perfection and the classical dogma in the face of romanticism and its descendants. From about 1895 on, many poems published in the magazines were in more regular, less composite style, and contained fewer neologisms; the Baudelairian, Verlainian, and Mallarmean themes were brightened with mythological images or neo-Greek variations. Moreover, the reputation of *Trophées* contributed to the fashion of a precise technique, a more plastic art, and Hellenic settings. This pseudo-classicism reviving

*Literary society founded for the purpose of preserving the Provençal dialect. (Translator's note.)

†*Revue encyclopédique*, Dec. 26, 1896. As early as 1892 Saint Antoine (?) pointed out in *Ermitage* that *the term Romanism seems to designate a quartet of Parisian poets and the Félibrige movement, which is of course more important.* . . . In 1893, in the same magazine, Stuart Merrill mentions *a tumultuous crusade of a few meridionals against the gods of the North.*

the half-dead Parnassus and drunk on the charms of Alexandria—
Les Chansons de Bilitis appeared in 1894, and *Aphrodite* two years
later—aroused the protest of Maurras, who in the name of Athens
accused Hérédia of "savage" polychromy and the embalming of
corpses. But these intermediate works, at a time when classical
culture, even among those who were imbued with it, clashed with
modern habits and needs, were in reality unavoidable; they are all
the less surprising if we consider that Maurras had always displayed
keen admiration for the poems of Anatole France and Jules Tellier,
who are situated half-way between Parnassus and romanticism.

As for the somewhat later works that reflect the combined influence of the symbolist (especially the Mallarmean) tradition and
of Moréas and Maurras, it might have been rather difficult to
anticipate them in 1894. And yet ... today it seems obvious that
some of Paul Valéry's youthful poems represent a slightly "Romanized" Mallarmeism, in which a distant echo of Racinian music can
be heard. Conversely, one cannot help noting, in the Romanic poems
of du Plessys, de la Tailhède and even of Ernest Raynaud—not
to mention Emmanuel Signoret—an occasional arabesque, a bold
runon line or anacoluthon that is reminiscent of the most skilful
verses of *L'Après-Midi d'un Faune*. Take, for example, the beginning
of this parenthesis in *Dédicace à Apollodore* by Maurice du Plessys:

> *Tel, gardien du noir fleuve, un pâtre ami des lunes*
> *Rêve, la flûte aux dents, sous les feux de la nuit ...*

> So dreams the guardian of the black river, herdsman and friend of
>   the moons,
> His flute at his lips beneath the fires of night.

And these negations, in a sonnet of La Tailhède:

> *Pourtant, ce n'est ton doigt ...*
> *Ni cette fleur sans prix, la cyprienne rose*
> *Ni l'oiseau séculaire élevant haut mon voeu ...*

> And yet, it is not your finger ...
> Nor this priceless flower, the Cyprian rose
> Nor the bird of the ages raising high my desire ...

Thus, while everyone was ridiculing the Romanic "barracks,"
poets such as du Plessys or de la Tailhède seemed to point a furtive

finger in the direction which was later taken by the "neo-Roman" poets who pitched their tents half-way between Moréas and Mallarmé.

2.

Although somewhat more belated and confused, the naturist protest was no less significant than that of the Romanic poets; it seems to answer an even more imperious need, and manifests something as elemental as a physiological rhythm. It was concerned less with art and style than with action, life, "real" life—the life that one must take the trouble to live. To take refuge in oneself, to turn one's eye on oneself, in order to satisfy a desire for purity and negative perfection, or from fear, or weariness, or disgust with existence, but most often from an almost erotic desire to espouse all the inner stirrings of the self—such was the attitude par excellence of ultra-modern symbolism. "Narcissus was perfectly beautiful—and that is why he was chaste; he scorned the nymphs—because he was in love with himself. No breath troubled the spring, as all day long he bent tranquilly over it to contemplate his image . . ." writes Gide in his *Traité du Narcisse* (January 1891).

The poets vied with one another in turning out muffled plaints and litanies, detailing a morose delight in being unable to discover in themselves the strength to live. Thus, in *Tel qu'en songe*, Henri de Régnier, lost in a forest of legend, slowly wove a secret chrysalis for his soul, a closed house; but the golden flower that gleams in the woof is one of those that are picked only in dreams. Narcissus scorning the nymphs, infatuated with himself—the psychologists could not have chosen a better symbol for the tendency to introversion.

But new men were approaching who would involve Psyche in less purely spiritual adventures. It was in 1895 that the new trend made its appearance; the following year, Maurice Le Blond published his *Essai sur le naturisme** which opens on a comminatory

*On January 10, 1897, *Figaro* published the manifesto of Saint-Georges de Bouhélier. Little magazines were founded in Toulouse, Aix and Brussels (*L'Effort* in Toulouse, with M. Magre, J. Viollis, Marc Lafargue; in Paris, Ch.-L. Philippe printed his writings in *L'Enclos*; in Aix, Joachim Gasquet edited *Mois dorés*; Brussels saw the publication of *Art jeune*, with Henri Van de Putte and André

note: "Enough! Baudelaire and Mallarmé have been admired long enough!" And further on: "Our elders preached the cult of unreality, the art of the dream, the search for the new shudder. They loved venomous flowers, darkness and ghosts, and they were incoherent spiritualists. As for ourselves, the Beyond does not move us, we profess a gigantic and radiant pantheism." And he concluded with this creed: "We will rejuvenate our individuality in a universal embrace. We will return to Nature. We will seek healthy, divine emotion. We don't care a fig for art for art's sake." In short, this was a position more ethical than literary. Return to nature, rejuvenation, emotion and simplicity, the full life, the love of mankind—what difference did it make that all this was not new in the field of expression? Once again, art was not the main point.

And then there was Charles-Louis Philippe who exclaimed (in a letter written in 1897): "What we need now is barbarians. One must live very close to God without having studied books, one must have a vision of natural life.... Today begins the era of passion." This ardent desire was quite properly emphasized by André Gide in the lectures he devoted to Philippe some twelve years later when that young writer died. This would doubtless have been a logical position: to reject the heritage of the past and place one's hopes upon fresh sensations and discoveries. But the theoreticians of naturism, less bold, more respectful of historical values, strove to prove the titles of nobility and the national significance of their movement. "A return to the lustral waves of tradition is imperative," wrote Maurice Le Blond; unfortunately his enthusiasm left him little leisure to define exactly the elements of this tradition. Shortly afterward, Adrien Mithouard in *Occident*, Maurras and his young disciples, Barrès and other doctrinaires, undertook, by means of rigorous exclusion and selection, to trace in the past the French line par excellence and to circumscribe in advance the area of acceptable enrichment.

Moreover, according to the naturists, "Thought is not a toy for

---

Ruyters) which followed the lead of the *Revue naturiste*; *La Plume* opened its pages to Le Blond; in the *Mercure*, Andrée Viollis commented upon the new movement with sympathy; *Ermitage*, with André Gide and Henri Ghéon, was not at all hostile, and one of its columnists, Edmond Pilon, can be considered an early adherent. On naturism, one may profitably consult *Vingt-cinq ans de la littérature française*, edited by Eugène Montfort (cf. particularly v. II, 200).

sophisticates, and poetry is not a pastime of mandarins. They are functions and have a utilitarian aim." From all quarters came old and new variations on the theme of the social mission of the poet, "master of joy, beauty and wisdom" and "guarantor of public health." Was this not a revival of the tradition of utilitarian and Saint-Simonian romanticism? Martino observes correctly in *Parnasse et Symbolisme* that although these poets writing at the time of the Dreyfus Case were consumed with the need for social action and protested against romanticism and its Baudelairian descendants, their desire to escape into reality and the world, and their humanitarian dreams were perhaps not essentially different from the aspirations of George Sand, Michelet, Quinet, and still less from those of Hugo.

In all these preoccupations it is barely possible to discern the first outlines of a general aesthetics and poetics. Bouhélier readily admitted this: "What is called naturism is more a morality than a doctrine of art"—an ethics, we have said, productive of life and passions, of virtual poetry, but apt to inspire the most varied works. For this reason, all those connected with official naturism—if we discount novelists such as Eugène Montfort and Charles-Louis Philippe—published nothing that was not largely surpassed in scope and interest by the works of independent writers who looked on the activity of the "school" with sympathy or distrust. These were Adolphe Retté, who at an early date undertook a campaign against Mallarmé; Francis Viélé-Griffin, who succeeded, without rebelling against anyone, in combining life and dreams in his very first poems (Le Blond in his *Essai* refers to Viélé Griffin as a "herald of joy"); and finally Francis Jammes. Before the publication (in 1897) of his *De l'Angélus de l'Aube à l'Angélus du Soir*, Jammes' youthful verse had breathed a new impressionism that "savored of savagery." Soon afterward Paul Fort freed himself from an atmosphere of anguish and nightmare, and Verhaeren dared to raise his eyes to the "faces of life" in the hope of exorcising the phantoms of his mind. And consider the titles of the collections of poems that were published from 1897 on—*L'Age d'Or* by Marc Lafargue, *Les Chansons d'Aube* by Henri Ghéon, *Les Voix de la Montagne* by Michel Abadie, *Clartes* by Albert Mockel, *La Chanson des Hommes* by Maurice Magre, *Les Poèmes ingénus* by Fernand Séverin, *Les quatre Saisons* by Stuart Merrill, *Le Jardin des Iles claires* by André

Fontainas; and a short time later the Countess de Noailles published *Coeur innombrable, Ombre des Jours*, and *Eblouissements*. There is not one of these titles that does not evoke a human song, a radiant light.

However, I incline to think that the work of the last years of the nineteenth century, in which desire is exalted for its own sake in the most direct way, yet with a variety of resources which merge into the most homogeneous style, will remain in the eyes of the future the breviary of ardent wisdom which Gide called *Les Nourritures terrestres*. The intoxication with life, which this work seeks as a sovereign good, is that of man restored to a state of blissful destitution and compelled to feel everything anew: "It is not enough for me to *read* that the sand of the beaches is soft, I want my bare feet to feel it. I have no use for any knowledge that is not preceded by a sensation." There is perfect indifference toward the so-called social aspect of existence, a will to start from scratch, to reject the acquisitions and the dead weight of habit as well as the common forms of life, in order to create a new man, less attached to his present self than ready to engage upon a new path of development, less eager to fulfill than to transcend himself. For some time it was the fashion to regard Gide as a naturist, but this was a provisional classification. The fate of *Les Nourritures terrestres* was that of all books that are in advance of their times, and its influence, at first covert and intermittent, was fully effective only after other works had paved the way for it.

These new influences that contributed, between 1897 and 1914, to a vast triumphant movement, are extremely numerous and varied, and those which are perhaps the most powerful transcend the domain of literature. I shall cite three names so well known that any comment on their singificance is superfluous—Whitman, Nietzsche, Bergson.

First read in the original, translated partially and piecemeal beginning in 1899, Whitman later found in Léon Bazalgette a disinterested disciple who undertook to prepare a complete French version of *Leaves of Grass* (1908); but even before this, some elements of his poetry and ethics had penetrated into important works such as those of Viélé-Griffin, Paul Claudel, Verhaeren, and very probably of Gide. Thereafter Whitmanian accents were perceptible in the works of several poets, from Valéry Larbaud to Duhamel and Vildrac, from André Spire to Apollinaire. In the imagination of many readers, the vagabond of America's open roads was associated with that other tramp, Rimbaud. And a simple aesthetic theory was born from his morality, the morality of a man consubstantial with his poetry, who "asks for nothing better or more divine than real life" to raise him to a state of perfect euphoria.

The essential contribution of Nietzsche, who has often been misunderstood, was not a specific idea, but an almost organic affirmation of life and the power of man, exactly what was needed to justify the most contradictory experiments provided they were "lived."* If this is so, it may be somewhat inconsistent to blame a disciple for having betrayed his master's thought. Such a message, aiming primarily to establish that truth is to be found only in man's impulse to destroy himself in order to be reborn, was not only in harmony with the love of reality and life that characterized part of the generation of 1900, but also helped to reconcile their vital need for a spiritual synthesis with the passionate meditation of Mallarmé and above all Rimbaud. Thus it became possible to formulate an "ambivalent" attitude toward the world, which gratified the need for both affirmation and destruction, and which combined these two tendencies into a Dionysiac pantheism.

As for Bergson, a study of his influence, in the proper sense of this term, would be extremely difficult in the field of modern poetry. For the philosophy of *l'Evolution créatrice* also drew its dynamism from the deep vitalist current that it later helped to enrich and direct: by and large, the analogies between the works of Bergson and those of the poets testify to a kinship between speculative thought and literature, but do not warrant the conclusion that they are related as cause and effect. Moreover, the basic approach of the Bergsonian philosopher, his search for concrete reality beyond (or before) the conceptual and symbolic apparatus of language, is close to that of the poet. Correspondences can be established both in 1889 and in 1907 between the *Essai sur les Données immédiates de la Conscience* and *l'Evolution créatrice* on the one hand, and the condition of poetry, or a certain kind of poetry, in the respective periods. Bergsonism, which was auscultation of the self before it turned to the universe, seems to have developed along a curve parallel to that

---

*In *Prétextes*, Gide wrote: *In France the influence of Nietzsche preceded the publication of his work; it found the soil prepared; otherwise it might not have* "taken"; *at present, it no longer surprises, it confirms.*

followed by the general development of literature in the same period.

A survey of the Schools—most of them without any real importance—which succeeded each other in Paris at the beginning of the twentieth century (Humanism, Somptuarism, Paroxysm, Integralism, and even Unanimism and Futurism) shows that, however diverse their intentions, they participated more or less in the *élan vital* which at that time carried French thought like a tidal wave toward "the possession of the world." Simultaneously, in southern France, a poetry of regular form but pantheist inspiration was turning to account the teachings of the Romanic school, of Maurras and sometimes of Mistral, seeking a synthesis of classical tradition and naturist exaltation.

This is additional proof that the poetry of an epoch cannot be considered by itself, as a distinct and autonomous activity; it plunges its roots into the lives of individuals and through them into the life of social groups; on some occasions it perhaps expresses something as elementary as an instinct and as little reasoned as those occult revolutions through which one people after another, in a rhythm recalling the rhythm of the heart, becomes attached to or detached from itself, other peoples, the world. As for the decade or two that separate the aftermath of symbolism from the year 1914, there is no doubt that they witnessed among the young European generations the birth and growth of an optimism, a faith in life, a confidence in the future, and even a devotion to civilization and its conquests, fully as strong as the enthusiasm which animated the French and foreign romanticists on the eve of the revolutions of 1848. In France, subsequent events destroyed these hopes; the wave broke against the cliff of August 1914. The poets had lyrically vowed to embrace blindfolded Life and the real world, and had accepted the risks of this adventure in advance. But the war, with its frightening novelty, compelled the people and most of the poets, to seek an inner homeland in the mind and in dreams, just as they had done in the period of symbolism.

CHAPTER THREE

The Poetry of the Young Century

1.

The century dawned gray. There were well-known poets, schools, ephemeral groupings, but no definite movement, no original slogans. The coryphées of the generation of 1885, from Régnier to Viélé-Griffin and Verhaeren, each following his own path, gradually moved away from their youth, resumed contact with the tangible world, and discovered the social world. Their poetry came to resemble the diverse forms of naturism and followed the beaten track of the French literary tradition. The most recent and most genuine "novelty" was Francis Jammes' *De l'Angélus de l'Aube à l'Angélus du Soir*, published in 1897.

Out of respect for their masters and loyalty for their first ideal, these writers, who in 1900 were between thirty and forty years old (approximately; Samain died in 1900 at the age of 42, Verhaeren died at 45, and Paul Fort at only 28), continued to call themselves symbolists, as though everyone were in agreement as to the meaning of the term "symbolism."

One strain of their poetry can be described as an indirect lyricism: the emotions and desires of the self are represented in images, allegories, emblems, godlike figures, heroic masks, and occasionally developed in the form of fables, dramas, and characters. This applies especially to Henri de Régnier and Viélé-Griffin.

Then there are the poets who, instead of sublimating their sentimental inspiration into pure beauty or mystical élan, express their human emotions candidly or with pathos. Paul Fort, Stuart Merrill (after 1900), Viélé-Griffin (in his short pieces), Samain, and Jammes wrote elegies, songs and chansonettes about everyday joys and sorrows. However, Verhaeren's *Campagnes hallucinées* and *Villes ten-*

taculaires (1905) contain the elements of an epic legend of modern life and man; and the social and humanitarian poets, whether influenced by him or not, grouped themselves around him.

Finally, with Francis Jammes, and occasionally Paul Fort and Viélé-Griffin, came a poetry of nature, rejuvenated by a new sensibility and impressionistic vision; in fact, this "naturist" poetry was the most direct protest against the aestheticism of the 1890's and the cult of artificial paradises.

Of these three principal currents, the first is nothing but the extension of a certain symbolist tradition which is itself linked with the Parnassians and shows a predilection for historical or mythological themes. Régnier's poetry, for example, is deliberately turned toward a celtic or Hellenic past already poetized by time and legend,—a fantasied past that emerges from a dream, so that the atavistic memories that haunt the poet's imagination are reflected in it as in "their own correspondence." This is clearly one of the favorite attitudes of the symbolist Narcissus. True, in *La Sandale ailée* or *Le Miroir des Heures* nature does cast off its veils, and the god of love stands alone in a tragic atmosphere; but these poems, with their Parnassian or classical rigidity, often lack the music and harmonious rhythm of *Jeux rustiques et divins*. After 1900, Régnier continued to write exquisite poems, showing that his art remained what it had been from the outset, a refined product of very ancient culture. Hence its great seductive power, but perhaps also its weakness: a self-complacent revery that only plays with aesthetic form runs the risk of petrifying, of yielding to foreseeable rhythms, of becoming imprisoned in a setting it has constructed as its own tangible and sumptuous replica. And a fortiori, many imitators will see in all this only a vein to be exploited.

As for Viélé-Griffin's dramatic poems and short epics, they seem, during the first years of the century, to have been chiefly appreciated for their dynamism and perfect eurythmy. In their free stanzas the isolated verse yields its autonomy to a vaster movement, which suggests a stylization of the human gesture or an inflection of the natural voice. This poetry is not only psychological and visual, but also "spoken" and consequently anti-Parnassian.

It would be easy to go back as far as Verlaine, Laforgue, Maeterlinck, Corbière, let alone Nerval and Aloysius Bertrand, to enumerate the nineteenth century sources of the popular or medieval theme of *Ballades françaises*. Actually, one of the merits of the symbolists, "poets of the soul," was that, like the romantics,they were interested in the so-called primitive forms of art and attempted to revive the spirit of folklore. This current of popular lyricism, in which a grain of Villonesque madness seasons the sweet memory of the *lais* and *complaintes*, the *chansons de geste*, and the dreams of chivalry (and ribaldry), was kept alive by Paul Fort, Viélé-Griffin, Fagus, and Tristan Klingsor, and influenced Guillaume Apollinaire. However, even before the naturists had preached the reconciliation of the poet with life, the genius of Paul Fort unfolded; an intoxication with life, based on a vague pantheism, had taken hold of him, and like a gifted story-teller he improvised on all human pains and pleasures.

But it was chiefly Jammes and Verhaeren who, after the demise of symbolism, represented the new alliance between the spirit and nature. Most of the experiments that preceded or followed 1900 were undertaken with a view to such an alliance. The poets had forgotten the roads that lead to the spiritual homeland of Baudelaire and Mallarmé or to "the other world" of Rimbaud, or pretended to have forgotten, or shunned them like precipitous paths on which their lives would be endangered. Was there not a homeland quite near by, clearly visible, fresh and bright, where beings with real bodies came and went, where the very shadows were luminous, where there were some souls with a real "vocation for happiness"? The poetry of Baudelaire's and Mallarmé's disciples, because it detached itself from the tangible world and pursued a dream, ended by becoming bloodless. Jammes infused it with new vigor, and Verhaeren poured into it a wine as red as blood.

Jammes' purpose was to make poetry flow back from "the ideal" and the dark background of the mind into the world of simple things and feelings. Symbols and allegories vanished before his clear gaze, external things began once again to live for themselves, outside the poet's mind; moreover, he divested them of the hardness, dryness and dreariness with which the naturalistic novelists had endowed them; a new spring swelled the buds, once more freshness and innocence transfigured nature like a morning dew. This is still naturalism, but a naturalism that does not exclude poetry, but on the contrary finds it everywhere, draws it from the shoddiest scene and the most wretched human being. Once again everything was worthy to be written about. Between 1897 and 1917, more than one young writer could doubtless have said what Alain-Fournier wrote in a letter to Jacques Rivière: "As for myself, Jammes authorized me to say many things that otherwise I would not have dared to say . . ."—not necessarily the most individual things, but rather the most commonplace or reputed to be such. And now let the poem follow the sensation, let it be once more, as it was for Verlaine, "the good fortune brought by chance"; the rest is mere literature.

Finally, it must be recalled that Verhaeren evolved morally from an attitude of acceptance to an attitude of rejection; his task, after he had overcome the temptation of neurasthenia, was to tame himself little by little to this modern world, which he had hated ever since he ceased to recognize in it the work of God. There are few examples of such an attempt to "transmute values," of so explicit a will to strike the spark of joy from suffering. If Verhaeren now refused to condemn anything that existed, it was only that he might go one step further and embrace "ardent and contradictory life." But it is important to note that this strong trend to extraversion was only in keeping with the general intellectual trend from the symbolist period to the first world war. "What everyone experiences in Verhaeren," wrote Marius-Ary Le Blond in the *Mercure de France* in 1904, "is passion." It would be hard to account for Verhaeren's large audience and the many echoes gradually aroused in and outside France by the author of *Forces tumultueuses* and *Multiple Splendeur* solely by the aesthetic merits of his work. What Verhaeren proclaimed above all was proud intoxication of the twentieth century European on the eve of the catastrophe—man's glory and his pact with matter.

In fact—except for Jammes and Fort, who were younger, and Verhaeren who perhaps alone of his generation effected a true renewal of himself—most of the poets of the post-symbolist period had, by 1900, undertaken to humanize, regularize, we might even say popularize, in the noblest sense of the term, the relatively esoteric poetry that they had cultivated ten or fifteen years earlier to please a restricted and, in a sense, conniving public. This tendency is manifest in Samain, for instance, though it must also be said that the author of *Le Jardin de l'Infante* had from the outset skilfully wielded the grace and glamor of a composite style designed to charm the

imagination of those who still regretted the guitars of elegiac romanticism. But in the others as well, it was a composite art that
triumphed, to the satisfaction of compilers of anthologies and most
of their readers—an art which continued to call itself symbolist but
which amalgamated poetic virtues inherited from the Parnassians
and even from the picturesque or sentimental kind of romanticism.

2.

To read the programs and manifestoes of the magazines founded
during the first years of the century, seeing the care they take in
defining and redefining French and Latin values and the terms
"classical" and "classicism," one might suppose that at that time
intellectual and literary nationalism was advancing full sail.* Yet
the younger schools of poetry preferred the formulas of Maurice Le
Blond and his friends—life, nature, reality, mankind. "We want an
art that sings of human life, of all human life," declared Fernand
Gregh, apostle of humanism, and later in the introductory poem of
Clartés humaines (1904) he sang:

> Mais à mon tour j'aurai connu le goût chaud de la vie;
> J'aurai miré dans ma prunelle
> Petite minute éblouie,
> La grande lumière éternelle;
> Mais j'aurai bu ma joie au grand festin sacré;
> Que voudrais-je de plus?
> J'aurai vécu,
> Et je mourrai.

*In December 1901, for example, Adrien Milhouard published the first issue of
Occident which broadly defines an Occidental, Christian-inspired classicism opposed
both to the theories of the Romanic school and to the *naturalistic and sentimental
excesses of the romantics*. *Minerva*, founded in 1902, was distinctly conservative and
immediately opened its pages to Maurras and Bainville. *Renaissance latine* (first
issue, May 15, 1902) cared little for poetry, but unreservedly exalted everything
Mediterranean. In 1903, Eugène Montfort became editor of *Les Marges* in which
naturism lived at peace with some stronger opinions borrowed from Maurras.
Indeed, it was the doctrine of Maurras, adopted by *l'Action français*, that more or
less directly fertilized most of these expressions of national or aesthetic con-
servatism; later, in 1908, it led to the creation of the literary and political *Revue
critique des Idées et des Livres*.

But I, too, shall have known the taste of life;
Mine eyes will have beheld
For an infinitesimal dazzling moment
The great eternal light;
I shall have quaffed my joy at the great sacred feast;
What more could I desire?
I shall have lived,
And I shall die.

The two currents born after the decline of symbolism (and in opposition to symbolism) continued to provide sustenance to intellectual life, but both were changing. Naturism, which had sprung from a deep desire to accept reality and human experience, underwent endless metamorphoses and finally became a simple vital optimism; Romanism, on the contrary, became more circumscribed, concentrated, refined, and developed into a kind of neoclassicism.

On the face of it, nothing seems more heterogeneous than the work of the rising generation of poets, who were between twenty and thirty years of age in 1905. Some tried to follow in the wake of the great symbolists. *La Chanson d'Eve* (1904) seems to justify their efforts. In a pre-Raphaelite atmosphere, shot through with hesitant flashes of light, soon submerged in a diaphanous mist, Van Lerberghe evokes a mysterious Eve who gradually takes possession of a world of dreamlike fluidity. But the latest production of Henri de Régnier, Jammes, Samain, Charles Guérin, and the Comtesse de Noailles rather invited the young poets to renounce the bold attempt to realize a synthesis of the various traditions of sentimental romanticism from Lamartine to Hugo, Coppée, and Verlaine. After the upsurge of the years from 1885 to 1895, a kind of ebbtide tended to bring poetry back to an intellectual substratum anterior to Baudelaire and Rimbaud, even though some of the works composed on this basis did discreetly profit from the stylistic acquisitions and "techniques" of symbolism. Most of the new poets were not so much interested in evincing any striking originality or even in expressing their temperament, as in cultivating a linguistic consciousness that was scrupulously French, and in adapting themselves to the well tried forms of the national spirit. Some seductive intermediate products thus resulted from a meeting of several traditions. True, this poetry often strikes us as reminiscent, but this should not blind us to its charm, nor to the stirrings and "sincere" hopes of souls still uncertain of themselves, divided as they were between a *fin-de-siècle* melancholy inherited from romanticism, and a will to live, startled at its own boldness.

Among these efforts, some of which led nowhere, it is difficult to choose. Louis Mercier, a sober and pure poet, followed the tradition of Catholic romanticism and that of Lamartine; Fernand Gregh, at first a Verlainian, later returned to Hugo, specifically to the collections of eloquent meditations that Hugo produced at intervals between 1830 and 1840; nor do I think that François Porché would have denied his romantic Origins; Roger Frêne, author of *Sèves originaires* (1908), can be regarded as one of the most gifted exponents of naturism; the poems of Léo Larguier are firm and measured, nourished by the "masters" from Homer and Virgil to Ronsard and Hugo, and basically respectable in their means of expression. There is little doubt, however, that the most interesting poets of the young century, those who articulated the inner voice, somewhat veiled and nostalgic (and incidentally, provincial) of an era that was not entirely lost in admiration for itself and the Eiffel tower, steered an almost deliberate course toward a minor, elegiac lyricism.

The elegiac vein that runs through the works of Emile Despax, Charles Dérennes, Abel Bonnard, even of Léo Larguier (to cite but a few names) derives from the tradition of intimate poetry, the tradition of *Méditations*, and of *Muse française* by Marceline Desbordes-Valmore; or one might even go back to Parny, Léonard, Chénier, the dreams of the Golden Age at the end of the eighteenth century, and by another road, to Fénélon and Racine. After 1825, this current inspired the melancholy of Sainte-Beuve and the tenderness of Maurice de Guérin; it also nourished the sadness of the *Nuits* and the exaltation of Georges Sand, while *Graziella* and *Raphaël* carried it to the point of insipidity. Later it branched out in several directions, and vanished, one might have thought, had it not reappeared in *La Bonne Chanson*, in the religious and erotic complaints of Verlaine.

What creates a bond between poets as different from one another as Samain, Jammes, and Charles Guérin, writing shortly before 1900, is precisely their elegiac sensibility. One might add to this group Louis Le Cardonnel, a serene Christian whose slow-moving and luminous poetry rises to the level of prayer, and even Henri Bataille, who dwells in a late autumn mist, full of trembling shadows and inchoate stammerings. Charles Guérin, who was a distinguished elegiac poet, but nothing more, played for some time the part of mentor to the younger writers. To be sure, he showed a certain complaisance toward a despair inherited from Musset, de Vigny, Baudelaire; but he would not have been able to maintain the tone of passionate meditation that characterizes his poems if a real illness had not rent him to his very depths; all his efforts to live proved powerless to wrest him free from the circle of his solitude. Incidentally, the decadents, if not the symbolists, knew and cultivated this romantic anguish that ravages a suffering body, and the naturists' optimistic will to embrace reality did not succeed in dissipating it; Samain, for example, who found "infinite sweetness" in "broken things," was, shortly before his death, more than ever enchanted by this *mal de siècle* of the declining century. In *Le Chariot d'or*, we read:

> J'entendis s'élever une voix solitaire
> Qui vibrait dans le soir comme un beau violon;
> En me penchant un peu, dans un noble salon
> Où flottait un passé d'Eloas et d'Elvires,
> Je vis, à la lueur vacillante des cires,
> Un visage de marbre avec de lourds bandeaux,
> Et de grands yeux brillants de larmes aux flambeaux.
> Anxieux, j'écoutai . . .

> I heard a solitary voice
> That vibrated in the evening like a beautiful violin;
> And bending over a little, in a noble salon
> Where hovered a past filled with Eloas and Elviras,
> I saw by the flickering candles
> A face of marble with heavy braids of hair
> And great eyes glistening with tears in the light of the torches.
> Anguished, I listened . . .

Silence, music in the night, a poet questioning himself and questioning the shadows, the answer that does not come, a loving complicity with mystery and sadness, waiting protracted to the point of tears—this whole atmosphere created by the "heavy heart" of

late adolescence, recurs, almost unchanged, in a poem from
La Maison des Glycines by Emile Despax:

> *L'ombre suavement s'ouvre au chant qui prélude.*
> *Jeanne pâlit. Je tremble en regardant ses mains.*
> *Sommes-nous plus divins, ce soir, ou plus humains?*
> *Seul, Beethoven le sait au ciel. O solitude.*
> *Sur terre, cette voix . . . ailleurs partout, la nuit . . .*
> *Tout l'Océan qui songe et tout l'azur qui luit.*
> *Harmonieux semeurs d'extase, doigts des femmes,*
> *Comme vous enchaînez, en vous jouant, nos âmes*
> *De liens délicieux qu'un seul mot doit briser.*
> *Un ange, en se penchant, beaux doigts, vous a baisés;*
> *Un instant vous avez touché ses boucles blondes.*
> *Silence . . . Mais ces vents, cette mer, ces rumeurs . . .*
> *Oh! respectez, vents fous, respecte, mer profonde,*
> *La nuit élyséenne et ce chant qui se meurt. . . .*

> Suavely the shadow opens to the preluding song.
> Jeanne turns pale. I tremble as I look upon her hands.
> Are we more godlike tonight, or more human?
> Nobody knows but Beethoven in heaven. O solitude.
> On earth this voice . . . everywhere else, the night . . .
> The whole ocean dreams and the whole sky glitters;
> Feminine fingers, harmonious sowers of ecstasy,
> How easily you enchain our souls
> In delicious bonds that a single word must break.
> An angel bent down and kissed you, lovely fingers;
> For one moment you touched his blond curls.
> Silence . . . But these winds, this sea, these sounds.
> Oh, respect, mad winds, respect, deep sea,
> The Elysian night and this dying song. . . .

The style of this effusion, just as in Samain and Guérin, is moulded
by the need for an expression that is both pathetic and musical; but
Despax, taught no doubt by Jammes, interrupts his rhythms more
than the others, and within each verse multiplies the stops, the
organ points, which enable the emotion to radiate and the poem
to escape from the regularity of oratorical cadences. As for the
sentimental theme, it belongs so much to the period and to elegiac—
and provincial—poetry of the years between 1900 and 1905,

that we find it again, in a piece by Léo Larguier entitled *Minuit*:

> *Pendant que je dormais, n'as-tu pas sangloté*
> *Mon coeur? Que veux-tu donc? voici la nuit d'été . . .*
> *Un lointain violon, d'une plainte lassée,*
> *Déchire le silence. Oh! cette étrange voix*
> *Douloureuse, obstinée et toujours offensée!*
> *J'ai soudain le désir de pleurer dans les bois,*
> *De marcher le front nu dans une immense allée . . .*
> *Je me lève en tremblant . . .*

> While I slept, did you not weep,
> My heart? What then do you disire? Here is the summer night.
> A distant violin rends the silence
> With its weary plaint. Oh, this strange sorrowful
> Voice, stubborn and always offended!
> Suddenly the desire takes me, to weep in the woods,
> To walk bareheaded down an endless forest path,
> I arise trembling . . .

This "distinguished" tone, this style of "carrying one's heart on one's sleeve," of exhibiting one's feelings and impressions by naming, describing them—I was about to say: by analyzing them—instead of suggesting their nature through images, in the manner of the symbolists, everything in these lines, down to the distant violin, leads us step by step to the salons of the period of the *Muse française* and its noble sentimental intimacies—to the living, musical wellsprings of elegiac romanticism.

The first years of the century, however, were also the years of "feminine romanticism," to borrow a term from Maurras. Renée Vivien, Madame Lucie Delarue-Mardrus, Madame Gérard d'Houville, the Comtesse de Noailles, Marie Dauguet, and later to a lesser degree, Cécile Sauvage, as well as others among the poetesses of yesterday, knew "the glory of being oneself" and the new delight of singing, in a major more often than a minor key, and with an unprecedented frankness, the most secret, most feminine part of their being. Needless to say, they were distinguished from one another by more than mere nuances. Several of them, more sentimental than sensual, especially Madame Lucie Delarue-Mardrus, display a rather coquettish modesty. As for Madame Gérard d'Houville, who happened to be the daughter of Hérédia, the sister-in-law of Pierre Louÿs, and the wife of the author of *Médailles d'argile*, she inherited a certain decorative symbolism, which was part of her family tradition, so to speak. Incidentally, Maurras himself, in consideration of the beautiful classical poem on Charon and the Styx, was unwilling to condemn her poetry, as his doctrine would have required. We can only approve this weakness, even though the soft Tanagra figurines that Madame Gérard d'Houville created are quite clearly Alexandrine. Moreover, she composed poems that were more spontaneously human, romantic if you will, but sober and unpretentious, on her anxieties and unfulfilled hopes, and on the elusive and strange discoveries that a woman bent upon achieving self-knowledge makes in her own soul. Here is a passage from *Epitaphe*, the last selection in *Poésies*.

> *Je veux dormir au fond des bois, pour que le vent*
> *Fasse parfois frémir le feuillage mouvant*
> *Et l'agite dans l'air comme une chevelure*
> *Au-dessus de ma tombe, et selon l'heure obscure*
> *Ou claire, l'ombre des feuilles avec le jour,*
> *Y tracera, légère et noire, et tour à tour,*
> *En mots mysterieux, arabesque suprême,*
> *Une épitaphe aussi changeante que moi-même.*

> Lay me to rest in the woods, that sometimes the wind
> May rustle through the trees
> And shake their boughs like waving hair
> Over my grave, and shifting with the bright or darkening hour,
> The shadows of the leaves, mingled with light,
> Will trace upon it in mysterious words
> A supreme arabesque, delicate and black by turns,
> An epitaph as changing as myself.

It is the Comtesse de Noailles who surpasses all other members of this group in power and productivity, as well as the response she aroused. Though it is true that she lived a pathetic inner drama which ended in the angry revolt of her last books of verse—and today, we might say, in her death—her contemporaries were chiefly impressed by the delirious poetry of her first works, in which a temperament ravaged by sensations overflows without restraint. It is quite understandable that her influence should have coincided with that of Jammes. But how far apart they are! Jammes is never submerged by his sensations; in the face of them he preserves his artistic aloofness and is able to record the arabesques of his impressions with the light touch of a Far-Eastern poet. On the contrary, the Comtesse de Noailles is always wholly stirred by the world, it dominates her like a passion. Powerfully attracted by a pantheist vision, she comes close to a very profound experience of the universe. Yet perhaps she lacks imagination and a sufficiently acute sense of spiritual life. She finds it difficult to remain for any length of time above the stormy feeling born of the effervescence of her senses. Her poetry, like herself, clings close to the carnal earth.

Sometimes, as in *Les Eblouissements*, she succeeds in opposing the universe, in holding her own against its assaults, through her heroic resolution to feel ever more fully:

> *Glauque matin, chaos d'azur*
> *Opaque et dense comme un mur!*
> *L'écumeux et mol paysage,*
> *Comme une armée au bleu visage*
> . . . .
> *Bondit sous mon regard*

> Sea-green morning chaos of blue
> Opaque and dense as a wall!
> The foamy and soft landscape
> Like a blue-faced army . . .
> . . . .
> Leaps as I behold it

At such moments, when the demon of eloquence or an instinct of conquetry does not lead her astray, the Comtesse de Noailles gauges her words and associates them in such a way as to translate the confused language of sensations. She invents synthetic images that remind one of Rimbaud's striving for a "word" accessible to all the senses. True, Hugo remains the first of her romantic masters, it is his example that she is most prone to follow, nevertheless she owed much to modern impressionism, and she must be classified as a descendant of Baudelaire in the sense that she is one of those poets who seek to express the direct action of things on the human body. Thus she learned to write poetry that seems to accord with vegetative nature, and that seethes and brims over like a life-giving fountain.

Most of the women of this poetic generation—I also have in mind Colette, in the field of prose—are characterized by their willingness to accept their own nature and the data of their senses, to "entrench themselves in their essential differentness," and to admit things that men have never been able to find in them; they are also characterized by their style, which is no less "feminine," and their almost feline art of luring words into caressing sentences. If need be, an accommodating Hellenism provides them with an easy alibi; this is true of the Comtesse de Noailles, of Madame Gérard d'Houville, and (though in a different context) of Renée Vivien who required a Greek background for her Lesbian dreams. Most often they are satisfied with finding, anywhere *in* the world (and no longer *outside* it, like the author of *Le Voyage*), something to feed their "sensual, mystical, and *clairvoyant*" delirium. The male, his love and the love he inspires, occupy a relatively small place in this feminine lyricism. It is the universe of things and sensations, the delights of the self, that attract and fixate the inner gaze of these women, which the image of human beings never succeeds in holding for any length of time. Exacting and egotistical, they seek constantly to expand their empire, to indulge their enjoyment of themselves to the point of rapture, they dream of a marriage with the powers of the earth. A desecration, says Maurras, who wonders "whether we must have Bacchantes." But no doubt some freedom must be left to the genius, the personal demon. The Comtesse de Noailles indisputably had such a demon, which soon tore her away from the pantheist exaltations of *Le Coeur innombrable*, and revealed to her, some time after Maurras had defined the morality of feminine romanticism, a new heaven and a new hell: to the passion of living there were added the passions of love and, in her declining years, the thought of death. Perhaps "she was made to be dead," as Jean Cocteau said so profoundly of this woman, who bent the bow of life to the breaking point to keep from feeling the emptiness of a heart which only the possession of the absolute could have filled.

To sing the most intimate part of herself without desecration or aridity, it would seem that a woman must refrain from taking refuge within her jealously guarded femininity, and open herself to desire, to the ardent need of forgetting herself. Then the most direct confessions, like those of Cécile Sauvage, can remain natural and free from any suspicion of exhibitionism:

Je suis autour de toi comme l'amande verte
Qui ferme son écrin sur l'amandon laiteux,
Comme la cosse molle aux replis contonneux
Dont la graine enfantine et soyeuse est couverte.

La larme qui me monte aux yeux, tu la connais,
Elle a le goût profond de mon sang sur tes lèvres.

. . . .

Ecoute, maintenant que tu m'entends encore,
Imprime dans mon sein ta bouche puérile . . .

I am round you like the green almond
That encloses the milky kernel in its jewel case,
Like the soft husk with the downy folds
That covers the childlike, downy grain.

The tear that comes to my eyes, you know it,
Has the profound taste of my blood on your lips.

. . . .

Listen, while you still hear me,
Imprint your boyish mouth on my breast.

The reality of love is stronger than the reality of the flesh in this maternal and childish speech, this whisper more profound than any thought.

(And due place, an eminent place, should be given to the few poems left by Catherine Pozzi [published in the magazine *Mesures*] and first of all to the ode entitled *Ave*, a noble and radiant hymn to "most exalted love.")

Could these young poets of the new century revive the great adventures and passions of romanticism? For this, they would have had to find in themselves the fuel for the anguished hallucinations, the despairs and sadness of a spirit raging and pacing the floor in its prison—all the resources which gave rise to the rhapsodies of a de Musset—or else find a way out, transcend pure humanity, press forward to the pre-mystical states which favor the flight of exalted poetry. The Comtesse de Noailles was perhaps the only one of these poets who had it in her to attempt a heroic existence. Still, Paul Drouot, in the incomplete fragments of his prose poem, *Eurydice deux fois perdue*, occasionally opens the gates of those solitary regions. But only to exceptional beings is it given to attempt such exhausting ventures. The others, often those who are most civilized, spontaneously avoid the tragic, and what they ask of poetry is primarily to increase their pleasure, to lend a refined embellishment to life, without disclosing its dangerous depths. In sum, the neo-romaticism of the 1900's was successful in the field of elegy, because it was natural for a tender sentimentalism impregnated with noble literary memories to express itself in an intimate, moving, and musical poetry. Moreover, this neo-romanticism encouraged a feminine lyricism charged with sensations.

"It is a poetry too close to the average tone to arouse anger," wrote Rémy de Gourmont in 1905. He was a keen but unsympathetic observer. The elegiac poets, who were free from aestheticism and able to avoid the stylistic methods and mannerisms of the minor symbolists, succumbed to the spell of "poetic atmospheres" and vague emotions, but they have lost the key to the metaphysical lyricism originating in Baudelaire. As for the poets of sensation, for them the world ceased to be an *incitamentum*, an intellectual stimulus, and often lured them into its toils, ensnared them like a bird-catcher, so that they could not detach themselves from tangible objects, from everyday existence. There were others, however, who more or less successfully strove to restore the literary traditions of romanticism at its best.

CHAPTER FOUR

The Awakening of Meridional Poetry

It has often been observed that there have been relatively few French poets of southern ancestry—poets writing in verse, that is. It was not until the sixteenth century that a great writer was born in a land of Provençal speech, in the person of Marot. Later the very men who glorified humanist and Mediterranean thought—Chénier, Leconte de Lisle, Hérédia, and, in more recent times, Moréas—were all born under the tropics or near the Aegean Sea. The great romantics, except for Gautier, came from the center or north of France; symbolism was of Parisian and Flemish origin (with a slight admixture of American blood), and deliberately oriented itself toward the Celtic northwest and the Germanic east, extending to Scandinavia and the Russian plains. We recall with what contempt Huysmans, in *Là-bas*, relegated the provinces in which a southern dialect is spoken to a world outside of France; and in 1905, Robert de Souza wrote almost as cavalierly in the first issue of *Vers et Prose:* "In a way, symbolism is an awakening of the true French literature of the north against the deplorable meridional usurpations." De Souza was no doubt attacking the inspiration and aesthetics of the Parnassus.

Be that as it may, around 1900, the southern-dialect provinces, and primarily Provence, suddenly became, and remained for a period of several years, the favored home of a certain lyrical quality; there occurred an "awakening of the true French literature of the south" brought about by a number of poets, from Emmanuel Signoret to Joachim Gasquet and Lionel des Rieux, and from Marc Lafargue or Pierre Camo to Fernand Mazade. And why not include as well Royère, Toulet, Derême, Vérane, Alibert and even Valéry, Despax and Dérennes, natives of Languedoc, and Leo Larguier, of the Cévennes region, and those northerners, who were conquered by the

Mediterranean: Paul Castiaux, Théo Varlet, and others? But it would be absurd and paradoxical to apply a rigorous new "theory of climates." Common sense and the facts bid us relate to a natural milieu and the spirit of this milieu—in this case, the southern regions—only those poems which it deeply influenced and which proclaim this influence.

Mistral and the poetry of the Félibrige had far more to do with initiating this current than Moréas and his Parisian "Romanic school." A new national consciousness born in the southern-dialect provinces invited the poet to draw fresh vigor from a feeling of everything that tied him to the mores, people, forms of these happy regions, to the modes of thinking and feeling of the Mediterranean world. But it must be noted at the outset that this spiritual acceptance of the milieu and historical past of a civilization was also enjoined upon the "naturists" by Maurice Le Blond, in a hardly different form, when he formulated the prerequisites for a reconciliation of the self and the external world. Moreover, to plunge into local sources, and into the Latin or even Hellenic origins from which they derived, led inevitably to a certain classicism, perhaps more comprehensive than that of Maurras, but at bottom quite close to it. Thus, the two ideas of a return to "nature" and of a return to the humanistic tradition found a favorable climate in southern France where they were grafted on each other and bore fruit. At the same time the great example of Mistral and his followers offered the prospect of a large-scale literary decentralization, thanks to which the "regionalist" poets, living far from Parisian fashions and influences, attached to their local homelands as the poets of the *Pléiade* were attached to their Vendômois or Anjou, would each play his part in a symphony of provincial France. This was only a daydream, perhaps, but it seemed alluring at a time when Barrès was offering the educated bourgeoisie his aesthetic of the soil and the dead.

Marc Lafargue and Pierre Camo developed from the "School of Toulouse," as the contributors to *Effort* were smilingly called about 1900. Though differing from one another in their essential nature, both started out with poems of a somewhat indolent facility and abundance—pleasant variations of the naturist pattern; then under the impact of *Stances* and neo-classicism, they submitted to the so-called Romance influence, Lafargue to that of Ronsard and Chénier, and Camo to that of Malherbe and Tristan—although Camo today cultivates a more complex poetry, which has something of both Mallarmé and Valéry. Lafargue will no doubt leave behind the memory of a tender Epicurean who evoked a world of voluptuous and subtle delights, bathed in light and shadow:

> *Enlace-moi de tes beaux bras, ô jeune amie . . .*

> Enfold me in your beautiful arms, o young beloved . . .

We are reminded of Ronsard inviting Marie de Bourgueil to take her pleasure with him. There is nothing here that has not been seen before . . . but youth is reborn each spring, and Lafargue's best poems have precisely the touching grace of youth.

> *Tout le prix de la vie est dans la volupté*

> The entire value of life lies in pleasure

was also the credo of Pierre Camo. But his pleasure was more secret and somber, perfumed with exoticism, with a strain of Moslem languor. Camo who lived in Madagascar was a French Catalan, and his ardor was mingled with an element of aridity, of haughty pride, of Spanishness; his dream flickers back and forth, from the balmy shores caressed by the trade winds to the rocky Pyrenees, harsh and bare under the blue sky and the snow.

It was the sky of Provence that brought to full maturity the exuberant classicism out of which Maurras modeled the profile of his frail goddess. But the man who seemed predestined to realize these potentialities died at the age of twenty-eight, during the winter of 1900, "stifled by misery and the night." A child poet bathed in an almost apostolic candor—"has not mankind lived long enough to dispense with what has been called evil?"—Emmanuel Signoret was both a mystic of pure beauty and perhaps the only French poet to make Pindaric sublimity the habitual climate of his soul. Shortly before his death he succeeded in taming, in making an ally of that "fury" which had led so many pseudo-classicists to the abyss—I mean to say, to the most resounding, most distressing rhetoric. Having rejected one by one the accessories which he had at first borrowed from Banville and the Parnassians, and which encumbered his first works; gradually forgetting the principles of art and the reminiscences that burdened his memory, he finally found his own style, a perpetual surge toward the heights:

> *Dans les neiges, miroirs courbés sur les abîmes,*
> *Une stérile nymphe a miré ses longs yeux!*
> *Triste reine des monts purs et silencieux*
> *Contre mon sein mortel craindrais-tu de descendre?*
> *L'éternel désespoir fait ton regard si tendre!*
> . . . .
>
> *Aux bords où je naquis et que tu peux connaître*
> *Les purs sanglots des vents animeront ta voix;*
> *La myrte et les lauriers y composent des bois;*
> *Une épouse y cueillit la fleur de mes années;*
> *Mes fils y grandiront; les Muses y sont nées!*
>
> *Habitante des monts dont le coeur m'a parlé,*
> *Reine au front de mélèze et de buis noir voilé,*
> *Puisque ta belle lèvre à ma lèvre s'assemble,*
> *Qu'en mes vers gémissants tout ton désespoir tremble!*
> *Mon épouse!... Mes fils!... O tristes intretiens!...*
> *Pleurons près des torrents!... Mêle mes pleurs aux tiens!...*
> *Notre amour concevra quelque jeune harmonie,*
> *O Nymphe pour jamais à ma douleur unie.*

In the snow, a mirror overhanging the abyss,
A sterile nymph gazed at her long eyes!
Sad queen of the pure and silent mountains
Would you fear to descend to my mortal breast?
Eternal depair makes your gaze so tender!...
. . . .

On the shores where I was born and which perhaps you know
The pure sobbing of the winds will animate your voice;
There the woods are of myrtle and laurel;
There, a wife gathered the flower of my years;
There my sons will grow up; there the Muses were born!

Mountain-dweller of whom my heart has told me,
Queen whose forehead is veiled in larch and boxwood
Since your beautiful mouth is joined to my mouth
Let all your despair tremble in my moaning verses!
My wife!... My sons!... O sad colloquies!...
Let us weep by the torrents!... Mingle my tears with yours!...
Our love will conceive some young harmony,
O nymph for ever united to my pain!

(From Poésies complètes p. 275)

Signoret liked to abandon himself to a verbal delirium, to gain his effects by discontinuous and sometimes plainly gratuitious notations that add up to an atmosphere of translucent vapors, in which one hears the roaring Provençal sea and the vibrant Provençal air. This mystery made of dazzling light, these lyrical arabesques that surge up and break without regard for oratorical cadence, herald Valéry, a Valéry that is to Signoret what a metaphysical and hyper-conscious poet can be to a spontaneous poet, imprisoned by his intuitions, and lost in a solitary intoxication.

Signoret was able to achieve this lyricism only in flashes. Joachim Gasquet, his disciple, strove for it throughout his life, and sometimes found it, though always on the verge of a torrential eloquence:

> Un soir, en contemplant le jeu divin des ombres
> Sur la face des lacs où soleil descend,
> Sans le savoir, j'ai bu, vainqueur des charmes sombres,
> Au coeur unique où bat la source de mon sang.
>
> . . . .
>
> O, douceur de l'Amour, depuis tu me tourmentes!
> Je vois gonfler ma vie aux sources des torrents.
> Les pins, les flancs ouverts, tombent dans les tourmentes
> Et moi, les mêmes mains m'enlacent dans les vents.
>
> Comme un monde céleste où s'enflamment les plaines
> Et dont le pur éclat attire les oiseaux,
> Au bord de l'horizon luisent les mers lointaines,
> Et mon sang brûle en moi comme l'air sur les eaux.
>
> . . . .
>
> Des rocs, des fleurs, des eaux, ruisselle en moi la sève,
> Mes cheveux sont trempés de l'encens des forêts,
> La palpitation des germes me soulève,
> L'Universel Chasseur me crible des ses traits.

One evening, while contemplating the divine play of shadows
On the face of the lakes where the sun sets,
Unknowing, I vanquished somber spells,
And drank of the one heart where beats the source of my blood.

. . . .

O, sweetness of love, you have tormented me since!
I see my life swelling at the torrents' springs
The pines, with open flanks, fall amid storms,
And the same hands clasp me in the winds.

Like a celestial world where the plains are ablaze
A world whose pure radiance attracts the birds
The distant seas gleam at the edge of the horizon
And my blood burns in me like the air on the waters.

. . . .

The sap of the rocks, the flowers, the waters, flows within me,
My hair is drenched with the incense of the woods,
The throbbing of the seeds exalts me,
The Universal Hunter riddles me with his shafts.

(*Chant doré*)

Is the call that resounds in this hymn that of Maurice de Guérin's *Centaure*, Hugo's *Satyre*, of the early poems of Rimbaud? Actually, Gasquet's poetry is akin to the pantheist poetry of the great romantics; most often it is human, full of pathos, enclosed in the circle of joy and suffering. Here, then, is a classic writer of the south, whose romantic ancestry (in the domain of emotion and flamboyant rhetoric) cannot be doubted. But the term "classicism" lends itself to no less confusion than "romanticism": in a broad sense it denotes a doctrine of art and an ethics that do not call upon man to sacrifice anything of himself, except perhaps his taste for disorder and his secret desire that irrational forces will triumph over him. It was Joachim Gasquet who in 1903 published his *Chants séculaires* with a preface by Louis Bertrand, which is a manifesto in behalf of a Mediterranean and classical poetics, also founded on the Greco-Latin ideal, but less rigorous than that of Maurras. Later, in 1921, prefacing with a programmatic text an anthology published in honor of an ephemeral group, the new *Pléiade*, Gasquet proclaimed his desire to take upon himself as much as possible of nature and of life, to cultivate all his enthusiasms, on the sole condition that this superabundance must be ordered and integrated in a beautiful form.

As a mater of fact, most of the Meridionals could not feel at ease in the neo-classicism whose severe image was traced by Maurras (who was the friend and teacher of many of them, particularly of Gasquet). Some of these poets supported his doctrine by a misunderstanding. Their temperament, their taste for the Latin *copia*, their attachment to carnal nature, their receptivity to the message of death and dissolution that lives in the torrid light-seared air of Provence, all this prevented them from truly worshipping the atticism put forward by Maurras—or at least their work disavowed what their reason sometimes approved. Thus developed the romantic classicism of Gasquet and certain of his associates. I am referring particularly to Xavier de Magallon who today embodies these tendencies, a poet of strict form and classical intention, but indisputably a descendant of Hugo.

Moreover, if there was an old master whom they recognized, it was not Racine, La Fontaine, or Malherbe, it was Ronsard— Ronsard who on three occasions influenced modern poetry, each time in a different way, depending on which aspect of his work was stressed. The "Romanists" of 1894 regarded him primarily as the "laurel-chewer"; the lyricists of the south such as Lafargue, Gasquet or Pize, were attracted by the poet of rebirth and of nature, while the "neo-Romanists" or "Gallicans," from André Mary to Fernand Fleuret were the disciples of the satirist.

Thus far it must be admitted that this great lyricism of the south, the possible French equivalent of Mistral and the Félibrige poets, has produced only rough outlines or disconnected fragments. Moreover, the Félibrige poetry was popular in origin and profoundly autochthonous, while most of the Mediterranean poets writing in French have been products of a refined intellectual culture and have drawn on various sources. It must also be noted that the diverse modern attempts at epic poetry have been clearly urban in inspiration, following in the wake of Zola, Verhaeren, and Whitman, and not of Mistral. In the realm of pastoral poetry, however, one or two pieces by Louis Pize, and particularly some of the *Eglogues* by F.-P. Alibert offer us a glimpse of Virgilian beauty, abundant and serene. Quite naturally, this *lactea ubertas* is blended with barely perceptible, perfectly assimilated elements originating in Ronsard, Chénier, or Lamartine—the Lamartine of *Harmonies*, of whom Joachim Gasquet, speaking in the name of his group, said "that by a kind of sublime intuition he anticipated our entire aspiration" (he was doubtless referring primarily to such poems as *La Vigne et la Maison*).

It has been said that nothing is more mysterious than light. The man of the South likes the "golden darkness" that invades Valéry's youthful *Parque* the moment she closes her eyes. Though many poets of the southern-dialect provinces acknowledged the precepts of Maurras and Moréas, others yielded to Mallarmism. Through his encounter with Aubanel, Mallarmé had in a way surmised the possibility of this marriage of North and South, and *L'Après-midi d'un*

Faune showed the direction in which the reconciliation should be attempted. As early as 1894, Raymond de la Tailhède tried to fuse Romanism and Mallarmism in his *Métamorphose des Fontaines*, perhaps the first example, among the moderns, of that pastoral lyricism in which the meridional poets excel. Then came Jean Royère of Aix, soon leader of the group he formed in the shadow of *La Phalange*, his magazine; and finally F.-P. Alibert who carried Mediterranean Mallarmism to its highest development. But there was also Fernand Mazade who though a Hellenizing and quasi-Parnassian poet, admits "that we must content ourselves for a moment with the detour of the obscure sign," and adopts, in *La Chimère et les Ombres*, an allusive style consonant with a poetry of philters and magic. Thus it was not long before "the true literature of the South," through some of its best-known representatives, betrayed the mission with which an orthodox neo-classicist would have charged it —but betrayed it perhaps in order to fulfill it in a way more compatible with our times.

Nevertheless, this literature contributed to the literature of all France a specifically Mediterranean spirit, which is rather hard to define, but which seems to be characterized by an exalted feeling for nature, experienced as a cosmic power in which man participates, a power now vivifying and inducive to action, now crushing and luring like the void itself, but always a mute, invincible, inexorable power whose designs are unfathomable—the fatal image of a tragic *Ananke*. A similar experience, occurring in a place accessible to the "call of the Orient," could lead to passive ecstasy, to mystical union. Restricted to a rough outline, mastered by reason, disciplined by the meditations of Virgil, Lucretius, Ronsard, and Mistral, it gave rise to a "metaphysics of the soil," which is a kind of realism. On the aesthetic plane, this nature—and particularly its recurrent images, the cypress, the oak, the plane-tree, the olive, the tree pure and simple, symbol of all realized life—suggests ever more strongly the idea of an organic literary creation, characterized less by an order imposed from outside than by the fact that it is inhabited by a cohesive population of cells, endlessly drawing "from the very bowels of the earth, the profound waters that the summits require." This is no doubt a classical teaching, but such classicism is eternal.

CHAPTER FIVE

Under the Sign of the Helmeted Minerva

The first years of the century were characterized by a revival of nationalism among the cultivated middle class. This class was concerned with its own survival. Thinkers supplied it with ideas — for years it had enjoyed no such atmosphere of festivity. The programs and manifestoes of the new magazines defined specifically French values, and advocated the creation of a classical literature. Some of the essential features of Mediterranean lyricism, as well as the measured romanticism of many poets around 1905, would remain inexplicable without the increasing ascendancy of Jean Moréas and particularly the success of the so-called reactionary doctrine (in both literature and politics) forged by Charles Maurras. The eclectic Romanism of the 1890's was gradually replaced by a full-fledged integral traditionalism. However, Moréas was an independent poet; his influence happened to accord with that of the political-minded writers, but his only true pleasure was "to hold Apollo at the tips of his ten fingers."

Paging through *Enone, Eriphyle*, and *Les Sylves*, although these date from 1893 and 1894 and follow closely the first manifestations of Romanism, we soon realize that this admirer of the minstrels and imitator of the *Pléiade* moved gradually from Ronsard to La Fontaine and Chénier. Let us read the opening and closing lines of *La Plainte d'Hyagnis*:

> Substance de Cybèle, ô branches, ô feuillages,
> Aériens berceaux des rossignols sauvages,
> L'ombre est déja menue à vos faîtes rompus,
> Languissants vous pendez et votre vert n'est plus.
> Et moi je te ressemble, automnale nature,
> Mélancolique bois où viendra la froidure.

Mais la Naïde amie, à ses bords que j'évite,
Hélas! ne trouve plus l'empreinte de mes pieds,
Car c'est le pâle buis que mon visage imite,
Et cette triste fleur des jaunes violiers.
Chère flute, roseaux où je gonflais ma joue,
Délices de mes doigts, ma force et ma gaîté,
Maintenant tu te plains: au vent qui le secoue
Inutile rameau que la sève a quitté.

Substance of Cybele, o leafy boughs,
Aerial cradles of wild nightingales,
The shadow has dwindled at your broken summits,
You hang down languishing and your green is gone.
And I am like thee, autumnal nature,
Melancholy wood to which winter will come.

But no longer do I seek out the friendly naiad, and on her shores
Alas, she no longer finds my footprints,
For my face has grown like the pale boxwood
And the sad yellow bloom of the wallflower.
Beloved pipe, reed that puffed my cheeks,
Delight of my fingers, my strength and my gaiety,
Now you make plaint: to the wind that shakes it
A useless branch bereft of its sap.

(Poèmes et Sylves)

The opening invocation is reminiscent of the elegy *Aux bûcherons de la Forêt de Gâtine.* The comparison of the boxwood and the wallflower might also recall, with its Ovidian grace, the plaints of the lover of Cassandra and Helen. But it is of La Fontaine that we are reminded by the lightness of these imponderable words, so gently reduced to their intellectual and sonorous essence; piano without pedal, somewhat metallic in tone, with a secret melancholy charm. And a verse such as *Et moi je te ressemble, automnale nature* clearly foreshadows the Moréas of later years.

In the *Stances*, "there is nothing, and it is well." In these words Moréas doubtless proclaimed his intention to cease treating a particular subject; but to those who know how to listen, his song expresses his soul. However, it took a strange fanaticism to salute this book as a flawless masterpiece: its Muse often stumbles, its cadences clash, and only a few of the poems are free from awkwardness.

Nevertheless, it would be a great mistake to regard the *Stances* as a pastiche, a mere literary exercise as some have, done; it is by patient work on himself that the poet created an accord between his own spiritual path and some of the great commonplaces of poetry.*

By ordering his life and subjecting it to his critical judgment, he entered upon the path that characterizes the stoic on the moral plane, and the classicist on the literary plane.

The *Stances* are primarily poems of regrets, of solitude. Moréas' pessimism is continually fed by the nostalgia of exile. Whatever he may do, whatever stir there is around him, a single rhythm fills his life, the rhythm of "his great, resonant, somber and lonely heart." The last blaze of the day, the nocturnal shadows, a bird's call, the echo of his steps on the Paris streets, everything convinces him that he is alone on a barren earth. To him objects and forces are mere witnesses of his existence.

But if he humanizes nature, he does not go as far as to become fused with it, like the romantics. On the contrary, he feels that he must strongly establish himself at the highest point of his being and raise his sense of his fate and his solitude to the most acute awareness if he is to treat nature as an equal, with the noble familiarity of a Petrarch and a Ronsard.

For the sake of this confrontation the poet, instead of losing himself in the cosmos, exalts what is most human in him, and his poetry, when nothing extraneous enters into it, rises like pure unadorned song. Despite his pride he looks on the withered leaf and the faded flower as the most appropriate symbols of his life. He fears death — although he is always ready to face it — yet he accepts his fate with all his wounded soul, betrayed by the world, but stoical. Here the dividing line between poetry and morality is blurred; as Moréas increases his mastery over himself, he is better able to discipline his words; in his eyes, to compose a perfect verse is to work toward one's own inner perfection. Having finally stripped his self of all dross, having reduced it to its elementary and classical simplicity, he confines himself to meditating on two or three ideas rooted in

* I believe it is Emile Godefroy who first drew attention to the sustained meditations echoed in the *Stances* (*Vers et Prose*, June–July 1906).

the very depths of his emotional life, and to expressing these ideas in his poetry. Thus, the commonplace is imposed upon him as an ineluctable necessity.

These commonplaces are rather those of romanticism than of humanism. As early as 1899 Charles Maurras saw that in *Stances* the entire romantic soul, "a hundred years of fever, nostalgia, melancholy . . .," was incorporated in the classical element of French poetry. It is a despairing soul, which uttered perhaps its noblest confession in the second poem of Book VI:

> *Solitaire et pensif j'irai sur les chemins,*
> *Sous le ciel sans chaleur que la joie abandonne,*
> *Et, le coeur plein d'amour, je prendrai dans mes mains*
> *Au pied des peupliers les feuilles de l'automne.*
>
> *J'écouterai la brise et le cri des oiseaux*
> *Qui volent par les champs où déjà la nuit tombe.*
> *Dans la morne prairie, au bord des tristes eaux,*
> *Longtemps je veux songer à la vie, à la tombe.*
>
> *L'air glacé fixera les nuages transis*
> *Et le couchant mourra doucement dans la brume.*
> *Alors, las de marcher, sur quelque borne assis,*
> *Tranquille je romprai le pain de l'amertume.*

> Solitary and thoughtful, I shall walk the roads
> Beneath a sky without warmth, abandoned by joy,
> And, my heart full of love, I shall take
> The autumn leaves in my hands under the poplars.
>
> I shall listen to the breeze and the cries of the birds
> Flying over the fields where night is falling.
> In the cheerless meadow at the edge of the sad waters
> I shall think long of life, and of the tomb.
>
> The icy air will freeze the clouds in their places
> And the sunset will die gently in the mist.
> Then, weary of walking, I shall sit on some mile-stone
> And tranquilly break the bread of biterness.

Here, as in some others of the *Stances*, we have doubtless the most original achievement of Moréas—a certain transition from the lyrical to the tragic, a certain sublimation of the individual and his inner romanticism, by which the content of the poem is transmuted and suffused with a classical light.* And if he could endure life at all, it was in the last analysis, because of this work to which he devoted his energies and his sense of the eminent dignity of the poet, in whose eyes the world exists only "to serve as a pretext for his songs." This is a truly Pindaric pride, and it was the only wall that Moréas could erect against nothingness.

The *Stances* offered an example of pure language and style without, however, justifying all the fastidiousness of the purists. Coming after a century in which a number of illustrious models seemed to justify the worst verbal excesses, Moréas was led to rehabilitate the faculties of discrimination, to take words at their full meaning, to say less in order to suggest and feel more. This was a good remedy against the exhaustion of the literary language that inevitably results from the tendency to over-expressiveness manifested in so many modern works. Moreover, it marked a "Hellenic" protest against the Latin bent for verbalism and rhetoric.† But this is a difficult task for him who is first to undertake it, for he inevitably incurs the risk of appearing dry and barren. Whatever may be said in favor of his denuded style, Moréas seldom avoids this danger.

The specific beauty of *Stances*—and this accords with the teachings of Maurras—lies in the turn of phrase, the syntax, the balance, that is to say, in the movement of thought and in the relations which the poet establishes between its elements. While the poets of the romantic and symbolist tradition strain their ingenuity to devise new images—and the image finally becomes the "glorified body" in which poetry is incarnated—Moréas uses sound images, but there is nothing startling or overpowering about them; his main concern is with the "disposition" of the elements, which in his eyes is the criterion of all true beauty. Moreover, he believes that by patient elaboration perfect intelligibility can be achieved. Obscure sensations, desires, passions, suffering, all the "given" elements of

---

*It is known that Barrès asked the classicists to grant him *the honors of war* (in *Le Voyage de la Sparte*). Moréas answered him: *All of us are more or less romantics. And as for those banners, let us keep them! But let the breath of Athens dispose their folds in conformity with the* only *rhythm, which might still reveal nuances and modalities.* (Quoted by Emile Henriot, in *Tribute to Moréas*, in *Revue Critique des Idées et des Livres*, March 25, 1920).

†Cf. the essay of André Thérive in *Revue Critique des Idées et des Livres*, March 25, 1920.

life must be eliminated in favor of a symbolic, almost abstract, pattern. Thus the supremacy of reason over reality is asserted. This represents a notable intellectual and moral advance; but does not such treatment expose poetry to the risk of degenerating into the formula, the aphorism, in a word, the gnomic style? Striving primarily to satisfy the intellect, it is less capable of arousing the imagination, it loses its power over the reader, who is affected only in the cultivated parts of his sensibility. The well-ordered poetry of Moréas moves us most when it suggests the disorder that preceded it, and it is to this disorder that it essentially owes its significance and humanity.

2.

During this period, the ideas of Maurras were definitely taking a political turn. For the theorists of *l'Action Française*, literature and poetry are only subordinate activites; however noble and exalted they may be, their ultimate purpose is to serve as "institutional forces," which contribute to integrating the individual into the social body. And it is undeniable that a considerable number of the contributors to *la Revue Critique des Idées et des Livres*, who claimed to be working in behalf of a rebirth of classicism, were originally seduced by Maurras' political arguments, and only later went over to literature.

The doctrine of neo-classicism, whose intellectual method was defined as an "organizing empiricism," is built upon very narrow foundations. It rests on the conception of a "correct balance," a state of equilibrium between barbarism and the decadence that supposedly existed in Athens during a brief span of Greek history and during twenty or thirty years of French history under Louis XIV. If this doctrine is thus reduced to its core, and formulated in terms of historical reality, its "mythological" aspect soon becomes apparent. It took very skilful "tailoring" to justify a conception of Hellenism which gives no place to Dionysus, and which prefers a helmeted Minerva to Apollo himself. And as for the seventeenth century, it must not be forgotten that the achievements of the great classicists were individual. Moreover, the classical concept of perfection is connected with a certain idea of man. Is true any hope of reviving this *homo classicus*? For this is the crucial point; the modern writer is asked to effect a complete transformation of his being, to work constantly upon himself, to maintain an unceasing intensity of the mind. Such an effort is indispensable because this classical man today no longer has any direct relation with the "nature of thing," and can exist only outside this nature and against it. The inner "re-creation" of such a man is no doubt possible, by way of exception, for critics, men of letters, intellectuals living chiefly by the intellect. But in poets, instinct and sensibility must normally be dominant over critical awareness, regardless how much store is set by taste and the will. Therein doubtless lies the secret error of neo-classicism considered as a generating principle of works of art.

Actually this doctrine satisfied a social, moral, and intellectual need. Many Frenchmen, in the face of the rising tide of ideas, emotions, dreams, that had been unleashed by European romanticism, felt lost, and it seemed to them that the only means of restoring the threatened balance in and around them was to reject all this flood of matter and life, and to confine themselves to the exploitation of traditional, tested, and already classified ideas, ideas that had been French or naturalized as French for centuries. This falling back on old reserves, in search of an anterior order, justifies Suarez who said: "What they mean by 'classical' is imitation, and of this they are unaware." To return to that past, to a past pre-judged sound and pure, such was the restless and unavowed desire of the majority of Maurras' young disciples. For them, as Fernandez points out, "classicism was a certain way of having been classical," which might be alluring for its elegance or the exquisite refinements it makes possible, but which enables one to dodge the most difficult part of artistic creation, the transition from *experience* to expression. And if they accepted this kind of renunciation, it is because often they had very few things that imperiously demanded to be said.

Thus, despite Maurras, there was a rebirth of a new variety of Alexandrinism (characterized, it is true, by clear-cut forms), and with it academicism, that shadow of authentic classicism. As early as 1896, Lionel des Rieux had declared: "Only the order of our ideas is ours, not the elements that compose these ideas. To create is never anything but to combine. We cannot help imitating. And it will be granted, I presume, that a French poet should rather choose his models among the writers who carried French literature to the highest point of perfection than to lower himself to those who have taken to clothing protozoan ideas in a Negro syntax." Very well; but we do not accept their premises; to see nothing but "ideas" in poetic experience and to make creation a mere "combination" of ideas, is to negate poetic experience itself.

3.

Those who bear all the burden of an aesthetic doctrine, those who live by it and die by it, are the well-intentioned disciples, the docile arrangers of clichés. It is only yesterday that the "salutes to Versailles" and the prayers to Pallas Athene, "virgin with limpid eyes," went out of fashion. Fortunately, the true poets always rediscover poetry. In our case, it even happened that this doctrine, which was ruinous to many, enabled one or two writers to achieve a kind of Doric beauty, a type of poetic and moral heroism, which defied the world and condemned success.

But if the traditionalist poets are legion, there are only a few orthodox neo-classicists whose work has any value. We shall not count among them humanists such as Frederic Plessis and Pierre de Nolhac, or Auguste Angellier who could justly claim to be a French Petrarchan, or even Charles le Goffic, a Romanized Celt, although Maurras praised him for having given "a precise voice, a classical and Latin voice to the uncertainty of things." Even Moréas' former companions, while they more or less progressed along the path he had prepared for them, did not feel obliged to cling to pure classicism, to eschew all independence or any compromise with more recent traditions. Ernest Raynaud chose a sinuous path; and Raymond de La Tailhède, having sacrificed to the shades of Lebrun-Pindar in panegyric songs, came to profess an admiration for certain aspects of romanticism which gradually led him to eclecticism, and carried him, perhaps against his will, to a point not far removed from the Parnassians. The cult of Hellenism and the preoccupation with plastic form facilitates this development.

In any case, the best poet of the School, beside Moréas, was indubitably Maurice Du Plessys. Enamored of nobility and aristocracy, eager to "keep his spotless escutcheon." Du Plessys, whose unlucky fate reminds one of de Vigny's Chatterton, represents pure "Romanism" or rather *the* Romanist, *the* medievalist, perfectly at home in every period and every dialect of northern France, and capable of writing at will in the idiom of *La Chanson de Roland*, in the manner of Jehan de Meung, Eustache Deschamps, or François Villon. This was a magnificent and preposterous game played by a man who was starving and who carried the cult of poetry to the point of mysticism. Alas, Du Plessys is not as far removed as it might seem from "the accursed ones" celebrated by Verlaine.

But, aside from the archaizing poet who sometimes spoke Greek and Latin or Romanic in French, there is in him a classical elegiac poet. The best of his "modern" verses combine a refined musicality with intellectual fullness. As early as 1896, in his *Etudes Lyriques*, Alcandre adjures Carinice in the following words:

> *Se peut-il que tant d'heur laisse en sorte un front sombre?*
> *Dis-le-moi, mon amour, et saché-je à quoi tient*
> *Que ton âme á tes yeux s'épaissit comme l'ombre*
> *Qui tremble au pied de l'arbre à l'heure où la nuit vient.*

> *Votre peine, colombe, attriste la nature,*
> *Dîtes-moi de vos yeux l'inquiète pensée:*
> *Viens, consens que nos fronts mêlent leurs chevelures,*
> *Et dis-moi que ma voix charme une âme blessée!*

> Can it be that so much happiness leaves you brow dark?
> Tell me, my love, that I may know why it is
> That your soul deepens in your eyes like the shadow
> Which trembles at the foot of the tree at the hour of nightfall.

> Your sorrow, my dove, saddens all nature,
> Tell me the anguished thought of your eyes:
> Come to me, press your forehead to mine,
> And tell me that my voice charms your wounded soul!

(Le Feu Sacré, p. 89)

Such accents, so different from the course of everyday life, are situated in the poetic firmament somewhere between Malherbe, Maynard, Tristan, Racine on the one hand and the final stanzas of *La Maison du Berger* on the other. But Du Plessys, thanks to the ardent conviction that sustains him and his science of language, escapes from the pastiche; his classicism (like that of Moréas) is the fruit of a tenacious effort to defeat all baseness of thought, and to create in himself, by an act of faith in the virtue of perfection, a heroic life.

Unfortunately, felicitous mements are rare in this work;

Du Plessys is an inspired writer, and however highly he may value patience and discipline, he, like so many others of his group when the Muse abandons them, sometimes recklessly exploits all the resources of rhetoric. Instead of real frenzy, we are then confronted only with the machinery of frenzy and icy transports reminiscent of the deliberate fury of the eighteenth-century lyricists.

As for Charles Maurras—the poet, not the critic and prose-writer—his admirers could scarcely resist the temptation to elevate him to the rank of a great master. Thus, they praised to the skies some of his works that hardly deserved such honor, for example, his "historical ode" on the *Bataille de la Marne*, a big, cumbersome (and unfinished) affair in which ardent partisan sincerity runs aground on the worst of artifices. His *Mystère d'Ulysse*, a fairly good example of Alexandrine poetry, reveals the laudable intention of reconciling poetry and Sibylline didacticism. There is no doubt that Maurras has a rich poetic sensibility, a whole concert of inner voices, a desire for the rhythmic beauty which alone is capable of ordering life, amidst the buzzing of diligent bees, in a flood of light. But his lyricism, always restrained, appears in his poems only at long intervals; in *Découverte* it carries the accents of a grave confession full of pathos:

> La vie entière m'apparut,
> Sa dureté, son amertume
> Et quelque lieu qu'on ait couru,
> Cette douceur qui la parfume.

> Enfant trop vif, adolescent
> Que les disgrâces endurcirent,
> A mon automne enfin je sens
> Cette douceur qui me déchire.

> Presque à la veille d'être au port
> Où s'apaise le coeur des hommes
> Je ne crois plus les pauvres morts
> Mieux partagés que nous ne sommes.

> Je ne conduis vers mon tombeau
> Regret, désir, ni même envie,
> Mais j'y renverse le flambeau
> D'une espérance inassouvie.

The whole of life appeared to me,
Its hardness, its bitterness
And, wherever one may go,
This sweetness which perfumes it.

Too eager as a child, as a youth,
Hardened by misfortune,
In my autumn at last I feel
This sweetness that rends my heart.

Almost arrived at the haven
Where the heart of man is appeased,
I no longer think that the poor dead
Are better off than we are.

To my grave I shall not carry
Regret, desire, or even longing,
But it is there I will cast down the torch
Of an unquenched hope.

(Musique intérieure)

But I believe that the great poetry of Maurras will continue to be found chiefly in the prose of Anthinéa or in the preface to *Musique intérieure.**

While Moréas traveled intellectually through the successive stages of French poetry, from the time of the minstrels to the century of Malherbe and Racine, while from about 1900 to 1910 neo-classicism was becoming established, a few so-called neo-Romanist or Gallic poets, lured by the primitive Romance spirit, attempted to rejuvenate and reinvigorate the doctrine of the School of 1891

---

*Now that we can read *Quatre poèmes d'Eurydice*, this judgment strikes me as too peremptory. Nowhere else had Maurras revealed such consummate mastery of style, and in no other verse has he shown greater purity of *diction*. By a kind of necessity, the theme of *Découverte* recurs in the most beautiful piece, *Reliquiae Foci*.

Lorsqu'au vent du déclin nos cendres se soulèvent,
En heureux tourbillons vers les cieux bien-aimés,
Le coeur reste jonché de désirs et de rêves,
Que la flamme a mordu et n'a pas consumé.

When in the wind our ashes rise
In happy whirls to the beloved skies
The heart remains littered with desires and dreams
That the flame has bitten but has not consumed.

and provide it with a scientific foundation in philology, history, and folklore.

Their native domain extends from the chivalrous and legendary Middle Ages to the epoch of Villon and the pre-classical period of Ronsard and Régnier. We can imagine them repeating after Théophile: "Malherbe (or Moréas) worked well, but he worked for himself." These neo-Romanists are clearly Gauls, lovers of the "caverns and fountains" that charmed Ronsard, the Vendômois, they were facetious, satirical, rebellious; if they had lived under Louis XIV, one would have met them not at Versailles, but in the manor of some provincial squire, making merry, and reading, contrary to the advice of Boileau, *Les Folâtries*, or other "gay tales" dating from the time of the *Pléiade*. Old style libertines in short, they very consciously devised an aristocratic literature that could please only the few.

Moreover, they had their reasons for preferring the "Gallic" to the classical language: it is richer, abounding in words full of sap; one can find in it, as Hugo writes, "all those magnificent Greek, Latin, or Spanish etymologies, like pearls and corals under the waters of a limpid sea"; the spirit of bygone customs and legends survives in a host of its phrases; finally, its syntax is freer than that of modern French. Also, history proves that the lyrists under Louis XIII tried to preserve the syntax of the *Pléiade* despite Malherbe. La Fontaine "imitated"; Racine was forced to defend his archaisms against the pedants; Fénelon and La Bruyère stated expressly that they regretted the lost liberties of Renaissance French. It seems that an aesthetic need led a number of poets, among the greatest, as late as Chénier, and if you will, Sainte-Beuve, to adopt a vocabulary and syntax that lagged behind contemporary usage.*

Following their example, the Romanists of today cultivate archaism, in the conviction that purely French but forgotten words, if placed under a favorable light, may acquire a youth and suggestive poetic power that other words have lost through everyday use. It may be argued that such a language is artificial, since it was "made," and has no relation to its time. This is true;

---

*André Therive has insisted on this fact on many occasions; cf. especially *Du Siècle romantique* (Nouvelle Revue Critique, p. 160).

but every literary idiom, and especially every poetic idiom, is always more or less artificial, while this language is at least natural in that it contains no neologisms and includes only a minimum of "learned" words, while its "nobility" consists primarily in its having a great number of "popular" words. Even so, one can foresee no great future for the "high French" that André Mary has been trying to elaborate, a kind of dead language, a κοινή, which in his eyes must be clearly distinguished from the "low French" that he leaves to "the current usage of business and politics." Such a venture can scarcely lead to anything more than isolated successes, the fantasies of scholarly poets.

Another neo-Romanist, Fernand Fleuret, a satirist sparkling with racy verse, wrote in the language of Régnier and Théophile, as though striving to achieve the Gallic lyricism suggested by Villon and Ronsard, but which for various reasons could not bear all its fruits in the seventeenth century. There is no modernism in André Mary, a profoundly original poet, though a disciple of Moréas and Maurice Du Plessys. The work of this scholarly poet, grammarian and philologist is imbued with a nature, the rustic and woodland nature of olden Burgundy, and with a spirit of piety toward whatever bears witness to the permanence of things and the mystery of their existence. André Mary's most accomplished poems are perhaps to be found among his *Rondeaux*, "revived from the work of the rhetoricians of the time of the Valois";* personal feelings are embodied here in a verbal music which is outdated only in appearance:

> Mélancolie en peine en l'ardeur des longs jours
> Où vont brûlant sans fin glycine et tubéreuse,
> Vit seulette, recluse en chartre douloureuse,
> Et voit parmi sa grille et regarde peureuse
> Les soleils dévorants éterniser leur cours.
>
> Mais quand vient que la noix est gaulée, au rebours,
> Levant ton front moins triste où ta ride se creuse,
> Pour les noires cités tu laisses ta chartreuse,
> Mélancolie.

*Published *somewhere on earth, in the year MCMXXIV of the Incarnation of Our Lord* (typography F. Didot); most of them reproduced in *Poèmes.*

Par la grêle qui sonne et bondit dans les cours,
Par bourrasques, frimas et brume catarrheuse,
Sous le manteau rayé de la pluie octobreuse,
Dans l'âtre où je tisonne une bûche cendreuse,
Tu viens me visiter, douce, à pas de velours,
        Mélancolie.

Melancholy, languishing in the ardor of long days
When wistaria and tuberose burn without end,
Lives all alone, secluded in sorrowful cell,
And looking out from its bars, timorously watches
The devouring suns on their eternal course.

But when the time comes for the beating of the nut trees,
Then, less sad, raising your furrowed face,
You leave your cell for the black cities,
        Melancholy.

Through the hail crackling and leaping in the courtyards,
Through squalls and frost and rheumy mists
In a cloak streaked by October rains,
On the hearth where I poke at a half-burnt log,
You come with velvet steps to visit me,
        Melancholy.

        (*Poèmes*, p. 177)

What a strange and unexpected turn for a fixed form; "hyperbole," Mallarmé would have said, and indeed the poem recalls *Prose pour des Esseintes*:

Car j'installe, par la science,
L'hymne des coeurs spirituels
En l'oeuvre de ma patience . . .

For by science I insert
The hymn of spiritual hearts
Into the work of my patience . . .

In any event, this defense and illustration of archaism achieved by André Mary and Fernand Fleuret was not in vain—for a considerable number of poets of humanist culture conceived the idea of expressing themselves and sometimes of expressing the spirit of our times by calling on certain of the resources of the old language. This archaizing strain included part of the work of Vincent Muselli, Léon Vérane, and Charles-Théophile Féret (who in this case is an initiator rather than a pupil). Following Fernand Fleuret, several satirists practiced the burlesque invective. There even developed a bantering, raillard (to use a term of the *Pléiade*) genre, which established its own rules and themes, a genre somewhat comparable to Marotism, a movement long-lived during the classical centuries, for reasons that are perhaps related to those which insure today the success of this unmodern poetry, not the least interesting among the types that were grafted on the tree of "Romanism."

Today it seems established that though integral neo-classicism might serve as a useful platform for the dogmatic criticism of Maurras, Pierre Lasserre, and Henri Massis, it could not by itself bring forth a living literature. Order is valuable only if it is achieved by a victory over rebellious matter, if it marks the end and completion of a slow process of inner maturation. In their weakness, the neo-classicists made the idea of order the very basis of their work, and thus doomed themselves to "making" poetry without ever having "lived" it, and to regarding poetic creation as a kind of exercise in higher rhetoric. Only one or two of them managed to put their souls into the game they were playing. Far from steering a course toward a Hellenic or Racinian art, most of them resurrected the palest shades of the Parnassians, the phantoms of academicism, or clung stubbornly to an artificial and verbal pseudo-classicism which made one regret the eloquence of J.-B. Rousseau and Lefranc de Pompignan.

It may be said without unfairness that the success of neo-classicism in the pre-war period coincided with a certain blunting of the "sense of poetry" in the minds of the reading public, in favor of a renewed understanding of the moral and rational beauties that abound in the French seventeenth and eighteenth centuries. This observation may help us to bear in mind the real benefit conferred by this movement of literary "reaction." It succeeded where the good intentions of the professors often failed—thanks to it, the classical beauties and many of those that had preceded them and made them possible, from the Middle Ages to the Renaissance, were restored to full light, and this to the great advantage of the writers themselves. A sustained and serious contact (not confined to high school or college years) with the masterpieces anterior to the nineteenth century gave our contemporaries a lesson in style, in the most elevated sense of the word—

a lesson in style and by the same token a new taste for sobriety, for purity of line, a hatred for the turgidity born of romantic and impressionistic tendencies, and present in so much of modern literature.

But, needless to say, such virtues, classical if you will, were not foreign to Baudelaire, Mallarmé, and the better symbolists—or to several of the romanticists. On this ground, fruitful encounters were bound to take place between the old aesthetics and the new which represented primarily the art of Baudelaire and of Mallarmé.

Rimbaud, Nouveau, Verlaine, Delahaye

BOOK II

In Search of a New French Order

Valéry by Picasso

CHAPTER SIX

Neo-Symbolism

1.

"Who is still a Symbolist?" Edmond Jaloux asked Stuart Merrill* in 1905. At that time Baudelaire was no longer cited as an authority, and Mallarmé even less; the importance of Rimbaud had not yet been realized, and Claudel was almost unknown. But having gone to one extreme, the pendulum was about to swing back. Moreover, the influence of the great lyricists of the second half of the nineteenth century continued to be felt under the surface. Young poets among those who began to write toward 1900—Léon Deubel, for instance—cultivated the emotions and ambitions of the "accursed poets." While the most serious among the newly founded magazines generally inclined toward Latinism and classicism; while the *Mercure de France* printed the most varied productions, and while the *Ermitage* opened its pages to many trends, the little magazines, often ephemeral, applied themselves to resuming contact with one or the other of the symbolist traditions. Thus the *Festin d'Europe*, to which Guillaume Apollinaire, André Salmon, Henri Hertz, and Max Jacob contributed, revered Alfred Jarry and other dangerous divinities, and paid tribute to an intellectual and emotional disorder capable of begetting the best and the worst, as well as to a strange taste for the dream world and the marvelous. At the same time, René Ghil, who was stubbornly pursuing his experiments in verbal instrumentation and scientific poetry, grouped around himself a few faithful adherents.

In the first volume of *Vers et Prose* (1905), Robert de Souza felt it

*Cf. *Stuart Merrill*, by Miss Marjorie Henry. In 1908, Stuart Merrill wrote to André Fontainas: *Yes, to be sure, symbolism seems to hang fire as a result of the defection of many of its members as well as because of public indifference. . . .*

necessary to demonstrate that the only living School—against which the "grave-diggers fumed in vain"—was symbolism, which had attained its fullest flowering in the latest works of Verhaeren, Viélé-Griffin, Jammes, Gide, Charles Guérin, Moréas, Paul Fort, etc. This is a singularly varied cohort, unless we ascribe to symbolism the limits and characteristics of lyricism itself.*

Heterogeneous from its beginnings, symbolism had changed completely in twenty years; by 1905, it was a matter of choice whether to recognize and salute it everywhere or, on the contrary, to take pleasure in enumerating the movements or "schools" that had supplanted it. If one wishes to speak of a neo-symbolism, one must await the foundation of *La Phalange* (July 1906).

This is not to imply that *La Phalange* was exclusively a polemical magazine demanding a rigorous orthodoxy of its contributors. Nevertheless, the convictions of Jean Royère, who edited it until 1914, were too definite to allow of eclecticism when the validity of the ideas, to whose defense he devoted his life, was questioned. His doctrine may have varied in the course of the years, it may have grown top-heavy with philosophical formulas or swathed in clouds, but the general themes of his criticism none the less contributed to rehabilitate some of the aesthetic "truths" that Baudelaire had borrowed from Poe, and that were illustrated by Mallarmé—and more recently by Valéry. There is no doubt that the so-called pure poetry controversy developed on ground prepared by the campaigns of *La Phalange*, and that most of the arguments and examples brought forth were familiar to its old readers. The very expression "pure poetry" (in the sense given it by Valéry) was currently used by the entourage of Jean Royère. And it was he who declared as early as 1911: "Even though it has at all times had illustrious defenders, the method of enthusiasm is worthless in poetry . . . "

But while l'Abbé Bremond made poetry subservient to Christian mysticism, Jean Royère posited it as an absolute. "Symbolism was nothing other than the will to penetrate poetry in its essence," he said. And later: "The poets who constituted the symbolist generation

---

*To convince oneself of this one need only thumb through the successive volumes of *Vers et Prose* (1905–1914), originally established to rally all symbolist forces, but soon transformed into an anthology reflecting almost every aspect of poetry.

all regarded their art as an *absolute*." Finally, there is this sentence in which something of English romanticism seems to live again, and which so clearly anticipates the propositions of some of the present champions of pure poetry: "Poetry is, in its own way, lofty and philosophical, since it feeds on ideas, but on *poetic*, i.e., sensible ideas; in brief, it is religious. Its essential *obscurity* is due to the fact that it is the history of a soul and that it seeks to comply with the mystery of that soul; but this obscurity is luminous. . . ." No better defense can be made of hermeticism and natural mysticism, of which the poetic work is the sensible expression. . . .

> *Seule en l'accablement de la Crypte écroulée*
> *Sous le bélier de la lumière—mon désir*
> *Parallèle trouant enfin le mausolée*
> *Des ténèbres—je fais le rêve de saisir*
> *L'Essence . . .*

> Alone in the dejection of the Crypt, crumpled
> Under the ram of light
> My parallel desire piercing at last the mausoleum
> Of darkness
> I dream that I seize
> The Essence . . .

Unfortunately, the doctrine that Jean Royère today calls "Musicism," however interesting it may be, encourages the poet to confine himself to linguistic and formal explorations. It is true that the work of Baudelaire or Mallarmé ended in such explorations, but it began elsewhere, in that "intimate experience," which penetrated to the very heart of the "poetic and pure world of consciousness," and which by its nature cannot be directly communicated. To assert, with Royère, that "poetry is verbal creation, nothing more" or "today one is a poet in the very degree to which one is an artist" is to foster misunderstanding. Whatever miraculous virtue one may be justified in attributing to stylistic devices and figures, they belong on careful examination to the human realm of rhetoric and not to the superhuman realm of poetry. Despite the refinement of their material and the sustained tone of their incantations, the poems of Jean Royère and the writers of his group strike the reader as expressions of an art too skillful at exploring the marvels of language. Here is a charming quatrain by Louis de Gonzague Frick:

> *L'avion ennemi semble touché,*
> *Et gire, est-ce la chute, ô coup de dé,*
> *Mirage, cette nerveuse avalanche,*
> *L'azur n'en fait qu'une sandale blanche . . .*

The enemy plane seems to be hit
And spins, is it falling, O throw of the dice,
Mirage, this nervous avalanche,
The blue sky but turns it into a white sandal.

And this tercet of a more manifest preciosity, by Gaspard-Michel:

> *Le flux rouge à flots rougeoie à travers le verre*
> *Du vitrail haut, crépuscule sur le calvaire*
> *Enguirlandé des parfums de la primevère . . .*

The surging red flood glows lurid through the pane
Of the high church window, dusk on the Calvary
Wreathed with the perfumes of the primrose . . .

To end finally in this, signed by André Breton:

> *D'or vert les raisins mûrs et mes futiles voeux*
> *Se gorgent de clarté si douce qu'on s'étonne.*
> *Au délice ingénu de ceindre tes cheveux*
> *Plus belle, a n'envier que l'azur monotone,*
>
> *Je t'invoque, inquiet d'un pouvoir de manteau*
> *Chimérique de fée à tes pas sur la terre,*
> *Un peu triste peut-être et rebelle plutôt*
> *Que toute abandonnée au glacis volontaire*

The golden-green ripe grapes and my futile vows
Gorge themselves on a light soft beyond belief,
In the candid delight of wreathing your hair,
Fair one, who need envy only the monotonous blue sky,—

Anguished by the power of a chimerical
Fairy cloak, as you step on earth I invoke you
A little sad perhaps, and rebellious rather
Than quite abandoned to the wilful slope.

(Mont-de-Piété)

In the eyes of the surrealist of today this imitation of Mallarmé
is doubtless a sin of youth, in any event, a sin of aestheticism. The

exclusive cult of beauty and infatuation with words had already done a disservice to the symbolists of 1885 — for indeed poetry feeds upon life and meditations on life far more than upon meditations on language. But the latter are indispensable, and it would be wrong to underestimate the studies of Jean Royère and his collaborators. If *La Phalange* had survived 1914, it would have offered a safe haven to *La Jeune Parque.**

La Phalange also contributed to bringing into favor a neo-impressionism originating in Verlaine, Jammes, and sometimes in Laforgue and Henri Bataille, but applied to the mystery of great spaces and ocean vistas rather than to the human world of emotions. Let us examine for instance, the delightful author of *Cartes Postales*, Henry Levet (who died in 1906):

> L'Armand Béhic (des Messageries Maritimes)
> File quatorze noeuds sur l'Océan Indien . . .
> Le soleil se couche en des confitures de crimes,
> Dans cette mer plate comme avec la main . . .

> The Armand Béhic (of the Maritime Freight)
> Scoots along at fourteen knots over the Indian Ocean
> The sun sets in a jelly of crimes,
> On this sea flattened as though by hand.

(Poèmes)

Consider also the work of John-Antoine Nau, a poetry of the ocean and its shores, charged with nostalgia and pervaded with the need of escaping from a limited life:

> Debout au bossoir — buvant la fraîcheur saline
> Toute la douceur de l'océan dans mes yeux,
> Je te vois approcher en vapeur opaline
> Et ta forme, vaguement connue, se dessine
> Presque familière et presque mystérieuse.

> Standing at the bow, drinking the salty freshness
> With all the sweetness of the ocean in my eyes
> I see you approaching in an opaline vapor
> And your shape, vaguely known, is outlined
> Almost familiar and almost mysterious.

(Hiers bleus)

*In 1912, Thibaudet published his work on Mallarmé. *The idea of this book,* writes the author in his preface of 1926, *was born toward 1910, in the milieu of* La Phalange.

In these fluid verses (are they really alexandrines?) which wind and unwind in so soft a rhythm, Valéry Larbaud correctly sees the expression of "the modern geographic sense." Incidentally, it is in the direct vicinity of Levet and Nau that we must place Valéry Larbaud as a poet, or, if one prefers, his overseas hero, A.-O. Barnabooth, an offspring of Whitman, but humanized, Frenchified, ironical, polished by a seasoned Epicureanism, and a billionaire.

> J'ai senti pour la première fois toute la douceur de vivre,
> Dans une cabine du Nord-Express, entre Wirballen et Pskow.
> On glissait à travers des prairies où des bergers,
> Au pied de groupes de grands arbres pareils à des collines,
> Etaient vêtus de peaux de moutons crues et sales . . .
> (Huit heures du matin en automne, et la belle cantatrice
> Aux yeux violets chantait dans la cabine à côté.)

> I felt all the sweetness of life for the first time
> In a compartment of the Nord-Express, between Wirballen and
>   Pskow.
> We were gliding through meadows where shepherds
> At the foot of groups of tall trees like hills
> Were dressed in dirty raw sheepskins . . .
> (At eight in the morning, in the fall, the pretty singer
> With violet eyes was singing in the next compartment).
>   (Les poésies de A.-O. Barnabooth)

Almost all modern influences, from Rimbaud to *Nourritures terrestres*, are here assimilated, converted into fresh blood. And these supple sentences, plane-surfaced and caressing, teach the enjoyment of the moment, *carpe diem*. The gliding motion of the luxurious train, a steamship whistle, an encounter with a flower girl, a certain warm rain on the sea of Marmora—none of this is exploited for the purposes of a facile picturesqueness or eroticism, each secretes an essence that is the very perfume of life and becomes an object of poetic delectation. But this book—which served as a model for the poems with which Paul Morand, during the war, prefaced his *Nuits*—has still another merit, namely, it paves the way for the development of what might be called the awareness of the conditions of man's actual and planetary existence, an awareness which is an integral part of the "modern geographic sense," and without which the poetry of the "great out-of-doors" and the wide open-spaces appears decidedly devoid of pathos and philosophical resonance.

In his freed or free verse, John-Antoine Nau (like Vielé-Griffin) makes abundant use of mute vowels, thereby achieving a special kind of lightness, of velvety softness. This original prosody attracted the attention of many writers, probably of Valéry Larbaud, and surely of Guy Lavaud, who is also a poet of the sea and the sky, but whose poems seem to have been born at the confluence of Mallarmean symbolism and impressionism, the two principal currents which carried the *Phalange*. In reality, Guy Lavaud is primarily an elegiac admirer of Jammes and passed from the sentimental elegies of his first volumes of verse to marine and astronomical elegies. But although his images seem to be borrowed from the external world, his poetry evokes spiritual landscapes, a delicately woven fabric, whose appearance has an indefinable element of freedom and intangibility. One is tempted to say that it partakes of the nature of the atmospheric elements, of clouds about to be condensed into rain, of drops of rain beginning to crystallize, of foam, of snow. . . .

> *Cette étoile perdue dans un nuage blanc,*
> *Cette lumière bleue et ce vol ravissant,*
> *Ces pâleurs détachées, on dirait d'une rose,*
> *Ce ne sont ni des fleurs ni des anges qui volent.*
> *C'est le secret tourment des ardeurs et des feux*
> *(Comme un coeur en aurait pour des yeux merveilleux),*
> *C'est un astre qui brûle et souffre et se contracte,*
> *Et la Nuit, inclinée et pensive, regarde*
> *Tout cet incendie rouge, éclos depuis des ans,*
> *S'épuiser, s'épurer dans l'ombre qui descend,*
> *Et comme nos amours, dans notre sang, s'apaisent*
> *Jusqu'à n'être que songe et soupir, et caresse,*
> *Redevenir, perdu dans un nuage blanc,*
> *Cette lumière bleue et ce vol ravissant.*

> That star lost in a white cloud,
> That blue sheen and that enchanting flight,
> Those detached pallors, as of a rose,
> It is neither flowers nor angels that are flying.
> It is the secret torment of ardors and passions
> (As of a heart for marvelous eyes),
> It is a planet burning and suffering and contracting,

> And the Night, bowed down and pensive, looks on
> As the red fire that burst forth years ago
> Dies down, cleansed in the falling shadow;
> And just as love, in our blood, is appeased
> Till it is nothing more than a dream, a sigh, a caress,
> So, lost in a white cloud, the fire becomes again
> That blue sheen and that enchanting flight.

(Poétique du Ciel)

One might criticize this poetry for stopping half-way in its striving for a cosmic beauty that is only suggested and that one would wish were "inspired." Guy Lavaud is too logical to renounce balanced symmetries, regular constructions, consistent metaphors, all that fine needle-point which satisfies the aesthetic conscience of so many French poets. But we must be thankful to him for concealing the "secret torment" of his heart by patiently interlacing, as though in pursuit of a noble entertainment, those gracile fibers that compose his poems. Coming after Mallarmé, and before Jean Cocteau and certain "cubists," he shows the use that a subtle intellect, capable of circumventing reality, can make of sensory data when it transposes them and integrates them in a system of relations and correspondences.

2.

Tancrède de Visan, in his Bergsonian studies on modern lyricism, interpreted poetry as a kind of irregular metaphysics and defined the essential role of the image, which tends to symbolize concretely, to embody, a "state of mind" developing in time. The poet must not aim at embroidering a linguistic veil that will separate him from the true reality residing in himself. His only legitimate intention is to penetrate into the heart of this reality. Even though he fails despite his efforts, even though the images he finds can, in the last analysis, be no more than symbols—not Being itself, but something which is, however, more than a mere indication or sign, something in which Being participates—his duty is, nevertheless, to devote himself to expressing this ineffable Being as directly as possible. The symbolist aesthetic, T. de Visan concludes in a seeming paradox, "is one that aims at dispensing with symbols"; that is to say, it repudiates the indirect symbol, consciously elaborated, and invites the poet to approach naked nature and draw it into the flow of his images. He maintains that the concrete language of the poem, by giving us an intense feeling of reality, ultimately gives us an insight into reality which surpasses in authenticity the knowledge we might obtain through any arrangement of concepts. And Bergson had written earlier, in his *Introduction to Metaphysics*: "No image will replace the intuition of concrete time, but many diverse images borrowed from very different realms may, by their converging action, direct the consciousness to the precise point where a certain intuition can be had. By choosing images as disparate as possible, one will prevent any of them from usurping the place of the intuition it is commissioned to call forth, because in such a case it would immediately be chased away by its rivals." Thus, a certain mode of philosophical knowledge, the one advocated by Bergson, and a certain quality of poetic experience would seem to be singularly similar. "If Bergson is a precursor," wrote Jean Florence in *La Phalange* (in 1912), "it is because he recognized the absolute in the subjective." A precursor, and also the continuator of a long tradition which includes all the mystics, along with a number of philosophers. (This text of Bergson obviously reminds one of Suso's remarks quoted in our introduction.)

But to have the intuition of the absolute is to experience God in oneself or life as such, an awareness of the total universe, a sense of existence in its most elementary, least determined aspect. Here we join the great traditions of mysticism and of inner romanticism. Indeed, T. de Visan was not merely characterizing symbolist poetry from 1885 to his own day, but defining some of the conditions of poetic experience. He himself quite well realized the relations obtaining between poetry, as he understood it, and for example the poetry of the German romantics. He might only be criticized for having referred to Régnier, Viélé-Griffin, Paul Fort and the so-called symbolist generation, when the works of his younger contemporaries, Claudel, Saint-Pol-Roux, Apollinaire, Fargue, and Milosz would have provided better justification of his theories.

It is the sense of inner time, of existence, not of an existence drowned in the universe, but limited, concentrated in a soul whose distress and least stirrings are made perceptible to us, that constitutes the charm of Léon-Paul Fargue's youthful poems. An equally profound and vibrant music dwells in the poetry of O.-V. de L. Milosz—long sentences, yet simple and apt, breathed out by life itself, with slightly eccentric yet inevitable images. It is thus that the soul appears to itself in the gray dawn:

> L'esprit purifié par les nombres du temple,
> La pensée ressaisie à peine par la chair, déjà,
> Déjà ce vieux bruit sourd, hivernal de la vie
> Du coeur froid de la terre monte, monte vers le mien.
>
> C'est le premier tombereau du matin, le premier tombereau
> Du matin. Il tourne le coin de la rue et dans ma conscience
> La toux du vieux boueur, fils de l'aube déguenillée,
> M'ouvre comme une clef la porte de mon jour.
>
> Et c'est vous et c'est moi. Vous et moi de nouveau, ma vie.
> Et je me lève et j'interroge
> Les mains d'hôpital de la poussière du matin
> Sur les choses que je ne voulais pas revoir.
> La sirène au loin crie, crie et crie sur le fleuve.

My spirit purified by the numbers in the temple,
My thought barely recaptured by the flesh,
And already this old muffled, wintry sound of life
Rises from the cold heart of the earth, rises to my heart.

It is the first dung-cart of the morning, the first dung-cart
Of the morning. It turns the corner of the street and in my mind
The cough of the old scavenger, son of the ragged dawn,
Opens the door of my day like a key.

And it is you and it is I. You and I again, my life.
And I get up and I question
The hospital hands of the morning dust
On things that I did not wish to see again.
The siren wails far off, it wails and wails on the river.

And further on:

> Te voici donc, ami d'enfance! Premier hennissement si pur
> Si clair! Ah, pauvre et sainte voix du premier cheval sous la pluie!
> J'entends aussi le pas merveilleux de mon frère;
> Les outils sur l'epaule et le pain sous le bras,
> C'est lui! C'est l'homme! Il s'est levé! Et l'éternel devoir
> L'ayant pris par la main calleuse, il va au-devant de son jour . . .

Here you are then, childhood friend! First neighing so pure
So clear! Ah, poor and holy voice of the first horse under the rain!
I hear also the marvelous step of my brother;
His tools over his shoulder and his bread under his arm,
It is he! It is man! He has arisen! Eternal duty
Has taken him by his callous hand, and he walks to meet his day . . .

In this poem man's fate speaks from the beginning of time. The glamor of beauty is superfluous here; the purity of these sentences is like a gift of the high springs that nothing can blemish because it comes straight from that "nameless land" whose call was no doubt heard by Alain-Fournier; it is a region before rather than beyond all thought, where feelings thrive easily and trace their curves, unconstrained by the necessities of life and reflection. This is the inner homeland in which arise the dreams, fables, legends, the *Maerchen* of the German poets which Novalis referred to as "a scattered dream, an ensemble of marvelous things and happenings, a musical fantasy, the harmonious sounds of an Aeolian harp, nature itself"—the nature wherein man rediscovers himself and rediscovers all men. From this homeland, romanticism drew the elements with which it both gratified and maintained its nostalgia.

Milosz has recently left us. Let us appreciate his greatness and the quality of this boundless inner silence that speaks in some of his poems. Let us be grateful to him for having sung as Rilke sometimes sang, and for having proved that, despite linguistic barriers, communication is possible between the secret domains of different literatures, and that by dint of love and patience it is possible to discover paths leading to the very depths of European sensibility.

At the beginning of the twentieth century more than one poet was moving toward these musical solitudes, following the example of Verlaine, the early Moréas, Laforgue, Maeterlinck, and Paul Fort. Such were Tristan Klingsor and Fagus; the former played with the erotic and sentimental themes of the courtly and Gallic traditions; the latter, a greater poet, spiritual brother (however modern) of Villon, of the medieval lyricists, the authors of the *soties* and the mystery plays, a religious mystic and a mystic of the flesh, fettering himself with all the sins, yet always aspiring to the highest peaks.

> *Tu hais orgueil et félonie*
> *Sur toute chose.*
> *Tu es le lis où Dieu repose:*
> *Tu es rosier qui porte rose*
> *Blanche et vermeille . . .*
> *Ha! Dame vierge nette et pure!*
> *Toutes femmes, pour ta figure,*
> *Doit-on aimer.*

> Thou hatest pride and felony
> Above all things.
> Thou art the lily on which God rests:
> Thou art the rosebush bearing roses
> White and red . . .
> Ah! Lady Virgin pure and clear!
> For the sake of thy countenance, one must
> All women love.

This poem is not by Fagus, it is by Rutebeuf. Fagus answered him, seven centuries later:

> *Lune immense en nos insomnies,*
> *Fée des anges, reine Marie,*
> *Vers vos bras me voici venu,*
> *Tel que Jésus enfant et nu:*
> *Voyez comme faible et soumis*
> *S'est voulu le Sauveur promis:*
> *Comme lui, soyez-nous propice,*
> *Qu'en retour il nous affranchisse,*
> *Pâques fleuries, Pâques fleuries!*

> Vast moon of our sleepless nights,
> Fairy of angels, Queen Mary,
> To your arms I am come
> Like Jesus, the naked babe,
> See how weak and submissive
> The promised Savior made himself:
> Like him, smile upon us,
> That in return he may liberate us,
> Flowery Easter, flowery Easter!

> (*La Guirlande à l'Epousée*)

In Klingsor and Fagus, the gates of the kingdom of enchantments are only half-opened. To make it live fully in one's poetry, one had to be more detached from art, from all transmitted literary form,

from the world, from oneself. It was one of the privileges of
Apollinaire, that new Nerval, to hear "the song of the distant flute,"
that song always interrupted, always resumed, whose melody came
to him from a very obscure past.

To make possible a subjective lyricism such as Tancrède de Visan
tried to formulate, what was needed was a rebirth of poetic imagination rather than a return to one or another romantic or symbolist
tradition. It was essential that nature should become, as Baudelaire
had phrased it, a dictionary of forms, a forest of symbols; that the
whole universe should strike roots in the poet's heart in such a way
that invisible bonds, like sensitive nerves, might connect his images
with the living core, the center of the self.

The traditionalist poets, with a few exceptions, used images and
metaphors which were listed in the civil register of literature, and
which the "educated" reader greeted with the same satisfaction
one feels when "giving a name" to a face. There was next to nothing
in their poems that did not benefit from being recognized as an echo
of something heard before. They refused to engender creatures without a respectable home or place of origin, dwelling in a truly alien
world in which they would not have found normal appearances or
literary reminiscences. But others worked in the shadow, to raise
harvests of images. Saint-Pol Roux, "the Magnificent," continued
to treat words with freedom, untiringly inventing flamboyant metaphors. As early as 1886 he created the models of the linguistic
precipitates in which he was to specialize:

> Le désert s'oubliait dans l'urne des margelles;
> La palombe ramait par les ors du matin:
> Les coteaux d'Ephraim belaient dans le lointain;
> Un paradis montait des fientes de gazelles.

> The desert forgot itself in its stony urn;
> The ring-dove sailed slowly through the gold of the morning:
> The slopes of Ephraim bleated in the distance;
> A paradise rose from the droppings of the gazelles.

> (*Bouc émissaire*)

Thus for a long time he brewed the natural essence of Rabelais,
Hugo, Rimbaud, then sifted them, filtered them, as Mallarmé would
have done. As early as 1900, the inspired poet succeeded in fusing
these same influences (especially those of Rimbaud and Mallarmé),

in *Connaissance de l'Est*. However, it is to the great odes of Claudel (1905) that we owe the true revelation of this type of poetry, timeless yet consonant with symbolism and naturism—this poetry which, in a surge that seemed to borrow the secret of its force from the elements, sent forth foaming images, sparkling in their meta-morphoses, mingling the sensuous and the spiritual in an ever-renewed synthesis.

Yet these images—a fact of prime importance for this revival of Baudelairean aspirations—do not aim at evoking some sort of trompe-l'oeil, some fantastic domain of illusion, fit to beguile the love-sick reader. Their effect is rather to make the so-called real world appear as a "sham world." "Man seems to inhabit only a fairy-land of vague indices, slight pretexts, timid provocations, distant affinities, enigmas," Saint-Pol Roux asserts. But the poet penetrates the primordial, he is the decipherer. It is the function of images to reveal in a flash, to make sensible to the heart, the occult reality which the veil of appearances, normal perceptions, easily definable feelings, clear ideas, conceals from us. Claudel believes that he holds from God his "spirit of Creation and image-making"; Coeuvre, his mouthpiece in *La Ville*, is an "ambiguous" man, like the man who "recrosses a river" and tells of everything he has seen on the other side.

For the time being we only wish to indicate a direction. The es-sential fact is this, that in many poetic circles the attraction of mystery was progressively increasing at that time, and that a belief in the particular efficacy of poetic experience in this respect was spreading. Thus, in 1909 Jules Romains, who cannot be suspected of excessive sympathy for the symbolists, emphasized in a lecture at the Salon d'Automne on "direct poetry" (i.e., a poetry that "dispenses with symbols" and aims at the apprehension of reality), the will of the moderns to discover the "subterranean springs," the "spiritual depths." There was a growing belief that we are surrounded by the Unknown and that it slips even into the most brightly illumined thoroughfares of our soul. To make poetry an instrument of know-ledge, was exactly what had been advocated in the teachings of Baudelaire, Mallarmé, and Rimbaud.

CHAPTER SEVEN

The Marriage of the Old and the New Aesthetic

1.

Between some of the traditions of symbolist origin and the classical values restored by Maurras and illustrated by *Les Stances* there were possibilities of agreement that paved the way for the formation of intermediate currents. That is why, in Mallarmé's lifetime, it was possible for R. de la Tailhède and Signoret—not to mention the poems of Pierre Louys and the sonnets of the young Paul Valéry— to seek their paths on the borders of Romanism and Mallarmism (and sometimes of the Parnassian School). Shortly afterward, Adrien Mithouard, who was one of the first to publish Claudel, Milosz and Alibert (in his magazine, *L'Occident*), pleaded the cause of a new French order. Indeed, he heralded the attitude which, by the advice of Gide, became that of *La Nouvelle Revue Française* in its early days (in 1909). Arguing against Pierre Lasserre, it declared that we must not, out of pigheadedness, abandon all so-called romantic feeling, or timidly renounce "everything strong and exquisite bequeathed to us by the late nineteenth century"; it affirmed the need for a modern classicism, that is, a new effort of integration, a new synthesis.

It is perhaps between the aesthetics of pure poetry, in its Mallarmean aspect, and a certain classical aesthetics tending toward preciosity, that the conciliation proved particularly interesting. In their art (if not in their inspiration), Racine and La Fontaine were closer to preciosity than one might think. As soon as Mallarmé smiles, he comes close to them (in his *Vers de Circonstance*); or consider his *Placet futile*; the purpose is always to reject all oratorical amplification, to complicate the linguistic apparatus by lightening it, to increase the suggestive and figurative power of the words. Mallarmé's heterodoxy—his barbarism, in the eyes of the purists—consisted in breaking the regular syntactic relationships and contriving new ones; his "Romanist" disciples of today, in order to escape from logical discourse and prose, prefer to resort to archaism (or Latinism and Hellenism), which enables them to remain French (in fact or in theory), but more freely and more variedly than is permitted by modern usage, which is often poor in its rational rigidity. In both cases, there is the intention of elaborating a purely poetic idiom (in syntax at least as much as in vocabulary) upon the margin of the everyday tongue, an idiom more or less equivalent to that "special style," which Ronsard wanted to create for his odes. André Thérive, the foremost theoretician of this aesthetics, called it a "stylistic of anti-prose," which forbids the exposition of facts and concepts, which forbids description proper no less than didacticism.

In Mallarmé as in the classical masters (and Moréas), matter tends to evaporate, the mind seizing hold of the sensation to project it halfway between the concrete and the abstract; impressionism in the broad sense, at least in Mallarmé, can thus sustain a spiritual poetry whose elements bathe in a single atmosphere of thought and are disposed on one plane, although perhaps not without breaks—discontinuity making it possible for the poet to escape from oratorical logic—but without any of those sudden changes of tone, which the romanticists of the Hugo school boasted of having introduced into their works. While it is likely that not all subjects are equally suitable for such poetry, it obviously does not exclude any subject *a priori*, and the rarity of an emotion, its modernity, will not prevent a skilful poet from expressing it in a sustained language that endows it with artistic value. This takes us rather far away from classicism in the sense of Maurras, which implies a certain concept of man.

Actually, it is the exceptional importance of the problem of expression in this type of poetry that provides the most solid bridge between the classical teachings and those of Mallarmé and Baudelaire. The poet's task is not to externalize himself, to pour out his life by becoming absorbed in the movement that animates it, but to sublimate the immediate data of existence by means of his sensibility and intellect—a skilful aristocratic art in which one may sometimes discern certain traits of preciosity and alexandrinism.

However, this meeting of classicism and symbolism takes place almost exclusively on the terrain of formal aesthetics. The Maurrasian idea of *homo classicus*, his morality and philosophy, are not necessarily implied in these attempts at conciliation, however cautious they may be. And of the two Baudelairean traditions, that of the hyper-conscious poet, the deliberate creator (stemming from Poe) and that of the mystic (an independent and sometimes unwitting disciple of the occultists), only the former is here in question. These lucid, "artistic" poets do not aspire to "attain to the unknown" through the instrumentality or help of poetry, as Rimbaud demanded, nor, consequently, do they make metaphysical claims. For the same reasons, if they practice Rimbaud's "derangement of all the senses," they would find it difficult to maintain, as they wish to, control over their emotions, sensations, and work. Poets such as Alibert, Muselli, Toulet, Dérême and others doubtless remain to a certain degree skeptics at heart—unless they adhere to the certainties of Catholicism, and this perhaps is the normal outcome of their skepticism, of their refusal to trust man and his ability to attain, without grace, and sometimes by slippery paths upon which the demon casts his shadow, to any absolute whatever.

Paul Valéry is undeniably related to this Mallarmean classicism. François-Paul Alibert represents the Mediterranean and even Virgilian aspect of this poetry. A certain Latin fullness, which is his strength in many passages, is sometimes also his weakness; his sentences are then protracted beyond measure, striving too long before they reach the point. This abundance, despite appearances, is at the bottom quite different from oratorical breadth—Alibert's poems are often invocations or discourses—they are always compact, their elements are concentrated and intermingled; the severest criticism that may be made of them is that their density and magnificence are often chiefly verbal.

It would, however, be extremely unfair to regard Alibert as primarily a rhetorician. He has his demon, a natural and inborn force—*vis poetica*—which speaks from the very depths of his being and seizes hold of him in his entirety, like a Panic power, a sacred fury, partaking of obscure instinct. But Reason is vigilant, a reason which is neither common sense nor the queen of a desert land;

which does not consider itself the mistress of life, superior to
Necessity. It is only an ordering reason: its function is to forge the
chains between which the burning lava will pour. Alibert's
originality consists in his ability to express passion without weaken-
ing it, to sublimate it in a chastened and noble language:

> Toi qui peux, beauté nocturne
> Aux insaisissables traits,
> Si bien garder les secrets
> De notre amour taciturne,
>
> Saurai-je ici quel démon,
> Sous ma contrainte muette,
> Vient consommer ta défaite
> Et ton suprême abandon?
>
> De tant de grâce complice
> D'un cygne mol et charmant
> Dont l'aile onduleusement
> Près de moi s'étire et glisse,
>
> Il ne reste, quand la nuit
> A son opaque mystère
> Soudain ton corps solitaire
> Et sa blancheur a réduit,
>
> Que ta seule indifference
> . . . .
> Entends mon coeur qui se brise
> De son contraire désir
> Et d'une ardeur à plaisir
> Cent fois quittée et reprise.
>
> De quoi sert-il seulement
> Que ta lenteur me prolonge
> Par je ne sais quel mensonge
> Un aussi rare tourment?
>
> Chair silencieuse et sombre,
> Est-ce toi? Ne vais-je pas
> Plutôt avancer mes bras
> Vers le fantôme d'une ombre?
>
> Hélas, comme au premier soir,
> L'âme et la bouche serrée
> Par l'épouvante sacrée
> De mon exécrable espoir

J'attends et je me consume . . .

You, nocturnal beauty
With elusive features
Who can so well keep the secrets
Of our silent love,

Shall I know here what demon
Under my silent constraint
Consummates your defeat
And your supreme surrender?

Of so much yielding grace
As of a soft and charming swan
Whose wing undulously
Stretches and glides beside me,

There remains when the night
Suddenly reduces your solitary body
And its whiteness
To an opaque mystery,

Only your indifference
. . . .

Hear my heart that is breaking
With its adverse desire
And with an ardor
A hundred times abandoned and resumed at will

But why must your slowness
By I know not what lie
Prolong for me
So rare a torment?

Silent and somber flesh,
Is this you? Shall I not rather
Hold out my arms
To the phantom of a shadow?

Alas, as on the first night
My soul and my lips tightened
By the sacred fear
Of my execrable hope

I wait and consume myself. . . .

(*La Guirlande lyrique: Nocturne*)

The further the poet advances in the portrayal of elementary emotions, the closer his style, by a kind of proud modesty, comes to the abstract. And it is not a little surprising to see this intense lyricism developing on a restricted foundation and accommodating itself to rigid conventions; the rules of versification, the requirements of tone, all the premises of the problem involved in a poem to be composed, function as freely chosen obligations which, far from inhibiting the growth of the work, allow it to fill all the space allotted to it and to order itself as a homogeneous totality.

In Alibert's poems—those that have reached the point of maturity—each element is related to each other element; a rhythm "harmonious and slow" commands the poem's progress, like the rhythm of a river as it approaches the sea, like the rhythm of those trees of the south which became the poet's friends and which for him reflect the image of his destiny. For Alibert's poetry is not the poetry of the exile who would like to *fuir, là-bas fuir* (escape, escape out there beyond);* his pessimism and his serenity full of pathos are those of a Mediterranean, of an "ancient" nurtured on Lucretius and Virgil; his pantheist ardor and gift for communing with things express themselves in a form that is largely traditional, but the Sibylline beauty of which reflects an entirely modern conception of poetry.

The design to marry symbolism with classicism and draw from them a supreme art fusing thought and poetry into a pure language radiant with the fires of a lofty Reason, can be inferred from the poems of several neo-Romanists of our time. This is particularly true of Jacques Reynaud and Henri Charpentier. Reynaud is almost Malherbian (like Lucien Dubech who is usually regarded as one of the neo-classicists); Charpentier is more of a Mallarmean (or Valeryan), he is obsessed by the idea of a gnomic lyricism, although it is embodied in figures and fables and strewn with exquisite verbal inventions. For these two poets, as for Alibert, poetry becomes something different from a game of skeptical minds. "If it achieved its goal," Henry Charpentier wrote recently in a manifesto published in the first issue of the magazine *Latinité*, Jan. 1929, "it would be

*Like Mallarmé, his master, whom he sometimes directly imitates in some pieces. Cf. especially *Midi* (in NRF of July 1926), (NRF of Dec. 1, 1927), and *Sémélé* (NRF of August 1, 1929).

identified with complete Knowledge. It would be both intuition and logical architecture, Dream and Reason, a flash illuminating the enigmas and depths of the universe and Man." This lofty ambition, enhanced by a kind of Pindaric pride, inspired a poetry that is deliberately lofty and thrives on familiarity with the gods:

> Où s'en iront les suprêmes idées?
> Le dernier homme, à qui laissera-t-il
> Le flambeau d'or des ères fécondées
> Par tant d'amour anxieux et subtil?
> O long effort! O savoir éphémère,
> Tu n'es plus rien! ... La grande nuit primaire
> A résorbé ton esprit volatil.
>
> Et toi que j'aime, absolument perdue!
> Douce Eve, encor frissonante, à quoi bon
> Toute mon âme à ta chair suspendue?
> C'est vainement que nous aurons, d'un bond,
> Franchi la borne assignée à la vie :
> Tu vas périr, Nature, inassouvie,
> N'ayant conçu que l'être moribond.

What will become of the supreme ideas?
To whom will the last man bequeath
The golden torch of eras fertilized
By so much anxious and subtle love?
O long effort! O ephemeral knowledge,
You are nothing now! ... The great primal night
Has absorbed your volatile spirit.

And you whom I love, now utterly lost!
Sweet Eve, still quivering, to what end
Does my whole soul hang on your flesh?
In vain shall we cross in one bound
The limit assigned to life:
You shall perish, Nature, unfulfilled,
Having conceived only moribund being.

(*Odes et Poèmes*)

2.

In his introduction to the anthology of "whimsical" poems published in *Vers et Prose* in October 1913, Francis Carco, after making his bow to Paul Fort, defined his own position and that of his group, placing it to the right of André Salmon, Apollinaire, Max Jacob, Henri Hertz, somewhere near Toulet and Tristan Klingsor "who gave a less hetero-geneous character to fantasy." Apollinaire's group must be con-sidered separately—it was the avant-garde that led poetry toward a certain literary cubism, which in turn paved the way for the new art of the post-war years. Jean-Marc Bernard, who figures among the "whimsical" poets in *Vers et Prose*, might be regarded as a neo-classicist, while Vincent Muselli and Léon Vérane might well be called neo-Romanist poets. Thus the movement extends on a wide front; after the armistice of 1918, the poets of this group continued together for a few seaons, largely in honor of P. Toulet, whose memory they wished to preserve.

But whatever master they chose, and whatever the various sources of their poetry, the *fantaisistes*, or whimsical poets, are moderns in spirit. They bade farewell to legends; as for regrets, pleasures, griefs, how could they forget them? No sooner do their dreams try to soar than they are caught in the troubled atmosphere, in the strong and bitter odor that hangs heavy over the landscape of our time. One must accept this twentieth century existence as it is; can poetry sustain itself by anything other than true sensations and emotions? In this sense impressionists, these poets are related to Jammes, Verlaine, Laforgue, even Corbière, and to the Rimbaud of the earliest poems; in short, to the decadents rather than the symbolists.

They are the libertines of modern bohemia; bohemians of the provinces whose wretched festivities plunge these young men into boredom; civil servants or soldiers, who love nothing so much as poetry and nothing so little as their trade; bohemians of Paris, who first gravitated to the *Lapin agile*, in Montmartre, before settling (toward 1910) in Montparnasse. The strange goddess, Fancy, oscillating between realism and chimera, awakened in the course of a sleepless night or under the pink and gray light of one of those morning twilights immortalized by Baudelaire. Several features of this contemporary bohemia remind one of the bohemia of Baudelaire and Banville, or of the *Jeune-France* movement; but the *fantaisistes* of today, even though they may have preserved something of romantic sentimentalism, have resolved to be without illusions. They know that people are no good. They have no thought of upholding the rights of art, passion or justice for the benefit of mankind. They love with-out believing in love, without believing in happiness, and a sense of modesty, the memory of former tears, and a certain self-detachment prevent them from opening their hearts without irony.

This humor, less natural than deliberate, or natural only as a result of a deliberately adopted habit, a humor that for a moment enables the poet to escape from the burden of his life, to pierce its illusions, to judge it, and to rediscover a possibility of free play, of freedom on the margin of oppressive reality, constitutes perhaps the only common characteristic of these minds which in other respects are quite different from one another. It is doubtless Laforgue, more than any one else, who set them the example of this theatrical atti-tude. At all events, we must not assimilate this irony to that of the German romantics. It does not lead them to those heights where the poet, having cast off his self and all sensible reality, sees everything transfigured and idealized. To yield to the inducements of the imagi-nation would, in their eyes, be one more illusion, in the trivial sense of the term (moreover, they lack the resources to undertake so long a voyage). The only liberty that is available to them and that they demand is the power to lengthen a little the tether binding them to real life, to compose their countenances and their poems in such a way that a slight vibration at the surface will suggest the beat of their hearts.

But this self-mastery cannot accommodate itself to a loose literary form. Even in disorder, they must control themselves. Because of their attitude toward life, these poets were led to adopt, if not a classical doctrine, at least a strict and sometimes elaborate syntax, a sharply defined style, a regular, or deliberately irregular meter. Whether they have inherited it from Verlaine, Mallermé or Moréas, their predilection for short pieces and simple rhythms reveals their desire to compose perfect and self-sufficient syntheses.

These aesthetic preoccupations explain why the *fantaisistes* sought an ancestry older than the "accursed" poets of the late nineteenth century, older than Banville or Nerval, and went back as far as the libertine France to which they are also linked by their moral noncon-formism, their skepticism, and their irony. From Villon to Marot, Régnier, Maynard, Voiture, La Fontaine, Voltaire, even Chaulieu and Parny, the road that traverses the middle or lower regions of Parnassus is adorned with light beauties, more or less officially recognized, possessed of a bewitching French charm. These poets of old, with their regulated, disingenuous imagination, were also wits; their poetry is like a sparkling froth of intelligence, and as for their "philosophy," not very Christian, and colored by Epicureanism, it is none the less "national."

Thus it came about that poets such as Toulet, Roger Allard, Dérême, Pellerin, or Carco, turning to a past anterior to romanticism, found teachers of thinking and writing, whose stylistic lessons did not contradict those of the modern "Abstractors of quintessence" — Baudelaire and Mallarmé. But it will be observed that in the lives of these poets and artists there is no place for metaphysics or mysticism, or for any ambition except to produce an accomplished work. Does not this conception of art as an entertainment and of the poet as a useless "player of ninepins" amount to one more attempt to return to classicism, this time by another road?

As far as I know, P.-J. Toulet has left behind no sonnet that would illustrate the dictum of Boileau; but he did write ten-line stanzas, quatrains, "flawless" couplets and *contrerimes* composed of two octosyllabic and two hexasyllabic verses, the former alternating and riming with the latter. It is delicate poetic woodwork. The whole is made of nothing:

> *O nymphes, regonflons des souvenirs divers . . .*
> O nymphs, let us bring back to life various memories . . .

says Mallarmé's Faun. Similarly, Toulet most often works on memories; and it is the faintest and most remote memory that lends itself to the surest magic; his poems are undisturbed by passion, the stanza is suspended motionless between heaven and earth like an irradiated bubble, a flake of foam spared by the wind. Yet there is nothing in this poetry that would remind one of the lifeless, diamond-inlaid gems of the Parnassians:

> *Douce plage où naquit mon âme*
> *Et toi, savane en fleurs*
> *Que l'Océan trempe de pleurs*
> *Et le soleil de flamme;*
>
> *Douce aux ramiers, douce aux amants,*
> *Toi de qui la ramure*
> *Nous charmait d'ombre et de murmure,*
> *Et de roucoulements;*

Où j'écoute frémir encore
Un aveu tendre et fier
Tandis qu'au loin riait la mer
Sur le corail sonore.

Sweet shore where my soul was born
And you, flowering savanna
That the Ocean drenches with tears
And the sun with flame;

Sweet to the dove, sweet to lovers
You whose foliage
Charmed us with shade and murmurs
And with the cooing of doves;

Where I can still hear throbbing
A tender and proud confession
While far off smiled the sea
On sonorous corals.

(*Les Contrerimes*)

As in a sea shell, one perceives a murmur of regret and nostalgia.

All of Toulet's poems, even—and particularly—the most ironical, end in a minor key, and bear witness to the fact that life is bitter and futile. And yet, he assures us, his soul yearned only for "dreams and flowers." There was something of de Musset in his dandyism, in his facetious, disenchanted manner; like de Musset he nursed in his heart the exacerbated suffering of the *enfant du siècle* who destroys himself and softly bemoans his inability to love. Libertinage, skepticism, irony, a culture pushed to the ultimate refinements, had shattered his youth; but a new century did not rise for him; the old century was drawn out, to die slowly in boredom and impossible dreams. Pierre Lièvre, in an important study published in *Divan* (May 1920), has noted that lyrical despair is the essential quality of Toulet. His poems are reminiscent of Alexandrine epigrams, of what Chenier called *quadri* or of the Japanese *hai-kai*—of an exquisite product preserving ancient aromas.

Je me rapelle un jour d'été blanc, et l'heure
Muette, et les cyprès . . . Mais tu parles: soudain
Je me rapelle un jour d'été blanc, et l'heure
D'une source un peu rauque, et qu'on entend qui pleure.

I recall a white summer's day, and the silent hour
And the cypresses . . . But you are speaking: suddenly
I dream, my eyes closed, of a muted brook
Beyond the garden, and I hear it weeping.

(Les Contrerimes)

One word more or one word less, and everything would fall into
dust. The most secret pathways of sensibility, the sinuous paths of
memory rise to the surface to be combined into an image of inex-
tricable beauty. It is obviously impossible to translate something
that is nothing but form and music. However, Toulet is not a
decadent, but a classicist inclining toward preciosity;* there are no
mannerisms in his verse, no graceful effeminacy, it is on the contrary characterized by such syntactic brevity and flexibility that the
poem darts forth like an arrow when the bow is released. A few
chosen notations evoke a state of mind severed from the course of
time and projected on a background of silence, the silence of a heart
that refuses to abandon itself and that is intoxicated, in solitude,
with the subtle perfumes prepared for it by a magician of the word.
As for life and pleasure, let them remain outside:

Toute allégresse a Son défaut
Et se brise elle-même.
Si vous voulez que je vous aime,
Ne riez pas trop haut.

C'est à voix basse qu'on enchante
Sous la cendre d'hiver
Ce coeur pareil au feu couvert,
Qui se consume et chante.

Every joy has its flaw
And shatters itself.
If you want me to love you,
Do not laugh too loudly.

It is in a low voice that one enchants this heart
Under the winter ashes
Which, like a smouldering fire,
Consumes itself and sings.

(Les Contrerimes)

*R. Allard, in a note published in La Nouvelle Revue Française, Apr. 1, 1921,
likens him, not without reason, to Saint-Gelays and Voiture.

The tradition of *art*, and the cult of form, which the influence of Toulet parallel to that of Valéry (continuing that of Mallarmé and Moréas) maintained during the years following the armistice of 1918—against the Dada movement and surrealism—are no less brilliantly represented today by poets such as Vincent Muselli or Roger Allard, fantastic, archaizing, precious, occasionally Baudelarian, but undeniably original. Scholarly, in possession of all the *French* resources offered by literature from Charles d'Orléans to Maynard, Tristan and Mallarmé, detesting all emphasis, with a penchant for allusive sentences and meanders, for concealed, Sibylline perfections, they work patiently to extract the rarest philters from their emotions.

In the range of full deep tones, it is perhaps Muselli who has most molded in pure traditional metal some of the "charms" so rare in serious literature before symbolism.

There is nothing more complex and more delicate than the internal architecture of his stanzas which embody the most multiple relations of meaning and sonority between interlocked elements, between down-beats and up-beats. The arrangement of words assumes the character of both inexorable necessity and capricious gratuity that seems to combine the orderly qualities of the old aesthetics and the virtues of surprise sought by the moderns.

> Tout un orchestre de drapeaux
> Et la barque parée en reine!
> Des fleurs, des flûtes, des flambeaux,
> Et de rubans flottante chaîne!
> Vins et liesse: à pleine haleine
> Le rire danse en vos ébats,
> Mais apaisez cette lumière,
> Joyeux rameurs, chantez plus bas,
> Au fil de l'an fuit la rivière!
>
> Qu'as-tu fait des jours les plus beaux,
> Mouton qu'as-tu fait de ta laine!
> Qu'a-t-il fait ce coeur en lambeaux:
> A tels roseaux pleure ma peine!
> Où vont la source et la semaine?
> Amour, Hélène et leurs appas?
> Une heure encore et la dernière,
> Plaisirs qui ne reviendrez pas!
> Au fil de l'an fuit la rivière.

Qu'importent les demains nouveaux,
Onde, incessament, qui m'entraîne
Fiers instants promis à la faux,
Eclairs sombres au noir domaine!
Si court-on que la course est vaine!
C'est la mer et c'est vous, hélas!
Votre voix, déjà coutumière,
Cloches d'Ys qui sonnez quel glas!
Au fil de l'an fuit la rivière.

ENVOI

Princesse, est-il une prière
Qui, nous tirant de ces combats,
Exorcise, unique et plénière,
Le temps, l'espace et les climats!
Au fil de l'an fuit la rivière!

An entire orchestra of flags
And the boat decked out like a queen!
Flowers, flutes, torches,
And the floating chains of ribbons!
Wines and merriment: Full-throated
Laughter dances in your revels,
But dampen this light,
Joyous oarsmen, sing softly.
The river flows down with the year.

What have you done with the best days,
Sheep, what have you done with your wool!
What has this tattered heart done:
My sorrow weeps to the reeds!
Whither go the fountain and the days?
Love, Helen, and their lures?
One more hour and the last,
O pleasures that will not return!
The river flows down with the year.

What matter the new tomorrows,
Wave which unceasingly carries me,
Proud moments promised to the scythe,
Flashes of light in the black realm!
However you race, the race is vain!
It is the sea and it is you, alas!

Bells of Ys, how familiar your voice,
What knell are you tolling now!
The river flows down with the year.

ENVOI

Princess, is there a prayer
That, freeing us from this battle,
Might exorcise, alone and fully
Time, space and the climes!
The river flows down with the year.

(Published in *Les Nouvelles Littéraires* of Sept. 5, 1931)

There is a Villonesque element not only in the form of this *Ballade de Contradiction*, but also in its theme, emphasized by the refrain "the river flows down with the year" which answers the question of the old lyrical poet, "But where are the snows of yesteryear?" Here, even more than the words and images, it is the tone and certain verses of an extraordinary aptness ("Proud moments promised to the scythe"), which betray a lofty and somber mood. A poet without real talent might have taken this mastery as an end in itself. But alas, there is no fear of such a poet creating a school. Possession of an art so difficult requires a never-ending apprenticeship which very few today would care to undertake.

Muselli attacked varied genres and styles, without ever yielding to the legitimate pleasure of doing again what he had done well once before. Almost the same might be said of Roger Allard who seemed predestined before the war to create a synthesis of Voiture or Malleville and Mallarmé. No one has a keener eye for observing the disappearance of a ribbon

> ... *en le peu profond*
> *Remous d'écumeuses dentelles*
> *Mourant aux rives les plus belles.*

> ... into the not very deep
> Eddy of foamy lace
> Dying at the most beautiful shores.

(From *Poésies légères*, 1911–1927)

But this malicious indiscretion saved him from pasturing the sheep of a new *Guirlande de Julie*; it was rather libertinage that lay in wait for him, a very elaborate libertinage ...

Folle coquette qui te fies
Aux charmes que tu vérifies

Foolish coquette relying
upon charms that you verify.

(Ibid.)

This epigram on a coquette examining herself in the morning
light applies to his own poetry. Then, Maynard seems to have impressed upon him the value of a more direct touch: his stanzas stand
out clearly or are interlinked like the ellipses traced by a dancer;
each in turn rises like a graceful balloon in a melancholy sky:

Adieu, la raquette sonore,
Les cris anglais, les gestes blancs!
Le seul jeu de ce jaune octobre
Est de s'embrasser sur les bancs.

. . . .

Je vois la campagne cauchoise
Se fleurir d'un coup de fusil,
Bouquet pâle auquel cherche noise
Un zéphir à demi transi:

Est-ce un braconnier dans la plaine
Ou le pistolet de Werther?
Mon coeur est ivre de sa peine,
Ma bouche a le goût d'hiver.

Farewell, noisy tennis racket,
English cries, white-flannel gestures!
The only game of this yellow October
Is to kiss on the benches

. . . .

I see the countryside of Caux
Blossom with a gun shot,
A pale bouquet with which a half-frozen
Zephyr tries to pick a quarrel:

Is it a poacher in the plain
Or the pistol of Werther?
My heart is drunk with its sorrow,
My mouth has the taste of winter.

(Adelaide, in L'Appartement des jeunes Filles)

This is sensual poetry, but it is governed by an exact mind, skilled
in handling words and rhythms. Such beauties, though minor, are

none the less remarkable. Actually, the traditional distinction between the light and the serious is no longer valid. The particular gift of Toulet, Muselli, Allard, the best among the *fantaisiste* poets is their power to open the gate to dreams with a single image, and without ever "scaling the heavens," to call forth a tragic flower of poetry beneath our feet. In his *Elegies martiales*, Allard traced with a delicate pencil the face of a young generation promised to love, and carried off by death, in a world where "nothing lasts" and where war seems to have taken its place among the inevitable evils:

> *En tous les lieux où la guerre nous lie,*
> *Je vois pourrir au soleil, à la pluie,*
> *Les jeunes corps par vos mains caressés:*
>
> *Ne filez plus, fileuses de leurs deuils,*
> *Ils sont vêtus de rayons et de feuilles.*
> *Vos beaux amants et vos doux fiancés.*
>
> *J'ai vu le peu que c'est de bien mourir,*
> *Que rien ne dure au-delà du désir*
> *Et qu'il n'est pas d'angoisses infinies;*
>
> *Heureux celui qui passe avec l'Été*
> *Et dans son sang retrempe sa beauté,*
> *S'il aima mieux sa chance que sa vie.*

> In all the places where war binds us,
> I see the young bodies caressed by your hands,
> Rotting in the sun and rain:
>
> Spin no longer on their shrouds,
> Your handsome lovers and your gentle betrothed
> Are clothed in sunshine and in leaves.
>
> I saw what a small thing it is to die well,
> That nothing lasts beyond desire
> And that there is no infinite anguish;
>
> Blessed is he who passes with the Summer
> And retempers his beauty in his blood,
> If he loved his fortune better than his life.

> (*Blessures de Guerre et d'Ailleurs*)

This is very different from the shattering anguish of Jean-Marc Bernard's *De Profundis du Combattant*, this last cry of a man about to be cut down by machine gun fire and buried in the mud; here, the spirit has freed itself from the flesh, it contemplates the hecatomb and dreams of man's fate.

The Bohemian poet par excellence during the first years of the twentieth century was Francis Carco. As often the case with Verlaine and Jammes, he seems at first to have scarcely any style; the various elements—the reflection of a face, the sighing of the wind, a lamp in a bar—seem in his poems to assemble themselves at random. This disorder is more apparent than real, it conceals an extremely sure touch in the choice and disposition of broken chords and interrupted movements. The tradition of intimate romanticism survives after so many avatars in this moving poetry full of mist and rain, which develops into a disturbing elegy whenever the poet's cynical perspicacity permits it to do so.

After 1918, following the example of Toulet and Jean Pellerin, and under the influence of the disoriented times, *fantaisiste* poetry adopted a swifter and more jarring cadence. Stifling to an ever increasing degree its sentimental impulses, cutting short its sharp sallies, it occasionally achieved a striking expression of that "modern mind" which the disciples of Apollinaire were striving in their poems to "intercept" like a radio wireless message. Especially Jean Pellerin, in the octosyllabic ten-line stanzas of his *Romance du Retour* brought out what is perhaps the principal element of this post-war *fantaisisme*—the constantly renewed surprise that suggests to the reader the essential incoherence of modern life and civilization. Heterogeneous notations which succeed one another as on a film strip are ingeniously interlaced in a single stanza, and all these distinct touches never constitute a simple psychological tonality. Yet several confessions full of pathos, veritable oases of intense poetry, rise from this whirlpool of images; they are soon interrupted by a backlash of irony, as in the following passages from *Le Bouquet inutile*:

> J'ai pleuré par les nuits livides
> Et de chaudes nuits m'ont pleuré.
> J'ai pleuré sur des hommes vides
> A jamais d'un nom préféré.
> Froides horreurs que rien n'efface!
> La terre écarte de sa face
> Ses longs cheveux indifférents,
> Notre vieux monde persévère.

> *Douze sous pour un petit verre!*
> *Combien va-t-on payer pour les grands?*

> I wept on livid nights,
> And hot nights wept for me.
> I wept for men forever empty
> Of a preferred name.
> Cold horrors never effaced!
> The earth pushes her long,
> Indifferent hair from her face,
> Our old world perseveres.
> Twelve pennies for a little glass!
> How much must we pay for a big one?

When Jean Pellerin diverts himself with descriptions, he chooses scenes of obvious novelty:

> *Quarante-chevaux qui s'ébroue,*
> *Arrêt. Le chauffeur va charger*
> *Avant de partir une roue*
> *Amovible. Un noble étranger,*
> *Boyard ou camérier du Pape,*
> *Monte. La craintive soupape*
> *Elève un murmure brisé;*
> *Ses soeurs chantent avec ensemble,*
> *Mais elle, doute, appelle, tremble*
> *Sur un cylindre ovalisé.*

> A forty-horse-power snorts, and stops.
> Before going on the driver
> Must pump up the spare tire
> A noble foreigner,
> A boyar or papal chamberlain,
> Gets in. The apprehensive valve
> Utters a broken murmur;
> Her sisters sing in chorus,
> But she hesitates, cries out, trembles
> Upon an ovalized cylinder.

What is astonishing here is the attempted amalgam of poetic cadence and modern subject matter. The spectacle of the machine has much more often inspired writers to produce lyrical effusions or exalted dithyrambs than such neat little sketches. But the manner of the *fantaisistes* remains traditional in its very oddities and audacities.

These experiments have been widely imitated and in this respect Pellerin is one with Carco and even Toulet. Today there is a poetry that is regular in its syntax and prosody, but devotes itself to portraying moral and material disorder. Street scenes, prostitutes, bars, fair grounds and their burlesque characters provide it with disquieting images. Banville and Baudelaire may be said to be the precursors in this field, and there is a visible thread connecting the *Odes Funambelesques* with many an odelet by Léon Vérane, for example:

> *Chabaneix, vous souvenez-vous*
> *De la gargotte à Montparnasse,*
> *De ces flacons de vins d'Anjou,*
> *De cette maritorne grasse . . .*

> Chabaneix, do you recall
> The joint at Montparnasse;
> Those flagons of Anjou wine,
> That fat sloven . . .
>
> (*D'un Soir à Montparnasse,* in *Le livre des Passe-temps*)

All in all, this is a Bacchic ode, quite clearly revealing the design of the most scholarly among the *fantaisistes*—the "Romanizing" libertines—to renew the minor themes of humanism by contrasting man's "eternal" sentiments with the most prosaic (in appearance) and most ephemeral elements of the contemporary setting. One might point out all kinds of rapprochements and interesting compromises, in this intermediate realm where *passéisme* and modernism willingly ally themselves, sometimes so charmingly. Marcel Ormoy writes elegies in the manner of Ronsard; Philippe Chabaneix, for more than ten years, has been distributing among his "tender girl friends" the amiable effigy of a French cavalier treading his way between roses and kisses, while Georges Gabory, Jacques Dyssord or René Chalupt clothe their stanzas in Harlequin garb. These three poets, with their ellipses and arabesques, achieve the art of a prestidigitator who can decorate a poem at will with the accessories of an *avant-garde* painter or a rococo boudoir. The antecedents and equivalents of this genre can doubtless be found in Toulet or Pellerin, as well as in the cubists or pseudo-cubists of today, poets and painters such as André Salmon, Apollinaire, Picasso, or Marie Laurencin.

Les demoiselles d'Avignon
Ont une rose à leur chignon
Et des bas de soie à fines mailles
A leurs pieds mignons.

. . . .

En revenant de Villeneuve
Elles quittent leur robe neuve
S'il leur plaît de feindre l'ébat
Des naiades du fleuve,

Offrant douce proie au pinceau
Du peintre Pablo Picasso
Qui s'est, pour les surprendre nues,
Caché sous un arceau.

The young girls of Avignon
Wear a rose in their chignon
And finely meshed silk stockings
On their dainty feet

. . . .

Returning from Villeneuve
They drop their new dresses
If they feel like imitating
The frolics of the naiads in the river

Offering sweet prey to the brush
Of the painter Pablo Picasso
Who, to catch them naked unawares,
Has hidden under an arch.

(*Les Demoiselles d'Avignon* by René Chalupt)

To balance this, we find in Tristan Dérême an opposite tendency which brings him ever closer to the old masters. The core of his nature is an elegiac sentimentalism which does not seem very different from the tender romanticism of Francis Jammes, during his melancholy youth. But Jammes himself, and Laforgue as well, helped him to strangle the chimeras and to adopt the mask of humor that he was to retain for many years. His feeling that there was nothing new to be seen or felt, his awareness of the automatisms and perpetual repetitions that are the woof of what we take to be our personalities, gave emphasis to the taste for caricature and pirouetting that appeared in his earliest poems. But even so, true emotion occasionally insinuated itself between sallies of deliberate triviality:

> *Chambre d'hôtel morose et vide. Un oeillet penche*
> *Et touche le miroir triste où tu contemplas*
> *Ta gorge nue.* Eau chaude —— Eau froide. *MM. les*
> *Clients sont priés de régler chaque dimanche.*
>
> *C'est dimanche. Réglons les comptes du coeur*
> *Rideaux jaunes et noirs, quel funèbre décor!*
>
> *Tu n'es plus là. J'ai lu Delille et l'Annuaire*
> *des Téléphones, pour ne plus songer à tes*
> *Sanglots . . .*

A hotel room empty and mournful. A carnation leans over
And touches the sad mirror where you gazed
At your naked bosom. *Hot water —— Cold water.* Guests
Are requested to settle their accounts every Sunday.

It is Sunday. Let us settle the accounts of the heart.
Yellow and black curtains, what a dismal setting!

You are no longer here. I have read Delille and the Telephone
Directory, to stop thinking of your
Sobs . . .

(La Verdure dorée)

But for the last few years Tristan Dérême has abandoned modern themes to compose elegies (dedicated to an absent Clymène). Their flowery graces and sustained sytle sometimes remind us of the elegies rimed for another Clymène by the poet of the nymphs of Vaux:

> *Sur le sureau qui penche au bord de la prairie,*
> *Les poules pour dormir poussent leur bec sous l'aile;*
> *La lumière du soir berce l'herbe fleurie,*
> *Les girouettes, la tonnelle*
> *Et les roses d'avril dont les anthologies*
> *T'enseigneront les epithètes,*
> *Et cependant, seul et dans l'ombre, tu t'entêtes*
> *A composer des élégies.*
>
> *Une lune nouvelle entre les cheminées*
> *S'elève, douce, et glisse aux branches des troènes;*
> *Pourquoi rêver encore à des rives lontaines*
> *Et nouer à ton coeur des guirlandes fanées*
> *Quand rit un pâle azur au calme des fontaines?*

Il n'est plus un oiseau qui jaillisse des feuilles;
La platane les garde en ses ténèbres fraîches;
Mais des songes que tu recueilles
Empennant de brûlantes flèches
Tu fais autant d'oiseaux qui tendent vers les nues
Le furieux élan de leurs plumes dorées,
Et qui heurtant eu ciel des vitres inconnues
Retombent sur ton coeur, les ailes déchirées.

On the elder-tree that stoops at the edge of the meadow,
The hens put their beaks under their wings to sleep;
The evening light cradles the flowering grass,
The weathercocks, the arbor,
And the April roses whose epithets
The anthologies will teach you,
And yet, alone and in the shadows you persist
In composing elegies.

A new moon between the chimneys
Rises gently, and glides toward the privet branches;
Why dream of distant shores
And tie faded garlands to your heart
When a pale blue sky laughs by the calm springs?
No bird soars from the foliage;
The plane tree holds them in its fresh darkness;
But of the dreams that you gather

Fitting them with burning darts
You make as many birds which press cloudward
With the furious impulse of their golden feathers
And clashing against unknown windows in the sky
Fall back upon your heart, with torn wings.

(*Le Livre de Clymène*)

Here, once again the sentimental romanticism prolonged by
Verlaine and the symbolists is harmonized with the more severe
lesson of Moréas and his school. Tristan Dérême's fantasy today is
a regulated scientific operation which enables the poet, without ever
disclosing himself or even confining himself to "treating a subject,"
to turn all the "classical" resources to the task of capturing the
essence of poetry. His felicitous manner and the discreet irony by
which he seeks to show that the exercise is of no consequence, add
further charm to the delicate embroideries by means of which he
diverts his thoughts from his surroundings.

Yet such indifference to the contemporary world remains rather exceptional among these poets most of whom devoted themselves to composing "circumstantial verse." With the exception of Alibert who embodies the extreme tendency to Mallarmeism, of Henry Charpentier and his group with their Mediterranean lyricism and perhaps of Vincent Muselli, with his somber gravity and heroism, they scorn the search for a certain "depth," which, sentimentally or spiritually, seemed to the romanticists and symbolists, or to most of them at least, the central point of the soul, from which the universe appeared to the poet in its correct and indispensable perspective. What they borrow from the symbolists is not a faith or an aesthetic of form, but stylistic procedures and a particular way of making a brief stanza vibrate and tingle in a halo of music. We shall not hesitate to see in them the successors — and often the conscious successors — of the light poets both worldly and irregular, who produced gallant or witty poems about the very sincere griefs or the trifling pleasures of their existence. The style, the epigrammatic accent, the gift of unpredictable associations flashing like a spark, of the sally — that is certainly the principal quality, renewed from the classical centuries, of the modern *fantaisistes*. The scene has changed, perhaps the hearts as well, still suffering from a hundred and more years of desires and dreams, but wit, prompt and lucid, springing up at the borderline between sensibility and intelligence, is still capable of polishing reliable weapons for the poet refuses to yield to delirium.

CHAPTER EIGHT

Paul Valéry, or the Classic of Symbolism

It is the tradition of the hyperconscious poet, the *fabricator*, that Valéry wished to follow. He chose Apollo against Dionysus. In his eyes, Leonardo da Vinci and Edmond Teste, those two examples of "the man of intellect," represent hyperbolical images of himself, and what he at one time dreamed of being, or, as Thibaudet says, pretexts for meditating on "the supreme possibility of the human mind," for imagining "a kind of abstract locus of genius." Valéry says of Leonardo: "I felt that he had discovered the central attitude from which the undertaking of cognition and the operations of art are equally possible." (*Introduction à la méthode de Léonard de Vinci*). Thus on the horizon of his thought, there glitters the mirage of omnipotence. "A man who has never attempted to make himself like the gods, is less than a man" (*Moralités*).

The proper object for a man of intellect, Valéry thinks, is to distinguish himself from everything in the self that is not pure consciousness. For what is a thought, a particular feeling, a sensation that lingers on, or a certain desire, what are all these phenomena of *inner* life, when the mind looks upon them, if not *external* things? Things that are born and die, that are transformed, that replace one another, and from which the mind must separate itself in a process of continuous "exhaustion"; which it must reject as impure and fluent in order to remain itself, aware of itself, identical with itself. Then nothing subsists but a "closed palace of mirrors" and a "solitary lamp" (*Introduction à la méthode*). "I am in being, and seeing myself; I am seeing myself see myself, and so on," as M. Teste formulates it; an image of consecutive mirrors carried to infinity.

For such a mind everything can become an object; for example, our personality which the romantics regarded as the sovereign good of the individual, as the subject par excellence, and which in reality is nothing but a *thing*, an accidental event, "deserving to figure with all other accidents of the world," a "game of nature, a game of love and chance." And where shall we find our soul, or what is called our soul, elusive among so many desires and impulses that nature arouses in us, and can it be taken for anything but a myth among other myths?

At the end of this intellectual asceticism, the pure *self* tends to become a cosmic point, an anonymous power, without any individual support. Valéry bears witness to this: *the man of intellect* "must knowingly reduce himself to an unlimited refusal to be anything whatsoever." Thus in order to achieve absolute self-awareness, we must tear ourselves away from nature and life, we must constantly negate them in ourselves. Seen from this angle Valéry might be defined as a mystic of a strange kind, infinitely anxious to free himself from all emotional and spiritual life (in the usual sense), a mystic of self-awareness, "daughter of faceless being":

> *Temple du Temps, qu'un seul soupir résume,*
> *A ce point pur je monte et m'accoutume,*
> *Tout entouré de mon regard marin;*
> *Et comme aux dieux mon offrande suprême,*
> *La scintillation sereine sème*
> *Sur l'altitude un dédain souverain.*

> Temple of Time summed up in one sigh,
> To that pure point I ascend and accustom myself,
> Wholly surrounded by my sea gaze;
> And as my supreme offering to the gods,
> A serene scintillation sows
> Sovereign contempt upon this altitude.

> (*Le Cimetière marin*)

But how difficult it is to sustain this ecstasy!

Indeed, the world constantly invades the mind. Perceptions, emotions, ideas, pleasures and sufferings, things of the inside and outside, together form in us a "familiar chaos," which is nevertheless monstrously alien. Nothing is clear in the soul or in nature, and the mind glides by inertia along beaten tracks, imagining that it knows what most often it only recognizes because it has already perceived or felt that thing without ever penetrating its real nature.* Consciousness is awake only intermittently; to bring it back to itself, a shock, an intrusion of the unknown, is required. But these ever-renewed assaults of the world, while imperiling the mind, afford it the means of salvation, of escaping from its slumber, of being reborn, of becoming equal for a moment to all movements and forms, of taking their imprint, and then of distinguishing and separating itself from them. Here is M. Teste at the theater:

> *Il ne regardait pas la salle. Il aspirait la grande bouffée, brûlante, au bord du trou. Il était rouge.*
> *Une immense fille de cuivre nous séparait d'un groupe murmurant au delà de l'éblouissement. Au fond de la vapeur, brillait un morceau nu de femme, doux comme un caillou. Beaucoup d'éventails indépendants vivaient sur le monde sombre et clair, écumant jusqu'aux feux du haut.*

> He did not look at the hall. He was breathing in the great burning wave of air at the edge of the hole. He was red.
> An immense copper girl separated us from a whispering group beyond the dazzling glare. At the heart of the vapor glittered a naked fragment of woman, soft as a pebble. Many independent fans were alive against the somber clear world which foamed to the fires on the ceiling.

> *(La Soirée avec M. Teste)*

The most active contemplation is carried on before everything dies away in phosphorescence. But if the mind at last rediscovers itself and recoils, it is only after pushing to the extreme the awareness of the individuality and specificity of things. It will dispose of them at will, perceiving analogies, arranging and disarranging connected wholes.

As a matter of fact, Valéry seeks to compel his mind to assume some of the prerogatives of nature; for fear of automatisms, and in order to attain a higher freedom, he tries to substitute himself for nature, to convert its accidents into opportunities. To abandon oneself to inspiration, to hidden forces, is to cast one's line and wait for miracles. Is it not advantageous and economical to prepare favorable encounters in broad daylight?

Most people see with their intellect much more often than with their eyes. Instead of colored spaces they take cognizance of concepts. For them a cubic whitish form, tall, and pierced with reflections in glass is immediately a house: The House! (Introduction à la méthode)

In this, the proud poet deludes himself, Nature cannot be replaced. One can only extend the luminous kernel of the *self*, project light beams even further. But the darkness persists. The attempt to reduce everything to thought is only a snare, and this cannot be changed by the keenest of Valéry's paradoxes. We are confronted with a man who has made up his mind to be interested only in his own functioning; but, as Paulhan says, "what he shows the absence of, is only what he has refused in advance to see." Moreover, it sometimes happens that Valéry, with an instructive inconsistence, bows before the evidence: "To seek is only to put oneself in the condition of being able to find by some accident or some slumber. It is to prepare the field for the happy spark." This is enough to raise the whole question again: for then there are things that are given us; or perhaps we give them to ourselves but without knowing it, without being able to detect their subterranean sources.

More must be said. However "available" he means to be, however absent from everything that is not pure mind, Paul Valéry is continually and invincibly attracted by his soul and his body—our thought in its seeming spontaneity and freedom being perhaps nothing but an almost uninterrupted dream, a sequence of myths that are like the interpretation of our internal and external sensations. Tenderly attached to his soul and his body, attracted by them as Narcissus, bent over the deep water, is attracted by his image, tempted by this alien and incomprehensible life, by these lovely colors that it projects one knows not how at the sunset of consciousness, seduced by this life, and taking pleasure in this weakness— not without regretting and desiring the altitudes, the "pure point" of absolute contempt and the perfect vacuity of the consciousness that rejects life—such is for us the image of Valéry. Two states of being—or of nonbeing? there is no deciding because they condition one another—two conflicting states appeal to him—that of the simple, the stable, the nontemporal, and that of the multiple, of the changing, of duration, in short, of things which beset the mind. Almost all his work bears witness to this oscillation. Just as underneath clear thought, which believes in its own self-mastery, there subsists the unconscious and chance, so underneath the will to abstract oneself from there persists the will and the need to live. For it is not only as a spiritual exercise that the *self* strives to become aware of all its sensations. "Some men," says Valéry, "experience

with a special delicacy the pleasure of the individuality of objects."
(*Introduction à la méthode*). In vain does his mind strive to look upon
his soul and even his person as objects, in vain does he say: "I — that
am neither somebody nor someone else; the fact of forgetting shows
that I am no one" (*Analecta*, cxix). Despite all this, nothing could prevent this cry, this *passionate* interrogation (our emphasis): "O who
will tell me how through existence *my person* has been preserved in
entirety, and what thing has carried me, inert, full of life, and charged
with spirit, from one boundary of nothingness to the other?" (*A.B.C.*,
in *Commerce*, 1925).

Nascitur poeta. Paul Valéry is a poet. He had to be one by nature
for the genius of poetry in him to survive so many contrary ventures,
above all the "mad desire to understand," which consumed him
from his twenty-second year on. And if Valéry consented to lend
himself to the game of poetry, and even to devote all his energies to
it, it is because he profited by it. This "exercise," as he liked to call
it, permitted him to feel his power. "It is a game," he says, "but a
solemn, regulated and significant game; the image of what one
ordinarily is not" (*Littérature*). To construct a poem is to construct
oneself. The poetic art has as its counterpart an art of self-fulfillment
by means of the acts which beget the poem, an art of overcoming
"that familiar chaos" (i.e., the disorder of psychological life), of conferring a form, a style, upon that which "lacks it by nature," i.e.,
upon thought.

But this exercise is effective (with regard to the author) only if it
is difficult. Convinced that aesthetics and personal ethics are identical, Paul Valéry believes that the birth of a beautiful work is favored
by the author's voluntary submission to a great number of precise
and complex conditions — to begin with, the precepts of traditional
versification — which may have only conventional value, but which
compel the mind to spend itself against the constraints imposed
upon it, to sacrifice useless "finds" and to maintain itself in a superior
state of tension and inner cohesion. By observing all the rules of
the game, however arbitrary they may be, by making the poem a
system of inextricably interlinked and consubstantial thoughts and
sounds, the writer prevents the dispersal of his psychological energies and at the same time increases his chances of producing a successful work.

And what if by accident so much labor and so many deliberately accepted constraints did not secure the best possible poetic result? Valéry dares to answer: "I would infinitely rather write something weak in full consciousness and complete lucidity than give birth to a masterpiece of the most beautiful kind by means of a trance and outside myself." (*Lettre sur Mallarmé*). This is perhaps a capital sin against poetry. Out of pride and hatred for the irrational, the poet refuses treasures that might come to him from a world that is not governed by his clear and sovereign thought. He does not consent to hold himself responsible for the gifts of nature. Nevertheless nature works for him, and this is indispensable, as he himself is well aware; it pleases him to challenge nature, to try to escape from himself through paradoxes. This is lost labor. There is much truth in the saying of Abbé Bremond that there is in Valéry something of "the poet in spite of himself." The worst of it is, indeed, that Valéry's avowal, which we have just quoted, reveals a resolve of his entire being. But it must also be granted that Valéry, because of his prejudice in favor of absolute lucidity, gives us very little information about his "total functioning"; "what we think," he himself observes, "conceals from us what we are."

Does an attitude so extremely intellectualistic require that the poet express *ideas?* This might be feared if we forgot the profound inclinations existing in him side by side with his will to hyperconsciousness. A disciple of Poe, Baudelaire and Mallarmé cannot believe that the object of poetry is to communicate ideas to others, and that didacticism under any form belongs to any realm but that of prose. Valéry, like Mallarmé, instead of treating words as instruments of exchange capable of transmitting thoughts—and perishing once this function is performed—groups them according to their powers of suggestion, of psychological creation. In his eyes, the poet's mission is to act upon the reader's total self, to ravish it, to arouse in him, more effectively than would nature, certain extraordinary activities and emotions. Far from being a rational song, the poem, extracted from life, always ambiguous like life, represents a kind of supernature (in a nonmystical sense) in which the pressure of several atmospheres prevails. Moreover, we need only listen to Valéry defining poetry, to be ourselves carried to the antipodes of intellectualism: "Poetry," he said one day, "is an attempt to represent or to restore, by articulate language, *those things or that thing*, which tears, cries, caresses, kisses, sighs, etc. try obscurely to express." (*Littérature*.)

He is, then, concerned with cutting a path to the primordial, the fundamental, with going back to the very sources of life to discover "what we are" underneath what we think. Valéry's very skepticism, his distrust of ideas considered as superficial products, useful but unauthentic, separates him from any rationalist poetics. Let us recall *Aurore*. It evokes ideas under the aspect of secret spiders in the darkness of the self. "See," they say to the poet . . .

> *Regarde ce que nous fîmes:*
> *Nous avons sur tes abîmes*
> *Tendu nos fils primitifs,*
> *Et pris la nature nue*
> *Dans une trame ténue*
> *De tremblants préparatifs . . .*

> See what we have done:
> Over your abysses
> We have spun our primitive threads,
> And captured naked nature
> In a tenuous web
> Of trembling preparations . . .

But the poet answers:

> *Leur toile spirituelle,*
> *Je la brise, et vais cherchant*
> *Dans ma forêt sensuelle*
> *Les prémisses de mon chant.*
> *Etre! . . . L'universelle oreille!*
> *Tout l'âme s'appareille*
> *A l'extrême du desir . . .*

> Their intellectual web,
> I break it, and I set out to seek
> The premises of my song
> In my sensuous forest.
> Being! . . . Universal ear!
> All my soul embarks
> To the sail of extreme desire.

(Aurore in Charmes)

In this image the spirit does something quite different from "rehearsing its proofs" (Rimbaud); it turns resolutely to the obscure

fringe that surrounds the luminous center of consciousness. Thus
everything—his poetic art as much as his critique of ideas, and
the almost voluptuous attraction exerted upon him, willy nilly, by
the irrational powers of the self and the universe—conspires to
direct Valéry, the Apollonian poet, to the nocturnal depths of man.
If he is the poet of consciousness, as he has been called, he is not
in the least the poet of formulated, codified knowledge—a poet
of ideas—but of knowledge in process of being born, of still embry-
onic ideas, of all the states intermediate between the unconscious
and the conscious. Valéry patiently gathers scarcely perceptible
plants, which, however, sink their roots into the very depths—and
which, if permitted to grow, might become clear ideas, good for
prose, but bad for poetry.* This slow ascent, this transition from
night to day, constitutes one of the main themes of his poetry.
Consider the palm tree which does not know itself "between the
sand and the sky"; sometimes rigorous thought becomes alarmed
and despairs of a growth whose laws elude it, a growth which dis-
appoints its expectation:

*It is worth while to re-read the following page from *Introduction* (text of 1919):
*Between the vividness of life and the simplicity of death, dreams, disturbances, ecstasies,
all the half-impossible states which one might say introduce approximate values, irrational or transcendent solutions into the equation of consciousness, interpose strange
degrees, ineffable variations and phrases—for there is no name for things among which
one is quite alone.*

*Just as insidious music harmonizes the licenses of sleep with the coherence and
concatenation of extreme attention, and produces a synthesis of momentary but intimate
beings, so the fluctuations of psychic balance make perceptible aberrant modes of existence.
We carry within us forms of sensibility which cannot be successful, but which can be
born. These are moments snatched from the implacable critique of time; they do not
resist the complete functioning of our being: either we perish, or they dissolve. But
the monsters of reason are monsters full of lessons—and so also are these transitory
states; they are areas in which the familiar continuity, connections, mobility are modified;
empires where light is associated with pain; magnetic fields where directed fears and
desires assign strange circuits to us; material that is made of time; abysses literally
of horror, or love, or tranquillity; regions oddly soldered to themselves, non-Archimedean
realms that defy motion; perpetual sites in a flash; surfaces which become hollowed
out, conjugated to our nausea, inflected beneath our least intentions ... It cannot be
said that they are real; nor can it be said that they are not. He who has not gone through
them does not know the price of natural light and the most commonplace surroundings;
he does not know the true fragility of the world which is not related to the alternative
of being and nonbeing—that would be too simple!*

N'accuse pas d'être avare
Une Sage qui prépare
Tant d'or et d'autorité:
Par la sève solennelle
Une espérance éternelle
Monte à la maturité!
Ces jours qui te semblent vides
Et perdus pour l'univers
Ont des racines avides
Qui travaillent les déserts.
La substance chevelue
Par les ténèbres élue
Ne peut s'arrêter jamais
Jusqu'aux entrailles du monde,
De poursuivre l'eau profonde
Que demandent les sommets.
Patience, patience,
Patience dans l'azur!
Chaque atome de silence
Est la chance d'un fruit mûr!
Viendra l'heureuse surprise:
Une colombe, la brise,
L'ébranlement le plus doux,
Une femme qui s'appuie,
Feront tomber cette pluie
Ou l'on se jette à genoux!

Charge not with avarice
The Sybil who is preparing
So much gold and authority:
Through the solemn ferment
An eternal hope
Is rising to maturity!
These days that seem to you empty
And lost to the universe
Have greedy roots
Which cut through the wilderness.
The hairy substance
Chosen by darkness
Can never stop pursuing
Even unto the entrails of the earth
The deep water
Demanded by the summits.

Patience, patience,
Patience in the blue sky!
Each atom of silence
Is the chance of a ripe fruit!
The happy surprise will come!
A dove, the breeze,
The softest touch,
A woman leaning,
Will unleash the rain
In which man throws himself on his knees!

(*Palme* in *Charmes*)

In this poem, imperious reason disarms itself and there rises a hymn of gratitude to the forces which are active only in the shadow, without and against reason, a hymn to nature and spontaneous creation. This is an extremely valuable admission, of which there are several instances. In reality, Valéry pursues two callings, alternately or simultaneously.

This, no doubt, is why the same theme recurs in *La Jeune Parque* and *Cimetière marin*, which are in many respects Valéry's most important poems. There is a conflict between two opposite attitudes—the "pure" or absolute attitude of consciousness retrenched in its isolation, and the "impure" attitude of the mind which accepts life, change, action, and which, renouncing its dream of perfect integrity, allows itself to be seduced by things and chained to their metamorphoses. The overwhelming majority of the developments of *La Jeune Parque* and most of the "subjects" of *Charmes* can be considered in relation to this essential theme.

La Jeune Parque and *Cimetière marin* both end in the triumph of life. In the former we see a fabulous being, half girl and half goddess returning into the sea. While the "inevitable stars" dwindle, it seems to her after the temptations of the night that the first whiteness of dawn "illumines the torments of an ancestress." Will she live on, she who for a moment desired death as the only means of escaping from impure things? But now she is wounded by "the sharpest air"; a "summons of the sea" seems to strike her face; skimming over the waves, the rays of the sun fill her very thoughts with "a glare of icy sparks." Once again bitten by life, she yields, she surrenders, she worships:

Je te chéris, éclat qui semblait me connaître,
Feu vers qui se soulève une vierge de sang
Sous les espèces d'or d'un sein reconnaissant.

I cherish you, brilliance that seemed to know me,
Fire toward which rises a blood virgin
Under the golden guise of a grateful heart.

Is it correct to speak here of a triumph of life? It is rather an acceptance of an existence that will remain precarious. Really to live would be to lose oneself in one's desire, in one's act, to become one—and cease to see oneself. That is no longer possible. From the day when consciousness awakened in man, he began to feel himself separated from the whole, isolated, exiled, in a universe to which he clings with all the fibres of his body and his soul, but which remains alien to him. It is impossible to escape from this dualism which consciousness has introduced into life, to abandon oneself to the world without reservations, but also to abstract oneself from it. To veer and tack, to accept compromises, to seek intermediate paths between the mind and things, sometimes closer to the mind and sometimes to things, such is the fate of man.

In *Cimetière marin*, the sea symbolizes, as it does in *La Jeune Parque*, movement, unconscious and creative life; it also symbolizes the soul, living, desiring, obscure, formless. Meditation having come to a standstill, the mind seeing only illusion everywhere, even in movement, it is the sea which by the breath and foam that it projects into the slumbering body awakens the soul, carries it into the magic circle of the universe, and compels it to surrender for a moment, and to live.

Non, non!... Debout! Dans l'ère successive!
Brisez, mon corps, cette forme pensive!
Buvez, mon sein, la naissance du vent!
Une fraîcheur, de la mer exhalée,
Me rend mon âme... O puissance salée!
Courons à l'onde en rejaillir vivant!
Oui! Grande mer de délires douée,
Peau de panthère et chlamyde trouée
De mille et mille idoles du soleil,
Hydre absolue, ivre de ta chair bleue,
Qui te remords l'étincelante queue
Dans un tumulte au silence pareil,

Le vent se lève! . . . Il faut tenter de vivre!

No! no! . . . Arise! Into the next era!
Break, my body, this pensive form!
Drink, my bosom, the birth of the wind!
A freshness exhaled by the sea
Gives me back my soul . . .
O saline power!
Let us run to the waves and spring forth alive!
Yes! Great sea endowed with deliriums,
Panther skin and mantle riddled
By a thousand sun idols,
Absolute hydra, drunken with your blue flesh,
Biting once more your glittering tail
In a tumult resembling silence,

The wind rises! . . . We must attempt to live!

What an extraordinary recapture of movement! Nowhere else perhaps has French decasyllabic verse attained such richness of expression. And what a boon, what relief, this temporary return to chaos, this surrender to delirium and time! Alas, once the drunkenness is gone, there is again a task to be faced, a venture: "we must attempt to live." Consciousness returns, and with it questions, doubts. To be or not to be? The problem is not posed in these terms. One is doomed to be imperfectly and miserably subjected forever to the conditions of all human life.

Paul Valéry declines the title of poet-philosopher which he has been awarded by public opinion. He likes to say that philosophy is defined "by its apparatus and not by its object"; the incompatibility obtaining between the language of the pure poet and the technique of the philosopher suffices, he thinks, to show how monstrous is the idea of a philosophical poetry. But must we adopt Valéry's criterion? If it is true that modern philosophy tends to define itself by its apparatus, it is permissible to think that this should not be a source of pride. The author of *La Jeune Parque* seems to us—in his best passages—a poet philosopher who does not lack an *object*. To be sure, he never treats or raises problems that are, strictly speaking, metaphysical. But a very profound experience bearing upon the relations between soul and body, the unconscious and the conscious, leads him by a necessity of his nature to create what he modestly calls philosophical "color," an atmosphere; in fact, it is much more, namely, the psychological and vital movement that compels the formulation of these problems and makes their solution urgent and infinitely remote. Foreign to all didacticism, his poetry can never be divested of its pith, can never be "translated." The poem as a whole invites us to philosophical reflection, without ceasing to progress in the chiaroscuro of images and music, without ever losing contact with the sources that animate it, and without breaking the sweet bonds of blood that hold it suspended.*

And yet the drama that is played here is one of the most general imaginable: it is that of the *Jeune Parque*, of Valéry, and in a sense, of mankind. By dint of deepening oneself and overlooking accidents in order to apprehend only the essential, one ultimately transcends the personal and particular, and finds one's way back to the universal. Mallarmé had already set the example of this transmutation of the romantic poetry of the self into a poetry of the mind; most of his poems produced at a mature age are on a level other than the lyrical. If Valéry's is superior in this respect, I believe it is because his poetry is much more sensuous, at least in its felicitous parts. If the "pure" attitude has as much attraction for him as for his master, things and emotions obviously seduce him more than they did Mallarmé. He relates the pleasure they create in him to real objects, not to lifeless Platonic effigies, "pure and suave ideas," less present than absent. It is the feeling for psychological concreteness, in relation to an infinitely subtle feeling for the weight, color, and extra-intellectual qualities of words that enables him to infuse his verses, even the most abstract of them, with that savor and secret vibration which give the reader an immediate poetic shock and pleasure, even before his intellect has had time to question itself.

Thus, however eager Valéry may be to look at his soul and body from the outside, however extended the marvelous meanings which can sometimes be read into his work, and for which Valéry declines all responsibility ("there is no true meaning of a text"), nevertheless man is always present in his supra-lyrical and "philosophical" but concrete poetry. In all his verses there resides a certain essence always similar; "a profound *note* of existence," says Valéry, which

*And in my sweet bonds suspended by my blood, says the *Jeune Parque*.

once heard, dominates all the complexity of the conditions and varieties of existence" (*Introduction à la methode*). And this grave and continuous note, though tender and noble, is not gay at all. It has the accent of a complaint, a weariness, a nostalgic regret. It betrays the disillusioned hope of a solitary self which has no respite unless it progresses another step toward self-knowledge and self-love, but which knows in advance that its quest is doomed to have no end, to remain without result, and without effective reward.

Consider his favorite theme of *Narcisse*. According to Valéry, it symbolizes the confrontations of man and consciousness. But the "delicious, desirable and icy demon" which is traced in the water, an image constantly destroyed by the movement of the nymphs, this demon is inaccessible. Either the mind wears itself out in the quest of it:

> *Mes lentes mains dans l'or adorable se lassent*
> *D'appeler ce captif que les feuilles enlacent*
> *Et je crie aux échos les noms des dieux obscurs.*

> My slow hands in the charming gold grow weary
> Of calling this captive whom the leaves enlace
> And I cry to the echoes the names of obscure gods.

> (*Narcisse*, first version)

or, going down deeper, armed with all its vigilance, it believes that it sees nothing but an unfathomable emptiness. Madame Emilie Teste is concerned over the meditations of the man who is her husband: "Will he find life or death, at the end of his attentive efforts?——Will it be God, or some frightful sensation of his own miserable matter?" (*Lettre de Mme Emilie Teste*). There is the same sadness in *La Jeune Parque*: words akin to the foregoing express similar feelings:

> *Leurs fonds passionnés brillent de sécheresse*
> *Si loin que je m'avance et m'altère pour voir*
> *De mes enfers pensifs les confins sans espoir.*

> Their passionate foundations glitter with dryness
> As far as thirsting I advance to find
> The confines without hope of my pensive infernos.

Narcisse found in the investigation of the self a "treasure of impotence and pride" or even "boredom." The *Jeune Parque*, too, speaks of boredom, "the clear boredom," the boredom that has become "the prey of her gaze." Socrates in *L'Ame et la Danse* defines the boredom of living with greater precision still: "This perfect boredom, this pure boredom ... this boredom, in short, which has no substance other than life itself, and no second cause but the clearsightedness of the living." It is necessary to recall that in one of the most beautiful passages of *La Jeune Parque*, the poet, reputed dry and pitiless, evokes the birth and slow progress of a tear:

> *Tu procèdes de l'âme, orgueil du labyrinthe.*
> *Tu me portes du coeur cette goutte contrainte,*
> *Cette distraction de mon suc précieux*
> *Qui vient sacrifier mes ombres sur mes yeux,*
> *Tendre libation de l'arrière-pensée!*
>
> . . . .
>
> *D'où nais-tu? Quel travail toujours triste et nouveau*
> *Te tire avec retard, larme, de l'ombre amère?*
> *Tu gravis mes degrés de mortelle et de mère,*
> *Et déchirant ta route, opiniâtre faix*
> *Dans le temps que je vis, les lenteurs que tu fais*
> *M'étouffent ... Je me tais, buvant ta marche sûre ...*

> You proceed from the soul, pride of the labyrinth.
> You bring me from my heart this constrained drop,
> This diversion of my precious life-blood
> Which rises to sacrifice my shadows in my eyes,
> Tender libation of the thought back of the mind!
>
> . . . .
>
> Whence do you come? What labor ever sad and ever new
> Draws you, tear, from the bitter shadow?
> You climb my mortal, mother's steps,
> And your slowness, stubborn scythe
> That rends your path in my lifetime, chokes me ...
> I fall silent, drinking your sure progress.

This is a very human music, and it may be said that it, too, proceeds from the soul. After this it matters little that Valéry affects to be disinterested in the "subjects" of his poems, that it pleases him to look on poetry as a mere exercise. This voice and its sadness "without hope" are unmistakable. As a man the poet obviously suffers from the lack of anything genuinely real in his own center, on which to base himself; being evades him endlessly, faceless, closed, heterogeneous. True, "one must attempt to live";

but for one who has once been seduced by the mirage of absolute self-knowledge and self-mastery, life is only a lesser evil. In *l'Ebauche d'un Serpent*, Valéry clearly states the revealing words. He accuses the Sun:

> *Tu gardes les coeurs de connaître*
> *Que l'univers n'est qu'un défaut*
> *Dans la pureté du Non-Etre.*

> You prevent men's hearts from knowing
> That the universe is but a flaw
> In the purity of non-Being.

Already Mallarmé held life to be, if not a mistake, at least an evil, an impurity, a deterioration. He would have subscribed to Valéry's "infernal" paradox: "There is nothing so beautiful as that which does not exist"—indeed, he strove to confer a positive value on non-Being, to give reality to absence, and he dreamed of a poetry without matter, as close as possible to nonexistence, a poetry that would be the "musician of silence."

The pride of consciousness constitutes the misfortune of consciousness. By refusing "to be anything whatsoever," one runs the risk of being reduced to a faculty of transpositions, substitutions, "without any real foundation." If there is a tragic point in Valéry's destiny, which decisively affects his poetry, it is this—that he seems unable to conceive of the pure mind and what confronts it (souls, things, the universe) except in intellectualistic propositions. The mind tends to become a "power without an object," incapable of proving its existence to itself. And however much the poet may love the universe, and caress its forms and faces, the mind consents to see in it only an enemy, a flaw, a blemish. But poetry, and especially a poetry of consciousness such as this, can be born only on the frontier between the mind and things, the conscious and unconscious, the rational and irrational, at their points of contact. Valéry's predilection for the "pure attitude" and perfect intellectual availability make such contacts difficult. If they occurred in spite of this, it is because he sometimes "tried to live," to forget and to lose himself. Like *La Jeune Parque*, like man before being bitten by the serpent, he did not close himself in the world of hyperconsciousness. He knew blessed moments of abandon, thanks to which his poetry could mature like the fruit of a magnificent and paradoxical accord between a thinker and a poet who are not always one and the same man, the thinker aiming only at understanding, and the poet prizing poetry only in so far as it affects all being, and does not seek primarily to be understood.

It is superfluous to note that Paul Valéry is not an initiator opening paths toward a new poetry. Like the classic poets, his mission was rather to fulfill. Beyond any question, valuable lessons of style can be drawn from his work, and his meditations can serve as a starting point for infinitely suggestive reflections. But his position involves more than one danger. Anyone trying to develop it would doom himself to remaining "on this side" of poetry or to destroying creative poetic states in himself. It is impossible to go further than he did; to purify the mind still more would be to sterilize it. That is doubtless why poets younger than he, many of whom were his intimates, strove, if not to do exactly the opposite of what he did, at least to adopt methods in every respect contrary to his. Valéry's influence on the poetry of today is perhaps above all an influence by reaction. And who knows whether in his latest years he did not multiply his intellectualistic propositions (on aesthetics) with the unavowed intention of criticizing his unfaithful disciples? But in such cases each side succeeds only in involving itself more completely in its own position.

CHAPTER NINE

Paul Claudel, Bard of the Total World

1.

To leave Valéry for Claudel, means to move into another solar system, to yield to the lure of a hierarchized universe, in which everything has value and meaning. It is to pass from the island of pure consciousness to a solid and concrete order of pure "things," created and sanctified by an omnipotent God. By the same token, it is to renounce the idea of the sovereignty of the solitary mind. The soul, *anima*, returns to its castle at the highest point of the personality; it ceases to be an object, an occurrence, it ceases to belong to the immense realm of the external world; it is a queen, but a queen aspiring to be dispossessed by that "someone in myself who is more myself than I" of whom Claudel speaks in his *Vers d'exil*. Claudel certainly does not lack subject matter, will, material. He does not lack the inspiration that carries the soul toward matter. Matter, he says, is "a black clamor," awakening at the source of Being and transformed into "an intelligible explosion" (*Cinq grandes Odes*).

Christianity, Romanticism, Hellenism (as different as possible from the Minervian Atticism of Maurras)—Claudel seems to follow all these paths at once in quest of a certain primitivism, of a communion with the Mothers. He allied himself with the elements, abandoning himself to the night, the earth which gorges its children with milk during their sleep, entrusting its life to "primal matter" par excellence, to "the eternal, salty sea, the great gray rose" (*Cinq grandes Odes, L'Esprit et l'Eau*), the breeding place (*le lieu*) of all seeds; while the ship furrows it with its prow, it communicates an orgiastic joy to the poet and inspires him with the desire to dissolve in that "which rises and falls. . . ."

"Only the first gulp is difficult" (*Ballade*). But since his twentieth year Claudel has not weakened in exorcising this Dionysism illumin-ed by a remote ray from Orpheus or Zarathustra. This will to power has been "converted." Among the paths that might lead him to the very "pulse of Being," the Christian has chosen that which is the only one. In his eyes only that path is sure which leads man to see God in the Church. And if he has chosen it to the exclusion of any other, it is because it gave him not only salvation but also the possibility to live, to believe in the world, and to function as a poet. That is the capital fact. For his almost organic certainty that "to live is an amazing thing, a powerful thing," proved incapable of overcoming the physical horror of nothingness that we find in many of his works, especially the earliest. If the world is build on a vacuum, without foundations, it ceases to *be*; it disintegrates at the touch like ashes. Even the great enterprise, the great folly of "Tête d'Or" would seem to be a mere distraction. And Besme, the engineer in *La Ville*, to whom the earth has been given that "he might build railroads on it," repeats in the end like a death knell, "Nothing is, nothing is. . . . " So clear a vision of death makes any attempt to live illusory; all that remains of man is his pride burning alone over the abyss.

Claudel has given some indication of his spiritual itinerary during the last years of his adolescence. There was first of all the revel-ation—"I suddenly had a shattering sense of God's innocence, of His Eternal Childhood"—then the harsh and long unsettled struggle for an accord between faith and thought, the building of an entirely homogeneous personality, man and poet welded without a seam. And then Rimbaud, even while kindling his dream of power, "breached his materialist dungeon," and gave him the air of the supernatural to breathe, an intoxicating perfume capturing all the powers of the soul forever by its enchantment. From then on it could be said that

> *L'homme a terminé sa suprême entreprise. Et il ne prévaudra point*
> *contre la puissance qui maintient les choses en place . . .*

> Man has ended his supreme undertaking. And he will not pre-vail against the power that holds things in their place . . .
>
> (Conclusion of *Tête d'Or*)

No doubt Claudel had to experience the supreme temptation, leading to the supreme sin, whereby man conceives himself as his own end, before he could achieve supreme victory; henceforward, the poet had the certainty of God, and thus entered into the true possession of life; creation presented itself to him no longer as a network of phenomena or a complicated billiard game set up in a vacuum, but as a glorious universe, in its full physical and meta-physical reality. This is the infinite value of the sacrifice, of self-renunciation: to forget oneself is not only to gain the "other world," but also this one, in so far as it finds its principle and its goal in God: life becomes "truly alive," and things recover their earthly density and their divine essence. Forgetfulness of self is also to win joy, that extraordinary Claudelian joy which bursts out in "a kind of solar jubilation." He writes in *Tête d'Or*:

> *Mais rien n'empêchera que je meure du mal de la mort, à moins que je ne saisisse la joie . . .*
> *Et que ja la mette dans ma bouche comme une nourriture éternelle, et comme un fruit qu'on serre entre les dents et dont le jus jaillit jusque dans le fond de la gorge . . .*

> But nothing will prevent me from dying of the disease of death, unless I grasp joy . . .
> Unless I put it in my mouth like an eternal food, like a fruit that you crush between your teeth, and its juice gushes deep down in your throat . . .

(Théâtre, I, 278)

Fruit of absolute certainty, joy eternally renewed! One need only open one's eyes, hold out a hand in the sunlight, to understand with complete certainty. And then everything is simple, one has the right to laugh, to yield to the memories of a peasant childhood and the promptings of a Homeric imagination. Such is the virtue of joy. In Claudel's most somber dramas, *Echange* and *Le Pain dur*, it is the absence of this joy that is intolerable and that makes the souls and objects as dry as the parched desert. In this respect, Claudel differs from nearly all romantic poets. Nothing in him evokes that covert or loudly proclaimed despair, that despair which feeds on itself. He has none of that quivering nostalgia of the whole being, obsessed by the inaccessible blue sky and seeking to gratify its hunger in the mysterious unknown. Innocence and salvation can be nowhere but in God. Along with joy, the poet rediscovers his homeland. Things are not deceptive; the essential is to know what they mean; they are infused with spirit, they are something more and better than signs: "There is no radical separation between this world and the other world. . . . Actually things are at least a part of what they signify" (*Positions et Propositions*). For the contemplative soul, the very feeling of their presence is a revelation:

"In our vulgar hours we use things for practical purposes, forgetting the pure fact of their being; but when at noon, after a long period of work through branches and thorns, I penetrate historically into the heart of the glade, and set my hand on the burning summit of the great cliff, the entry of Alexander into Jerusalem is comparable to the immensity of my realization" (*Art poétique*). What Mallarmé said of the "words of the tribe" upon which he dreamed of conferring "a pure meaning," Claudel says of things themselves. Aesthetic and mystical vision become identical. It is because things live primarily in God, with an absolute life, and because they are "of God a partial image, intelligible and delectable" (*Positions et Propositions*), that the poet must discard the thick crust of habit and ancestral convention to grasp reality in its nakedness. Thus Claudel's faith permitted him to strengthen all the bonds attaching him to the earth. His mysticism and realism merge into a mystical realism. His customary procedure is different from that of San Juan de la Cruz, for example, who dwells for a moment on images only to expel them from his thought along with all sensation, and to advance ever farther into the night until he reaches the unique and sublime light. Nor has he followed the poets in their revolt, and he has not striven like Rimbaud to tear himself loose from the world. Claudel's mission is to reconcile the mind and the world. He will renounce no thing or image; he needs all the mythological apparatus of the Roman Church, with its pomp and decorative beauty, to serve as a support for his thought. And he is pleased to note that "in Japan the supernatural is by no means different from nature; it is literally super-nature, that region of superior authenticity in which the raw fact is transferred to the realm of meaning" (*L'Oiseau noir dans le Soleil Levant*).

But this very statement shows us to what degree his realism is transcendent. The object of his desire is the spirit of nature; the idea that reveals the meaning of the fact is omnipresent God. "It is this divination of the spiritual in the sensuous, which will express itself in the sensuous, that we call poetry," says Jacques Maritain.

However profound his delight in these things which surround him, in his sense of the united carnal and spiritual elements that constitute their being, there comes a moment when he feels "that need of man . . . which is to escape from happiness" (*Ode jubilaire pour le six-centième Anniversaire de la Mort de Dante*). Then everything becomes perishable in his eyes, a strange transparency gradually deprives reality of its substance; he seems as though suspended between heaven and earth, at the mercy of a breath:

> *Une fois de plus l'exil, l'âme toute seule une fois de plus qui remonte à son château . . .*

> Once again exile, once again the soul all alone climbing back into its castle.

A profound feeling of inner emptiness takes possession of the soul:

> *Ici, je n'entends plus rien, je suis seul, il n'y a que ces palmes qui se balancent.*
> *Ce jardin mystérieux à Votre image et ces choses qui existent en silence.*

> In this place I hear nothing more. I am alone, with only these swaying palms.
> This mysterious garden in Thy likeness and these things which exist in silence.

> (*La Messe là-bas*)

They hardly exist at all, they are far off, and the silence is so dense that only a voice from the beyond might break it. Only the water of grace can satisfy the soul and give it something that is more than happiness. Through faith and sacrifice of the self, the poet has gained possession of the world and life; but the sacrifice of the world and of life serves in turn as the key to a *vita nuova*.

It is not in vain that Claudel strove for four years and more to implant his faith in himself like a tree and to follow the development of his beliefs to their ultimate ramifications. On one occasion he expressed thanks to Mallarmé for having asked in the face of the world of things, "What does this mean?" Man must know the meaning of the universe, in its totality and in each of its parts. Several writers have expounded the broad outlines of Claudel's metaphysics—the deeply "felt" metaphysics of a poet, who desires, however, to keep it within the shadow of the dogmatic edifice of the Church. At its basis we find once again the idea of the unity of the world, and the idea of general correspondence, of the co-operation of all beings and all things. Nothing exists, and nothing must seek to exist by and for itself—hence the sin of man, the original sin of man, who refuses to forget himself—each element must maintain an infinitely complex balance with the whole and contribute to the perpetual creation of harmony. All things "compensate one another," says Claudel; they are meaningful only through their relations to all the others, just as in a painting each color acquires its value only through its multiple relations to the other colors. It is an organic conception of a universe assimilated to a living being and not at all mechanical. Moreover, nothing is really repeated, "the same causes never produce the same effects," for no cause can be isolated from all the others; "each time we draw a breath, the world is a new as it was when the first man drew his first breath of air" (*Art poétique*). Thus the miracle is permanent and necessary, it is the rule, and the poet is exalted in the face of this universe rediscovered, restored, in its living integrity, in its absolute primitiveness:

> *Salut donc, ô monde nouveau à mes yeux, ô monde maintenant total!*
> *O credo entier des choses visibles et invisibles, je vous accepte avec un coeur catholique.*
> *Où que je tourne la tête*
> *J'envisage l'immense octave de la Creation!*
> *Le monde s'ouvre, et si large qu'en soit l'empan, mon regard le traverse d'un bout à l'autre.*
> *J'ai pesé le soleil ainsi qu'un gros mouton que deux hommes forts suspendent à une perche entre leurs épaules.*
> *J'ai recensé l'armée des Cieux et j'en ai dressé l'état.*
> *Depuis les grandes Figures qui se penchent sur le vieillard Océan*
> *Jusqu'au feu le plus rare englouti dans le plus profond abîme . . .*

Hail then, o world new in my eyes, o world now complete!
O entire credo of things visible and invisible, I accept you with a catholic heart.
Wherever I turn my head
I envisage the immense octave of Creation
The world opens, and however wide its range, my gaze encompasses it from one end to the other.
I have weighed the sun like a fat sheep slung on a pole between the shoulders of two strong men.

I have taken the census of the heavenly hosts and I have made
their inventory
From the gray Figures that bend over aged Ocean
To the rarest fires buried in the deepest abyss.

(Cinq grandes Odes: L'Esprit et L'Eau)

Only man among all living beings can be conscious of this drama
constantly enacted and constantly creating itself, of the *meaning*
of things in this one and finite world. Indeed, Claudel's only
subject, the only "object of his poetry," is this universal drama.
Reduced to himself, the individual is of little importance; what
gives him value is his form, the place he occupies, his fate, his
meaning. It is futile to dwell excessively on the particularities of
persons, on their characters, since they are involved in an immense
action that transcends them as the spirit transcends the flesh. This
action is represented not only in Claudel's plays but in his poems.
The latter progress toward the resolution of a conflict, toward the
conquest of a harmony between voices that oppose and answer one
another. There is a dramatic quality in them; just as in his plays,
the expression of the person, circumscribed in its earthly and
psychological nature, is not the final aim, so the expression of
personal, individual feelings is not considered sufficient justification
for a poem. The romantic poetry of the self is transcended. In this
universe where objects existing in themselves are no longer simple
representations of the mind, the human personality and all living
beings can be seen only in terms of the universal. The real aim is
always to find their cause and meaning.

Such is the task of the poet, chosen from among all men. God
has granted him the privilege of "attention," of "ascertaining," of
"gathering together in his mind" all figures. "Gradually there
dawned upon me," says Claudel referring to the years of his con-
version, "the idea that art and poetry are also divine things." A
priest, if you will, the poet is also a seer (in Rimbaud's sense).
But while for Rimbaud the seer is like an angel of Lucifer while for
Rimbaud he is "the great sick man, the great criminal, the great
outcast," for Claudel his mission is that of a prophet working under
the eyes of God to make for Him, as an offering, an image of His own
work. Moreover, he has in him a divine spirit, a certain power which
participates in that of the Word; by naming an object, he evokes it,
creates it . . .

Dieu qui avez soufflé sur le chaos, séparant le sec
de l'humide, sur la mer Rouge, et elle s'est divisée
devant Moïse et Aaron.

. . . .

Vous commandez de même à mes eaux, vous avez mis dans
mes narines le même esprit de création et de figure . . .

God who breathed on the chaos, separating the dry from the wet
on the Red Sea, and it divided before Moses and Aaron

. . . .

In the same way you command my waters; in my nostrils you put
the same spirit of creation and form . . .

(*Cinq grandes Odes: L'Esprit et l'Eau*)

Interpres deorum, as in the fabulous times of Orpheus and Muse-
aus . . .

Is this a mere lyrical exaggeration? There are a score of indic-
ations to the contrary. This belief in the magical virtue of the word,
in the omnipotence of formulated thought, is part of the heritage of
the "primitive mentality" that subsists in each of us in the substructure of the mind. Throughout the nineteenth century, despite
science, the various occult traditions preserved this heritage and
transmitted it to the great lyricists—particularly Hugo, Baudelaire
and Rimbaud—in the very heart of whose thought it bore fruit. The
essential principle here—and it matters little that as a rule it is
not consciously recognized as a truth—is that there can be no
evocation, and consequently no poetry in the thing. One recalls
the solemn pronouncements of Baudelaire in his study on Th.
Gautier: "There is something sacred in speech, in the word. . . . "
Beyond a doubt Claudel would subscribe to such an assertion. For
he transposes to the Christian plane, sanctifies, as it were, one of
the most important and most obscure beliefs of the romantic and
post-romantic lyricists.

Recently Claudel has told us without lyricism how he explains
the phenomenon of poetic creation: "Poetry is the effect of a certain
need to create, to realize through words, the idea that one has had
of a thing. Consequently the imagination must have a vivid and
strong idea (even though at first and necessarily imperfect and
confused) of the object it proposes to realize. Moreover our sensibility must be placed in a state of desire with regard to this object,

and our activity must be aroused by a thousand dispersed touches and, in a manner of speaking, summoned to respond to the impression by expression" (*Lettre à l'abbé Bremond sur l'inspiration poétique*, reprinted in *Positions et Propositions*). This expression—the poem—must be literally a deliverance. But this deliverance can take place only if the imagination has gratified the desire—then we have a blessed catharsis by which the soul knows that it is released from all the weight that had oppressed it. In this spiritual operation, words and rhythms function as instruments. Man's whole being is called forth by "dispersed touches"; then invaded by a something that is the sense of reality, it will have no respite until it has poured all its desire—which by the same token is realized—into a certain composition of words and rhythms. The purpose is, says Claudel, to constitute "a kind of equivalent or *preparation*, soluble in the mind, of a spectacle, or of an emotion, or even of an abstract idea" (*Positions et Propositions*). And this precisely is the poetic alchemy, an indefinable process, which can be assimilated to a veritable "sacred action"; this "preparation," which is the poem, represents the glorified body which the spirit takes as its nourishment and which thus infuses the spirit with the certainty that it possesses reality. No doubt, this transmutation is fully effective only in exceptional cases, and usually one must be content with approximations that confer a greater or lesser degree of liberation. (Moreover, the question should be considered from the standpoint of the reader, whom the poet must set in motion by induction, whom he must "move" by means of language as a real thing would move him.) But the central fact is that poetic creation, considered in its essential principle, appears here as a fundamentally vital reaction.

We must not, however, see in Claudel an unconscious poet prophesying in the darkness. The example of Proust, after Baudelaire, would be sufficient to remind us that the intelligence can be made to serve a quasi-mystical art. What a fine point the mind needs to trace the skilful verbal hieroglyphic which will serve as a symbol of deep emotion! Claudel assures us that "in this very breath—inspiration—in this desire, order and intelligence are involved." On the other hand, he does not aim at capturing immediate life, in its raw materiality, at its source, but at elucidating all things, at restoring their authentic meaning. Such a design prevents the poet from making a selfish catharsis the goal of his work, even if this catharsis might give him a superhuman joy. Everything in the work, and the work itself, must serve. Everything in it "means" something, as does the universe, in its least parts. Those fancies which seem gratuitous, those light embroideries—who knows whether they have not a meaning of which the author who amuses himself in following them may not be aware? Thus, this Claudelian poetry, whatever may have been said of it, and whatever it appears to be, aims at a superior intelligibility, sometimes by strange and difficult detours. It aspires to be penetrated, understood, as much as felt; or rather, to be both felt and understood (*comprehendere*), to feed both mind and soul.

In such a poetics, the metaphor has a most important function. It is the contrary of a play on words, it is a manner of gaining an insight into the universe, and of proclaiming this insight which refers to a "second logic," since the first logic uses the syllogism as its instrument. "And do not speak of chance. The way this grove of pine trees is planted, the form of this mountain, are no more an effect of chance than is the Parthenon or this diamond over which the lapidary has grown old ... " (*Art poétique*). The poet raises his eyes and sees. He sees, he feels the "infinite relation" between this object whose ephemeral contour is traced before him, and all other objects. "No one thing remains alone," he says, "for I associate it with another in my heart" (*Cinq grandes Odes: L'Esprit et L'Eau*). It follows that the principal task of the metaphor is to bear witness at every moment to the totality of the world, to its perpetual primitivity. The *Odes*, the *Cantate à trois Voix*, like the lyrical fragments of the dramas, advance on a broad front, comparable to that Rhône River (to which Claudel devoted one of his most beautiful hymns) which drinks from the springs of a hundred glaciers lost in the heights. One image gathers its complementary images around it:

> *O grammairien dans mes vers! Ne cherche point le*
> * chemin, cherche le centre! mesure, comprends l'espace*
> *compris entre ces feux solitaires!*
>
> . . . .
>
> *Que je maintienne mon poids comme une lourde étoile à*
> * travers l'hymne fourmillante!*

O grammarian in my verses! Seek not the path, seek the center!
measure, understand the space comprised between these solitary
fires!

. . . .

Let me like a heavy star sustain my weight through rousing hymns.

(*Ibid., Les Muses*)

The cosmos is thus constantly evoked, made present, indisputable.
Within this metaphorical language, the spiritual mingles with the
carnal like water which in secret penetrates a porous substance;
"continuity never ceases, any more than does the continuity of the
soul in the body" (*ibid., L'Esprit et L'Eau*); the visible and the invisible stand surety for each other's existence and the reality of
matter bears witness to the reality of the soul:

Esprit perceptible aux sens! et vous, ô sens à l'esprit devenus perméables
et transparents!

Spirit perceptible to the senses! And you, o senses that have become
permeable and transparent to the spirit!

(*Cantique des Parfums*, in *Cantate à trois Voix*)

But this mystical realism in which all things form a monolithic
unity requires a special prosody. The problem is always to preserve,
even in the most elaborate verbal constructions, something, the
essential part if possible, of the vital and spontaneous reaction
which releases the poetic operation. Since "one does not think in a
continuous way," since "our thinking apparatus . . . supplies a
disjointed mass of ideas, images, memories by flashes, jolts" (*Réflexions sur le vers français* in *Positions et Propositions*). Claudel defines
the "natural" verse as "an idea isolated by blank space" that is to
say, a group of words that carry a certain psychic charge. It follows
that all spoken language is made of "verses in the raw," and that
the verse, far from being what definition and tradition make of
it—a product of art—is rather a simple element, gushing forth
from the spirit. Coeuvre says in *La Ville*: "I defined (the verse) in
my heart of hearts as this double and reciprocal function by which
man absorbs life and finally breathes forth in its place an intelligible
word."

This assertion seems paradoxical chiefly because Claudel uses
"verses" (in contrast to common usage) to mean the distinct

elements of spoken prose; but today an aesthetician like Pius Servien has reached a very similar conclusion: "The verse is that part of a rhythmic (and not necessarily versified) text," he says, "which goes from one natural division to the next; it is an aggregate of syllables inserted between two silences with no silences, except for very slight ones, within itself." Similarly, the two are agreed that every French sentence is composed of "a number of iambics whose long element is the last syllable of the phoneme, and the short element is an indefinite number . . . of indifferent syllables that precede it." But while Claudel discerns verses in the least accented, least eloquent spoken language, according to Servien we have a verse only when the mind, having reached a superior state of tension (the lyrical state), is lifted by its own movement, and spontaneously expresses itself in sentences whose rhythmic structure is clearly indicated.

   Be that as it may, Claudel's prosody is based upon this idea of oral poetry, of natural gesticulation of thought.* To manifest the dynamism of the mind, each paragraph should form a distinct ideational and rhythmic unit. Jacques Rivière has quoted the first words of Cébès, at the beginning of *Tête d'Or* an exposition of the theme of the whole act, comparable to the leitmotiv of a Wagnerian overture. It is a true representation of living thought, first chained to the depths, then bursting forth in spurts, then gradually relaxing and taking a freer rhythm:

> *Me voici,*
> *Imbécile, ignorant,*
> *Homme nouveau devant les choses inconnues,*
> *Et je tourne ma face vers l'Année et l'arche pluvieuse, j'ai plein mon*
>   *coeur d'ennui!*

> Here am I,
> Stupid, ignorant,
> A new man before unknown things,
> And I turn my face to the Year and the rain ark, and my heart is full
>   of torment!

---

*In theory if not always in fact. It is known that Claudel wrote regular verses (cf. *Vers d'exil*) and that he attempted a compromise by composing—chiefly for his religious and liturgical poems—a kind of verset or rather rimed or assonanced distich, of variable length, almost always greater than that of the alexandrine.

But every day those who seek to progress outside the paths traced by that second nature which is habit or literary tradition, are accused of going against nature. Some have called Claudel's style an almost entirely artificial creation. It is, however, undeniable that most of his sentences condemned as tortuous or alien to the French intellectual tradition tend to reproduce the movement of the first psychic crystallizations and that these spontaneous products are determined by affectivity. Metaphorical density, syntactical structure, and even phrases condemned by grammar, everything that distinguishes the Claudelian idiom from ordinary French or academic French, is largely accounted for by the poet's intention of putting all the resources of language and poetry at the service of the total reality that he wishes to express.

But let us not oversimplify the problem. If only these intentions are considered, the style of *Grandes Odes* or *Cantate à trois voix*, for example, will be appreciated in an arbitrary and incomplete fashion. In Pindar or Virgil, Claudel particularly enjoys the "delicious" juxtaposition of "words which have no logical relation" (*Positions et Propositions*). He has been affected by literary influences, the ancients as well as Mallarmé and the Anglo-Saxon lyric poets, yet they have not diminished his loyalty to the immediate, but rather justified it, and perhaps on certain occasions corrected it, making it possible for the raw elements, without losing any of their authenticity through this work of refinement and harmonization, to be brought forward into a light which transfigures them and lends them the patina and irridescence of the highest poetry. Only this can make possible such evocations as the following, which I find almost at random in *Cantate à trois voix*:

> Je me souviens! c'est une nuit comme celle-ci,
> Quelque part au centre de l'Europe, dans un vieux parc royal, sous le tilleul bohème,
> Nous étions là devant quelques coupes, une douzaine prêts a nous séparer.
> Et l'on ne voyait dans la nuit que le point rouge d'une cigarette aux lèvres de deux ou trois.
> (Tous sont morts)
> Et éclairant le beau col nu à la petite oreille soudain l'éclair d'un diamant
> Comme une grosse goutte sous d'épais cheveux noirs empruntée à des eaux immatérielles.

Et l'on n'entendait rien que dans les avenues immenses le roulement sourd d'un équipage,

Et le dialogue bien loin, aux deux extremités de ce jardin, d'orchestres opposés,

Dont le vent faible étrangement tour à tour unissait et divisait les cuivres.

I remember! It was a night like this

Somewhere in the center of Europe, in an old royal park, under the Bohemian lime-tree,

There we were with a few cups before us, a dozen of us ready to separate.

And in the night I saw only the red point of a cigarette at the lips of two or three.

(All are dead)

And lighting the lovely bare neck, on the little ear beneath heavy black hair, suddenly

The flash of a diamond like a great drop borrowed from immaterial waters.

And I heard nothing except the muffled rumbling of a carriage in the boundless avenues,

And the dialogue far off, at the two ends of the garden, of opposed orchestras,

Their brasses strangely divided and united by turns in the feeble wind.

Nevertheless there is something more than pure music here; or else let us say that this music follows the lines of an ethereal architecture. This is almost always the case with Claudel. His seemingly least controlled effusions, his freest fantasies, turn away as though by instinct from inner chaos, from all the vagueness of elementary life, and outline the first beginnings of an order. Everything in creation, as he conceives it, tends to the act, to being, aspires to maturity of form, to the flowering of matter and spirit. Similarly, "the aim of art is the discovery of wholes." This murmuring music, or else this utterance of words full of vigor and rural force, all this must enter into a monumental organism, must become closely articulated, then more flexible and charged with thought, in order to compose an oracular discourse, a dramatic prayer, a concert of alternating voices which free themselves from the particular, from space and time. The image of the French country cathedral suggests itself naturally. Born of the earth, still held by the earth, of which it has the robustness, there is nevertheless nothing in its immense body, even in the slightest statuette of the least ornamental spandrel that does not bear witness, that does not manifest an intention, that does not teach in its own way and does not proclaim a truth to the centuries. Everything in it rises, soars, everything is attracted along the curves of the arches to the summit where reside the bells that seem borne by the sky.

In Claudel's work certain essential pieces stand out for their high spirituality. Imperceptibly, by a continuous gradation, by a progressive filtering, one passes from the carnal and from nature to the supernatural; but "the supernatural itself is real," says Péguy; similarly, eternity can here be breathed; filth is made transparent and the lyrical transfiguration becomes an act of thanksgiving. I am referring particularly to the lofty passage which concludes *L'Annonce faite à Marie*. Claudel's extraordinary achievement, here and in other pieces, seems to me to consist in this, that he was able to sustain an atmosphere of beatific clarity without sacrificing any earthly accident and reality in his vision. Claudel's Christian genius succeeded in re-creating and deepening the sublimity achieved by Hugo's genius in those last verses of *Booz endormi* which evoke the golden sickle of eternal summer in the night sky. Perhaps, in reference to such rare beauties, one may say of him what he once said of Dante: "Alone among all poets, Dante depicted the universe of things and souls not from the standpoint of the spectator, but from that of the Creator, by attempting to situate them definitely not in the framework of the *How* but in that of the *Why*, by judging them in a sense, or rather by appraising them with regard to their ultimate ends" (*Positions et Propositions*). There are pages of Claudel in which every face and image is turned in the same direction, magnetized by the same desire, the desire for the ultimate ends.

Claudel declared one day that he desired to "gather up all images," that he wished to be "the gatherer of God's earth" (*Cinq grandes Odes*). While the "pure" poets maintain, with Paul Valéry, that "what must be said in poetry is almost impossible to say well," it would seem that he undertook to show that a poet, today as formerly, can say everything or almost everything, above all that he can say what he must say, and that it is weakness to renounce saying what must be said in order to say it better.

His entire work is an attempt to effect a vast synthesis through the multiplicity of his means of expression (which often belong to prose more than to versified poetry), through the variety of the genres and tones that he intermingles, and through his solemn resolution not to reject any element of the universe but to bring forth poetry from every "subject" and every thing. Claudel, who has sometimes been represented as a disorderly creator, has the stuff of a conciliator. What is most striking in his nature is his balance. It is a living balance, born of a clear-sighted mastery of opposing impulses, an attempt to reconcile different literary traditions, a way of seeking a new order beyond opposites, without losing anything of their virtues. Is this the picture of a classicist? In a way perhaps, but not in any historical sense, at least with reference to French literature. For the deep sources of Claudel's poetry and the models he has chosen are not to be found in the epoch of Louis XIV. The modes of thought and life put forward by his poetry, his mystical realism, his flamboyant catholicism, his sense of drama, the theatrical aspect (most often nobly theatrical) of his creations, even the lyrical ones, his passion and tension— everything contributes to make him a great baroque poet, harmonized in the French manner, nourished by diverse humanistic currents. The dithyramb celebrating Rubens in *Le Soulier de satin* is an important clue. We may say that Paul Claudel, however modern he may be, occupies the same position in an imaginary France of 1600 as Calderon really occupied in Spain. Post-medieval, pre-classical and especially pre-Cartesian—for his whole being is averse to the philosophy of the pure mind—he seems to bring to French literature what fate did not grant it at the appropriate time, as it did to Spain despite the Renaissance, and also to Elizabethan England, in a different domain.

It is characteristic of this universal poet that he does not indulge, or indulges only occasionally, in individual lyricism. The "days" that he describes, the great "action" that takes place on all the stages of the world and that holds all his thoughts, is outlined on a fresco far vaster than that of any particular psychological life. By virtue of the same movement that carries him toward objectivity, and makes him leave his self to achieve a total and nontemporal vision of things and destinies, he progresses to the dramatic and the epic, where the essential is to evoke the divine or demoniacal forces, the omnipotent Spirit that breathes life into earthly forms.

But in the foreground of the picture or the scene, nothing suffers from this change of light, from this removal of the center of gravity. No more than his religion leads Claudel to mutilate his being in any way, does it invite him to discard anything that exists. His anti-Jansenism forbids him to dig an abyss between the universe of nature and that of grace. Pascal's saying on the silence of the infinite spaces arouses no echo in him.

> *Ainsi le ciel n'a plus pour nous de terreur, sachant que si loin qu'il s'étend*
> *Votre mesure n'est pas absente. Votre bonté n'est pas absente . . .*

> Thus the sky holds no more terror for us, since we know that as
>   far as it extends
> Your measure is not absent. Your goodness is not absent. . . .

> (*Cinq grandes Odes*)

Moreover these spaces are not infinite, and God is everywhere. Motivated by a kind of artistic impartiality, by a very human feeling of the possible, which is nourished by his love of life, Claudel depicts ugliness, buffoons and infamous characters. All this part of creation vegetates and subsists by divine permission in the shadow of grace:

> *Nulle chose n'est inutile puisqu'elle sert à expliquer le Paradis . . .*

> Nothing is useless since it serves to explain Paradise. . . .

What an unusual and noble tolerance.

I think it is fair to consider Claudel the most powerful poet France has had since Hugo. Some of the fundamental features of his work go counter to the spirit of the century, and it is not surprising that his influence so far has not been as far-reaching as might have been expected before the First World War. But if it is true that the rising generation has a taste for concrete thought and tends toward a spiritualist realism, it is permissible to think that the poet's wish will be fulfilled more than once:

> *Faîtes que je sois comme un semeur de solitude et que celui qui entend ma*
>   *parole*
> *Rentre chez lui inquiet et lourd.*

> Grant that I be like a sower of solitude and that he who hears my
>   word
> Return home restless and burdened.

2.

The very inspiration of Claudel's work is contrary to our times, but the poems of Charles Péguy are more basically old-fashioned and anachronistic. Reading them we forget that symbolism, the Parnassian school, and even romanticism ever existed. Here litera- ture is joyfully and openly humbled before Christian theology and mysticism. Motivated by a need opposed to those of the moderns who strive to isolate poetry as a pure essence, Péguy holds it to material things, to moral and religious values. At all times, his major intention is to integrate as many elements as possible in the sacred, to realize in his whole being a perfect unity of thought and action without ever losing touch with an entirely spiritual center of gravity and indulging in fragmentary undertakings. That is why it is difficult to distinguish the prose writer and pamphleteer in him from the poet, and to consider separately the "mysteries," published between 1910 and 1914, which he composed as confes- sions and works of piety.

In our time, a man's thought—"and nothing is as grave and serious as thought"—gravitating around a very small number of mystical problems presents an extraordinary spectacle. Péguy's problems are those of Christian life, of grace, and of return to inno- cence, full purity, primal youth—not an innocence in conformity with nature, à la Rousseau of Rimbaud, nor the blessed "state of the children of the Sun," but a divine innocence, that of "the first earth and the first clay." Only in this respect, if it is true that nine- teenth-century poetry transmitted to our century an "unquenched hope of innocence" (to use the words of Giuseppe Ungaretti), can Péguy be said to share in the subterranean life of his epoch. The misery and age of the world oppress him, and he, too, tries to voice a dream of paradisiac existence. But his crusade is Christian. His entire effort was concentrated upon resistance to "aging" and "hardening" (habit, as his teacher Bergson would say), and upon the discovery of that superhuman lightness and joy which must characterize sainthood. When he addresses Geneviève, his sentences soar, freed from all the weight of sin:

> Sainte que rameniez tous les soirs au bercail
> Le troupeau tout entier diligente bergère,
> Quand le monde et Paris viendront à fin de bail,

Puissiez-vous d'un pas ferme et d'une main légère
Dans la dernière cour par le dernier portail
Ramener par la voûte et le double vantail
Le troupeau tout entier à la droite du Père.

Saint who led back each night
The entire flock to the fold, diligent shepherdess,
When the world and Paris come to the end of their term,
May you, with a firm step and a light hand,
Through the last yard and the last portal,
Lead back, through the vault and the folding door,
The entire flock to the right hand of the Father.

                                        (*La Tapisserie de Sainte-Geneviève*)

This mystic is also a realist. He has no respite (and gives words no respite) until he has made present and tangible all the miracles that have ever taken place, all the hidden mysteries, everything that occurs beyond the reach of our senses. But he does not know the secrets of a poetic alchemy like that of Claudel, the spectacular clashes of words that give the reader a sudden jolt, like the very electricity of reality; perhaps he distrusts the "whiteness" and innocence of this magic; he takes the longest path; his heroes multiply precise statements, material details—and they care little if they are verbose in the eyes of those who judge them—in order to recreate what once existed, and at last to possess the truth in a soul and a body . . .

Car le surnaturel est lui-même charnel
Et l'arbre de la grâce est raciné profond
Et plonge dans le sol et cherche jusqu'au fond
Et l'arbre de la race est lui-même éternel.

For the supernatural itself is carnal
And the tree of grace is deeply rooted
And plunges into the soil and explores it to its depths,
And the tree of the race is itself eternal.

                                        (*Eve; la double Racination*)

"Continuity between soul and body never ceases," said Claudel — nor between the lowest and the highest, earth and heaven. And even in the intellectual act, no discontinuity must exist. If Péguy looks with suspicion upon the magician's art of the poets, he is also averse to the Cartesian art of reasoning by means of logical chains of which only the final term is retained. To be able to *believe* in his idea, to assimilate it truly, and to let it ripen within him, he must inter-weave all of its elements in an unbreakable tissue, he must associate and knit together his propositions in such a way as to incorporate a *tranche de durée*, a segment of time in the Bergsonian sense, in his unconscious life. A short quotation from *Le Mystère de la Charité de Jeanne d'Arc* or from *Le Mystère des saints innocents* can hardly show the hesitations, delays and advances of this thought given entirely to self-conquest. The resultant passages are essentially unbalanced, without elegance of form or "distinction"; they bring us a crude beauty, full of knots and slag, but beside which the "products of art" often seem over-sophisticated. The lyrical and epic novels of C. F. Ramuz supply other examples of this harsh and strong poetry, animated by a breath that seems to come from a supernatural beyond. Both illustrate the benefits of a return to the primitive, to that concrete and spoken poetry, to which Claudel gave so much place in his work.

But Péguy is doubtless the only poet in whom one can find a certain familiar, unadorned, earthly sublimity, which approaches the highest spirituality. Here Péguy, the man, speaks to a friend: "I have made a pilgrimage to Chartres. I am a native of the Beauce region. Chartres is my cathedral. I had no training in this sort of thing. I walked 144 kilometers in three days. Ah, my friend, the Crusades were easy! I am sure that we would have been the first to leave for Jerusalem and that we would have died on the way. To die in a ditch is nothing; truly, I felt that it is nothing. We are doing something more difficult than that. The steeple of Chartres can be seen across the plain, at a distance of 17 kilometers. From time to time it disappears behind a rise in the ground, a line of trees. The moment I saw it, I was in ecstasy. I no longer felt anything, neither fatigue, nor my feet. All my impurities dropped at once...." From the memory of those days this poem was born.

> *Etoile de la mer, voici la lourde nappe*
> *Et la profonde houle et l'océan des blés,*
> *Et la mouvante écume et nos greniers combles,*
> *Voici votre regard sur cette immense chape.*
>
> . . . .

Etoile du matin, inaccessible reine,
Voici que nous marchons vers votre illustre cour,
Et voici le plateau de notre pauvre amour,
Et voici l'océan de notre immense peine.

. . . .

Deux mille ans de labeur ont fait de cette terre
Un réservoir sans fin pour les âges nouveaux.
Mille ans de votre grâce ont fait de ces traveaux
Un reposoir sans fin pour l'âme solitaire.

Star of the sea, here is the heavy sheet,
And the deep swell and the ocean of wheat,
And the moving foam and our full barns,
Here is your gaze on this immense cape.

. . . .

Star of the morning, inaccessible queen,
Behold we are walking toward your illustrious court,
And behold the plateau of our poor love,
And behold the ocean of our vast affliction.

. . . .

Two thousand years of toil have made this land
An endless reservoir for new generations.
A thousand years of your grace have made these labors
Into an endless resting place for the solitary soul.

(*Présentation de la Beauce à Notre-Dame de Chartres*)

The spirit of ancient Christianity and of poetry rise from a single spring. This is quite unlike Claudel's grand organ. We hear a voice quite close to the ground, it comes from a furrow, but it rises heavenward, like a lark.

CHAPTER TEN

The Poetry of the Men of Good Will

1.

Unanimists, Whitmanians, poets of the Abbaye—they have been thus variously designated, those men of good will who began to write shortly after 1900, but none of these terms fits more than two or three of them; several never frequented the Abbaye of Créteil, and only a few were disciples of Jules Romains who in turn owes but little to Whitman. In its early stages, before it was checked by the war, when it was developing parallel to the neo-classicism and neo-symbolism of the *Phalange*, the movement of the men of good will seems to have been a kind of post-naturism related to Verhaeren, Paul Fort, Jammes (and Maeterlinck), and strongly influenced by democratic and socialist ideology.

It is difficult to reduce these rather heterogeneous tendencies to a common denominator. But all these poets more or less consciously turned away from symbolism and intellectualism. They were unable to remain aloof from the world, to yield to the attraction of artificial paradises, or to resurrect a legendary past for their private enjoyment. In their eyes the present, the real world supply the heart with tangible satisfactions. Hence their antipathy for the symbol, which was only too often an indirect mode of expression, and for the poets of 1890; hence also their enthusiasm for Ch. L. Philippe's trenchant formula quoted by André Gide in a lecture published in 1911: "The time of sweetness and dilettantism is over. What we need now, are barbarians." Gide commented: "The curious thing is that it is through culture that [Philippe] becomes aware of the *legitimacy* of this feeling." Duhamel, and later Arcos, gave their own interpretation of it: "He meant that we must renounce bookish art and give an account of our own experience."

This concept of experience, closely akin to that of William James, is here the central point. Experience becomes a sense of certainty that penetrates one's whole being and stirs one like a revelation; a state of euphoria that seems to give the world to man and persuades him that he "possesses" it. But it is accessible only to those who free themselves from habitual vision, from utilitarian convention, and who, in the words of Duhamel, gain deeper knowledge of "that virtual abyss which separates sensation from perception." To become a barbarian by means of patient and progressive deintellectualization is, first of all, to receive sensations and to leave them a certain amount of free play, not to place them in a logical framework and not to attribute them to the objects which produced them; it is a method of detaching oneself from an inherited civilized form in order to rediscover a greater plasticity and expose oneself to the imprint of things. It is, in short, the same order of problem as Bergson tackled in his considerations on art.* For Duhamel and his friends, just as for Claudel, poetry does not reside in dreams, in vagueness, in the imaginary; it resides in reality, but an authentically experienced reality that is not simplified and conventional. The difficulty lies in expressing one's experience "as directly as possible, without imposing the constraint of rhetoric on it and without dissimulating it under the garlands of melody." Here Duhamel clearly repudiates romantic eloquence as well as the verbal music so beloved by the symbolists. Such an aesthetics foreshadows a candid and crude poetry.

But by 1905 the time was past when the symbolist Narcissus tended to cast doubt upon the existence of others. Human presence, more stirring than any other, was to give this poetry its original color. Even Vildrac, to be sure, would not deny that there is "a

*See, for example, *Le Rire* (pp. 155 ff.): *What I see and what I hear in the external world, is simply what my senses extract from it to guide my behavior. . . . In the vision which they give me of things and myself, the differences useless to man are erased, the similarities useful to man are emphasized, the paths of my action are traced in advance. These paths are those which mankind has trodden before me. Things have been classified with a view to the benefit I can draw from them. And it is this classification that I perceive, far more than the color and form of things. . . . And further: Art has no other object than to discard virtually useful symbols, conventionally and socially accepted generalities, in short everything that conceals reality from us. . . . It is a misunderstanding on this point that gave rise to the debate between realism and idealism.*

natural hostility," among men as Valéry put it, but friendship among men is also a natural thing, and deep in the human heart there is a secret need for effusion and confidence. Herein is revealed the human benefit of an experiment in communal living such as that attempted at the Abbaye of Créteil, or of an unfeigned sympathy for "the white wine of La Villette." This hearty optimism does not spring from a false estimation of the world, but from a lively faith in "two or three divine things"; it does not feed on the worship of progress or on a puerile admiration for man's creations, but on a discreet concern for man's joys, sorrows, and patience. "If civilization is not in man's heart, it is nowhere," says Duhamel at the end of *Civilisation*; and as early as 1910 Jules Romains wrote in *Manuel de déification*: "Do not be amazed at the inventions of practical men. Use their machines, and despise them, the inventors and the machines. . . . Only the soul matters."

For these religious minds—although they reject all dogmas—life is ordered around a few privileged states in which the powers of the soul achieve an exceptional degree of coherence, "in which the universe speaks" (Baudelaire), showing its true contours, and in which the slightest accidents of life are colored by a metaphysical light. Romains calls it "the poetic sense of life," Duhamel calls it "lyrical life"—it is a state of grace accompanying the blessed catharsis, the purgation of the passions and the alleviation of human sufferings. What is the poem, then, but a means of self-exaltation, "self-beatification"? Henceforward, the goal of the poem is external to it, and its purpose is "to make everyone love his life, penetrate it and enlarge it."

This has been called a utilitarian art, revived from the days of the Saint-Simonists. And, to be sure, most of the poets of the Abbaye and their associates display something akin to the missionary spirit that animated the social poets of the nineteenth century; but unlike Lamartine, they do not set out "to popularize truths" by combining the useful and the pleasant through verbal ornaments, or even to point at the stars, like Chatterton—what they seek is joy. "If one had enough love," sings Vildrac in *Livre d'Amour*, a clump of lush grass or the cry of a bird would suffice to transfigure the most wretched landscape. The essential article of this Credo is that everything contains food for the soul, that he who seems to be the lowliest of men has his secret nobility. The value of this creed is measured by the worth of the man who professes it, and of his work. Vildrac probably owes to it the best pages of his *Livre d'Amour*, and Duhamel more than one striking passage of his poems and of *La Possession du Monde*. As for the sources of this belief, they may be sought in Maeterlinck (in his *Trésor des Humbles*), or in the Slavic sentimentality popularized in the West by the great Russian writers.

Even in the Parnassian period, Coppée and Manuel had attempted to rejuvenate the tradition of intimate lyricism by drawing poetic elements from everyday life seen in the light of a tender sympathy for man. Romains, Chennevière, and even Vildrac, it is true, follow from Verhaeren. But Verhaeren is a successor of Hugo, among whose disciples were Coppée and Manuel. Sentimental, popular lyricism, modern, humanitarian epic writing—these two currents which run through the unanimist and Whitmanian poetry of 1910 probably have a common origin in *Les Contemplations* and *La Légende des Siècles*, and more particularly in pieces whose subject is modern, such as *Les Pauvres Gens*.* And some of Zola's novels occupy an intermediate place between Hugo—particularly the Hugo of *Les Misérables*—and Jules Romains. Let us not overlook this continuity and these similarities between writers who might be thought to be quite distant from one another. Their kinship is hidden chiefly by stylistic differences; these heirs of Hugo distrusted oratorical amplifications and used a simple, unadorned language, which often struck ears accustomed to symbolist music as poor and discordant. On this point, Whitman's influence often supplanted that of Hugo; the poets consciously imitated his "effusive style," his monologue that retains the rhythm of spoken language, even during the lyrical invocation, but without sacrificing pathetic emphasis. A kind of fraternal communion is established between the poet and his reader; the poem develops into an irresistible confession, the confession of a man whose long contained fervor forces him at last to disclose his superabundant, misunderstood life to his fellow man, to the first comer. There is much to be said

---

*In Duhamel's *Propos critiques* we read (p. 139): *A poet speaks, he speaks of himself. Listen: he speaks for you. Come closer: he speaks of you.* And in the preface to *Les Contemplations*, Hugo writes: *When I speak to you of myself, I am speaking to you of you. How can you fail to feel it? Ah, you madman, who believe that I am not you!*

of Whitman's influence.* Consider the new poetry of the individual
as Whitman sees him, or who as Larbaud writes "has ceased to sulk
apart, or to coddle himself, or to cultivate his manias, or to worship
himself, but who lives in contact with other individuals, *en masse*":
or the poet's extraordinary familiarity with the cosmos, this exaltation of the subject perpetually filled with the joy of living, or again
his developments by juxtaposed appositions, by enumerations
which take on a panting rhythm—and you will realize that all
this was bound to affect such poets as Duhamel, Vildrac, Durain
(and even André Spire or Valéry Larbaud), who, each in his own
way, dreamed of discarding the glamor of words, of tearing the
veil, in order to discover a new happiness amidst the universe and
men . . .

> As to me I know of nothing else but miracles,
> Whether I walk the streets of Manhattan,
> Or dart my sight over the roofs of houses toward the sky,
> Or wade with naked feet along the beach just in the edge of the
>   water.

> (*Leaves of Grass*)

A fountain of youth offered to the world, a grandiose gesture
of welcome to the men of the future.

2.

"Only the soul matters," but we know next to nothing of its powers.
If we only knew how to cultivate it, thinks Jules Romains, as we
cultivate our intellect and body, and to hurl it into truly "spiritual"
ventures! Everything leads us to suppose that the mind has external
effects; for those who reject this postulate, the unanimist doctrine
is pure fantasmagoria. In the invisible world, hesitating, groping
contacts can occur. A man and woman in love may spontaneously
generate a new psychic force that remains largely unconscious.
The atmosphere of a family, a milieu, the soul of a crowd, can,

*Léon Bazalgette's book was published in 1908 (Mercure de France, publ.), and
his complete translation of *Leaves of Grass* in 1909; but by then Whitman had long
been known in France.

under certain conditions, become more than images—provided only that all the members of the group desire and believe together in the same thing. These souls born of the spirit disintegrate and are reabsorbed in the separate individuals as soon as the communion among them ends. Romains calls them "gods." For "we can only love a god younger than ourselves," he says, "who did not create us but whom we create, who is not our father but our son." Modern pragmatism, for its part, taught that man is capable of begetting the "divine" in himself. As for the unanimists' debt to Tarde and especially to Durkheim, we may recall that Jules Romains had his first "visions" at the age of eighteen when he had no knowledge of modern sociology. Moreover, his religious youth and his recent interest in the problems of parapsychology show that in addition to being a scientist, he is a mystic. But this poet, who is also a teacher and a philosopher, thought it advisable to formulate dogmas, to publish a textbook of spiritual exercises and prayers, and to compose a few formal demonstrations such as *Un Etre en marche*. He invited criticism and ridicule with a fine boldness. It might have been better if he had abstained from establishing a militant church and transforming all his intuitions into ideas.

"One day, after all, we will have to be mankind!" (*Il faudra bien qu'un jour on soit l'humanité*) Romains wrote at the end of *La Vie unanime*. Such is the ultimate goal of unanimism, which has a future. . . . This idea of a total humanity inspired a few fine, impassioned poems, such as *Pendant une Guerre* written during the Russo-Japanese war) about the revolt of a man too weak to experience a sense of living solidarity with those who die, and several fragments of *Europe*.

Like Claudel and Péguy, Romains does not think that poetry dwells in a remote land which one can enter only as a somnambulist, or that a poem must be an incantation, the voice "of another world," which reaches us only through crevices in the real world. In his eyes, everything can be said poetically. Every sensation, feeling, idea, every *fact*—once the appropriate vantage point and tone have been discovered—can become poetic, can show itself openly, if necessary with its train of proofs, with the verbal apparatus required to assert its outlines under an explicit light. (And mystery itself will be given its proper place.) But Jules Romains is no Lucretius. His abrupt, imperious verse, the harsh sonority of his consonants, and his gray imagery are so contrary to present tastes that the resistance he has encountered is not surprising. The public no longer takes to poetry laden with didacticism and showing how it is made. And yet this poetry has the great merit of existing strongly. If we try to negate it, it subsists nevertheless, like a real object, made to last, with the density and solid structure that have characterized so many French works.

It is infused with an epic spirit. It is frequently narrative. In *La Vie unanime*, written before the first World War, as well as in *L'Homme blanc*, things happen; events take place—struggles and conquests, fears and defeats, apparitions, miracles—internal or external events, directly involving things or the soul, but experienced like psychic facts that affect the deepest strata of the mind. In them the epic character of unanimism is reduced to a spontaneous intuition of human groups. Everywhere Jules Romains sees invisible presences, secret movements, underlying magnetisms, outlines of form in the formless, aggregates of psychic atolls; his literary problem is to give concrete shape to these intangibles. For this purpose he has created a special vocabulary with many abstract words expressive, as in Hugo, of the metamorphoses of matter and the soul. This intense dynamism constitutes an epic element; similarly, the mythological vision of a city, a crowd, a procession, a factory—all of these are seen as great fabulous beings living an elemental life. The miraculous element of the old epics, which had been curtailed by science, springs into life again animated by the breath of the poet for whom the world of the mind is the scene of true "miracles." Even the voyage theme, prevalent in Homer, Virgil, and their countless imitators, reappears in *Europe* and *Voyage des Amants;* and *L'Homme blanc* is built upon the idea of the migrations of Asiatic tribes moving ever closer to the "languor of the west wind" and the "mass of golden things" which occupy the entire horizon of the setting sun.

Thus past and future join, countries come closer to one another, the earth shrinks beneath a sky that speaks to it in signs. Romains moulds gross living blocks composing a vast schematic universe, at the center of which man stands firmly, drunk with a powerful, heroic happiness:

Hospenthal!
> O semaine sonore,
>> qui pends
A ma jeunesse comme une plaque de fer!

O nuits en métal noir
Qui étiez faites comme les gongs et les cloches!

Ce n'est pas sur un lit que j'étais étendu,
Ce n'est pas dans une chambre que je dormais,
Dans un agencement de planches et de poutres.

J'étais couché de tout mon long,
De toute ma joie
> Sur la rumeur de la Reuss.

Laisse-moi t'en parler, camarade chérie,
Tu étais là,
> Avec ton corps, avec le mien
Jouait distraitement une rumeur sans bords.
Les jours n'avaient pas moins d'ampleur ni d'excellence.
Il venait du soleil des fraîcheurs du torrent.
Midi gênait la terre à force d'être pur ;
Et sa lumière, où l'on frissonnait de tremper,
Coulait sur nous par la fonte d'un bloc de ciel.

Hospenthal!
> O sonorous week
>> that hangs
On my youth like an iron weight!
O nights of black metal
Made like gongs and bells!

It was not on a bed that I lay,
It was not in a room that I slept,
In a contrivance of boards and beams.

I way lying stretched out,
With all my joy
> On the clamor of the Reuss.

Let me tell you about it beloved comrade.
You were there,
> An endless clamor
Played absently with your body, with mine.
The days had no less amplitude or excellence.

From the sun came the freshness of a torrent.
Noon embarrassed the earth by being so pure;
And its light that made us shiver as we dipped into it,
Flowed over us from a molten segment of sky.

(*Europe*)

Here the poem is an act of "poetic cognition" of the universe. And this insight must believe itself to be absolute. "Sometimes we have mysteriously concrete insights," says Luc Durtain. "Our shifting boundaries are crossed, and an object or person penetrates almost physically into our own intimacy. . . . Things then cease to be simple objects, separated from others by those outlines, ineradicable as wrinkles, with which the old age of human thought seamed the world; once more they become or aspire to become what they are— deep, violent, ineffable, and bound to one another at the navel." This is a profound intuition of a real, irrational, directly perceived universe, or, at least, it expresses the hope of approximating such an intuition.

The foregoing poem does not contain any unanimistic formulas, strictly speaking. This is nothing unusual. In the works of Jules Romains we find a strain of lyricism which is not related to any system, and which might be classified as belonging to the "intimate" genre, were it not that the poet's self is disturbed even in its retreat by messages and appeals. One might say in general that his epic passages reflect a conscious and conquering attitude of the mind, while the lyrical passages reflect passive states, and even the failures and anxieties of the self when it is weak and incapable of creating gods. The *Odes* and the little book entitled *Amour, couleur de Paris* include a few remarkable pieces of this kind. Analysis reveals many classical traits in these short poems whose seeming terseness conceals the poet's patient quest for the most striking words, those which arouse the most profound echo in the soul of the reader. But unlike Moréas, for example, Romains reduces literary transposition to its barest essentials; it is the whole mind with its obscure powers, it is the flesh and the blood that murmur restlessly; the total self is here opposed to the classical idea of man, to the self stylized by tradition and culture. In a sense, no poetry is more realistic, more opposed to the imaginary; gushing forth at the very level of life; in a gray light it follows with silence steps the inner transformations that take place in a zone to which everyday language does not penetrate.

> Le monde attendait peut-être
> A la porte du dormeur;
> Pas de grâce pour les songes
> Ni de sortie derobée!
>
> Mais voilà qu'au lieu d'un maître
> T'accueille une délivrance
> Etrange, que le brouillard
> A nuitamment préparée.
>
> Toute limite est vapeur,
> Toute prison est fumée;
> La demeure et le chemin
> Sont, au pouvoir d'une aurore.
>
> Par l'abîme dont tu doutes
> Un homme est poussé vers toi;
> Vous glissez l'un contre l'autre
> Comme deux astres fuyards.
>
> Et des mouvements ondoient
> Au bord de ta solitude,
> Ruisselant de cette joie
> Qu'ont les créatures neuves.
>
> Mais avant que tu les nommes
> Compagnons de ton exil,
> Ils replongent d'un bond mol
> Dans le limon éternel.

The world was waiting perhaps
At the sleeper's door;
No reprieve for dreams,
No furtive exit!

But now instead of a master
A strange deliverance welcomes you,
Which the mist has made
During the night.

Every boundary is vapor,
Every prison is smoke;
The dwelling and the path
Are under the sway of dawn.

Through the abyss that you distrust
A man is driven toward you;
You glide toward one another
Like two fugitive stars.

And at the edge of your solitude
There is a movement of undulant shapes
Brimming over with that joy
Which belongs to new creatures.

But before you call them
Companions of your exile
They plunge back lazily
Into the eternal silt.

(Amour, Couleur de Paris)

The self is caught in a network of forces that infinitely transcend it; each of these intuitions leads us from psychology to metaphysics; if all things are "bound together at the navel," the roots of the human mind are outside man.

"We did not think that the poet should go less far than the philosopher into the secret of things," wrote Jules Romains defining his youthful ambitions (in his preference to the *Oeuvres poétiques* of G. Chennevière). This places his work at the center of the modern stream. Even an accord between Rimbaud and Romains is not inconceivable, since both have a vigorous, militant faith in the powers of the mind and share the idea that the poet by cultivating his soul will transform his poetic sense into an instrument of exploration and conquest. However, Romains is, in his own way, a positivist incapable of relinquishing the rudder, of progressing otherwise than step by step along a course he has charted; the refusal to yield to enchantments, which marks his works with a special obviousness and "efficiency," suffices to distinguish him from the disciples of Rimbaud.

Recently he has taken pains to define his position and the meaning of his "lesson," which is far removed from the surrealists, or from Valéry. I am referring to the preface to *L'Homme blanc* in which he so lucidly pleads the cause of an "open air" poetry, eloquent and full of flesh, capable of saying everything. It is a pity that the author of *L'Homme blanc* does not always rise to the height of such a purpose, and that he imperfectly fulfills the hopes which have been aroused by the occasional fragments he has published during the last ten years. I do not dislike the idea that a modern epic should conclude with an appeal in favor of a world republic, and with a glorification of the village schoolmaster; but how can one help thinking of the myths and the poetry that such ideas would have produced in the mind of Hugo? Prophecies, to be stirring, must have wings.

3.

Today, Romains, whether he likes it or not, is a novelist and playwright in the eyes of the public; Duhamel, having at first followed Whitman and then taken the direction of a more inward beauty in his *Elégies*, seems to have resigned himself to prose; and even Vildrac has shown himself a dramatist. Like a living spring that erupts into other channels, unanimism in the narrowest sense of this term, or more accurately the spirit of the "hearty" poetry which animated the companions of the Abbaye and their friends, spread into works nonpoetic in form. In this way a humanitarian message gradually found an exceedingly large audience.

But this transition from verse to prose (novels, plays) was no accident, nor did it result from any "careerist" considerations. It was predictable. Beyond question, the essential poetic act can conclude alliances; it can be consummated in combination with other, related activities, and I shall certainly not condemn social-minded, humanitarian poetry a priori. It is clear, however, that love for mankind, like all other feelings, must not necessarily transmute itself into poetry. The "good will" of the writers belonging to this group was first of all an ethical aspiration.

Only Georges Chennevière remained almost exclusively a poet until his premature death in 1927. His unselfishness and modesty perhaps account for the fact that he has not achieved the reputation he so fully deserved. Moreover, he did not have a manner of his own, a "specialty"; the charm of his poetry springs from a balance between various gifts, and his sound mind combined with his sense of proportion and infinitely sure sense of language saved him from all excess; he might even be regarded as one of the rare poets of our time (perhaps with Paul Fort and Jammes) who are innate *classicists*, without bookishness, poets in whom nature and art are in perfect accord. Chennevière's poetry is entirely human; in him even unanimism loses its rigidity and heroism; his soul stands uncertain on the frontiers of the self, and sways between doubt, anxiety, and joy:

> *O pauvre coeur insatisfait,*
> *Homme trouble, que faudrait-il*
> *A ton bonheur?*

> O poor unsatisfied heart,
> Troubled spirit, what do you need
> For your happiness?

One feels the presence of this question behind the words of the poem, like a tear behind the eyelid. His "nostalgia for the eternal" and his attachment to the transient create a certain pathos of the soul, which suggests simple images and even phrases; the words become motionless like still water; everything becomes transparent. . . .

> *Le Temps sommeille au fond de l'être*
> *Et les instants montent en bulles.*
> *Les nuages glissent.*
> *Une voiture dans la rue*
> *Fait un bruit si doux qu'on regarde.*
> *Le jour brûle en paix.*

> Time slumbers in the depths of being
> And the moments rise like bubbles.
> The clouds glide by.
> A carriage in the street
> Makes a noise so gentle one looks out.
> The day burns down in peace.

> (From *Chant à voix basse,* in *Poèmes,* 1911–1918)

This thirst for an impossible happiness accounts for Chennevière's decision to write "idylls" such as *La Légende du Roi d'un Jour*, which combined nature and the marvelous in the rhythm of a popular song.

The upheavals and disappointments of the first World War and the post-war period did not change men. It is rare that facts "speak," and that events teach us anything at all. The so-called lessons of history are the inventions of historians, and more especially of litterateurs. Despite appearances to the contrary, very few among those who do not think by proxy were converted in any sense whatever by the war. It has been called upon with some semblance of reason to justify the most varied doctrines. In the case of the poets of "good will," the years of terror that began in 1914 served as a touchstone for testing the depth of a conviction and the firmness of a kind and humane will. These poets did dare to challenge the wind of insanity. They did not repudiate any part of themselves. They refused to heap curses on the enemy. Even today this attitude is regarded by some as a sign of utopianism, a disgrace. From *Europe* to P.-J. Jouve's *Tragiques*, to Vildrac's *Chants du Désespéré* and Duhamel's *Elégies*, there have been a number of poems about the war or against it, bearing witness to an incurable suffering, a boundless despair, or the breath of revolt of those who refused to accept the crime. Contrary to a facile assumption, the epic inspiration is rather rare in these occasional verses, which are merely the songs of hours of wretchedness. As for the bellicose poems or the tirades to glory, there are only a few which do not sink into the ridiculous or the grandiloquent when seen against the whole of the poetic production born of the war. In such a connection even the most violent sincerity can express itself only in an artificial and turgid language. The best pieces are simply human and sorrowful, or else fantastic, hallucinatory (I am referring particularly to Guillaume Apollinaire) and free of all passion. It seems that warlike enthusiasm, the atmosphere of marching double time, does not "pay off" in poetry. Misfortune rather invites man to withdraw into himself and to protect his life like a wretched little flame in the midst of a lurid world:

> Sous un figuier d'Avignon
> L'ombre verte était sucrée
> Par les larmes d'une figue
> Ivre de béatitude.
>
> Je ne voyais point les fruits,
> Je n'entendais plus les guêpes
> Et le Rhône en vain chantait
> L'immortel mépris de nous.
>
> Je regardais dans le ciel
> S'éloigner d'un vol farouche
> La paix comme un grand oiseau
> Chassé du canton natal.
>
> Un tambour bourdonnait dans le fond d'un village
> Le silence en semblait à jamais offensé;
> Une rumeur nouvelle et barbare insultait
> Vos fleurs, ô grenadiers pâmés dans la poussière.

Je n'éprouvais pas ces choses :
C'était assez que d'étreindre
Toutes les années futures
Abreuvées de mille hontes.

C'était assez que d'ouvrir
Des regards désespérés
Sur un monde enseveli
Dans l'insondable tristesse.

C'était assez sous vos feuilles,
O beau figuier d'Avignon,
Que d'appeler le néant
Des suprêmes solitudes.

Under a fig tree in Avignon
The green shade was sweetened
By the tears of a fig
Drunken with bliss.

I did not see the fruit,
I no longer heard the wasps,
And the Rhone sang in vain
Its immortal contempt for us.

In the sky I saw peace
Flying fiercely away
Like a great bird hunted
From its native province.

A drum rumbled in the depths of the village,
And seemed to offend its silence forever;
A new, barbarian clamor insulted
Your flowers, o pomegranate-trees swooning in the dust.

I did not feel these things:
It was enough to embrace
All the future years
Drenched in a thousand infamies.

It was enough to open
Despairing eyes
On a world buried
In unfathomable sadness.

It was enough beneath your leaves
O lovely fig-tree of Avignon,
To summon the nothingness
Of the supreme solitudes.

(G. Duhamel, *Elégies*, p. 47)

This is lofty poetry, but in its expression there is a tendency toward prose. Shortly afterwards when Europe was aroused to the highest hopes by the Armistice, *La Vie des Martyrs* and *La Possession du Monde* moved innumerable hearts. But since then injustice has become the common aspect of established disorder.

Only Jules Romains saw his influence in the field of poetry increase after the war. Those who were most profoundly subject to it, like P. J. Jouve and Jules Supervielle resemble him very little today. He attempted, however, in collaboration with Chennevière to establish a real poetic discipline (I am referring to their work in the Vieux-Colombier Theatre), to combat literary anarchism, to propagate the use of "accorded"* blank verse, and to restore the principles of order that have assured the permanent survival of so many French writings.

A few young writers responded to his call and attempted to lay the foundations of a "modern classicism" (cf., for example Jean Hytier in his articles in *Le Mouton blanc*) and to work toward the creation of "an objective poetry of spiritual essence." I refer particularly to Jacques Portail, whose *Androlite*, a veritable *"summa"* of social-minded and unanimist poetry is nothing less than an epic narrative of the birth, life, and death of a localized civilization. For the most part these poets seek an epic and legendary expression of modern life and man, following in this the example of Jules Romains who, after his *Ode génoise*, composed *L'Homme blanc*. But they were subject to various influences; some of these most recent unanimists partake of a certain "expressionism," which brings them close to the poems of Drieu La Rochelle and Montherlant and the cubist writings of Blaise

---

*That is to say, provided with a large number of recurrent sounds which lend a certain unity and a special musical tonality to the whole poem. (Cf. *Petit traité de versification*, by Romains and Chennevière.) This prosody is fully in keeping with Romains' temperament and is well suited to certain genres of poetry—although in my opinion the actual rhythmic element is neglected, and although it seems possible that, once clothed in scholastic formulas, this method will become a rigid code.

Cendrars, and correspondingly removes them from the "classical" principles which Jules Romains' young disciples, contributors to *Intentions, Mouton blanc,* or *Navire d'Argent* professed before 1925. But even these adventurous developments were foreshadowed by the course previously taken by an independent such as Luc Durtain.

In Durtain we again find the intention common to Romains and his followers of abandoning perception for the sensation that is completely impure and bound up in things, that is to say, for the physiological and coenesthetic substructure of our inner life. His hidden hope is to experience the feeling of reality to the point of perfect euphoria, and to transmit it by means of a language as directly expressive as possible. But language, especially the French language, whatever effort may be made to carry it back to its living springs, to deform, break, and smelt it down until it no longer reveals thought, does not allow itself to be kneaded without resistance. The writer who tries to break this resistance runs the risk of arriving at a mode of expression that is both convulsive and schematic, at a kind of stylization in reverse. This is a danger that threatened several poets of this group, including Romains himself (at least in his beginnings). Those who resolve to revise the value of words in order to translate integral sensation (in defiance of "purity" and even of grammatical correctness), are in great danger of straining the language to the breaking point, until words are used merely for their powers of percussion. Even Verhaeren had already shown to what lack of nuance such a quest for the expressive can lead. In the case of Luc Durtain, so much obstinate rigor enabled him to write a few poems in which persons and things are actualized with admirable concreteness:

> De l'autre côté du mur, le tic-tac de l'horloge à poids
> Et l'haleine lente du lit qui enclôt les époux chargés
> Chaque éveil d'un devoir égal, mesuraient le répit nocturne;
> Dans l'étable, la vache, de droite à gauche broyant comme une chaîne
> L'herbe dure déjà mâchée, soufflait un souffle creux et doux.
> Puis les bruits du temps, puis le temps lui-même enfin s'abolirent,
> Et rien ne fut plus, dissous dans l'obscur, âmes, rêves, brutes, charpentes
> Maçonnées de pierre, ni le nombre des tuiles, ni le val ni le ciel.
> Nuit. Silence. O fin de chaque jour. Jugement dernier—absolu
> Qui ne trouve plus qu'un néant vaste, flottant comme une fumée . . .

On the other side of the wall, the ticking of the grandfather clock

And the slow breath of the bed which encloses the husband and
  wife
Charged with an equal duty at each awakening, measured the noc-
  turnal respite;
In the stable, the cow, grinding the already chewed grass like a chain
Breathed a hollow, sweet breath.
Then the sounds of time, then time itself was at last abolished,
And there was nothing, all was dissolved in the darkness, souls,
  dreams, beasts, beams
Covered with masonry, tiles, valley, sky.
Night. Silence. O end of each day. Last Judgment — absolute,
Which finds only a vast nothingness, floating like smoke . . .   (*Lise*)

But perhaps another poet, André Spire, no less independent than
Luc Durtain, succeeded in forging a more flexible and *vocal* verse,
capable of giving "the poet possession of other men." André Spire
has profited from the works of the modern phoneticians, from the
Abbé Rousselot to Marcel Jousse. His aim is always to communicate, to arouse in his fellow men affective states and even the
physiological reactions that are the substratum of the emotions—
or, to use his own words, to call forth "the conscious or imperceptible
motions accompanied by the feelings of pleasure, malaise, sweetness, suavity, disgust, which are manifested by the movements of our
features and by our gestures, and of which those other motions,
words,—and I am referring not only to the sound they make, but
to all the internal and external motions of the vocal apparatus,
lungs, larynx, glottis, pharynx, nose, palate, tongue, cheeks, lips—
are the living image. Through these, the motions, or emotions, of
our interior are transmitted to our exterior, and through the operation of speech, uttered or internal (mimicked), they are transmitted
to the interior of those who hear them, and this is a contagion,
a radiation, a true communion, a presence truly real. . . ." Thus art
consists in expressing a profoundly organic thought by means of
rhythms and words, in making it into a mimicked, gesticulated
thought, "a perceptible figuration."* The poem aspires to preserve

---

*As Delacroix is quoted as saying in *Traité de psychologie* by Georges Dumas.
Moreover, Pierre Janet writes: *What we call thought is not the function of any particular
organ. . . . The brain is only a switchboard. . . . We think as much with our hands as with
our brains, we think with our stomachs, we think with everything. . . . Psychology is the
science of man in his entirety.* (Passage quoted by A. Lafont, *Un initiateur en psychologie:
Marcel Jousse,* in *Les Cahiers du Sud,* 1927, p. 269.)

the essential power and authenticity of the emotional cry, of the not yet articulate language by means of which one "primitive" man acted upon another as "an organ upon an organ":

> *Quand midi t'allonge à terre*
> *Suant*
> *Les oreilles bruissantes,*
> *Au milieu des abeilles trépignant les lavandes*
> *Et les agaves turgescents,*
> *Au milieu des fourmis, des aiguilles de pins,*
> *Des résines, des gommes, des sèves condensées, des fleurs écarquillées,*
> *Et, qu'à tes pieds, la mer*
> *Dort abrutie entre les rochers rouges . . .*
>
> *Quand midi te colle à terre,*
> *Au milieu des oiseaux engoncés, muets,*
> *Ton linge brûlant ta peau comme le foyer d'une lentille,*
> *La gorge sèche, la bouche sans salive,*
> *La nuque éteinte, les yeux aveugles,*
> *L'esprit vide.*
>
> *Connais, connais ton Dieu?*

When midday stretches you on the ground
Sweating,
Your ears humming,
In the midst of the bees that trample down the lavender
And the swollen agaves,
In the midst of ants, pine needles,
Resins, gums, condensed saps, wide-open blossoms,
And when at your feet the sea
Sleeps stupefied among the red rocks . . .

When midday glues you to the ground,
In the midst of clumsy, silent birds,
With your shirt burning your skin like the focus of a lens,
Your throat dry, your mouth without saliva,
Your neck cramped, your eyes blinded,
Your mind empty.

Know you your God?

(André Spire, *Midi* in *Tentations*)

In general, the spirit of pre-war unanimist and Whitmanian poetry, mingled with elements of various origins, today inspires currents oriented first, toward a social-minded, humanitarian poetry, inclined to be satirical, militant, and revolutionary, and seemingly deriving from the indignations and oratorical impulses of romanticism;* and, second, toward that total expression of reality which we have just discussed; here we find a meeting ground for men as different from one another as Romains, Durtain, Spire, Jouve (in his poems written before 1920), and even Joseph Delteil. The aims of all these poets are extra-literary, moral, in every respect "vital" and favorable to the birth of an epical lyricism.

Of these poets, those whom we have called "expressionists" —without meaning to suggest a comparison with the German writers called by that name—stand closer than one might suppose to Claudel or Péguy, or to a prose writer like Ramuz. All of them are sensual men, who think with their bodies and compel their minds to cling to reality instead of dissipating themselves in dreams and the infinite. It cannot be denied that Romains, Durtain, and Duhamel were influenced by Claudel. But their spiritualism, and that of their successors, is immanent, not transcendent; for them the mind has no master; in an irrational world, perhaps inherently doomed to disorder, it is at the mercy of anyone who can capture it and use its powers. It is easy to perceive possibilities of agreement between this spiritualism, in which the gods are made of the same stuff as man, and certain "materialist" and monistic conceptions of the universe. Nothing is less "pure" (in Valéry's sense of the word) than this poetry which strives to render not only the flower of reality, but its deep sap, its dense undergrowth, and its entangled roots.

*See, for example, one of Chennevière's last works, a long poem entitled *Pamir*, published for the first time in NRF of Aug. 1, 1926; in various respects this work can be regarded as a significant attempt at a composition in an elevated style.

Ubu Roi by Jarry

BOOK III

Adventure and Revolt

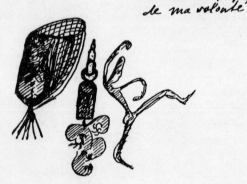

Manuscript page of *Apollinaire's The Assassin*

CHAPTER ELEVEN

The Origins of New Poetry. Guillaume Apollinaire

1.

To accept the present, to yield to the rhythms of the modern world and become aware of its newness, to say a passionate "yes" to "machine" civilization, such was the major ambition of Verhaeren. But consider the unanimists—coming after the naturists, the humanists, and Jammes—consider Claudel; at one point their designs coincide, a certain vital force pushes them into the midst of concrete reality, and it is in clinging to reality that they wish to live and function as poets. The manifestoes of Marinetti, with their prophecies bordering on hysteria, strike one as a disorderly echo of Verhaeren's credo: "Future, you exalt me as once my God exalted me!" An article in *Figaro* of Feb. 20, 1909, assures us that the poet of the future will sing only "the multi-colored, polyphonic currents of revolutions in modern capitals, the nocturnal vibrations of arsenals and shipyards under their violent electric moons, the gluttonous railroad stations swallowing smoke-ejecting serpents, and factories suspended from the clouds by the cords of their smoke. . . ." (Though, to be sure, Whitman, long before Marinetti, had made a locomotive the hero of one of his poems.)

Actually, the incoherent paroxysm of the futurists on the eve of the first World War was only the most recent avatar of a tradition dating from romanticism and the consequence both naive and barbaric of a legitimate desire, the desire to become adjusted to a universe in which man's power over the machine (and the power of matter over man) increases with every passing day. This same situation made it necessary for the new generation to put an end to the tyranny of emotion, to the "needs of the heart," the "aspirations of the soul," in short, to forget this nature with its outdated and monotonous charms—"What a failure this sunset is!" Fantasio had exclaimed. From now on, only one adventure was of any account, the adventure of twentieth-century man, slave and king of his machines.

Futurism, as conceived by Marinetti, hung fire in France, but it was not without influence, and it represents the hyperbolical image of a poetry of the "modern" world. In a sense, it is a "material-ist" poetry, lacking all style, nourished on raw sensations and moulded by external things; it is dynamic, its rhythm both regulates and is regulated by human action; it is a bundle of energies unfold-ing; finally, at its best it is epic. (As for the secret despair that is sometimes concealed in these flights into the inhuman, it is not always so completely muffled that it cannot be detected.) But though it was not long the style for young French poets to celebrate the future and the machine, many of them gave themselves to their time, accepting it as a fatality, mingling their lives with its life, absorbing "the climate of universal anxiety" (to use the phrase of André Salmon) to the point of suffocation. And in so doing they sometimes arrived at true poetry. For in this atmosphere of "vast twilight," in which they feel at home, there floats an impalpable dust which carries the germ of strange enchantments; at the center of an urban world, the poet feels within him a new sensibility and a reborn thirst for the marvelous. Among those manufactured objects with which man encumbers his life, he finds fetishes to populate his dreams. Once again, the boundaries were to be erased between inward life and the external world, between the self and the things which are said to be external.

The various currents of symbolist origin stand in contrast to these attempts at new conquests. Besides neo-Mallarmism and neo-impressionism, there survived a taste for the life of the "outcast," for moral and intellectual nonconformism, for the bizarre and the exceptional. The sensibility of several *fantaisiste* poets has been re-lated to the post-romantic and decadent tradition, and it is to the advanced wing of *fantaisisme* that the three poets belong, who con-tributed more than any others to shape the poetry of the war and post-war years—André Salmon, Max Jacob, and Guillaume Apollinaire.

The equivocal charm of Salmon's earliest poems is composed of mingled emotion and irony, nostalgia and cynicism, concealed innocence and pleasure in sin . . .

> *Romance! On n'est pas plus romance.*
> *Raillez, flûtes; toussez, tambours,*
> *Mon coeur, crapuleuse démence,*
> *A pleuré dans tous les faubourgs.*

> Romance—who could be more romantic.
> Jeer, you flutes; cough, you drums;
> My heart, with its lowdown madness,
> Has wept in every back street.

(Créances)

All his poems illustrate the poet's inability to adjust himself to society, to modern life, his feverish desire to get hold of the glittering keys that open the doors to fairyland. From the very first Max Jacob yielded to this desire to escape from himself, to "lose his countenance," *se décontenancer.* Apollinaire ventured no less boldly into the most eccentric regions of his mind. Crossing the barriers of unreality, he sometimes carves his poem in the stuff of dreams:

> *Les insulaires m'emmenèrent dans leurs vergers pour que je cueillisse des fruits semblables à des femmes. Et l'île, à la dérive, alla combler un golfe où du sable aussitôt poussèrent des arbres rouges. Une bête molle couverte de plumes blanches chantait ineffablement et tout le peuple l'admirait sans se lasser . . .*

> The islanders took me to their orchards to pick fruits resembling women. And the island drifted to fill in a gulf where red trees sprang at once from the sand. A languid beast covered with white feathers sang ineffably and all the people admired it and never grew weary . . .

(Onirocritique)

This piece of prose situated on a roundabout path which leads from *Aurelia* to the writings of the surrealists, bears the mark of truth as much as the most faithful "imitation of nature." It is one example among many of an oneiromancy inherited from minor romanticism and symbolism—a trend which slowly gathered strength until fifteen years later it became a veritable "torrent of dreams."*

**Vauge de rêves, Title of a manifesto by Louis Aragon (in *Commerce*, 2, 1925).*

At about the same time (in 1908), Jacques Rivière, before becoming the exegete of Rimbaud, composed his *Introduction à la Métaphysique du Rêve*. In view of the subsequent development of literature, this little-known piece is almost prophetic in character. He puts forward the exploration of the unconscious as the writer's goal, and advances the idea that genuine reality, "the vertiginous reality of the first ages," must be sought in the great "silent whirl of dreams," in "the somber and magical eddy where things become like living beings." And Rivière concludes: "I shall light the lamp of dreams; I shall descend into the abyss . . ."

This plea in favor of moral disorder, adventure, implicit in most of the writings of Apollinaire and his groups, appeared again, in a more insinuating form, in a number of disturbing utterances by André Gide. Side by side with the modern classicism that he propounded, he revealed a "demoralizing" ethics in *Les Nourritures terrestres*. To strive to make oneself "the most irreplaceable of individuals," is, for all practical purposes, to strive never to resemble one's fellow men, and, for some at least, not even to resemble oneself. This is a singularly attractive undertaking. A kind of underground spirit drives man to experiment with the extremest possibilities of self-metamorphosis. The question is whether it is possible to enrich one's nature and achieve a new awareness of one's total being by overruling the resistance of reason and habit, by forcing one's imagination to leap into the unknown, beyond any beaten track. This implies a readiness to destroy the traditional concept of man, and, first of all, to destroy one's own personal being, to let it be absorbed and lost in a *selva oscura*. And possibly poetry might profit from such an approach, possibly it might find a new and abundant material. More than that: this very activity, this mental proteanism, this way of living and constantly renewing one's life, *is* poetry.

This will to metamorphosis which Gide advocated, like Nietzsche before him, summoned men to accord the unconscious and the dream an ever greater place in the conduct of life and thought. Such a doctrine cast a retrospective light on the career of Rimbaud, on his stubborn pursuit of the origin and the definitive formula, and on the tragic adventure of Nerval. In the same period, another path led to Rimbaud. Whatever significance one may ascribe to *Une Saison en Enfer*, Claudel's preface to *Les Œuvres complètes* (reprinted in 1912) remains one of the most sober and most profound interpretations of Rimbaud's poetry. It was this interpretation and the idea that Rimbaud was "a mystic in the savage state" that served as the point of departure for Jacques Rivière in his attempt to demonstrate that the *Illuminations* give us objective visions of another world or of this world "in so far as the other one disorganizes it." Thus, the idea that poetic activity is a way to occult knowledge of a super-nature was, in the years preceding the world war, enriched by a mysticism and a spirit of revolt originating in Rimbaud.

We seem to be confronted with two opposite currents—on the one hand, the poets attempt to adjust themselves to positive reality, to the "mechanical" world of our era; on the other hand, they desire to shut themselves up in the enclosure of the self, in the world of dreams. But it must be observed at once that it is possible to "escape" or "take refuge" outside oneself as well as within oneself; either of these trends may imply conquest or flight. Moreover, and this is the main point, a whole area of contemporary facts supplies ample justification for the reconciliation of the real and the imaginary, the positive and the irrational, life and dreams, and in the light of these facts the opposition of the two attitudes just defined becomes a mere abstraction.

These facts, which are reflected in the approach of modern poetry, are the theses of modern epistemologists concerning the conditions and limits of knowledge, the psychological theories of the sub-conscious and the unconscious, and the relatively widespread belief or suspicion that within and without man there exist unknown energies upon which he can hope to act. Science can only be anthro-pocentric; it is always a vision of the world, it always rests upon *a priori* categories and axioms. Even the least pragmatic thinkers sometimes define it with Valéry—as an aggregate of recipes which are always successful. Reason seems to be a specialized faculty, which has slowly taken form through gropings, failures and mul-tiple experiments; and even if one does not go as far as Bergson and his disciples, according to whom reason is entirely directed toward action and utility, no one dares any longer to suppose that it can ever give us complete knowledge of reality. Consequently, the very concept of reality has lost the relatively simple meaning it had in the days of positivism. Once again, reality eludes us, it is infused with irrational elements, everywhere it overlaps our knowledge of it.

The universe *in itself* is inaccessible to us; and according to the anti-intellectualists, the more we try to express it in clear ideas, the less we grasp its essence.

Thus the poets find themselves authorized to accord a measure of confidence to the uncertain light of inspiration; this knowledge is perhaps as good as another kind of knowledge; and they are encouraged to perceive strangeness, mystery, the fantastic, in reality itself, whether it be the reality of the self or of the non-self. Caprice, arbitrariness, obscurity are happily legitimized. After all, say the philosophers to the poets: "Your feeling did not deceive you, you were instinctively right to take a stand against reason; its abuses of power are infinite in number, and it owes its very dominance to a usurpation." The opposition, traditional since romanticism, between the idea and life, the dream and life, can no longer subsist in the same terms. "Everything positive in life is bad, everything good in life is imaginary," wrote Nodier. This distinction is too simple. The most solid ideas are mere idols built on sand. What is called the real and the unreal, good and evil, are extremely relative standpoints from which to judge man and the universe. Beyond them, there opens the realm of the free mind, in revolt against self-evident truths. Already Dostoevsky, in his *Notes From Underground* and his great novels, opposed the assertions of common sense with a bold "perhaps." "I grant that two times two is four is an excellent thing, but if we must praise everything, I will tell you that two times two is five is also a charming thing." And our science is perhaps ignorance, our life death; perhaps we sleep during our waking hours, our eyes gazing at insignificant forms, perhaps we are prisoners outside ourselves without contact with reality.

Once again, a kind of mystical kinship is revealed among all things; everything tends to merge. The poet no longer "recognizes" the pictures that the tangible world unfolds before his eyes; they seem to him as strange, as abnormal as the most extraordinary phantasmagoria. And the events that develop within himself assert themselves before his inner eye with a concrete force that sometimes compels him to doubt everything else; are not the things said to be "imaginary" the real self-evident truths?

According to a formula of the German romantics, "the world is a dream and the dream is a world." Encounters take place between the facts of inner and external life; a harmony is revealed between the inside and the outside, signs answer signs; a hidden unity, capable of annihilating all objects and living beings can gradually be perceived beyond the phenomena which appeal to the senses and beyond the images which compose dreams. Suspended between the two worlds, the poet advances in a state of semi-ecstasy into the heart of reality.

There is nothing in all this that was not anticipated by the great lyricists of the second half of the nineteenth century. But at that time poetry was in advance of philosophy; common sense continued to be fully satisfied with the old antagonism between life and the dream—indeed, this antagonism was a literary cliché. But the attempt of the modern poetic movement to do away with it, the solutions both logical and extreme put forward by the modern poets, stand in direct relation to what has been called the crisis of the concept of reality.

2.

While the consequences of such a state of mind for art cannot be enumerated, we may emphasize the increasing contempt shown by many poets and artists for tangible appearances. In their opinion, the faithful reproduction of what is conventionally called "reality" is a futile task. All these things that our senses discover for us, all these everyday and utilitarian thoughts are in the end a mere setting, a parade, a way of not living. The whole world of the senses is vastly discredited. And here we undoubtedly find the clue to the peculiar humor that characterizes so many recent works. Flaubert already looked on life as a "sinister farce." A pessimist, permeated with a sense of the relativity and absolute insignificance of all things, finds it easy to see the intellectual and social comedy, which confers a utility and a value upon things and ideas, as a formidable mystification:

> It is one of our human superstitions that when we wish to speak with friends temporarily absent, we throw the written expression of our kind feelings into apertures especially made for that purpose, which resemble sewer vents; this after encouraging the tobacco trade, insidious as it is, with a small gift, and receiving in return

little images, no doubt sacred, which we devoutly kiss on their backsides. This is not the place to criticize the incoherence of these gestures...

(Alfred Jarry, *Gestes et Opinions du Dr. Faustroll Pataphysicien*)*

A few substitutions of terms, the replacement of a few consecrated epithets, suffice to show the absurdity of the most ordinary and least incoherent "gesture." Seemingly nothing has been changed, yet everything has been upset in a hilarious world.

Of this spirit of mystification and occult irony, the author of *Ubu Roi* was the most typical representative during the period extending from symbolism to contemporary neo-sybolism. Indeed, he always played the part of Ubu; the sententious, grandiloquent pedantry of each of his words was like that of his hero. The phrase that he repeated on every occasion: "It was as beautiful as literature, wasn't it?" shows sufficiently that in his eyes all the events of his life were situated on the same intermediate plane between reality and unreality as his literary reminiscences. Moreover, the very tasks of "pataphysics," the pompous science invented by another of his characters, Dr. Faustroll, is to investigate "the laws that govern exceptions and to explain the universe that supplements this one"; stated in less ambitious terms, it describes a universe which can be seen and which perhaps should be seen instead of the traditional universe..." Once again the mystification is instructive; the task is always to escape from the traditional vision of things and to take up our residence in that region of the mind, where they strike us as strange and incongruous. But Jarry's own life, unfolding as it did outside all social contexts, was itself an inexhaustible source of the fantastic and the grotesque, from which Salmon, Jacob, and Apollinaire drew abundantly.

Another consequence of the same state of mind, a consequence directly related to the foregoing, is that the image is born to a new life—at least it lengthens as much as possible (sometimes to the breaking point) the thread connecting it with the object. Instead of being attached to the object, of showing it, of making it tangible, the image now uses it as a springboard from which to leap into

---

*Perhaps it should be recalled that in France stamps are commonly purchased in the government tobacco stores. Tr.

space. It seeks to emancipate itself to an ever greater degree, until it denies its origin, and itself becomes an object.

Abundant examples of this process can be found in a collection of avant-garde poems (it was already apparent in Baudelaire, and even more so in Rimbaud). I shall quote one from *Les Spéculations du Dr. Faustroll* by Jarry, which shows the image in process of escaping from its explanatory function and conquering its full independece:

The River and the Meadow

> The river has a big flabby face, made to be slapped by oars, a neck with many folds, blue skin with green down. In its arms, over its heart, it holds the little island shaped like a chrysalis. The meadow in its green dress falls asleep, its head in the hollow of the river's shoulder and neck.

Obviously such images cannot be regarded as a means of attracting attention to a real meadow and river. The tangible world is used only as a pretext, a starting point, as raw material; the aim is to evoke plastic beings half human and half inhuman. It might be said that this is the ultimate consequence of subjectivism. But the problem is more complex than it may seem; while some poets want only to shuffle the cards and to create arbitrary and playful constructions, others believe that unapplied images are more than gratuitous inventions or consequences of a collaboration between the world and the poet, who confines himself to projecting on the screeen of language particular sensations which have meaning only in relation to himself. These poets believe that such images have an intrinsic value, that they "mean" something, that they are indices, signs, of an absolute reality. The most recent poets are inclined to assert that the data of their selves do not belong to them alone, and that a universal spirit manifests itself through them. But if such a design, discernible even at that time in many poets of various groups, has come into full light only in our day, it is because the cubist painters have given valuable aid to the poets.

Picasso, Braque, Derain and their followers no longer contented themselves with representing nature by deforming it, they strove to liberate themselves from the obligation to imitate anything whatsoever. The tangible world supplies the painter with materials disposed in an order which for the vulgar herd represents the sole reality; but the painter, like a demiurge, uses them to create another world. This process is similar to the one we have just briefly analyzed. Here, too, forms and colors live an independent life, and are disposed in accordance with an unexpected law. And in fact certain painters tend to interpret this purely plastic world as something quite different from an artistic lie, from a meaningless setting. In 1912 Guillaume Apollinaire maintained that "the painter tries to express the greatness of metaphysical forms" (*Il y a*); and many divagations on the fourth dimension derive from the idea that the painter rises to a superhuman contemplation of things which leads him to the threshold of a kind of Platonic universe, endowed with absolute being and having only an accidental relation to the artist's self.*

3.

The shadow of Guillaume Apollinaire lies across all the paths of French art between 1905 and 1920; and nearly every one of his poems gives one the impression of having been written by a different poet. Where shall we capture him? The moment we try to cast light on the field of his thought, we are beset by all manner of clouds. Concerning his personal predilections and the value he himself ascribed to his works, we are reduced to conjecture. Moreover, in view of his laziness and his lack of perseverance, his intentions are doubtful. We must also take into account his need to mystify people, although he often said that he alone was sincere. He was primarily an adventurer in thought; and this formula must be understood in its fullest sense—for he made real, exciting, dangerous things out of the notions of freedom, risk and adventure. But once he discovered a vein of ore, he left to others the job of exploiting it. "It was enough for him to write a poem that would give birth to poems

---

*Apollinaire, for example, wrote: *Greek art embodied a purely human conception of beauty. It took man as the measure of perfection. The art of the modern painters takes the infinite universe for its ideal, and it is to the fourth dimension alone that we owe this new measure of perfection which enables the artist to endow objects with proportions in conformity with the degree of plasticity he wishes to give them* (Il y a).

by others," wrote Soupault, "to publish a book like *Alcools* in which all the poetry of his time would find its orientation." Apollinaire himself boasted: "I sow my songs like seeds of grain."

If there is a permanent note that sounds throughout his life, if not throughout his writings, it is that of a tender and melancholy sentimentality which is sometimes reminiscent of Nerval, sometimes of Verlaine, and sometimes of Heine, and which draws nourishment from popular lyricism. Lays and complaints, ballads and romances haunt his memory. Their ancient tunes accompany "the inevitable descent of memories," perfumed with wonders. At the slightest sign, all his past awakens; the unloved lost child, the exile, or the traveler, is himself:

> *Mon beau navire ô ma memoire*
> *Avons-nous assez navigué*
> *Dans une onde mauvaise à boire*
> *Avons-nous assez divagué*
> *De la belle aube au triste soir.*

> My fine ship, o my memory,
> Have we not sailed enough
> In waters foul to drink ,
> Have we not wandered enough
> From joyous dawn to sad sunset.

> (*La Chanson du Mal-aimé,* composed in 1903)

But his narratives are soon lost in the violet mist of twilight. A few images emerge, and the whole is carried off in gusts of music:

> *Les souvenirs sont cors de chasse*
> *Dont meurt le bruit parmi le vent.*

> Memories are hunting horns
> Their sounds die in the wind.

> (*Cors de chasse*)

This is Apollinaire's magic spell. Two simple words suffice to create an atmosphere; the everyday, the trivial, the worn out themes are transfigured; the mystery that dwelled in them unknown to us is revived; and they recede, isolated in silence. And yet their pathos is not dissipated, but on the contrary concentrated; it becomes more human; every sentence, however weak, seems to be uttered for eternity. In the admirable poem entitled *Le Voyageur*, the familiar sentimental and personal romanticism is universalized and purified until it becomes a boundless song expressing a whole destiny:

> *Te souviens-tu des banlieues et du troupeau plaintif des paysages*
> *Les cyprès projetaient sous la lune leurs ombres*
> *J'écoutais cette nuit au déclin de l'été*
> *Un oiseau langoureux et toujours irrité*
> *Et le bruit éternel d'un fleuve large et sombre.*

> Do you remember the suburbs and the plaintive flock of landscapes
> The cypresses cast their shadows beneath the moon
> And that night in the decline of summer, I listened
> To a languorous and always irritated bird
> And to the eternal sounds of a broad and somber river.

This is an example of natural, native poetic purity freely flowing from a certain climate of the soul. Apollinaire's inspiration has often been called bookish; it is true that it sometimes led him astray; the influences to which he was subjected have also been enumerated; but he had a special gift, a charm; the stars willing, he created a fairyland with everything that life brought him.

Even in the trenches he lived the war in a dream, like a cosmic enchantment; he was like a child, full of wonder without concern for cause and effect. A night of bombardment is a "feast": the sky starred with rockets, the shells "color of the moon," criss-crossing and mewing, caressing "the soft nocturnal fragrance"—all these apocalyptic images captivated his heart. Even the old theme of the amorous soldier is revived with a "disarming" naiveté:

> *As-tu connu Guy au galop*
> *Du temps qu'il était militaire . . .*

> Did you know Guy with the gallop
> In the days when he was a soldier...

(Les Saisons)

Apollinaire was smiling and sighing, polishing rings for his loves, on the day when the shell struck his head. He survived for some months before he was carried off by the flu, but these months were not of his best. Whatever he himself may have said, his "blessed time" was that immediately preceding the war.

The greater part of Apollinaire's works, begun before 1900, derives from the symbolism of the end of the nineteenth century. The quatrains of the *Bestiaire*, the pleasant and nostalgic sketches of *Calligrammes*, exemplify the most gratuitous literary game. According to Jean Cassou, they are in the academic tradition of pure poetry, that of the old-time "describers," writers of occasional verse, who evoked at will the image of any object whatsoever. The Mallarmé of *Petits Airs* and *Loisirs de la Poste* is perhaps, in this respect, one of Apollinaire's direct predecessors. After the war, this charming fancy which does not negate nature, but uses it with the utmost freedom, was to seduce the most "advanced" of the "fantaisiste" poets, especially Jean Cocteau.

Alcools contains more ambitious symbolist poems, such as *Le Larron* or *L'Ermite*, almost regular in form and abounding in striking sonorities and rare words, sparkling in all their facets. These alexandrines are inflated with a certain Parnassian emphasis.

> *Un homme bègue ayant au front deux jets de flammes*
> *Passa menant un peuple infirme pour l'orgueil*
> *De manger chaque jour les cailles et la manne*
> *Et d'avoir vu la mer ouverte comme un oeil*
>
> *Les puiseurs d'eau barbus coiffés de bandelettes*
> *Noires et blanches contre les maux et les sorts*
> *Revenaient de l'Euphrate et les yeux de chouettes*
> *Attiraient quelquefois les chercheurs de trésors . . .*

> A stammerer with two jets of flame on his forehead
> Went by, leading a sickly people for the pride
> Of eating quail and manna every day
> And of having seen the sea open like an eye
>
> The bearded drawers of water, wearing black and white
> Headbands against evils and spells
> Were returning from the Euphrates and the eyes of owls
> Sometimes attracted the treasure seekers . . .

But this whole poem is undermined by a principle of disorder. The nobility of tone and the brilliance of the images are only a snare. A hidden drunkenness gives it an incoherence bordering on grotesqueness. Rimbaud in *Le Bateau ivre* and Jarry in several pieces of *Minutes de Sable mémorial* had already slipped into the temple of poetry in this manner, to shake its pillars and secretly profane its sacred objects. The sentence, instead of following an internal and external model, often seems to beget itself; it is carried away by a rhythmic and musical pattern, its "past" weighs upon it while light impulsions induce it to choose among several possibilities. But a stroke of the bow, says Rimbaud (in *Illuminations*), suffices to "release all the sounds and begin the new harmony"; an imperceptible incitement spins the whole poem on its hinges and turns the kaleidoscope upside down. In extreme cases, the poet has the feeling that he is no longer responsible for what he is writing, the illusion that the poem is composing itself.

In *Le Larron* or *L'Ermite*, to be sure, Apollinaire does not go so far; he holds the reins of his chariot firmly in hand, though nothing is lost through the constraints of the alexandrine meter and of the rhyme (which is often replaced by assonance). These constraints are all the more urgent because what he sets out to express is a precise "substance," anterior to the stanza and the verse; in these poems, where everything is instantaneous, they contribute to create an element of the unpredictable, of chance. And far from wishing to abolish this chance, Apollinaire like Mallarmé worships it. He strives to reveal the mysterious affinities existing between thought and language, to promote an exchange between the two, even by artificial means; in brief, he experiments with chance, the poetic element being essentially the arbitrary, the unforseeable, the free association that no reasoning can produce, the lucky find, the beautiful virgin image that the drunken bird carries in its beak. Baudelaire as an aesthetician had praised the poet who could accomplish exactly what he had decided on. But in the end the poet renounces choice and decision. Perhaps unbeknownst to him, his poems will mean something.

This is a new kind of poetic purity, quite different from that envisaged by Valéry. Similarly, it has been asserted that a painting which does not represent any object fulfills its plastic task more completely, and that music which is no longer expressive and has liberated itself from all pretexts is pure. It remains to be seen whether an art can subsist and live in an atmosphere rarefied to such a point. This no doubt is one of the most fascinating problems raised by modern art as a whole. More radical innovators coming after Apollinaire have shown us the full implications of this debate.

At a certain moment in his career Apollinaire came to regard the heritage of romanticism and symbolism as a dead weight. He had indeed from the very outset shuffled the rules "of the ancient game of verse."* But now he wished to free himself altogether, to reject the literature that prevented him from directly experiencing the ardent, new life of his time, he wished to reject the past, the memories and dreams that haunted him:

> A la fin tu es las de ce monde ancien
> Bergère ô tour Eiffel le troupeau des ponts bêle ce matin
> Tu en as assez de vivre dans l'antiquité grecque et romaine
>
> . . . .
>
> Tu lis les prospectus les catalogues les affiches qui chantent tout
>   haut
> Voilà la poésie ce matin et pour la prose il y a les journaux
> Il y a les livraisons à 25 centimes pleines d'aventures policières . . .

All in all you're tired of this antique world
O shepherdess, Eiffel tower, the flock of bridges is bleating this
    morning
You've had enough of living in Greek and Roman antiquity

. . . .

You read prospectuses, catalogues, posters all loudly singing
That is your poetry this morning, and for prose there are the
    newspapers
There are the the dime serials full of cops and robbers . . .

These opening lines of *Zone* bear witness to his attempt at liberation from the past. A poetry nourished on dreams would gradually be supplanted by a modernist poetry, whose aim would be "to exalt life in whatever form it may present itself" (*L'Esprit nouveau*, Apollinaire's manifesto published in *Mercure de France*, Dec. 1, 1918). Here we have the Whitmanian, futurist, prophetic aspect of Apollinaire. In the Europe of 1913, he looked forward to the future with confidence and candor. He no longer expected the alchemy of words to perform miracles. He scorned the music of words, just as he scorned legends. It is in things and events themselves that the wonder can be discovered, provided they are seen from a certain

---

*Pardonnez-moi mon ignorance
Pardonnez-moi de ne plus connaître l'ancien jeu des vers. . . .

Forgive me my ignorance,
Forgive me for no longer knowing the ancient game of verses.

(*Fiançailles*, in *Alcools*)

angle. This is not indifference, but rather a moral disinterestedness, a peculiar manner of wandering around objects, of finding the meaning of exceptions, and of inventing, as Jarry said, some kind of a universe "supplementary to this one."

Zone belongs to the genre of so-called cubist, synthetic, or "simultaneist" poems. Here, on a single plane, without perspective, without transition, and often without any apparent logical relationship, we find heterogeneous elements, sensations, judgments, memories intermingled just as in the flux of psychological life. But to forestall a possible misunderstanding, it must be pointed out that, while the painter constructs on his canvas an architecture that is intended to constitute an order different from that of nature, the composition of such mental films in poetry remains as a rule very free. It is rare to find in a poet the equivalent of the intellectual effort that characterizes pictorial cubism, as opposed to the relative passivity of impressionism. The painter André Lhote speaks of "the plastic utilization of the thunderbolt." In the case of Apollinaire and most of his "cubist" successors, this intellectual "utilization" is reduced to very little. However, an artistic intention subsists in the sense that the poet more or less deliberately chooses those parts of himself which he wants to externalize; despite everything, an arrangement takes place, and attention is focussed on an idea or image. *Zone*, for example, clearly reflects the conflict between poetry and anti-poetry, between the tendency to dream, which suggests rhythmic and musical phrases, and the "new spirit" which sets out to express life as such. Consequently, these cubistic pieces almost inevitably assume the character of a compromise, which amounts to saying that they are still works of art. This self-disguised art may be confined to a few finishing touches, it may also consist in the subtlest ruses and the most extreme refinements. For the intellect is not so easily dismissed, and it may appear in any garb. Laforgue, who in many respects foreshadows the cubists—as for instance in *L'Hiver qui vient* in his *Derniers Vers*—had already shown how intelligence could, if necessary, be substituted for spontaneous life. The desire to cultivate beautiful disorder would emerge again.

But the principle of the freedom of inspiration led Apollinaire to other adventures. Take, for example the poem entitled *Les Fenêtres* (in *Calligrammes*):

Du rouge au vert tout le jaune se meurt
Quand chantent les aras dans les forêts natales
Abatis de pihis
Il y a un poème à faire sur l'oiseau qui n'a qu'une aile
Nous l'enverrons au message téléphonique
Traumatisme géant
Il fait couler les yeux
Voilà une jolie fille parmi les jeunes Turinaises
Le pauvre jeune homme se mouchait dans sa cravate blanche
Tu soulèveras le rideau
Et maintenant voilà que s'ouvre la fenêtre
. . . .

O Paris
Du rouge au vert tout le jaune se meurt
Paris Vancouver Hyères Maintenon New York et les Antilles
La fenêtre s'ouvre comme une orange
Le beau fruit de la lumière

From red to green all the yellow dies
When the macaws sing in their native forests
Giblets of pihis
There's a poem to be written about the bird that has only one
   wing
We shall send it by telephone
A gigantic traumatism
It makes your eyes water
Here is a pretty girl among the young ladies of Turin
The poor young man blew his nose in his white necktie
You shall raise the curtain
And now the window opens
. . . .

O Paris
From red to green all the yellow dies
Paris Vancouver Hyères Maintenon New York and the Antilles
The window opens like an orange
The lovely fruit of light.

A hoax on the public, some will say. Perhaps.* But is it not the
poet's intention to use the world and the public and himself, as

---

*According to André Billy (*Apollinaire vivant*), Apollinaire composed this poem
in a café, with the collaboration of his neighbors; the first line, *From red to green
all the yellow dies* is supposed to evoke the "flow without honor" of a drink.

pretexts for a very special mockery? "The accidents of the world,"
said Flaubert (in his Preface to *Dernières chansons* by Louis Bouilhet)
"seem to you as though transposed for the benefit of an illusion to be
described, so much so that everything, including your existence,
strikes you as having no other use." But if reality becomes illusion,
the illusion is felt as real; it creates the fact, or at least it acquires
an accent which is no longer that of pure invention, of lies; it develops on an intermediate plane between dream and waking; the poet
can no longer abandon himself to it or withhold himself from it; he is
embarked on an adventure and his duty is to experience it. This is
a very particular mode of behavior, the psychology of which should
be closely studied. According to Baudelaire, the mainspring of
mystification consisted in "a kind of energy that breaks forth from
boredom and revery" (*Le mauvais Vitrier*, in the prose poems), at a
moment, that is, when attention turns away from the present, when
the forces accumulated in the unconscious are mobilized and erupt
into life, calling forth absurd or forbidden words, irrational or
dangerous acts. The creator of the mystification obscurely seeks the
beginnings of a new, abnormal, arbitrary fact; he can be satisfied
only with a provocation directly addressed to life; what life must be
compelled to answer through an accident with unpredictable consequences. The mystifier will be under the impression that he is
escaping from himself, from his past, that he "is losing the thread"
of his life, that he "is piercing a window in the wall of canvas," like
Mallarmé's buffoon. "When you are 'dry,'" Apollinaire advised his
friends, "write anything at all, begin any sentence, and push straight
ahead." One must compel chance and the unconscious to collabor-
ate.

It will be noted that aesthetics and ethics, life and poetry, are
here scarcely distinguishable. There is less distance than one might
think between Gide's "gratuitous act," symbolized by Lafcadio's
gesture of throwing his companion out of the train, to the "gratuitous" and yet inevitable images of the moderns. In both cases, man
appeals to a demon foreign to his normal self, enters into a pact with
him, and lets himself be seduced by him. For the mystifier himself
is the first who requires to be mystified. "Next to the pleasure of
being surprised," says Baudelaire, "there is no greater pleasure than
to cause surprise." Thus the most intense pleasure is that of being
surprised. As for Apollinaire, these conversation-poems, as he called

them, composed of heterogeneous and in a sense impersonal elements, seem to have provided him with the means of surprising, of mystifying himself. "The new is wholly in the surprise," he says. "That is what is newest, most alive about it." And in one of his poems he writes:

> Qui donc saura nous faire oublier telle ou telle partie du monde
> Où est le Christophe Colomb à qui l'on devra l'oubli d'un continent
> Perdre
> Mais perdre vraiment
> Pour laisser place à la trouvaille . . .

Who then will know how to make us forget this or that part of the world.

Where is the Christopher Columbus to whom we shall owe the forgetting of a continent

To lose

But to lose truly

To make room for a lucky find.

(Toujours in Calligrammes)

But must not everything be perpetually discovered? Must we first forget everything, and truly lose it, in order to discover? Is there not more of old age than of youth in this "revolutionary" spirit, is it not indicative of weariness with "an old world," of dryness of soul, of inability to discover the unknown and the mystery contained in the present, seemingly most ordinary life? It is possible that Apollinaire, thirsting for escape, suffered from a certain poverty of imagination. Clearly, he was preoccupied by a small number of themes, and he returns again and again to the same images. At the same time, his poetics of the arbitrary and the surprise, his eagerness to tempt chance by throwing his dice at every opportunity, after having destroyed all possibility of a regulated game, requires the constant presence of a teeming and subtle imagination, close to external objects but capable of freeing itself from them, and capable of metamorphosing them into all sorts of monsters and chimeras. Ultimately it is difficult to say—and this is not one of the least attractive aspects of the enigma he represents—whether Apollinaire might have been that great poet of whom he makes us think, or whether his poems with their equivocal, suggestive charm show him in a flattering light.

It must be said, in any case, that this revolutionary was not a mere negator; he was also a prophet, a "seer." If he encouraged "even hazardous literary experiments," it was because he thought that they would supply the material for a "new realism," which he was no doubt the first to call "surrealism."* He was perhaps also the first to have the idea of ceasing to compose works of art. "He was the last poet," writes André Breton. But there is still poetry.

Still during the period preceding his death, Apollinaire pleaded more than ever for pity:

> *Nous qui quêtons partout l'aventure*
> *Nous ne sommes pas vos ennemis*
> *Nous voulons vous donner de vastes et d'étranges domaines*
> *Où le mystère en fleurs s'offre à qui veut le cueillir*
> *Il y a là des feux nouveaux des couleurs jamais vues*
> *Mille phantasmes impondérables*
> *Auxquels il faut donner de la réalité*
> . . . .
>
> *Pitié pour nous qui combatons toujours aux frontières*
> *De l'illimité et de l'avenir*
> *Pitié pour nos erreurs pitié pour nos péchés*

> We who seek adventure everywhere
> We are not your enemies
> We strive to give you vast and strange domains
> Where mystery blossoms for all who wish to gather it.
> There are new fires of colors never seen
> A thousand imponderable phantasms
> To which reality must be given
> . . . .
>
> Pity us who fight forever on the frontiers
> Of the boundless and the future
> Pity us for our errors, pity us for our sins.

(La jolie Rousse, last poem in Calligrammes)

---

*In speaking of his drama, *Les mamelles de Tirésias* (1918).

CHAPTER TWELVE

Toward a Poetry of Modern Action and Life

1.

The *Sturm und Drang* period of modernism opened in 1909. The way had been paved for it by Verhaeren, Whitman, and the whole spirit of a century intoxicated with the brutal grandeur or ephemeral charm of "things that you won't see twice." In 1909 *La Vie unanime* was published. But Romains strove to impose order on his songs, and his intentions were actually spiritualist ones. Marinetti, on the contrary, advocated an integral futurism which would have produced only inorganic "works" if Apollinaire and especially Blaise Cendrars, between 1912 and 1914, had not attempted to give this poetry a kind of existence by capturing and guiding its potentialities. Pieces such as *Prose du Transsibérien, Panama*, and some of the "elastic poems" published here and there on the eve of the war, provided models for the next ten years. In the Berlin magazine *Sturm*, Blaise Cendrars printed his *Tour*:

> O tour Eiffel!
> Je ne t'ai pas chaussée d'or
> Je ne t'ai pas fait danser sur les dalles du cristal
> Je ne t'ai pas vouée au Python comme une vierge de Carthage
> Je ne t'ai pas revêtue du peplum de la Grèce
> Je ne t'ai pas nommée Tige de David ni Bois de la Croix
> Lignum Crucis
> O tour Eiffel!

> O Eiffel Tower!
> I didn't fit you out with golden slippers
> I didn't make you dance on crystal tiles
> I didn't dedicate you to the Python like a Carthaginian virgin
> I didn't clothe you in the peplum of Greece

I didn't call you Scion of David or Wood of the Cross
Lignum Crucis
O Eiffel Tower!

(From *Dix-neuf Poèmes élastiques*)

But it was the war that brought the break with the old world, with the age-old course of things. Abstract landscapes abandoned to death, orgies of iron and steel, cities that suddenly became cosmopolitan and devoted all their energies to overproduction, a victory that was "mechanical" as much as military—all these extraordinary things threw some writers back to the beliefs and watchwords of the past, which they accepted as the only possible framework for the French spirit; while others abruptly came of age, and felt their ties inexorably collapsing. Their eyes were opened to a civilization whose anonymous face they hoped to decipher; new myths found fertile soil in their minds which were deeply shaken by the events of the day—the myth of war, of revolution, of the machine, of speed, of the alliance between man and matter, of sports, but above all the love of action in the real world. This modern ideology, nourished on Nietzscheanism, exalted by the triumph of nationalism, "fascist" before the birth of Fascism, is strikingly illustrated by a book such as Drieu La Rochelle's *Interrogation*.

Then, freedom having been reconquered, people began to travel. Frenchmen visited Europe, America, Asia. They measured the greatness of the world, its resistance, they became familiar with the convulsions, malaise, psychological epidemics of a Europe and a human world which had lost their moral barriers. "When," Drieu La Rochelle lamented, "shall we cease to weep over the collapse of the old temples?"

Here the Dadaist crisis should be mentioned. Between 1913 and 1927, the influences are so entangled that nothing can definitely be isolated. Considered in itself, no doubt, Dadaism developed on a different plane, it led to another type of poetry, but its attempt completely to liquidate the past found a willing echo among the boldest of the French futurists, who were impressed by the linguistic exercises and games of Max Jacob and Pierre-Albert Birot in his magazine *Sic*, and beginning in the spring of 1918, among the young contributors to *Littérature*. Even before the war Marinetti had demanded the abolition of syntax and the liberation of words. Before the Dadaists, Apollinaire had arranged his words on the page with

the utmost whimsy in *Calligrammes,* and Pierre-Albert Birot had
composed a poem "to be howled and danced." As early as 1917,
Paul Dermée celebrated the Nord-Sud line of the Paris subway in
the following poem which seemed bold for only a few days:

> *De Montmartre à Montparnasse*
> *Cheval de Troie*
> *Pour la paix et la guerre*
> *Tu vas et viens NORD-SUD*
>
> *Coursier sonnaillant de lumières*
> *Voûte de chapelle*
> *Grotte aride*
> *Usine où l'huile coule sur les pièces d'acier*
> *Chambre des morts aux flammes de cierges GARES*
>
> *Refuges contre le beauté du ciel.*

> From Montmartre to Montparnasse
> Trojan horse,
> For peace and war
> You come and go NORD-SUD
>
> Steed clanking with lights,
> Chapel vault,
> Arid grotto,
> Factory where oil flows over steel bars
> Mortuary with candle flames *STATIONS*
>
> Refuges from the beauty of the sky.

(Spirales)

The direction implicit in this type of poetry is obvious. There is
no longer any prosody or metrics in the strict sense of the words.
Syntax is reduced to a few simple connections, and even disjointed
words are used. The most frequent figures are syllepsis and ellipsis.
In "former" times, these elements would have served as notes for a
poem to be composed; now they are no longer integrated into a
system of thought; the poet renounces *making* a poem of them. For if
poetry consists entirely in spontaneous conscious and unconscious
reactions, if it does not dwell in "the order and movement of
thought," and especially not in a deliberate order created by the
mind, but in free associations of images, why weaken it by filling
in the cracks with soft wax, why articulate it and hang it on a
logical frame? This line of reasoning, like many others, is consistent.

Does this mean that the poet deprives himself of the precious help supplied by rhythm? Not entirely; this poetry does not beat time like a metronome, but pulsates like the viscera. And the typographical white space which surround the notations represent the white spaces of thought, while it is condensing and coagulating. Only the psychic peaks emerge on the paper.

But it can be foreseen at this point that occasionally the futurist influences, especially those of *Calligrammes*, would be replaced by the influence of Mallarmé, specifically of his *Coup de Dés*. Mallarmé, Valéry tells us, "very carefully studied the effect of the distribution of white and black spaces, the comparative intensity of various types (even in posters and newspapers). . . . In his system, a page should appeal to the 'glance' that precedes and surrounds the reading, and should 'intimate' the movement of the composition; it must, by a kind of material intuition, by a pre-established harmony between our various modes of perception, or between the rhythmic differences among our senses, foreshadow what is going to take place on the intellectual level. He introduces a 'superficial' reading, which he connects with the 'linear' reading." The extraordinary development of publicity after the war and the vogue of the motion picture have even more strongly suggested the idea of a "surface" composition; it is as though the poem, as its psychological unity disintegrated, felt the need of conforming to a principle of visual unity. However, *Le Coup de Dés* presents a profoundly elaborated and *coherent* idea, and this alone suffices to distinguish Mallarmé from the modern futurists who disregard the internal constellations traced by pure thought, in order to make themselves more open to the imprint of things—they act like an anonymous plasma which yields to the slightest external motions. Moreover, a demon impels them to attach themselves—not to that nature so constantly loved or detested by the poets that it ended by becoming "their own correspondence," their soul—but to things manufactured by man, to the most artificial modes of life, to the skies of pitch and asphalt that envelop us and that are like an anti-nature which oppresses or exalts us.

The syntax of this poetry is as poor as its vocabulary is rich. It feeds on technical terms and slang, on colloquialisms and neologisms, on visual and motor images. The visual images as a rule are hallucin-

atory; they fixate some obsessive detail; most often they are approximations by exaggeration, making gestures seem mechanical and
giving visions, and an air of caricature. Recall *Lampes à Arc* and
Feuilles de Température by Paul Morand. But many visual images
are at the same time motor images; for in most cases the purpose is,
regardless of the pretext or occasion, to evoke conflicts or displays
of energy. Hence the hard, broken, hurried rhythms of these poems.
Drieu La Rochelle writes in *Auto*:

> *Double pulsation accordée comme une étreinte.*
> *Le bond du sang dans mes artères,*
> *Le bond des gaz dans le cylindre.*
> *Mon pied greffe un muscle à la pédale,*
> *Ma main est au volant une liane.*
> *L'auto allonge son ventre chaud au ras de la terre.*

> Double pulsation synchronized like an embrace.
> The leap of the blood in my arteries,
> The leap of the gases in the cylinder.
> My foot grafts a muscle to the pedal,
> My hand is a liana on the wheel.
> The car glides its warm belly along the ground.

> *(Fond de Cantine)*

A whole being is poured forth in this sequence of verbal dis-
charges. A profound accord is suggested between man and the
machine which the human body prolongs and animates.

However, a number of these images are "reversed," i.e., the
simile whose usual function is to illumine the object by associating
it with something familiar, is taken not from nature but from anti-
nature, from the products of human industry. In accordance with a
procedure that the Italian futurists erected into a system, the artificial becomes the normal, that which is most natural. Thus the old
alliance between the self and the landscape tends to be replaced by
a new alliance which might enable man to find himself in the maze
of machinery that is gradually coming to clothe the naked flesh of
the earth. Blaise Cendrars writes:

> *Toutes les femmes que j'ai rencontrées se dressent aux horizons avec*
> *les gestes piteux et les regards tristes des sémaphores sous la pluie . . .*

All the women I have met loom up on the horizon with the pitiful
gestures and sad eyes of semaphores in the rain ...

(*Du Monde entier*)

Anywhere in Paul Morand we can find passages like the following:

Sur les pavés
Où déjà s'établit une lune ovoide,
Un ciel magenta demeure décalqué parmi
Les tuyaux articulés et les arbres en celluloid.

On the avenue
An ovoid moon is sitting and
A magenta sky is stenciled among
The articulated pipes and celluloid trees.

(*Poèmes*, 1914–1924)

This brings us perhaps to the essential point with regard to the
nature and future fate of this poetry. To what extent is it possible
for man's mind to enter into, to assimilate a world transformed by
man, a mechanical world? Will a machine ever be able to *speak* to us
like the reddish brown of an autumn leaf or a wave breaking against
a shore. "In certain almost supernatural states of mind," says
Baudelaire (in *Fusées*), "the full depth of life is revealed in the
spectacle we have before us, however ordinary it may be. This
spectacle becomes its symbol." We know that a poet can find raw
material of a revelation in a horizon of factory chimneys or blast
furnaces. Similarly, the objects that fill our rooms, a vase, a lamp,
a trinket, a crystal paper weight ("a carousel of silences," says
Cocteau) have long had power to condense poetic emotion. There is
no ground for denying a priori that any form or object, a machine,
for instance, might one day make its way into the magic circle. Has
it not made its way into our dreams, sometimes stirring us with a
violence which proves it to be part of our inner lives? Unfortunately,
these emotions are not too varied. In most poems where the machine
appears, it symbolizes only power. Perhaps the monotony of these
affective reactions means only that the human unconscious needs
time to take full possession of a new entity; at first, fear, bewilder-
ment have the upper hand; then, gradually, a process of assimilation
takes place, and a closer network of spiritual analogies is woven
between the inside and the outside. Still, it is to be feared that these

"alliances" may remain imperfect forever, for man cannot hasten the obscure labor of the unconscious, while machines rapidly become outmoded; they belong to a domain of creations that exist only to be replaced and perfected. All the movements of our life are becoming accelerated, but probably this does not apply to our inner time, so that the poetic "efficiency" of the machine will always remain inferior. True, the plow and the sickle can make us dream endlessly; why should the dynamo not have this power tomorrow or the day after tomorrow? Because it will be obsolete or so changed as to be unrecognizable unless material progress slows down . . . .

Of course almost everything can become poetic. It may be maintained that any object at all will assume poetic quality under the proper circumstances, and surely the poet's powers of suggestion, his lyrical transfigurations can accomplish a good deal. But so far, precisely this has been the weakness of the modern futurists. The revelations of which Baudelaire speaks occur only "in certain almost supernatural states of mind," and sometimes it seems as though Blaise Cendrars and his imitators, with all their senses alert, present us with the image of a self whose forces are fixated upon signals coming from the outside, whose attention is focussed on the level of physical sensations, a self which no longer has the resources or the will to perform the spontaneous work of spiritual sifting and elaboration by which reality is transmuted into poetry. The eye of several poets of today, trained by painters, by the cinema, and by experience, has become an instrument capable of following the slightest change in the external scene with a marvelous promptitude; a refinement of the nervous system has made their whole bodies into powerful sounding boards; but their imagination, because it has remained in too frequent contact with the world of the senses, finds it difficult to concentrate, to dig a tunnel, an abyss in the mind, and to plunge into it. "Suppress the soul, the heart, etc . . . . or tolerate them only when absolutely necessary," says Max Jacob in his *Art poétique*. This undertaking is not without danger. The ultimate danger lies not so much in the subject matter of this poetry—however revolutionary or barbarous it may seem—but in the possibility that the very well springs of poetry may be dried up. Whether man will be crushed by things, and, first of all, by his own creations, or whether he will succeed in mastering them, is another problem which the poets must face.

2.

Several works written during the period under consideration reveal constructive intentions. Immediately after the war, constructivism was the avowed aim of the magazine *Esprit nouveau* which voiced the ideas of the cubist painters, of Apollinaire, and of certain architects. This composite aesthetics casts light on the work of Marcello-Fabri and Nicolas Baudin, the poets of "synchronism," or of Fernand Divoire who preferred a "simultaneism" the general principles of which were established by Martin Barzun as early as 1912. But it was the experiments of Blaise Cendrars that laid the foundations of a school. In *Prose du Transsibérien* or *Panama* a breathless poetry strives to emerge from the raw fact, from shattering events, or from the psychological reflex, the unforeseen association that is constantly transforming the self. "There is no truth other than absurd life shaking its ass's ears. Wait for it, lie in ambush for it, kill it" (*Eloge de la Vie dangereuse*). This is a summary philosophy capable only of favoring a lyricism of action, that would give the least heroic minds an illusion of direct and brutal contact with matter. With Cendrars one has the impression of embracing, of coming to grips with the harsh reality that Rimbaud discovered when he came of age (but Rimbaud, having discovered it, fell silent). But Cendrars too endeavors to balance masses, to order simple psychic realities as on an abstract canvas. His self seems to function only as a privileged center, in which all the cries of the world clash and are amplified, a sort of telegraph set receiving messages from everywhere.

There is in Cendrars the rough draft of an epic of modern life, of a certain modern life, that of the traveler, the adventurer breathing the free air of the world. This adventurer remains human, however, and mingles the themes of modernism with those of the lovers' journey and homesickness; he is a man whose pragmatic will is only an imperfect veil for his anxious prescience of, and secret desire for, disaster. At its best, this reckless game involving body and soul gives rise to a tragic poetry in an atmosphere of cosmic storm; the ultimate and only adventure is that of mankind revolving in the void like a monstrous top.

On this path toward the epic, we also find the post-war productions of André Salmon, particularly *Prikaz* and *Age de l'Humanité*.

His aim was to "restore emotion to the impersonal," to discover the poetry immanent in events, whether they relate to the Russian revolution or to the misfortunes of contemporary Frenchmen. Critical or moral judgment must be suspended; "we deliberately reject any intention to absolve, glorify, condemn," says Salmon in the prefatory note to *Prikaz* (1921), "we accept the fact on the plane of the marvelous." Half way between the poetry of Cendrars, in which the raw fact dominates, and that of Apollinaire who steers life toward the dream, Salmon refers constantly to an everyday reality, in which the most insignificant news item is illumined by an apocalyptic light or surrounded by a halo of mystery. Gabriel Bounoure calls it a poetry of the pure event, completely opposed to pure poetry in the sense of Mallarmé and Valéry, in whose eyes all events are prose. Salmon has defined it as a nominalist poetry, turned toward the particular, without reference to the absolute; it does not aim at an inaccessible, illusory aesthetic perfection. "Everything has always been a matter of circumstance." This modesty is touching, and even more moving are André Salmon's sense of the human, his love, his pity, and his feeling, strengthened by the war, for the human tragedy, the "H hour";

> Parti en guerre au coeur de l'été
> Vainqueur au déclin de l'automne
> Titubant d'avoir culbuté des tonnes
> Et des tonnes
> D'explosifs sur le vieil univers patiemment saboté,
> Tu vas avoir quarante ans,
> Tu as fait la guerre,
> Tu n'es plus l'homme de naguère
> Et tu ne seras jamais l'homme que fut à ton age ton père.
>
> Tu es avec ton couteau de tranchée
> Une nuit molle d'ombres
> Quand le ciel n'était que le vomissement fuligineux de la terre se consumant
> . . . .
> Coupé jusqu'au moignon les ailes pathétiques du temps,
> Ton heure c'est l'heure H . . .

Gone off to war in the heart of summer
Conqueror in the late fall
Reeling from having dumped tons

Upon tons
Of explosives on the patiently sabotaged old world
You're going on forty
You've been through the war
You're not the man you used to be
And you'll never be the man your father was at your age.

You with your trench knife
Are a night soft with shadows
When the sky was nothing but the fuliginous vomit of an earth
   devouring itself

.   .   .   .

They've cut the pathetic wings of time to the stumps
Your hour is H hour . . .

                                        (*Age de l'Humanitè*)

In these impassioned verses, eloquence is reborn, and it is
less romantic than Whitmanian. For the time of Art has passed.
Every word must have a sting, every word must continue to throb
with the fever that seized it during its tour through reality. By this
act of becoming poetically conscious of his epoch, André Salmon
anticipated the labor of time, the transfiguration of memory; he
revealed poetic or marvelous elements, like so many ultra-violet or
infra-red rays, in the present, in the most "historical" present.

This marvelous element is not that of the old poets. It lies in the
heart of the world, it is as disturbing as a bad dream. The sweetness
of living that A. O. Barnabooth tasted in one place after another
before the war is dead. But for several years now the violence of life
has also lost its power to exalt young writers. In most of them, at
least, the will to accept the great adventure of machine civilization
has weakened. More than one attempt to escape into the world of
things has ended in failure; the ideologies built upon the concept of
material progress have revealed their fragility; and the illusion of
man's power in a world of objects created by his industry has been
dispelled. A wave of anti-Americanism (in the philosophical meaning of this term) has more or less coincided with the ebb of modernism and futurism. And since 1924, surrealism, successor of Dadaism,
movements such as that embodied in the magazine *Philosophie*, and
other more recent directions, have oriented men's minds toward the
dream, toward concrete thought, toward a new mysticism, and contributed to discrediting the western idea of civilization. Up to a

certain point, the development of poetry is determined by the fate of the century.

As early as 1920, it should be said, Drieu La Rochelle was convinced of the puerility and poverty of pragmatism. According to him, machines are voracious slaves who betray man. The universe is not equal to "his vast appetite." It no longer satisfies him, and will satisfy him less and less, because "these are the last days of the earth's greatness." Having explored everything, devastated everything, having reached the edge of heaven, the limit, man will remain alone with his old dream, the dream of an Atlantis, the thirst for a happiness different from the happiness of possessing spoils.

> *Il tourne autour de la terre et la tête lui tourne.*
> *La ronde*
> *Danse extatique. La terre tournoyant gonfle comme la robe du derviche.*
> *Le cercle de toutes parts.*
> *Le cercle emprisonné dans son sort.*
> *Ta destinée est envoûtée par le trait ferme d'un dessin.*
> *Tu es inscrit dans une figure close.*

> He spins round the earth, and his head spins.
> The round
> An ecstatic dance. The spinning earth swells like the robe of a
>   dervish.
> The circle everywhere.
> The circle imprisoned in its fate.
> Your destiny is held in a geometric enchantment.
> You are inscribed in a closed figure.

> (*Rondeur* in *Fond de Cantine*)

Man is "on board with fifteen hundred million passengers," and he has no other object of desire than the earth.

The current discussed in this chapter lost its impetus as early as 1924, and produced no works of the first rank. This half-failure cannot be imputed only to external circumstances. Poetry is viable only if it succeeds in finding a form, its own form, an intimate order consubstantial with the poem. Only rarely is such an order present. These poets, too passive under the pretext of fidelity to the impression, ended by juxtaposing raw materials in their works. As soon as their faith in the virtue of spacing and other typographical artifices flagged a little, and as soon as the wish to be read overcame them, they cheerfully resigned themselves to writing good consistent prose more or less charged with poetic elements. This was the case with Drieu La Rochelle, Paul Morand, Blaise Cendrars and others. But it must be realized that the organic weakness of this poetry is that it is almost always enslaved by sensation, by external reality; the fountain of sparks of which their poems are made is called forth by external stimuli and accidental associations of images. Deep poetry grows like a plant which has its roots in man's whole being; such plants can be created by the most airy fantasy, and they can burst forth in a dream, but before this can happen there must be a certain spiritual ripening and tension, whether conscious or unconscious.

At present we may hope that these images of the world will find their way into the innermost spirit, we may wait for the moment of their metamorphosis, when they will become symbols—like fine crystals of hoar-frost settling on a wintry branch—and embody an eternal aspect of humanity, while losing none of their ephemeral strangeness. Perhaps tomorrow a great poet will come, a new Verhaeren—he will not be like the first one—who will advance on ground already tilled, and sing the epic of modern life and the modern world.

CHAPTER THIRTEEN

The Play of the Free Spirit

1.

Immediately after the war, dadaism rejected this modern civilization which the pseudo-futurists professed to accept; and the surrealists of 1924 based their faith in the absolute reality of the spirit upon an absolute negation of everyday realities. This violent reaction, this new attempt at escape would no doubt have taken a different form without the example of Apollinaire; if the most radical poetic movement of our time followed in the wake of the post-romantics of the second half of the nineteenth century, it is thanks to him (and to Jarry) and to his deliberate striving to take the path of Rimbaud and Lautréamont. At all events, a very free poetry developed in the entourage of Apollinaire. It distrusted the world of the senses and the whole human heritage, and its function seems to have been to find intermediate paths between life and dream, to establish a liaison between the avantgarde of 1914 and that of 1919. When its mission was accomplished, its left wing was supplanted by the dadaists; and the first impetus of surrealism made the whole movement a thing of the past. All that remains of it today is a few isolated poets, such as Max Jacob, Jean Cocteau, Pierre Reverdy—and Reverdy can be regarded as a pre-dadaist who has recently suffered the recoil of the movements that he helped to release.

Needless to say, such classifications are necessarily arbitrary, since these directions are always embodied in individuals each of whom follows his own path, and since the specific feature of this poetry, often called cubistic to mark its kinship with the paintings of such artists as Picasso, is its Protean elusiveness. We shall confine ourselves to discussing some aspects of this pseudo-cubism and indicating one or two avenues it has opened to the ebullient activity of a new generation.

These poets still feel the need of discrediting the positive universe. There is still no attempt to make the mind impervious to things; on the contrary, the poets seek occasions for close contact with the material world, but they strive to weave their sensations into a slightly diabolical game which will give rise to a sense of greater freedom. The poet cultivates this freedom by creating a void in himself, by "losing countenance," and in the end the game will be something like playing "Aunt Sally" with appearances. He will wander through the landscape with evil intentions, hoping to obtain a revelation of the fundamental disorder of the universe; to see in a flash the mad dance carried on by the herd of forms. This experience will leave in him an undefined anguish, akin to metaphysical anguish.

Liberation from reality was the aim of Apollinaire; and also of Max Jacob, no less strange as an individual, an extraordinary causeur, equivocator, mystic … In Max Jacob, nonconformism is carried to its ultimate consequences: man refuses to recognize himself in his own self. "A personality is nothing but a persistent error," he writes in *Art poétique*. It is irony, which supplies him each day with a key to escape from his prison, "an irony that is apparent or not, and that gives the work that distance without which there is no creation." And this brings ambiguousness to its climax. In Jarry humor preserved a certain logic in the absurd, a "professional" continuity; with Jacob it assumes such equivocal appearances, it has so many facets that it becomes extremely difficult to catch the poet in the act of being ironical, to define his attitude toward his work, and the position of the work itself. It may seem for a moment that the smile of the "stage director" will be revealed in a dark corner and gradually illumine the poem as a whole, but suddenly everything is blurred. Ariel, gleaming and dancing in the rainy dawn, suddenly changes into a grimacing demon scoffing at himself and destroying his own work. At other times Max Jacob makes use of the equipment of a magician, and handles mirror effects in such a way that his refuge becomes impenetrable:

> Les trois dames qui jouent du bugle
> Tard dans leur salle de bains
> Ont pour maître un certain mufle
> Qui n'est là que le matin.

L'enfant blond qui prend des crabes
Des crabes avec la main
Ne dit pas une syllabe.
C'est un fils adultérin.

Trois mères pour cet enfant chauve
Une seule suffirait bien.
Le père est nabab, mais pauvre.
Il le traite comme un chien.

Coeur des Muses, tu m'aveugles
C'est moi qu'on voit jouer du bugle
Au pont d'Iéna, le dimanche
Un écriteau sur la manche.

The three ladies who play the bugle
Late at night in their bathroom
Have for a master a certain cad
Who is only there in the morning.

The blond child who picks up crabs
Yes, crabs in his hand
Doesn't utter a syllable.
He is a son of adultery.

Three mothers for this bald child
One would be quite enough.
The father is a nabob but poor.
He treats him like a dog.

Heart of the Muses, you blind me.
It is I who am seen playing the bugle
At the pont d'Iena, on Sundays
With a sign on my sleeve.

(*Le Laboratoire central*)

The absurdity of people and things, a generalized absurdity, can be read in this poem, as though written with invisible ink.

In Jacob there is almost always an intention to mystify, that is, a need for gratuitous invention without reference to reality, or (more often) with a seeming realism that is only a lure; and the finished poem is meant to deceive, for it is never what it seems to be, either in its literary or moral aspect. What is it actually? "We are holding in our hands an unnamed object, endowed with some kind of monstrous and diabolical life," says Cassou. We, and no doubt the author, as well, will never know its identity, what it represents. We are similarly deceived by the universe, we never know what it "means." The irony here is like a defensive reflex of the mind, which refuses to believe in anything or to be "anything whatsoever." This movement of retreat and exhaustion can be observed in many modern poets, and first of all in Paul Valéry. If it is true that the desire to reject the word is one of the fundamental instincts of our times, it is interesting that two minds as different as Valéry and Jacob should meet at this point. Nor is it an accident if the author of *Laboratoire central* and *Cinématoma* likes to mimic the gestures of bourgeois common sense and to repeat clichés or sentimental trivialities with inimitable inflections; in this way he exorcises himself, he removes from his thought the dross which prevented him from achieving the state of spiritual vacancy that he loves.

Max Jacob's exercises are not without analogy in history. It was said of him that he revived the "macaronic" genre, that he gave a new youth to the skit and the *fatraise*. He himself calls many of his poems burlesque. In the seventeenth century, the burlesque writers, masters of travesty, "liquidated" the fables, images, sentimental themes, and the whole arsenal of metaphors which the poets of the preceding generations from Ronsard to Théophile used and abused. They did this by transposing them from the lyrical to the comic mood, and by paraphrasing them for satirical purposes.* One might say that Max Jacob devoted himself more or less consciously, and with far more shrewdness, to a similar venture. Coming after a great poetic century, and determined not to repeat what had been done many times, he parodied real poems just as he parodied the journalistic style. And in most cases it is impossible to recognize his models.

---

*In the first *Dialogue des morts* by Fontenelle, Scarron addresses Seneca as follows: *Oh, I see that you have not understood the perfection of jesting. It contains all wisdom. One can find absurdity in everything. I could even find it in your own works if I wished, and very easily too. . . . Does this not mean that absurdity dominates everywhere and that the things of the world are not made to be treated seriously? I transposed the divine Aeneid of your Virgil into burlesque verse, and there is no better way of showing that the magnificent and the ridiculous are so close that they touch each other. Everything resembles those tricks of perspective in which figures scattered here and there form, for instance, an emperor if you look at them from a certain angle; if you change your angle, the same figures represent a beggar.*

And yet this poet has now become an intimate of the angels . . . "Juggle no longer, Protagoras. Silence has come to you!" He composes mystical poems; his face no longer has its old grimace, he is unexpectedly calm and innocent:

> *J'attends la paix du soir dans tes plaines fertiles,*
> *Orléanais? faucille oubliée sur les champs,*
> *La Loire est l'éternel emblème des durs travaux d'Adam.*
> *O lointains du lointain? gris bleu pommelé d'îles,*
> *D'églises pommelé? villages endormis,*
> *Lointain d'arbres lointains sur l'océan fragile*
> *Des blés, soyeux espoir que Dieu bénit.*

> I await the peace of the evening in your fertile plains,
> Land of Orleans? Sickle forgotten in the fields,
> The Loire is the eternal emblem of Adam's hard labors.
> O remote, remote? blue gray dappled with islands,
> With churches dappled? sleeping villages,
> Remote, remote trees on the fragile ocean
> Of wheat, silken hope blessed by God.

> (*Voyages* in *Les pénitents en Maillots roses*)

Has Jacob really found his haven of grace? It is difficult to give oneself unreservedly when one has always tried to escape from oneself. So-called "freedom of mind" may be only the reverse side of a certain impotence, the result of an inability to possess anything, to create anything out of one's own substance; and then it becomes impossible to escape from one's ability to change indefinitely. Seen in this light, Max Jacob's adventure would assume the significance of a lesson; the refusal to crystallize, to adopt a form even temporarily, a refusal which amounts to a refusal to exist, would thus reveal all its intrinsic weakness. But we must be on guard against the temptation to fasten a formula upon a mind that has never ceased to play, to upset all predictions. It has recently assumed—with singular success—the person of the popular Breton bard Morven le Gaélique. But the bard does not sing his joys or sorrows. He lends his voice to the flayer of pigs, to the priest who has given his oath of loyalty to the First Republic, to the drunkard who has lost his hat, his fine drunkard's hat. This, I think, is the essential point: Max Jacob needs an object, a human being to whom he gives life, and who is not himself. And he will be even more successful if this being resembles the werewolf, the mad wind of the Breton moors.

2.

A poet who is so detached in the face of a world whose details and accidents are so utterly deprived of value, must welcome indiscriminately everything that is supplied to him by his sensations, his imagination, his dreams. An obvious realism, in the sense that has been traditional since the nineteenth century, characterizes this new whimsical poetry. Everything seems to be food for it, and everything is mingled in it, as in the showcase of a department store or the advertising section of the newspapers; Apollinaire boasted of this similarity in his *Manifesto* of 1918, and Max Jacob goes even farther if we take into consideration the fact that poetry, which for a long time has been trying to assimilate "ugly" images — and the most modern ugliness aroused the enthusiasm of the futurists — has almost always been averse to admitting the petty, the ridiculous. But the effort of these poets tends to transform the very concept of the ridiculous: either a general irony extends its limits to the infinite, or a certain absurdity which has been taken for granted, such as that of the Parisian suburbs before the war, suddenly reveals "unsuspected depths." The essential is the angle from which the spectacle, the event, the seemingly most insignificant news item is viewed. It is as though there existed a vantage point of the mind from which things could be discovered in their purely poetic, i.e., arbitrary and new aspect. But nothing is more difficult than to remain at this vantage point; and nothing is more difficult than to induce the reader to find this vantage point in himself and, by means that are not fallible or hypothetical to make him experience the shock without which the poem is for him devoid of life. It follows that the full effectiveness of this poetry is not objectively demonstrable and can be revealed only by individual experience. This is doubtless true of all genuine poetry, but in this case the complicity asked of the reader is of a special kind — he must have an exceptional plastic sensibility, infused with the atmosphere of an epoch. This is completely different from the labor of progressive penetration that is required in order to understand Mallarmé. The poems of Jacob, Cocteau, of Apollinaire in many instances, and of a great number of their followers, either affect the reader at once or do not affect him at all; strictly speaking this poetry does not contain a secret, and for this reason cannot be called hermetic; its ambition

is to be loved at first sight, and the danger to which it is exposed—
this is sufficiently clear after an interval of a few years—is that the
conditions needed for the transmission of the electricity with which
it is charged will no longer obtain in the future. Its best chance is
to find a reader endowed with a "sense of mystery" (as Cocteau
says) which is akin to that of the poet himself.

This mystery does not dwell in states of mind. Its presence can
rather be detected in unusual conjunctures—it is an occult relation
between seemingly unrelated events, a concatenation of unacknow-
ledged circumstances, an association of images produced by some
demon of analogy, defying all reason. The poem does not trace the
concentric circles of the dancer whose figures bring him back to his
starting point; it is animated by an internal dynamism, it presents
acts, facts. However, it moves on a plane which is not that of everyday life nor quite that of the dream; it subsists in an intermediate
zone, half way between the real and the unreal (or what is called
the unreal), the land of enchantments, of certain forms of mystification, and of the modern fantastic. There is always a psychological
"adventure," even when we can easily discern the sensation or the
optical error that produced the illusion; the poet's task is, as it were,
to transform his entire life into a sequence of adventures, of risks
to be taken, and of situations designed to convince him of the perpetual strangeness of the world. In a sense, it is a way of "cultivating
one's soul," of self-training, an attentive quest for the mysterious
and unforeseen, which may lead to discoveries and to all sorts of
artificialities. Here are a few images illustrating the fantastic
quality of everyday things in Jean Cocteau's poem *Dos d'Ange:*

> *Une fausse rue en rêve*
> *Et ce piston irréel*
> *Sont mensonges que soulève*
> *Un ange venu du ciel.*

> *Que ce soit songe ou pas songe,*
> *En le voyant par-dessus*
> *On découvre le mensonge,*
> *Car les anges sont bossus.*

> *Du moins bossue est leur ombre*
> *Contre le mur de ma chambre.*

A false street in a dream
And this unreal piston
Are lies fomented
By an angel from heaven.

Whether it be a dream or not a dream,
When you look at it from above
You discover the lie,
Because the angels are hunchbacked.

At least their shadow
On the wall of my room is hunchbacked.

(Poésies, 1916–1934)

Pierre Mac Orlan begins the second canto of *Simone de Montmartre* in a different tone:

Le corbeau, derrière un arbre
A l'entrée d'un bouqueteau borgne
Joue seul au poker d'as.
Il surveille d'un oeil vicieux
La route, les champs et la rivière.
Ainsi Georges, l'amant de Simone,
Le bout du nez livide, écrasé sur les vitres de "l'Electric-Bar"
Remue faiblement les dés dans sa main gauche
Et se déforme la bouche avec mélancholie.
Lui aussi surveille le hasard inestimable
Qui se faufile entre les trams et les taxis
Comme un pantin de laine au visage simple.

The crow behind a tree
At the entrance to a gloomy thicket
Plays poker with himself.
He watches with a vicious eye
The road, the fields, and the river.
Thus Georges, Simone's lover
The livid tip of his nose crushed against the windowpanes of the
    Electric Bar
Feebly shakes the dice in his left hand
And grimaces sadly.
He, too, watches imponderable chance
Slinking between streetcars and taxicabs
Like a wool puppet with a simple face.

(Oeuvres poétiques complètes)

In the most favorable case, the impression of mystery and the fantastic seems to spring spontaneously from life, and the poet does not have to trick himself into producing it. In Max Jacob's prose poems the extraordinary sometimes appears in the most natural way, especially in his visions of war (dating from 1909), revolution, universal catastrophe —probably oneirical (according to the author, prophetic) in origin:

> At night the outer boulevards are full of snow; the bandits are soldiers; they attack me with laughs and sabers, they rob me; I run away only to find myself in another square. Is it the courtyard of a barracks or of an inn? what a multitude of sabers! of lancers! snow is falling! someone pricks me with a syringe; it is poison to kill me; a skull veiled with crepe bites my finger. Vague streetlamps cast the light of my death on the snow.
>
> (*Le Cornet à Dés*)

It will be noticed that in these texts, especially the last, poetry is not dependent upon the words, the rhythm (Mac Orlan's free verse is nothing but prose), upon any "alchemy" whatsoever. The image is frequently replaced by direct notation; the language rests upon an oral foundation, often it does not even rise above the spoken sentence. By drawing upon all the clichés of the journalistic style, Max Jacob clearly shows his intention, shared by several poets of his group, to repudiate all concern with verbal creation. The poet is less and less concerned with evoking inner states of the self, or the color of a lyrical reverie, by weaving a network of metaphors, of "correspondences" between the tangible and the spiritual. The main thing is to gather together a few psychological "events" sufficiently uprooted (cf. the preface to *Cornet à Dés*), surrounded by a sufficiently wide margin, to suggest from the outset the presence of an irrational element in the very heart of reality, a disquieting aura, or even of that "universe" supplementary to the scientific universe which Jarry wanted to study by means of his science of pataphysics.

It is clear that the presence of this fluid can be manifested outside the poem. The short story, the novel have attracted Max Jacob, Jean Cocteau, Pierre Mac Orlan, Joseph Delteil, and a whole battalion of poets. The greater part of Cocteau's writings after 1920, and not only those which he calls "theatrical poetry," are a sort of projection made to be seen from a distance, under magnesium lights, of an ensemble of unusual gestures and strange revelations which constitute a code with entangled signs, and this code is the sparkling and enigmatic face of poetry itself.

3.

The principle of the absolute freedom of inspiration, proclaimed by Apollinaire, was ultimately bound to justify uncontrolled invention, spurts of unchecked thought (as both he and Jacob seem to have sensed several years before the war). This confidence in the mind left to itself was to occupy a prominent place in the surrealistic *credo*. Without going so far, Max Jacob (followed by a few post-futurists, including Blaise Cendrars) occasionally published "poems" which abound in instances of echolalia and punning, and seem like mere transcriptions of spoken monologue. It is easy to surmise the advantages of such experiments—an acceleration in the utterance of words; a feeling that the distance between thought and its expression (and the deformation of the thought through expression) is reduced, that the authenticity of words is increased; an opportunity to surprise oneself by permitting seemingly gratuitous impulses to reach awareness; and finally, an impression of being inhabited by an autonomous power which functions outside the conditions required for the existence of the "real" world.

However, none of the "cubist" poets has attempted to fill a book with this kind of improvisation. None has completely renounced composition, art. Quite on the contrary, Max Jacob has stated his desire "to externalize himself by chosen means." He felt that before mere drifting with the associational current could be erected into a method, he must make another step which would involve a radical change in the relationship between the creator and his work. To explain this restraint, one might mention several influences, and recall the constructive intentions of the cubist painters, and the unanimity with which many "advanced" writers express their admiration for clarity of form, purity of line, and sobriety and suggestiveness of expression. From the quatrains of Apollinaire's *Bestiaire* to the brief poems of the Chinese and the Japanese whose hai-kais were imitated in France, to Jules Romains' odes—not to mention the teaching of Gide, the example of Valéry, Toulet, and the always living cult of Mallarmé—a number of works (and precepts) coming from various directions seemed to illustrate more or less felicitously what Cocteau called "the aesthetics of the minimum." They encouraged the composition of self-contained poems, in which a great economy of means produced a very high poetic "efficiency." Thus Max Jacob formulated the "laws" of the prose poem in his preface to *Cornet à Dés* and wrote an *Art poétique;* while Jean Cocteau, after his "molting" which is described in *Le Potomak,* clung to a more or less regular meter. It is interesting in this connection to see old French qualities, renewed it is true, and an often charming taste, submitting to the demands of an art which was as little traditional as possible, at least in appearance.

Jean Cocteau, impertinent page boy of the Champs Elysées quarter, and "grand couturier" of the new spirit, was the Banville of this cubist "fantaisisme," and the spokesman par excellence of what he called the "classical Left." Cocteau has in him an aesthete nourished on Wilde, Mallarmé, Baudelaire. All the traditions of French art of the last seventy-five years meet in him and fertilize a marvelously ready mind, a little dry, and Parisian par excellence, a mind that might have been born in the eighteenth century under the sign of Voltaire. But he feels himself sufficiently rich to throw all these traditions overboard and to play the part of the prodigal son.

Like an acrobatic trick, his poetry tends to be self-sufficient, an aggregate of beguiling reflections, isolated, separated from things that have names, and beings that have bodies. "A poem must lose, one by one, all the cords that attach it to its motivation," he writes. "Each time the poet cuts a cord, his heart beats. When he cuts the last one, the poem is let loose, it rises by itself like a balloon, beautiful as such and without any bonds to hold it to the earth (*Le Secret professionel*)." Cocteau feels that he can discern this Platonic ascension of objects in quest of their essence in the art of Picasso. Similar ideas preoccupied his friends Poulenc and Auric, the composers. All this reveals the poet's conscious or unconscious Mallarméism; for him the poem is like a house of cards which must hold itself together with a minimum of matter and which achieves its maximum tension when the whole structure is in the gravest danger of sinking into insignificance. The raw sensation, caught in flight, is accepted only for its indicatory value; from each occurrence a prepared mind, that is, a mind capable of being perpetually caught by surprise, instinctively extracts a certain number of signs which are ordered into new relationships. References to "what is" vanish almost completely in favor of imponderable forms, which are truer than true nature.

This magic rests upon an infinitely delicate sense of analogies, governed by a hypersensitive nervous system. In the "meadows of inner silence" the poet sees a submarine flora and fauna, he hears a stellar music that follows the rhythm of his blood, and in this abyss he recognizes a projection of the unknown suggested by real things. "I am sick with being a man" (*J'ai mal d'être homme*), we read in *Le Cap de Bonne Espérance*. The sense of life and death, the vague hope of a possible deliverance, those are the sources of Cocteau's poetry at its best; the human sensations then find an echo in a mental desert where the voice of Mallarmé's swan is heard:

> Un combat de pigeons glacés en pleine figure
> Offerte à vos gifles, drapeaux
>
> Le gel qui gante
> Aquarium océanique
> Aspergé d'huile je suffoque
>
> Au bain marin
> Qui s'engouffre dans les narines
> Froide opulence
> D'eau de mer
>
> Péril de chute
> . . . .
>
> Halé
> Humé
> Mon corps interne se pelotonne
> Autour du coeur
>
> Pente infinie
>
> Vallonnements houle on recule
>
> Un roi des aulnes
> Entre les paumes
> Il masse, il caresse mon coeur
> Les sirènes silencieuses
> Dans la poitrine du pilote
> Enflent leur chanson aiguë

Le vol croissant signalé
Par les seuls viscères
L'appareil se hissait
A rien
Par flaques de hauteur.

Icy pigeons battling against my face
Exposed to your buffetings, flags

The frost which gloves
Oceanic aquarium
Sprinkled with oil I choke
In the sea bath
That surges into my nostrils
Cold opulence
Of sea water

Fear of falling

.   .   .   .

Parched by the sun
Sucked in

My inner body nestles
Beside my heart

Infinite slope

Rolling hills sea swell recoil

A king of the alders
Between his palms
Massages, caresses my heart
The silent sirens
In the pilot's chest
Inflate their strident song

Its gathering flight registered
Solely by my viscera
The machine hoisted itself
To nothing
Through pools of altitude.

(*Le Cap de Bonne-Espérance*)

In this "invitation to death" a poetry of physiological and visceral
origin is gradually released from the grip of reality and finally offers
a glimpse of the pulsation of its astral body in that inner sky where
Mallarmé cast his supreme throw of dice.

But often Narcissus, infatuated with himself, abandons the substance for the shadow. In Cocteau's love of prettiness, of the picture post-card, of over-civilized manners, a whole worldly heritage has survived the ascetic discipline to which he submitted when he was about twenty-five years of age. Instead of "catching by surprise the angel"—who awakens in his dreams—he sometimes contents himself with facile parades and beribboned arabesques. One of the temptations threatening this whole "classical Left" is that of preciosity. Yet it is a charming preciosity which it would be wrong to condemn on grounds of Puritanism; Marie Laurencin, "caught in a trap between the *fauves* and the cubists," as Cocteau says in *Poésie*, might be taken as a symbol of this tendency to catch images as one catches butterflies, to "mount" them with as few words as possible, to use but few colors, and to combine elegance and libertinage in a cloud of face powder. Before writing *Le Diable au corps* Radiguet was a master of this type of exercise:

> AUTOMNE
> Tu le sais, inimitable fraise des bois
> Comme un charbon ardent aux doigts de qui te cueille:
> Leçons et rires buissonniers
> Ne se commandent pas.
>
> Chez le chasseur qui la met en joue
> L'automne pense-t-elle susciter l'émoi
> Que nous mettent au coeur les plus jeunes mois?
>
> Blessée à mort, Nature,
> Et feignant encore
> D'une Eve enfantine la joue
> Que fardent non la pudeur mais les confitures
> Ta mûre témérité
> S'efforce de mériter
> La feuille de vigne vierge.

> AUTUMN
> As you know, inimitable wild strawberry
> Like a glowing coal in the fingers that pick you:
> Truant lessons and laughter
> Cannot be made to order.
>
> Does the autumn suppose
> She can fill the hunter about to fire upon her
> With the emotion that the younger months rouse in our hearts?

Mortally wounded, Nature
And still feigning
The cheek of a childlike Eve
Painted not with modesty but with jam
Your ripe temerity
Strives to deserve
The virgin fig-leaf.

(Les joues en feu)

This is an acid madrigal that touches neither the heart nor the soul. The charm operates elsewhere, in the regions of sensibility, wherein also lies the source of what is usually called wit. What is wit? asks Voltaire. It is "sometimes a new comparison, sometimes a subtle hint; here the abuse of a word presented in one meaning yet suggesting another; there, a delicate relation between two uncommon ideas; it is a peculiar metaphor; it is a search for something which an object does not at first reveal, but which actually is in it; it is the art of bringing together two objects separate from each other, etc. *(Dictionnaire philosophique*, article *Esprit)*." It is not surprising to learn that Radiguet named Malherbe, La Fontaine, Tristan l'Hermite among his masters. That a certain poetry which is assuredly not to be scorned, can arise from the surprises, detours, and thrusts of an extremely subtle and ironical intelligence, is sufficiently proved by the literature of the *ancien régime*. Lacking "mystery" and the "fantastic element," poets such as Radiguet, Pascal Pia, René Chalupt and others content themselves with a "witty" and impertinent view of things. Following in the footsteps of Max Jacob and harkening to Apollinaire's siren song, they join with Jean Pellerin, Georges Gabory, and the latest disciples of Toulet, to compose ballet figures of a bold rakishness; they are the extremists of the post-war *fantaisiste* movement.

Thus an important section of this literary cubism, however revolutionary it may be in principle, returns by detours to the tradition of the subtlest French intelligence, after a show of surrender to the unconscious and chance. It even falls into the pleasant defects of traditional minor poetry. Possibly the example of Toulet and Valéry, and the need to separate themselves from the nihilism of the dadaists helped these poets to appreciate the potential advantages of a freely accepted constraint.

In any case one can scarcely deny the existence of a line leading from the "precious" writers of the seventeenth century to the minstrels of art for art's sake, scornful of "ideas" and emotions, and to the present representatives of that special type of pure poetry based on a play of arabesques and *concetti*. Here again we are called upon to admire a "beautiful disorder" which in most cases remains "an artistic effect." But this art has made great strides in its ability to sham, and by a refinement of coquetry, to turn appearances against itself. One would never have guessed that Apollinaire's revolt would lead to this sort of literature.

CHAPTER FOURTEEN

Dada

1.

No doubt a great event, the war, was needed to create some enthusiasm for Rimbaud's desire to "change life" and to make young men look upon revolt against morality, literature, self-evident truths, and the everyday course of things, as the only acceptable attitude. Those who refuse to see in the dada movement anything but a Parisian scandal characterized by violence and buffoonery, will never understand the intense moral crisis of the 1920's and the current of anarchistic individualism, the refusal to be useful, that upset so many traditional slogans and age-old beliefs.

Without attempting to tell the whole story, let us recall that dadaism had at least three points of origin—(1) in the United States, with Marcel Duchamp and Francis Picabia; (2) in Zurich, where Tristan Tzara founded in 1916 a group which he called "Dada," a name that means absolutely nothing; (3) finally, in Paris, where in 1919 these men established contact with a few young writers who had been brought together by their universal suspicion and had just published (in March) the first issue of a magazine entitled, by antiphrasis, *Littérature*. The original purpose of Tzara and his friends seems to have been to organize an "enormous" mystification (aimed at the past, present, and future literary schools), employing the modern resources of publicity in behalf of a school whose intentions were entirely negative, "Ubuesques." Nevertheless, the ideas and sentiments of dada—and in saying this we do not underestimate what André Breton called "Tristan Tzara's admirable spirit of revolt"—seem rather French in origin, although the post-war psychosis saw the hand of Germany in the plot.

The contributors to *Littérature*—at least the younger ones, for the magazine at first opened its pages to Valéry, Gide, etc.—were

on an average twenty years of age in 1917, which in France was
perhaps the grimmest of the war years. Life itself undertook to
destroy whatever illusions they might have had about the "real"
world—: the regimentation of morals, the distortion of religious
feelings, a science that had celebrated its greatest triumphs in the
calculations of ballistics, the greatest "trahison des clercs" (betrayal
of the intellectuals) that mankind had ever seen—there was ample
ground for disillusionment. As for literature, it had fallen a prey
to military chroniclers. "We civilizations know that we are mortal,"
Valéry said a short time later (in *La Crise de l'Esprit*). Can dadaism
be called a wrecking enterprise? In the eyes of André Breton, Louis
Aragon, Philippe Soupault, everything had already been torn down;
dadaism could be only an inventory of the ruins, and a declaration
of the failure, or more accurately, the death of a civilization.

Dada thus appears as a desperate systematic skepticism leading
directly to total negation. Man is nothing. "Measured by the scale
of eternity, any activity is futile," says Tzara. And André Breton:
"It is inadmissible that man should leave a trace of his passage on
earth." Everything is of equal insignificance. "What is beautiful?
What is ugly? What is great, strong, weak? What is Carpentier,
Renan. Foch? Don't know. What is myself? Don't know. Don't
know, don't know, don't know." These words by Georges Ribemont-
Dessaignes are saluted by Breton as an act of great humility. To
utter any judgement, to claim to distinguish the true from the false,
is a mark of ridiculous presumption, for actually nothing can be
contradicted. At about the same time Einstein's theory was en-
couraging people to believe that everything was relative to circumstances, to man, and that nothing in the world had any importance
at all.

One may deplore these negations as paradoxical, puerile, insane,
inhuman; but it must be realized that at a certain moment they
were, "philosophically" speaking, logical and legitimate. Moreover
these opinions were in tune with the humorists of the Jarry school,
such as Jacques Vaché, whom André Breton met at Nantes in
1916, and whose shadow seems to have presided secretly over the
development of dada. Vaché defined humor as "a sense of the
theatrical and joyless futility of everything, when one knows."
In most cases, the idea of the infinite, which is always present, and
the certainty that convention or arbitrariness governs all our

actions suffice to convince man of the absurdity of himself and his life.

One of the essential preoccupations of the dadaists was to draw up an indictment of literature. According to them, the best literature is always imitation; the most sincere writers have always been dependent on others, have been prisoners of tyrannical traditions and, above all, of reason. It is impossible to know oneself, and the most clearsighted man imagines himself, composes and betrays himself before his mirror. Some of Paul Valéry's aphorisms seemed to justify the attitude of these young people who had admired the author of *La Jeune Parque* at a time of intellectual impurity and scarcity, and had been even his friends for a few seasons. "A work of art is always a forgery (i.e. it is a fabrication without any relation to an author acting under the influence of a single impulse). It is the product of a collaboration of very different states of mind." Or: "the slightest erasure is a violation of spontaneity." To this the ungrateful disciples soon retorted: "Let us then choose spontaneity, authenticity, let us act on one impulse, and renounce writing 'works'." For the time being, dada contented itself with acquiescing in such declarations of Valéry as the following: "The striving for a rhythmical, measured, rhymed, alliterated language comes up against conditions entirely alien to the pattern of thought (*Entretiens avec Fr. Lefèvre*)."

If every work of art is a forgery, it is not only because the man who composes it cannot possibly be sincere. In addition to the constraints of art, ordinary language is "the worst of conventions" because it imposes upon us the use of formulas and verbal associations which do not belong to us, which embody next to nothing of our true natures; the very meanings of words are fixed and unchangeable only because of an abuse of power by the collectivity: "one may very well know the word 'hello' and yet say 'good-bye' to the woman one meets again after a year's absence (André Breton, *Les Pas perdus*)." The "improper" word may express a feeling in a way that is quite satisfactory to the subject; in any event, its use is fully justified by the fact that it was spontaneously uttered. Even before the war, Jean Paulhan had made this kind of observation in his magazine, *Le Spectateur*. Now it was time to draw the consequences of these principles. As for the need to be understood, it was of small importance; writing was a private affair. And why write at all? The editors of *Littérature* asked modern writers this question. Solemn or pathetic answers were ridiculed; those approved were the modest or ironical answers, like that of Valéry, "I write out of weakness," or of Knut Hamsun, "I write to kill time."

Needless to say, the public understood none of all this. It demanded art, whatever it might be, and the most modern art, too; it saw gestures, and heard obscure, insulting, blasphemous words. The most serious critics raised the cry of madness, the more indulgent gently censured these young people eager to sow their wild oats, while the culprits themselves wallowed in "the aristocratic pleasure of displeasing." But this pleasure, and all other pleasures derived from the camaraderie and quarrels of Parisian literary life, could not suppress their sense of bitter joy, almost indistinguishable from despair—the joy of flaying a society that crushes man for the greatest evil of all, a civilization whose wretchedness had been bared by the war, in brief, a pseudo-reality which must immediately be proclaimed null and void. "Absolutely incapable of resigning myself to my lot, wounded in my highest conscience by the denial of justice which in my eyes original sin does not excuse at all, I shall not adapt my existence to the absurd conditions of all existence in this world. . . ." This haughty profession of faith opens André Breton's *Confession dédaigneuse*. Whatever use literature after 1919 may have made of these themes and this rhetoric—and fashion and snobbery often debased them—we must not ignore the tragic anguish they reflect. Even if all dadaist poetry were to sink into oblivion, a few sentences would still deserve to be rescued—sentences which are among the most striking ever written to express the precariousness of man's fate and the sorrow of him who is lost and cannot resign himself to his destiny.

Occasionally the writers of the group around *Littérature* use simple language, even in their poems. For instance, Louis Aragon whispers this *Air du Temps* to himself:

> Est-ce que tu n'as pas assez de lieux communs
> Les gens te regardent sans rire
> Ils ont des yeux de verre
> Tu passes tu perds ton temps tu passes
> Tu comptes jusqu'à cent et tu triches pour tuer dix secondes encore
> Tu étends le bras brusquement pour mourir

N'aies pas peur
Un jour ou l'autre
Il n'y aura plus qu'un jour et puis un jour
Et puis ça y est
Plus besoin de voir les hommes ni les bêtes à bon Dieu
Qu'ils caressent de temps en temps
Plus besoin de parler tout seul la nuit pour ne pas entendre
La plainte de la cheminée
Plus besoin de soulever mes paupières
Ni de lancer mon sang comme un disque
Ni de respirer malgré moi
Pourtant je ne désire pas mourir
La cloche de mon coeur chante à voix basse un espoir très ancien
Cette musique je sais bien. Mais les paroles
Que disaient au juste les paroles
Imbécile

Have you not had your fill of commonplaces
People look at you without laughing
They have glass eyes
You pass, you waste your time, you pass,
You count to a hundred and you cheat to kill ten more seconds
Abruptly you stretch out your hand to die
Don't be afraid
One day or another
There will be only one day to go and one day more
And then that's it
No more need to see men or the dear little beasts
They fondle from time to time
No need to talk to yourself at night to keep from hearing
The wail of the chimney
No need to raise my eyelids
Nor to hurl my blood like a discus
Nor to breathe in spite of myself
Yet I do not want to die
Softly the bell of my heart sings an ancient hope
I know the music well. But the words
Now what exactly were the words saying
Idiot.

(Le Mouvement perpétuel)

Is this a summons to silence, a summons to renounce all literature? Such was the teaching of Rimbaud. The idea of such a sacrifice
is tempting, but it is difficult to carry it out, to cease protesting, to
break one's pen. And then there was something else, something
different from an absolute negation, which gradually came to light in
the dada movement. After everything had been swept clean, a reality
remained. To be sure, it was not reason or intelligence or feeling,
but the obscure source of the unconscious which feeds our being and
which governs even our loftiest actions, the spirit. The first slogans
were soon enriched by the formula: dictatorship of the spirit. Zurich,
the birthplace of dada, is the city of Bleuler and Jung, psychologists
related to Freud; Louis Aragon and Breton had occasion to experiment with the methods of psychoanalysis. Here the essential is not
the thesis of pansexualism, but the theory (that had been advocated
by scientists such as Pierre Janet) according to which our conscious
activities are only surface manifestations, most often determined
by unconscious forces which constitute the substance of the self. And
as Jacques Rivière said, Freud emphasized "the hypocrisy inherent
in consciousness," the general tendency that "drives us to camou-
flage ourselves," to seek justifications of our words and acts, to cheat
at all times in order to make ourselves look more beautiful or at least
to "adjust" ourselves. His theory justified in attitude of systematic
distrust which curiously confirmed Valéry's statements on "forgery"
in literature and on the impossibility of being sincere. The influence
of Freud on the dada movement has sometimes been contested; possibly it amounts to little, but the meeting of the Viennese philosopher and the poets on this common ground is nevertheless a significant symptom.

We are now in a position to formulate the problem of art, more
accurately the problem of expression, as it appeared to the writers
of the *Littérature* group: only the unconscious does not lie, it alone
is worth bringing to light. All deliberate and conscious efforts,
composition, logic, are futile. The celebrated French lucidity is
nothing but a cheap lantern. At best the "poet" can prepare traps
(as a physician might do in treating a patient), with which to catch
the unconscious by surprise and to prevent it from cheating. The
goal was clearly indicated by Jacques Rivière: "To grasp our being
before it has yielded to consistency; to seize it in its incoherence or
better, in its primitive coherence, before the idea of contradiction

has appeared and compelled it to reduce and construct itself; to replace its logical unity, which can only be acquired, by its absurd unity, which alone is innate." As for art, it was repudiated, or at least there was no more question of any activity aiming at the elaboration, however free, of anything reminiscent of a finished work. Is this the ultimate outcome of the great romantic adventure which began in France on the day when an enemy of reason, of society, of civilization, of reality, an apostle of primitivism, declared that the only "perfect and full" happiness consisted in being absorbed in those regions of the mind which had remained intact and "innocent"?

2.

Our foregoing remarks have been a little in the nature of a theory of Dadaist poetry (if it is possible to combine such incompatible terms). Actually, the same label covered very different types of goods. André Breton became the center of a group of poets under the influence of Apollinaire, Jacob, Cendrars, and Reverdy. In 1919, to rebel against literature was inevitably to rally to a tradition. Hence the many criss-crossing paths one discovers if one leafs through the issues of *Littérature*.

A prominent place among these forerunners belongs to Pierre Reverdy who published his works in *Sic* and *Nord-Sud* during the war. In him we are fortunate to find someone who speaks simply of poetry that was not very accessible. "The poet," he says, "is in a difficult and often perilous position, at the cruelly sharp intersection between two planes, the plane of dreams and the plane of reality. Imprisoned in appearances, crowded into this narrow and moreover purely imaginary world with which the purely vulgar herd is contented, he transcends its obstacles to attain the absolute and the real; there his mind moves with ease. There we must follow him, for that which *is*, is not that dark, timid, and despised body that you absentmindedly run into on the sidewalk—it will pass like everything else—but these poems outside the form of the book, these crystals precipitated after the effervescent contact of the mind with reality." Only a "long, immense, and reasoned derangement of all the senses" can lead to this contact. Like Rimbaud, Reverdy aspires to reach the unknown, that is to say, the real. He dives into a narrow zone between dream and wakening life, and then walks "with ease" like a somnambulist in the middle of the world. Miracles await him there: the sun roams round a house, the sound of a bell dies away, a word is said, there comes a bird, or the wind, or a hand, or another hand holding snow. And the things on which people ordinarily spend themselves relapse into nothingness.

Thus there develops a poetry, which Reverdy calls "plastic." It is wholly mental plasticity, without picturesqueness or images of the accidental, an aggregate of dismembered sensations, of relationships from which all logic, as well as all human values, is banished. The meaning of human beings, of motions, is never revealed; everything remains anonymous; of a man who resembles him (and who resembles Coeuvre in *La Ville*) Reverdy says: "He does not relate his travels, he does not know how to describe the countries he has seen. Perhaps he has seen nothing, and when one looks at him he lowers his eyes or raises them to the sky, lest he be questioned." Each of his poems recomposes piecemeal a still life over which a strange anxiety hovers:

> Tout s'est éteint
> Le vent passe en chantant
> Et les arbres frissonnent
>
> Les animaux sont morts
> Il n'y a plus personne
> Regarde
>
> Les étoiles ont cessé de briller
> La terre ne tourne plus
> Une tête s'est inclinée
> Les cheveux balayent la nuit
> Le dernier clocher resté debout
> Sonne minuit.

Everything is extinguished
The wind goes singing by
And the trees shiver

The animals are dead
There is no longer anyone
Look

The stars have ceased to gleam
The earth no longer turns
A head is bent
Its hair sweeps the night
The last bell tower that has remained standing
Rings midnight.

(Les Epaves du Ciel)

Everything foreshadows the imminent threat of a metaphysical event, and one is compelled to cry out for a human pulsation, a human cry that might pierce the impenetrable, monotonous atmosphere.

It is impossible to conceive of a poetry more denuded than this, more unmindful of the glamor of words, of the grace of images. Very little is left here of symbolism and the derivative styles, of the "old poetic rubbish" from which Rimbaud strove to free himself. Pierre Reverdy is like a man who wishes to reevaluate all existing literary implements and methods — even the most common — and learns how to speak all over again. "Picasso," he says, "made up his mind to consider as nought the enormous mass of knowledge and experience that he had acquired, and called upon himself to learn everything — that is to say, to begin everything afresh." To begin all over again is the only hope of the young poets and moralists of despair. André Gide knew this well when, to please them, he published an excerpt from his *Nouvelles Nourritures* in the first issue of *Littérature*: "Tabula rasa. I have swept everything away. It's all over! I stand naked on the virgin earth, behind the sky which must be repopulated," and further on, he asks: "Ah, who will deliver our minds from the heavy chains of logic?" Between 1917 and 1919 there was a moment when Pierre Reverdy, more completely than Apollinaire and Max Jacob, and more even, than Jean Cocteau, seemed to embody this aesthetic and moral radicalism akin to that of the cubist painters, this profound ingenuousness. He greatly influenced André Breton and Philippe Soupault, and even more to Louis Aragon. His influence encountered that of Blaise Cendrars, of the post-futurists, and of modern publicity. In the Paris of the armistice, the language of posters and neon signs created new hallucinations. An ill wind, "the air of the times," tore everything from its place and carried it away in a whirl. But Reverdy and the post-futurists did not share the same orientation.

Reverdy gave an example of an intuitive art, seeking contact with a purely inner reality through a bind of second sight; the post-futurists summoned the poet to turn toward the modern world and let himself be molded by his sensations.

"Introversion" and "extraversion" are oversimplifications because they suggest an absolute opposition. For all practical purposes there is no great distance between a futuristic poem by Paul Dermée or Pierre-Albert Birot and a poem by Reverdy; both record only the downbeats of thought, disposing psychic islets and blots of poetry, as it were, on the page, and in more than one modernist the peripheral sensations emerge to the surface only after going through the "central laboratory" of the psyche. However, in theory there is an antithesis between the two attitudes, between a poetry of the world of the senses, which is temporal, and a poetry of the mind, oriented toward dreams and the nontemporal; the actual development of literature from 1915 to 1925 and beyond justifies this distinction.

As for the "absolute" dadaist poem, needless to say, it gives the reader a most striking impression of incoherence—"words at liberty," shreds of sentences, disintegrated syntax, and occasionally phrases borrowed from contemporary advertisements. Is this the voices of the unconscious? Or an application of the method advocated by Tzara: "Take a newspaper, take scissors, choose an article, cut it out, then cut out each word, put them all in a bag, shake . . .?" One wonders. No doubt the dadaists, too, hesitated between these two paths, that of mystery and that of mystification, between the "everything is at stake" and a taste for the feigned jest, between docile submission to the injunctions of the unconscious and a call for external accidents and verbal coincidences. It is true that most often these two paths merge, to produce a procession of unreadable litanies which would interest only a psychoanalyst.

But there are short poems bearing the dadaist label, which sum up a whole atmosphere:

> L'avion tisse des fils télégraphiques
> Et la source chante la même chanson
> Au rendez-vous des cochers l'apéritif est orange
> Mais les mécaniciens des locomotives ont les yeux blancs
> La dame a perdu son sourire dans les bois.

The airplane weaves telegraphic wires
And the fountain sings the same song
At the coachmen's rendezvous the aperitif is orange-colored
But the locomotive mechanics have white eyes
The lady has lost her smile in the woods.

In these lines by Philippe Soupault we feel something like a gust of fresh air on a spring morning in the Paris suburbs. For some time Tristan Tzara specialized in elucubrations strewn with lapses and burlesque strokes:

Un cristal de cri angoissant jette sur l'échiquier que l'automne.
Ne dérangez pas je vous prie la rondeur de mon demi-langage.
Invertébré.
Un soir de calme le beauté. Une jeune fille que l'arrosage transforma la route voilée de marécage.

.   .   .   .

Les Spartiates mettaient leur paroles sur la colline pour que les renards rongent et arrachent leurs entrailles. Un photographe passa. Comment, me dit-il, osez-vous galoper sur les champs réservés à la syntaxe? La parole, lui dis-je, a cinquante étages, c'est un gratte-dieu. C'était vrai, car le photographe n'était qu'un parasite de la compagnie générale des demangeaisons.

A crystal of anguishing cry casts on the chessboard which autumn.
Please do not disturb the roundness of my demi-language.
Invertebrate.
A peaceful evening beauty. A young girl that the sprinkling transformed the road veiled with swamp.

.   .   .   .

The Spartans used to put their words on the hill so the foxes could gnaw their entrails and tear them out. A photographer went by. How dare you, he said to me, gallop on the fields reserved for syntax? Words, I told him, have fifty stories, they are god-scrapers. This was true, because the photographer was only a parasite of Itches Ltd.

(Printed in *Littérature*, No. 5)

This is a mere curiosity and inconsequential.

By contrast, Paul Eluard used language in an unwonted way from the very beginning. Without forcing anything, naturally and simply, he diverted words from the things they usually signify; the most familiar of them seem to be reborn before one's eyes, to have regained

their innocence, to be prepared for any adventure; the varied possibilities they suggest and the new uncertainty concerning the scope
of their connection with their surroundings cleanse them of all sin
of utilitarianism. The following verbal drawing is entitled *Salon*:

>*Amour des fantaisies permises*
>*Du soleil*
>*Des citrons*
>*Du mimosa léger.*

>*Clarté des moyens employés*
>*Vitre claire*
>*Patience*
>*Et vase à transpercer.*

>*Du soleil, des citrons, du mimosa léger*
>*Au fort de la fragilité*
>*Du verre qui contient*
>*Cet or en boules*
>*Cet or qui roule.*

>Love of permissible fantasies
>Of the sun
>Of lemons
>Of the light mimosa.

>Clarity of means employed
>Clear glass
>Patience
>And vase to be pierced.

>From the sun, from the lemons, from the light mimosa
>To the extreme fragility
>Of the glass that contains
>This gold in balls
>This gold that rolls.

It is possible to be sure, to discern the equivalent of a subject
matter; but the subject matter is an intruder, and any reference to
an external reality casts a shadow on this sun, breaks this vase, this
glass, this light gold. An exchange takes place between a careful and
purified language and the reader's sensibility. On this point, Paul
Eluard explains himself in a few words appealing for their brevity
which at the same time inspires a certain regret: "Beauty or ugliness
does not seem necessary to us. We have always been much more
concerned with power or grace, with sweetness or brutality, with

simplicity or balance." We must also emphasize the following profession of faith: "Let us try, though it is difficult, to remain absolutely pure. We shall then perceive everything that binds us. And as for the unpleasant language which suffices the garrulous ... let us reduce it, let us transform it into a charming, true language...." In this state of purity and perfect abeyance that the poet tries to achieve, language renounces its interpretive function and aspires toward an autonomous existence, producing a confused illogical pleasure, an indefinable sensation of release from gravitation. "I dream of new harmonies," Gide wrote at that time, "of an art of words, more subtle and more frank, without rhetoric, which does not seek to prove anything." And André Breton writes: "A monstrous aberration makes relations."

We are perhaps entitled to cherish these verbal associations for the sake of the disinterested satisfaction they give us, for the new psychic precipitates they create by summoning thought to take pleasure in itself and to expand its capacity for dreaming. Poets, in any event, were irresistibly driven to this verbal chemistry, this melting pot in which some philosopher's stone was being engendered. "It is known now that poetry must lead somewhere." André Breton declared. In short, the question remains: are the linguistic accidents which occur whenever the poet breaks traditional associations without trying to reproduce a model or express a feeling, nothing but inconsequential games, or can they under some circumstances correspond almost in spite of us to something that has an authentic existence? Are we justified in ignoring them under the pretext that nothing in visible reality or in logical thought guarantees the value of such accidents, or must we rather regard them as outcroppings or signs of a reality of which we are unaware or only vaguely aware, as intermittent throbbings of a spiritual world in which all beings participate? Is it conceivable that we may for once escape from the relative world and find access, with the help of poetry, i.e., language, to the mysterious domain of the Mothers? It is with such arguments that dadaism countered the accusation that it was purely subjective. But these concerns lead us far away from the noisy negations of the initial period; all this mysticism, after contributing to the death of dada—which was to die of its own will—paved the way for its transformation and resurrection.

CHAPTER FIFTEEN

Surrealism

1.

"During recent years I have realized the damage wrought by a certain intellectual nihilism whose malice consisted in raising, upon every possible occasion, the broadest and most futile question of confidence." It was in these terms that André Breton toward 1924 turned away from his past and from Dadaism. He was determined to open a path for a new offensive onslaught "a wave of dreams": the quest for the marvelous and for integral poetry; cries of hatred against what is; aspirations toward a total freedom of the mind, all this thrown together pell-mell in a *Manifesto* alternately imperious and nostalgic.* Since then, in the magazines that he successively directed or "inspired" (*Révolution surréaliste, Surréalisme au Service de la Révolution, Variétés, Documents, Minotaure*, etc.), André Breton has applied himself to defining the only attitude which he considers "pure." Welcoming some writers, excommunicating others like a veritable Saint-Just of surrealism, he led his group—which today includes only two or three of the original elect—from anarchistic subjectivism to the "cult of the East," to a certain satanism colored with occultism, to a dialectical materialism, and finally to a doctrine that attempts to allot a proper place both to the inner universe of the spirit and to the world of external things.

At first sight this development seems rather disconcerting. Breton and his followers approve of the famous words of the Communist Manifesto wherein Marx asserts that the time has come to change

---

*If we were writing history, we should mention the fact that the surrealist movement, before it yielded to the impetus of Breton, had arisen in several places; and we should say something of the part played by Ivan Goll at that time.

the world which the philosophers have been trying too long and vainly to explain. But in their view the will to transform this world is not prejudicial to the will to know it. They strive to remain on the crest that separates these two activities, and it is possible that they still hope in this way to work toward an increase of the powers and possibilities of that Spirit, for the advent of which some of them were ready to sacrifice everything in 1925. A complete picture of surrealism must however include an account of the various heresies and heretics; in the camp of the revolution, poetic or otherwise, the nonconformists are not always the least interesting.

In the restricted sense of the term, surrealism is a method of writing; in the broad sense, it is a philosophical attitude which is (or was) also a *mystique*, a poetics, and a politics. The manifesto of 1924 defines surrealism in the restricted sense as follows: "A psychic automatism with the help of which we propose to express the real functioning of thought, either orally, or in writing, or in any other way. A dictation of thought without any control by reason, outside all aesthetic or moral preoccupations." Needless to say, this dictation—the writer confines himself to heeding the orders of "the voice"—takes place only under favorable conditions; the subject must ignore the surrounding reality, he must, to the greatest possible degree, close the doors (the senses) leading to the external world, put his reason to sleep and keep himself in a dreamlike state, then listen (but without deliberate effort) and write, write, following the accelerated course of his thought. The danger is that one may escape from the shadows for one second, emerge into a clearing, regain consciousness. There is no doubt that many poets had the impression of blindly obeying their stream of consciousness at privileged moments. But the feat is a difficult one. Moreover, it would be erroneous to reduce all the surrealistic modes of expression to automatic writing and to regard as "genuine" only texts written under dictation and without any control. "We have never claimed," André Breton admitted in 1932 (in a letter to Rolland de Renéville), "that any surrealist text was a perfect example of verbal automatism. It must be admitted that certain frictions can be discerned even in the least 'directed' texts. . . . A minimum of direction subsists, usually through the "arrangement of the text into a poem." . . . "Integral poetry," like Valéry's "pure poetry," remains a hyperbole, to use a term of Mallarmé.

André Breton and Philippe Soupault gave the title of *Les Champs magnétiques* to the first of their works which in their eyes deserved to be called "surrealistic." Here I shall quote a few beautiful and moving sentences, essentially lyrical, from the opening pages: "To-night there are two of us by the river that overflows with our despair. . . . We think of the glimmering lights of bars, of the grotesque balls in those shattered houses where we left the day. But nothing is more desolate than this light flowing gently over the roofs at five in the morning. The streets diverge silently and the boulevards come to life: a belated walker smiles not far from us. He has not seen our wild eyes and he passes softly. It is the sound of the milk wagons that dispel our torpor, and the birds soar heavenward in search of divine nourishment. . . ." Here we have plainly a romantic bohemian dawn; the amount of absurdity is infinitesimal. But most of the pieces in *Champs magnétiques* are made of different stuff; even though the syntax is correct, incoherence breaks out in every line; the ideas and forms that emerge as we read are constantly destroyed and negated by abrupt illogicalities: "Lovely mine explosions are in the offing, while upside down, the elegant ladies, leave for a trip to the center of the earth. Someone has told them of buried suns. Big chunks of created space rush full speed to the pole. The polar bears' watch shows the hour of the ball. . . ." Or: "In a glass full of a garnet-red liquid, an intense boiling produced white rockets which fell back in misty curtains. The men with dull eyes approached and read their fate in the frosted window panes of the economical dwellings. . . ."

"The vice called surrealism," writes Louis Aragon, "is the immoderate and passionate use of the drug which is the 'image.'" And indeed most surrealist texts disclose an incessant flow of images whose common characteristic is that they defy common sense. But long ago Baudelaire shocked academic critics by cultivating a certain "impropriety" of expression favorable to poetry (cf. Brunetière). Consider, for example, *La Chevelure*:

> *Fortes tresses, soyez la houle qui m'enlève . . .*

> Thick tresses, be the wave that carries me off . . .

Here the condensation is particularly strong:

> *Cheveux bleus, pavillon de ténèbres tendues*
> . . . .

Sur les bords duvetés de vos mèches tordues
Je m'enivre ardemment des senteurs confondues . . .

Blue hair, canopy of spreading shadows
. . . .

At the downy edges of your twisted locks
Ardently I make myself drunk with confused scents . . .

And in *Sed non Satiata:*

Je préfère au constance, à l'opium, aux nuits,
L'élixir de ta bouche où l'amour se pavane;
Quand vers toi mes désirs partent en caravane,
Tes yeux sont la citerne où boivent mes ennuis.

To constancy, to opium, to the night
I prefer the elixir of your mouth where love preens itself;
When my desires set out in a caravan for you,
Your eyes are the cistern in which my sorrows drink.

Lyrical transfiguration is achieved only at the price of logical incoherence, of a contradiction in terms. Needless to say, this phenomenon did not make its first appearance with Baudelaire; in every metaphor there slumbers a catachresis, and the magical power of poetry has always consisted first and foremost in unusual associations and in a supple, insinuating manner of using words. In the classical period, many examples of this can be found in the euphuists and the precious poets, both French and foreign, especially in Gongora. But with Baudelaire, "the first of the seers" as Rimbaud called him, the imagination became aware of its demiurgic function. Grafted on a mystical sense of "universal correspondence," it anticipates its immense task of revealing by means of images the essential kinship of all things, the participation of all things and souls in an all-pervasive mind, in the "dark and profound unity" of the whole. Most of Baudelaire's successors were not inclined to accept this metaphysics, but if we confine ourselves to an analysis of the use of imagery for the last seventy-five years, we must admit that the surrealist catachreses represent the terminal point of a perfectly clear line of development, the various stages of which are easily distinguished. Side by side with Rimbaud, Mallarmé, we must accord a prominent place to such poets as Lautréamont, Jarry, Saint-Pol Roux, and Maeterlinck (in his *Serres chaudes* he is the authentic precursor of post-war poetry), who for some time specialized in the search for verbal associations combining the physical and the spiritual—"the reseda of modesty," "the slow palms of my desires," or "the lavender herb of absences."

In the eyes of the absolute surrealists, everything is possible in the realm of images. For them the fallacy lies precisely in attempting to establish a rationally justifiable relation between the associated terms. The first romantics and their readers believed that the relation expressed by the image should be motivated; gradually, the area of the circle was extended, and the poets began to seek their equivalence at the end of the world; less and less applicable to the object, the image ceased to illumine anything whatsoever in the tangible world; ever less reasonable and useful, ever more independent and alien, it ended by assuming the aspect of an intrinsic creation, a "revelation." The definition given by Reverdy in 1918 seems to have been taken literally by André Breton's group—"The image," said Reverdy, "is a pure creation of the mind." Reverdy explained further: "The characteristic of the strong image is that it derives from the spontaneous association of two very distant realities whose relationship is grasped solely by the mind." And there is this most important reservation—"If the senses completely approve an image, they kill it in the mind" (*Le Gant de Crin*, pp. 32, 34)—and this seems to have been translated by the most intransigent surrealists as follows: "If the senses approve an image even in the slightest degree, they kill it." Paul Eluard said later: "The world must be desensualized."

In a note added in 1919 to the original text of *Introduction à la methode de Leonard de Vinci*, Paul Valéry maintained that all things were interchangeable ("everything is equal"), the characteristic of the mind consisting in its ability to associate "any" objects and forms. In the eyes of the surrealists, the unconscious spontaneously wields this power of substitution; but it does not confine itself to creating abstract relations; it makes objects participate in one another, it mysteriously identifies them. Thus, in the dream, the framework of the principle of contradiction is exploded; everything can replace everything else without losing existence and concrete power. The dissimilarity of objects is only apparent, it is only a product of reason and habit. "The unity of the mind rediscovered in the multiplicity of matter," such is the definition of the image according to the critic Pierre Guéguen, who goes on to say that "the image is nothing but a magical form of the principle of identity." Every surrealist text presupposes a return to chaos, within which there is outlined a vague super-nature; "stunning" chemical combinations between the most dissimilar words, and new possibilities of synthesis are suddenly revealed in a flash.

Thus there is a blossoming of highly poetic images: "In colored glasses . . . a fan of alcohol"; "When I am asleep my throat is a ring with a tulle signboard"* (Paul Eluard); "On the bridge the cat-faced dew rocked itself to sleep"; "the pretty carpentry of sleep" (André Breton); "delirium with crystal fingers" (Pierre Reverdy); and so many others. Let us note that these images, logically more or less absurd, by reason of their strangeness, more or less disconcerting to the senses, nevertheless produce sensuous representations; will-o'-the-wisps leap here and there, irradiations, Hertzian waves propagate themselves in the night. Whatever care the mind takes to isolate itself, it cannot help being fed by elements originating in the external world; it cannot tell its history, however inward it may be, without borrowing forms that have bodies and bear names. Similarly a fortune-teller must translate (and often betray) her obscure intuitions, which are ineffable as such, into phrases and fables. But the surrealist poet must obstruct any practical utilization of his language, and for this purpose he must use expressions devoid of any intellectual or sensuous evidence; in this way all references one may be tempted to find in the realm of clear ideas or the realm of familiar realities, will be rendered illusory. This is the difficult part of the task: to create, or rather to permit the involuntary, unconscious formation of a different kind of evidence, purely psychic if possible, appealing to a certain inner and poetic sense in us, which merges, perhaps, with our very sense of inner being.

---

*Is this a *dictated* image? Perhaps. But the unconscious has a good memory. At the end of the lullaby in *Jeune Parque*, there are the following lines:

> *La porte basse, c'est une bague . . . où la gaze*
> *Passe . . . Tout meurt, tout rit dans la gorge que jase.*

> The low door is a ring . . . where gauze passes . . .
> Everything dies, everything laughs in the throat that chatters.

2.

This undisciplined use of language raises certain psychological problems. It has been likened to what Bleuler of Zurich called autistic
thought, a thought which is illogical and asocial, in contrast to
"directed" thought, which aims at adjustment to reality. But for
Bleuler "autism" is clearly pathological; moreover, it cannot be
identified with the phenomena of automatism. It has also been
likened to the free and incoherent monologues that psychoanalysts
try to obtain from their patients. Finally, it has been likened to the
day-dream, so "vastly underestimated" as Léon Daudet* said, which
revolves in us almost constantly like a slow kaleidoscope creating on
the background of consciousness, amorphous, evanescent figures
whose destinies are mysteriously bound up with the effective stirrings of the self. But here again the question should be restated in
more precise terms, because the rudimentary psychic realities referred to usually exist outside language. Paul Eluard and André Breton
have recently applied themselves to simulating the linguistic delirium of certain types of mental patients, "without experiencing the
corresponding states of mind in the process" (*L'Immaculée Conception*, introduction). This is an important admission. It is as though
thought were like an impersonal plasma capable of yielding to the
least perceptible injunctions, of outlining any motions and uttering
any words. Let us imagine a stallion properly trained, who obed-
iently performs the most absurd tasks the moment he is ordered to
do so. "For me," André Breton says bluntly, "the most effective
image is the one that has the highest degree of arbitrariness, I
make no attempt to conceal this ..." (*Manifeste du surréalisme*,
1st ed.). From this point it is only one step to giving a completely
arbitrary direction to one's spontaneous linguistic production,

---

*In *Le Rêve éveillé* we read: *Dream is mingled with our everyday life, even in waking
hours, much more constantly and completely than oneirologists have supposed. In normal
persons the daydream (so vastly underestimated) is present almost continuously. Even while
we are engaged in a conversation or observing a beautiful scene, even while we act, or
think about some specific problem ... an important part of our mind is dreaming. ...
The dream must be regarded as a constant procession on the mental horizon of fragments
of memories, of all sorts of images ... premonitions, forebodings, and signs of an indisputable reality, whose mechanism is totally unknown to us.* Cf. also Jean Cazaux,
Surréalisme et Psychologie (Corti, 1938).

whether this leads to "arrangement into a poem" or to simulated psychosis.

In short, whether we study the surrealist texts from the standpoint of literature or of psychology, they are ultimately revealed to be products of culture, and of the most advanced culture—by no means resulting from the free exercise of a faculty or verbal invention shared more or less equally by all men.* Perhaps these are not "conscious"; but the subliminal memory of poets such as Aragon, Breton, Soupault, or Eluard teems with romantic and post-romantic reminiscences. It is extremely doubtful whether the surrealists have succeeded in producing an authentic image of spontaneous dreamlike thought. On the contrary, it seems that in many cases they have set in motion rather superficial mechanisms and have propagated a current of "literary" thought that is almost always "directed," even though this may be contrary to the will of the authors. "Black is not as black as all that," says Valéry's *Jeune Parque*.

We may go farther: some of the surrealist poems manufactured on the assembly line during the last few years strike the reader as capricious games, less entertaining than monotonous; their authors flout logic for the fun of it or from weariness, all the while taking a secret pride in the freedom of their frolics. And what shall we say of those "attempts at simulation," which reflect no element of the poet's state of mind? Nothing perhaps is more gravely symptomatic of their whole attitude than their acceptance of such a divorce between concrete experience and the word. The artistic "forgery" (Valéry's designation for any work of art) from which the dadaists swore to escape has merely been replaced by a psychological forgery. It seems to me that this experiment—recorded in the texts collected in *Immaculée Conception*—had to be carried out, and that it helps us to understand the attitude of indifference toward their products that one cannot help ascribing to so many surrealists. "The value of a work of art," says Pierre Reverdy, "is in direct proportion to

---

*In December 1933, however, Breton reiterated his original thesis: *The distinction of surrealism is to have proclaimed the total equality of all human beings before the subliminal message, to have constantly maintained that this message constitutes a common patrimony of which anyone can claim his share. . . . All men, I say, and all women deserve to be convinced of the absolute possibility, for themselves, of resorting at will to this language which is not supernatural at all and which is the very vehicle of revelation for us and for everybody.* (*Le message automatique,* reprinted in *Point du Jour.*)

the intensity of the poet's contact with his fate." This wise statement shows the dangers to which these writers are exposed—that of dropping the substance for the shadow and of emptying the word of its vital essence.

It would indeed be unjustified to reject and condemn a priori the surrealist methods and modes of expression. But it is important to realize that though their methods, especially that of automatic writing, may serve as a means of poetic expression and though, in theory at least, they shall be eminently favorable to the development of subterranean deposits of the unconscious in the form of images and symbols, they cannot be relied upon to perform this function infallibly and of themselves.

3.

But surrealism is not merely a certain manner of letting one's pen run on. André Breton and his friends pressed their explorations and investigations in various directions, and in their eyes their enterprises were of tremendous scope. As they see it, to break the accepted verbal associations is to attack the metaphysical certainties of the common herd, to escape from a conventional and arbitrary vision of the world. "Does not the mediocrity of our universe depend essentially on our power of expression?" (André Breton, in *Introduction au Discours sur le Peu de Réalité.*) A stereotyped language in which all freedom is strictly limited imposes upon us the vision of a stereotyped, hardened, fossilized world, as lifeless as the concepts that are intended to explain it. Let us recall Novalis, to whom nature was "a petrified magic wand." And what if the world we call real were nothing but an act of the imagination, "successful" thanks to some unknown process, what if it were an ancient dream which through habit, weakness, unforgivable inertia we permitted to congeal, and which holds us imprisoned today as in a chrysalis? Once again, we must open the windows, with the hope that we may at last penetrate into a world where freedom is infinite.

Surrealism in the broad sense of the term represents the most recent romantic attempt to break with "things as they are" in order to replace them by others, in full activity, in process of birth, whose mobile contours are inscribed in filigree in the heart of existence.

We may quote here the beautiful opening sentences of André Breton's *Manifeste*:

> The belief in life, in what is most precarious in life, in *real* life, as most would say, goes so far that in the end this belief is lost. Man, the incorrigible dreamer, from day to day more dissatisfied with his fate, laboriously surveys the objects that he has been led to make use of, and that have become his through his nonchalance or his effort, almost always his effort because he consented to work, at least he was not averse to risking his chance (or what he calls his chance!) . . .

Man, that incorrigible dreamer, is no doubt also an incorrigible child—"for it is perhaps childhood that comes closest to true life." Poets have long cultivated this tendency to suspect "reality," as their most precious faculty; now it becomes an absolute. A psychologist might denounce this as a confusion between the objective and the subjective, as reflecting a magic belief in the omnipotence of thought, as involving the notion that tangible reality has less "existence" than the world of the spirit, or rather that it exists only in the spirit, and depends upon it, and that the center of the cosmic nebula is the very soul of this Narcissus. All this of course is obscurely sensed rather than articulated. Nevertheless, the essence of the surrealist message consists in this call for the absolute freedom of the mind, in the affirmation that life and poetry are "elsewhere," and that they must be conquered dangerously, each separately, and each by means of the other, because ultimately they coincide and merge and negate this false world, bearing witness to the fact that the chips are not yet down, that everything can still be saved.

Since romanticism, since Baudelaire and Rimbaud, one might say, all these assertions are hardly new; and it might be added that they reflect mysticism, madness, a madness which is "natural," which can be explained psychologically, and classified in the history of literature or of the human mind. It is only too easy to dismiss the whole matter as "primitivism" and "infantilism" opposed to science and civilization, and to put it down as a symptom of a "regressive mentality." But have not many poets who were not mere versifiers, and not only poets of today and yesterday, arrived at similar ends? So many have thought for a moment that they possessed the world in a metaphor! With admirable ease they discarded all logical principles, identified opposites, breathed the breath of eternity into the present or into the past made present. They experienced this, concretely and irrefutably. And for the space of a moment, their readers experienced it as the truth. All these are facts.

The specific characteristic of the surrealists is this, that they aspired to be kings of a nocturnal kingdom, illumined by a strange aurora borealis, by phosphorescences and phantasms emanating from unfathomed regions. There is in them a deep nostalgia, and a desperate regret at the impossibility of going back to the "source" where potentialities exist side by side without excluding one another, to the chaos preceding all determination, to the central, anonymous, and infinite focus of the universe, whose searing flame Rimbaud felt in himself. I shall quote one single, but peremptory, passage from André Breton's *Second Manifeste*:

> Everything suggests the belief that there is a certain point of the mind where life and death, the real and the imaginary, the past and the future, the communicable and the incommunicable, the high and the low are no longer perceived as contradictions. It would be vain to look for any motive in surrealist activity other than the hope of determining that point.

Here we have the absolute revolt, the rejection of all self-evident truths, which was the very principle of dadaism, and the insane demands of a man who aspires to land "anywhere outside the world." Does this point of the mind, the determination of which is the goal of surrealism, really differ from God's hypothetical position relative to Creation?

Here the revolt assumes the same quasi-demoniacal character as in Baudelaire, Rimbaud, and particularly Lautréamont. Special circumstances and new massacres were required, no doubt, to bring about the present infatuation with the monster named Maldoror, born just before the war of 1870. Are his songs much more than an exercise of frantic simulation, are they anything other than "theoretical malice"—are they the fire of the furious archangel, hurling his blasphemies into an apocalyptic night? Is Lautréamont a mere psychological phenomenon, or is he a metaphysical event, the prophet of the "gospel of damnation"? Personally, I think that the essence of his work consists in the quality of his images, in the incomparable emotion these images release, and the fantastic aura they radiate. Because Lautréamont does not aspire to anything, because he does not anticipate a "sovereign good" beyond good and evil, he does not transmit a message, and the palinody of his *Poésies* only seemingly contradicts the semiparody of his *Chants*. The fact is, however, that by plunging into the hell of nightmares and verbal frenzy he came to satisfy the needs of an anti-Heaven. But it is not easy to conclude an alliance with Satan. Not everyone who wants to can meet him. Moreover, for many the revolt is hopeless and escape is impossible. "I don't believe in God," says Robert Desnos, "but I have the sense of the infinite. No one has a mind more religious than mine. I constantly run into insoluble questions. The questions that I am willing to admit, are all insoluble." At this point, one need only frown, to kindle a certain metaphysical flame in one's eyes. More than one has yielded to the temptation. But it would be puerile to deny the sincerity and the necessity of this revolt merely because there exists a snobbery of malaise and despair.

A few newcomers, though they hope for nothing and practice "systematic deception," advocate an approach which is indeed the only natural and positive approach left to the surrealist poet who worships the spirit—the approach of the mystics. A meditation on Rimbaud leads the contributors to *Grand Jeu* to the following propositions:

"By following a certain method called mystical a man can achieve the immediate perception of another world, incommensurable with his senses and irreducible to his intellect; knowledge of this world marks an intermediate stage between individual consciousness and the other consciousness. It is the common possession of all those who, some time in their lives, have wanted desperately to transcend the possibilities inherent in their species and have envisaged the mortal departure" (*Le Grand Jeu*, II).

This other, supra-individual consciousness, is the universal soul, of oriental philosophy and the occult science; this "mortal departure" is the farewell to all finite things, the loss of oneself, the final resolution of dualism, the fusion with the Whole, in short, the return, after exile in the particular, to the blessed unity of the mystics and that absolute nondetermination which is the sovereign good, but whose features are the very features of Nothingness.

Esoterism, transmitted and enriched by a tradition many centuries old, seems indeed to be the philosophy least incompatible with surrealism. The premonition of another world, a supra-real world which would absorb the internal and external, the subject and the object, a world whose messages might be intercepted by "dying to the world of the senses," by creating a void in oneself to suck up images born outside space and time, and marked with a prophetic sign, this premonition, this belief, seems to be the most normal consequence of the initial surrealist act of rejection and of their latent mysticism.

This was indeed the path they followed at first. They found their ancestors not only among the romantic and post-romantic poets—the true "inspired men" of the rationalist centuries—but also among the prophets and the illuminati. To Baudelaire, to Rimbaud, who in their eyes had been discredited by their Catholic exegetes (particularly the former; as for Rimbaud, had his *Bateau ivre* not achieved a deplorably public fame even in the salons?), they preferred Lautréamont because of their predilection for scandal and their desire to discourage bourgeois admiration. More seriously they took up Nerval—who alone among all Frenchmen did not content himself with merely "envisaging" the "mortal departure"; Hugo in some parts of his works (the least read), and among foreigners, William Blake, Hölderlin, and Novalis. How many "fragments" of Novalis were suddenly revived! But Novalis, like many German romantics of his period, was an "initiate," and his magical idealism bears the imprint of philosophical esoterism.

However, the orthodox surrealists gradually deserted this spiritualist position. Yielding to powerful influences, which also acted on the young writers grouped around the magazines *Philosophies* and *Esprit*—with whom they made common cause for a short time in responding to the "calls from the East" ("Orient, orient, you who have only the value of a symbol," wrote André Breton in 1924, with a quite indispensable oratorical reservation!)—they took the path, not without internal quarrels and dissension, leading to dialectical materialism and a certain form of communism. "What has characterized these recent years," Louis Aragon asserted as early as 1929, "is the agony and death of the individualism which was essential to the people of twenty years ago." What he actually meant was doctrinal individualism, for it is easier to "cover up the self" than to renounce it; and the ferments of anarchistic individualism, so specifically French, which have for so long been consubstantial with the romantic, symbolistic, and modern revolt, cannot possibly die out within a few years. Toward 1930, in any case, an attempt was made to rationalize surrealism. "No one has a mind more religious than mine," Desnos has formerly declared. These religious minds later strove to reject the idea of a super-nature, of a transcendent principle. The will "to change life" by the mind seemed to them inefficacious unless it was duplicated or even preceded by practical action designed to change the course of the world.

Was the lofty conception, which demanded that poetry represent the absolute of knowledge and life, to be abandoned? Was all this, despite the shocking and violent nature of the words used, merely an eccentric form of return to reason? It is difficult to give a definite answer to these questions. On the one hand, André Breton, in the face of the revolutionary opportunism, compromises, and "aria-tions" displayed by the communist factions, has always glorified principles, and has always advocated an aggressive attitude close to Trotskyism, but closer to utopianism. On the other hand, he has tried to combine two revolutionary attitudes, one social and the other spiritual, whose correlation cannot be established once and for all. He did, however, have the courage to say, and for this we should be grateful to him, that in his opinion the revolution could not be an end, that the only legitimate end was "knowledge of man's eternal destination," and that it was most important that everyone, after the social organization of life had been corrected, should become aware of "the real precariousness of man's fate." He thus preserved, with a sense of the relative and the absolute, the sense of tragedy and despaire.

If we consider the primary, essential attitude of surrealism, we shall probably conclude that never before in France (outside of France, there is the group of German romantics) has a *school* of poets so fully and so consciously identified the problem of poetry with the crucial problem of existence. As to whether this poetry contributes "revelations" in any degree universal, the question is naïve. How can we expect a school of poetry so far removed from common ways of thinking and living, to yield products whose value can be recognized "outside"? Did not Rimbaud quickly abandon the hope of awakening even one vocation?

Yes, no doubt, seen from the outside, so impertinent a striving can only end in failure. And it would also seem, that seen from the inside, the quest was doomed, that the "point of the mind," the ultimate word must vanish in this "hollow world" which eludes all attempts to grasp it. Possibly, the surrealists as a whole, orthodox or not, have been lacking in patience. They have tried to *force* the unconscious,* to conquer by violence secrets that might be revealed more readily to more artless minds. To advance on the path of true mysticism, Christian or not, they have lacked the power, and by this I mean, faith, any faith whatsoever; they have lacked perseverance, devotion to something more inward than the self.

It will be argued that many poets, as the Abbé Bremond showed, were pseudo-mystics, who drew virtues from their religious imperfection. But most surrealists can be reproached with indulging in compromise, with jeering at art while not daring to break with it except in words; they did not succeed in freeing themselves from their memories, habits, and literary bad conscience (though they pretended to be working on behalf of science and borrowed from Freud a mythology rather than his method). Their very images, their desire to be incoherent, prove that they find it hard to transcend the preliminary stage of negation, the break with the tangible and rational world. There is a fundamental disproportion, the design of an ironical fate one might say between the Promethean ambitions of Breton and his friends, their avowed resolution to "practice poetry" on the one hand, and the gestures and writings to which their great revolutionary impulses have given rise, on the other. This no doubt accounts for their doldrums as well as their invectives to convince the world that they are not "settling down"; this also accounts for their attempts to show by direct action on the social plane, that they were willing to stake their lives. We are dealing in the last analysis with a more or less openly avowed quest of *parousia*. Despite their alleged vocation for despair, despite Aragon's ablunt assurance that there "are no paradises of any kind," they are tormented by a desire to escape, to yield to another reality. They hesitate between action and poetry, between spiritual and temporal action. But it is only the soul (or what is called the soul) converted entirely into spiritual act and presence that can nourish that integral poetry, victorious over art, that unique truth, that marvelous and pure flower, which they dream of bringing into the world.

*One does not force the unconscious, wrote Franz Hellens as early as 1925, in Le Disque Vert.

CHAPTER SIXTEEN

The Surrealist Poets

1.

Fortunately there are men, or let us say poets among the surrealists. It is true that a doctrine can lead astray or even destroy a docile, overobedient author. But those who are something more than followers prefer to progress as free-lances; by unique means of their own they gradually gain possession of a remote, unnamed realm that henceforth will bear their name; a few resounding words, launched at an opportune moment, will, if necessary, reassure or alarm the disciples and academicians.

Thus, Louis Aragon who thanks to his extraordinary talent for prose is able to do exactly as he pleases, ventured to declare as early as 1928: "If by following a surrealist method you write wretched stupidities, they are wretched stupidities. And inexcusable" (*Traité du Style*). We may well wonder whether Aragon, a thinker, an inexorable logician, has ever been a surrealist except occasionally, and out of curiosity. What he prizes above everything is revolt; he joined the revolts of the dadaists, of the surrealists, and of the communists. Satirical and cynical, but a city dweller who needs society in order to flout it, he might have taken up the Voltairian tradition (read his *Anicet ou le Panorama*); no less easily, by merely following the aggressive, corrosive bent of his thought, he might have wielded that "demoralizing" power which Flaubert once dreamed of assuming, and at the same time left behind him a brilliant poetry of despair. For a long time, his fear of being snugly placed somewhere in a world irretrievably given over to stupidity, more or less close to those whom he abhors, as well as his love for disorder and his refusal to be interested in anything except his revulsions and hatreds, imprisoned him within a circle of blasphemies and monotonous vociferations. His thirst for scandal has been quenched successively by erotic fury and scatology; he has played rather well the part of the man with the knife between his teeth. According to Gabriel Bounoure, Aragon "realized that the most effective cleansing was cleansing by filth—the diversion of a great sewer into the Augean stables." The danger of this undertaking—as Rimbaud could testify—is that it is difficult to cleanse oneself of so much dirt later on.

It might have been supposed that Aragon would abjure the "cultivation of his literary gifts"—that he would be too proud to be concerned with his fate, his future, his existence—and that his *Paysan de Paris* would remain a solitary example in the field of prose. It is, in spite of everything, a lofty satire, a concrete evocation of the fantastic element in everyday life, where, as Baudelaire says, the "fate of the vilest things" is ennobled, where horror itself and wretched vices "are transformed into enchantments" (while his books of poems, *La grande Gaîté* and *Persécuteur persécuté* answer the call of Rimbaud—this is the time of the Assassins!).

But, once Aragon became a communist, it was the poet in him that he assassinated, and this without leaving a trace. Putting a strait jacket on his fury, the flamboyant anarchist is making good in the field of militant literature. What are the absolutely conformist and almost grimacing poems of the collection entitled *Hourrah l'Oural* (1934) but a way of taking leave of poetry? We say this not without regret; and at the same time we cannot deny that his recent novels, illustrating the doctrine of "socialist realism," have certain merits, even literary merits.

In contrast to Aragon, André Breton has linked his fate with surrealism for the last fifteen years. A prose writer, one might even say a writer of classical prose (by this I mean that he went to school and remembers what he learned), a master of dialectics and imperious formulas, Breton, even in the freest of his poetry feels really at home only in prose—and he once confided to his readers that it is second nature for him to observe the rules of syntax. Here it might be observed that "psychic automatism," since it requires an uninterrupted flow of words, normally leads to prose. To start a new line after a sentence, a complement, an epithet, already implies the intention to make "a poetic arrangement."

In Breton's quest for the poetic absolute, in the practice of surrealism, his intransigence is as extreme as it is in theory. You cannot follow him unless you consent to give ground and abandon yourself without reservation to a prose which ambles along at a regular pace, fluid and smooth as a piece of pliable wood without knots. His domain is that of the marvelous. "The marvelous alone is beautiful," he declared in his *Manifeste* of 1924. It is inherent primarily in images, whence it spreads to the atmosphere which becomes lighter, transfigured, pervaded by an abnormal ultra-violet or infra-red light. A vague restlessness, which sometimes turns into anguish, hovers over it like a nocturnal demon. Nothing is more stirring than certain "openings" which lead us into the heart of another world; a few words, and the estrangement is at its climax:

> *Si seulement il faisait du soleil cette nuit . . .*

> If only the sun were shining tonight . . .

or:

> *Un peu avant minuit près du débarcadère,*
> *Si une femme échevelée te suit n'y prend pas garde.*
> *C'est l'azur . . .*

> A little before midnight near the wharf
> If a disheveled woman follows you, pay no attention
> It is the sky . . .

or:

> *Le grand frigorifique blanc dans la nuit des temps*
> *Qui distribue des frissons à la ville*
> *Chante pour lui seul*
> *Et le fond de sa chanson ressemble à la nuit*
> *Qui fait bien ce qu'elle fait . . .*

> The great white refrigerator in the night of the times
> Which distributes shivers to the city
> Sings for itself alone
> And the substance of its song is like the night
> Which does well what it does . . .

> (*Le Révolver à Cheveux blancs*)

And this is the opening of *Un Epervier incassable*:

> The nocturnal round plays its customary sleight-of-hand tricks in the dormitory. At night, two multi-colored windows remain half-open. Through the first there enter vices with black eyebrows, penitent young girls are leaning out of the other. Otherwise nothing would disturb the entrancing cabinet-work of sleep. Hands covered with watery muffs are seen. On the big empty beds there is a tangle of bramble bushes, while the pillows float on silences that are apparent rather than real. At midnight . . .

It is almost always midnight, and even the sun in all its brilliance stands out like a blemish on the night. The weakness of this poetry is perhaps its incoherence; the marvelous is almost never given time to develop, or the symbol to organize itself into a continuous psychological vegetation, into a fable; the short waves of imagery are inexorably broken. We must assume that here André Breton follows a preconceived idea: he refuses to see anything but disorder in dreams (and consequently in poetry); and he is quite possibly mistaken. Would it be such a great evil if things became naturally "arranged"? Must nature be protected against itself, against its tendency to create organic wholes?

The beautiful novel entitled *Nadja*, which is allegedly a verbatim record of real events, several fragments of *Les Vases communicants*, and *L'Amour fou*, show us the marvelous becoming real. A man dreams his life and lives his dream. Facts most widely separated from each other in the eyes of reason become linked together with irresistible logic. Contacts shattering for the mind take place, launching frantic series of indefinite connections; the anguish of the old days and a tragic poetry are reborn; man's defenses are pulverized for an instant, and nothing conceals from him the threatening universe of signs. After Nerval, André Breton; but Breton does not take the ultimate leap; he is neither desirous nor capable of envisaging "the mortal departure." Once the spell is broken, he explains his hypotheses, his intentions, his determination to seek out, divining rod in hand, all the points of intersection between the positive world and the magic world (*Les Vases communicants*).

His intention is to remain on the crest, plunging into the abyss, his gaze armed with a second sight, conferred by love. I know of no other book in which the sense of the enigmatic, the occult, the quest for the "flaws" of life (among them "objective chance"), far from enslaving the mind to some chore of sterile decoding, achieves metaphysical scope more effectively than in *L'Amour fou*. Here, as elsewhere in Breton, the philosophy is not without blemish, but the poetry is indisputable when it achieves such fulness of existence. "Within the formless," a prose both fluid and resistant finds tangible points that lend direction to its grandiose waves. With augmenting *moral* intensity, it traces the image of a man. The surrealist adventure has brought him to those frontier regions where only repeated taps are perceived beyond the silence. We are reminded of Apollinaire's *Voyageur:* "Open this door on which I knock weeping."

2.

Verbal delirium reaches its probable climax in some of the poems of Robert Desnos. During the years following the dadaist crisis, Desnos applied himself chiefly to forming linguistic aggregates by simple mechanical procedures, aggregates for which he did not intend to be responsible, which were meant to be the outcome of an anonymous activity, and whose poetic properties were to be discerned only subsequently. It was a determined attempt to let words think for themselves; the results could be studied later. It was a fishing for miracles; but miracles are rare, and the method proved disappointing, at least for the reader.

Later, dreams supplied Desnos with the equivalent of an object, of a subject matter, however evanescent, whose existence was to be suggested by words. In the sequence entitled *Les Ténèbres* (in *Corps et Biens*) beautiful streaks of remarkably coherent dream poetry evoke the obsessive presence of those fabulous beings which in dreams take the place of material things and wander through the whole field of thought. But in Robert Desnos, the impact of the automatisms and the inertia of words "at liberty" produced the ultimate consequences of the "immense facility" inherent in surrealism; under the seeming discipline of the alexandrine or even of the rhymed or assonanced quatrain, a voice whispers or shouts a mad monologue, in which images drawn from the common store of romanticism, from Musset and Hugo to Apollinaire, emerge like strange islets. It is the final deception—the known and the unknown are mingled in a grimacing chaos, seemingly compounded of the fantasies of an overflowing collective unconscious. An engine is running in a vacuum, the mind having broken with words, having left them to all sorts of irregular loves which seem to produce a factitious and soulless lyrical exaltation. The experiment is interesting and was worth attempting, but once is enough.

There is none of this in Philippe Soupault whose poetry is entirely "inward." Taking refuge in himself and as though absent from himself, immobile, absorbed in a lucid slumber, the poet sees emerging from his depths, iridescent bubbles which sometimes reflect the gray things that silently vegetate around him. Here he is dreaming, his breath comes in gasps, he is, it seems to him, already "doomed":

> *Nuit chaude nuit tombée*
> *Temps perdu*
> *Plus loin que la nuit*
> *C'est la dernière heure*
> *la seule qui compte*
> *Forces diluées nuit secrète*
> *alors que le moment est proche*
> *et qu'il faut enfin encore*
> *se pencher vers cette ombre*
> *conquérante*
> *Vers cette fin vers ce feu*
> *vers ce qui s'éteint*
> *Souffles silences supplices*
> *Un peu de courage une seconde*
> *seulement*
> *et déjà s'achève cette lenteur*
> *Une lueur perdue*
> *Vents du ciel attendez*
> *Un mot un geste*
> *une fois*
> *Je lève la main.*

Hot night fallen night
Lost time
Beyond the night
It is the last hour
the only hour that counts

Diluted energies secret night
now that the moment is near
and again I must
bend toward this conquering
shadow
Toward this end toward this fire
toward what is dwindling and waning
Breaths silences agonies
A little courage just one second
and already this slowness is ending
A lost glimmer
Winds of the sky await
A word a gesture
once
I raise my hand.

(Condamné)

If poetry is precisely what eludes all determination, a musical aura, a universe of radiating waves, some of Philippe Soupoult's poems seem to retain the essence of this volatile spirit in their uncertain images. There is not a trace of rhetoric in this surrealism; it is an unadorned poetry, but chaste, its body has evaporated; and this surrealism itself, which is so little concerned with the techniques of the school, consists only in an effort to perceive the face of life at the frontiers of the mind. All this reflects Philippe Soupault's own personality, and continues the profound human note, the suppressed nostalgia, which, from 1920 on, characterized poems that were often dadaist only in name. He is in the sphere of influence of Apollinaire and Reverdy rather than in the tradition of orthodox surrealism.

For some time surrealism seemed to favor the emergence of new forms of eroticism in poetry. The elucubrations of the dadaists had been full of sexual symbols and conspicuously obscene words. This was no doubt required by the unconscious, which had recently been catechized by Freud. A breath of satanism from the forges of Maldoror, mingled with Baudelairian vapors, and the somber insights of the Marquis de Sade, added to the heaviness of the atmosphere. Lust and death, merging their charms and their fangs, danced together like two entwined serpents in the imagination of Roger Vitrac, Louis Aragon, Robert Desnos, and Georges

Ribemont-Dessaignes. For a full characterization of this aspect of the *mal du siècle*, one would have to cite other names. Between these moderns and Flaubert, Gautier, Petrus Borel, Philothée O'Neddy, the "Young France" of yesterday and of a century ago, there is a spontaneous subterranean tie, perpetuating the tradition of funereal, twilight romanticism.

> *Chair habile exil de la vie et de l'amour*
> *Deux grands squelettes s'invitaient*
> *et se broyaient bouche à bouche*
> *dans la vapeur du café et de la nuit*

> Flesh adroit exile from life and love
> Two great skeletons lured one another
> and crushed one another mouth to mouth
> in the mist of the café and the night

Elsewhere Roger Vitrac draws from the shadows images born in the murky sources of psychological life:

> *Les cloches revenantes les pâturages désolés*
> *Et le peuple affamé se mirant dans tes beaux pieds*
> *Je veille sur ton front cette feuille d'écume*
> *Et ma voix allume une statue de sang dans ton coeur.*

> The ghostly bells the desolate pastures
> And the famished people reflected in your lovely feet
> Over your forehead I behold this leaf of foam
> And my voice kindles a statue of blood in your heart.

(Humoristiques)

Clearly the design, shared by so many of our contemporaries, to empty the contents of the mind and the need to "confess everything," which can be read in Gide as well as in Proust, were here in agreement with the aspirations of the surrealists. In the post-war years psychologists and poets were united in their common will to draw the most beautiful monsters out of the darkness of the self. And since indeed everything is mingled in the self, and readily assumes the color of our vision, a vague Freudian bias sufficed to give the hues of eroticism to the entire substratum of life.

But it is in the writings of Paul Eluard that the new love poetry of the surrealists can primarily be found. Since about 1924 Eluard's thought has gravitated around the reality of love, or the reality of solitude, which is only the absence of love. It grasps ever more tightly and deeply that elusive point where the flesh and the spirit, realism and idealism—to use André Breton's terms—"are no longer perceived as contradictions."

It is metaphysical poetry in that it makes love a cosmic drama, in the resolution of which the whole universe is interested; it takes place in "the abysmal darkness which tends fully to a dazzling confusion" (*La Vie immédiate*) and only the presence of which can be felt, since the darkness itself remains inaccessible to the methods or formulas of psychology.

The climate of this poetry is purity:

> Still very young, I open my arms to purity. It was only a beating of wings in the sky of my eternity, a beating of the heart, of this amorous heart which throbs in conquered chests. I could no longer fall.
>
> "Loving love. In truth, the light dazzled me. I retain enough of it in myself to see the night, the whole night, all nights.
>
> "All virgins are different. I always dream of a virgin.
>
> "At school, she is on the bench in front of me, in a black pinafore. When she turns around to ask me the solution of a problem, the innocence of her eyes throws me into such confusion that pitying me she puts her arms around my neck.
>
> "Elsewhere she leaves me. She boards a ship. We are almost strangers to one another . . .
>
> (*Les Dessous d'une Vie ou la Pyramide humaine*)

There dwells in Eluard an ardent inexorable aspiration toward purity, toward the absolute of love. He does not know what he is, toward what end he is moving, what revelation awaits him—and always fails to materialize. In *Nouveaux Poèmes*, he sometimes abandons himself to sweetness, his joy breaks out and is prolonged in a tranquil luminous ecstasy:

> *Une femme est plus belle que le monde où je vis*
> *Et je ferme les yeux . . .*

> A woman is more beautiful than the world in which I live
> And I close my eyes.
>
> (*Capitale de la Douleur*)

This peace is precarious. One cannot establish oneself in love, where desire alternates with despair, presence with absence.

Solitude soon prevails in a mental universe where the mind spins amid deathly silence. "The new star of love" will not rise.

And yet, She comes closer, She moves away, always alive; nothing exists except in Her look, in a long dream in which night is mingled with day, in which all things are incessantly shattered, to be vainly reborn in a radiation of innocence duplicated by darkness, in an anguish sometimes interrupted by a humble and tender jubilation of the soul. A process quite different and far more serious than that of chivalrous love, however lofty, than idolatrous submission to a *domina*. Here we have to do with a spell, a "possession" that makes self-possession impossible, that makes solitude an ever-yawning abyss, and love a temptation stronger than life. And in the universal solitude nothing answers, no echo, no reassuring voice dropping from a transcendent beyond.

It is a poetry composed exclusively of downbeats, as Jean Cassou saw so well; it does not progress from one place to another, it does not traverse any space to connect psychological foci. Similarly, time is of no account; wholly in the present, this poetry aspires to establish eternity in the moment by breaking the crust of time. But this eternity consumes itself, this poetry, a miraculous fuel, destroys itself without leaving any definable residue. One seems to breathe a pure essence, imposed on the poet by another himself, blind, closed to the external world. It is hard to follow Eluard into his night, among images in which the external world is reflected only at rare intervals when the shadow of an object, the shadow of a hand, a hand, supply a gust of fresh air.

> *Devant moi cette main qui défait les orages*
> *Qui défrise et qui fait fleurir les plantes grimpantes*
> *Avec sûreté est-ce la tienne est-ce un signal*
> *Quand le silence pèse encore sur les mares au fond des puits tout au fond*
> *   du matin.*
> *Jamais décontenancée jamais surprise est-ce ta main*
> *Qui jure sur chaque feuille la paume au soleil*
> *La prenant à temoin est-ce ta main qui jure*
> *De recevoir la moindre ondée et d'en accepter le deluge*
> *Sans l'ombre d'un éclaire passé*
> *Est-ce ta main ce souvenir foudroyant au soleil.*

Before me this hand that undoes the storms
That uncurls climbing plants and makes them blossom

Is it with certainty yours is it a signal
When the silence still weighs on the pools in the depths of the wells in
   the very depths of the morning.
Never discountenanced never surprised is it your hand
That swears on each leaf with its palm to the sun
Taking it to witness is it your hand that swears
To receive every last shower and to accept its deluge
Without the shadow of a past flash of lightning
Is it your hand, this memory that blasts me in the sun.

(La Vie immédiate)

Gradually, not by agreeing to anything in the nature of a surrender, not by renouncing his destiny to be an "inward" poet, but by
being more artlessly himself, sufficiently alive and torn that he need
no longer concern himself with the surrealist methods of producing
the beautiful disorder of poetry, Paul Eluard found words still more
effective:

Les chemins tendres que trace ton sang clair
Joignent les créatures
C'est de la mousse qui recouvre le désert
Sans que la nuit jamais puisse y laisser d'empreintes ni d'ornières
Belle à dormir partout à rêver rencontrée à chaque instant d'air pur

. . . .

Mains qui s'étreignent ne pèsent rien.

The tender roads traced by your clear blood
Unite all creatures
It is moss that covers the desert
And night never can leave traces or ruts in it
Fair one to sleep everywhere to dream encountered at every moment
   of pure air

. . . .

Clasped hands have no weight.

One never wearies of repeating these verses in which all the love
of the world seems to be concentrated, then melted down, and
volatilized:

Nous conduisons l'eau pure et toute perfection
Vers l'été diluvien
Sur une mer qui a la forme et la couleur de ton corps
. . . .

O mes raisons le loir en a plus de dormir
Que moi d'en découvrir de valables à la vie
A moins d'aimer.

We guide the pure water and all perfection
To the diluvian summer
Over a sea that has the form and color of your body
.   .   .   .

O my reasons the dormouse has more reasons for sleeping
Than myself for discovering valid reasons for living
Unless I love.

(*Facile*)

Today, many years after Nerval, Paul Eluard is no doubt alone among French poets to express himself with such felicity. The traces of preciosity, the hothouse images (like the "lace of laughter," the "reseda of melancholy," which are after all charming) are becoming increasingly rare. In the depths of his heart there remains only the light of day, the sparkling of the flame. The poet is now present to the world, and unbelievably detached, present in a place where, once the catharsis has achieved total liberation, joy and sorrow merge, where nothing remains of suffering and disappointed hopes. The words pour forth as simply as the song of a bird, freshness, innocent words as on the first day, charming and perpetually felicitous. Here is man beyond all things:

> A delightful place. Torrents of verdure, clusters of hills, skies without shadow, vases of hair, mirrors of nectar, mirrors of shores, echoes of the sun, crystal of birds, abundance, deprivation, man with his porous hide is hungry and thirsty. Man, from the height of the idea of his death, looks pensively upon the beneficent mysteries.
>
> (*Juste Milieu* in *Donner à voir*)

The poet is he who inspires, says Eluard. He gives a soul to words such as grace, self-evidence. Some readers persist in speaking of barbarism when confronted with this poetry which obviously does not "want" to say anything, which strives only to realize its own fullness; it displeases them that so much assimilated culture should negate itself, that reason should disarm to make possible the flow of these radiant words. The glare of the recent Spanish conflagration lingers in the vision of this poet whose deep and innocent insight

enables him always to combine words infallibly, like crystal
spheres:

> *Je me souviens du redoutable océan de midi*
> *Je me souviens de la compagne bâillonnée*
> *Par le soleil duvet de plomb sur un orage d'or*
> . . . .
>
> *Je me souviens de cette fille aux cheveux jaunes aux yeux gris*
> *Le front les joues les seins baignés de verdure et de lune*
> *De cette rue opaque et dure où le ciel pâle*
> *Se creusait un chemin comme on creuse un baiser . . .*

I remember the redoubtable ocean of noon
I remember the countryside gagged by the sun
A leaden fuzz on a storm of gold

, ...

I remember that girl with yellow hair and gray eyes
Her brow her cheeks and breast bathed in verdure and moonlight
And that street opaque and hard where the pale sky
Dug a path for itself as one digs a kiss

(From Chanson complète)

3.

Of all the poets of the group in question, Tristan Tzara was the
latest to reveal his true nature. Since 1930 he has published
L'Homme approximatif, an epic poem, the only poem of great sweep
that can be legitimately connected with surrealism, *Où boivent
les Loups,* a collection of poems more lyrical in character, and
L'Antitête a collection of prose works written in the course of fifteen
years (beginning in 1916), which show a remarkable continuity in
the poet's effort to maintain himself in "muddled reality" just before
"it is conquered by dreams" (*L'Antitête*). Tzara, who seemed dedicated to humoristic games and the worship of the most insane disorder, has gradually, without renouncing any of his aspirations but
merely by deepening the disorder, taken the path toward massive
creations whose logical incoherence suggests not an internal order,
to be sure, but an intense dynamism, a *vis poetica,* a power that exerts
itself to "mould the hurricane" and to produce great verbal en-
sembles crackling with images.

It would be unjust however to represent Tzara as the conductor of one and the same orchestra always playing at full volume. Occasionally he sings *mezzo voce*:

> *Quelle est la belle au coeur d'eau*
> *Au coeur de l'eau changeant de peines*
> *A peine marchant de chanson en chanson*
> *Dévisagée le long des yeux*
>
> *Déraisonnée au long des îles ...*

> Who is the fair one with the watery heart
> In the heart of the water changing with hardships
> Hardly stepping from song to song
> Her face torn along the eyes
>
> Raving along the islands ...

(Où boivent les Loups)

But he rarely yields to "softness." Blood, death, the "grin of the earth," of the "viperine" earth, all the violent instincts, all the dark breaths, the sufferings of man, and sometimes hope, compose the tragic atmosphere whose density he experiences in his very flesh.

> *Elles sont mortes les étendues balayées par les trainées stellaires*
> *Qui grandissent à l'ombre ensanglantée*
> *Des oiseaux—îlots vivants dans le grouillement des récifs*
> *Où nous était donné l'amour en gage d'éternel*
>
> *La jeunesse noire aux yeux brillants a coupé la route du présage*
> *Ma jeunesse enchaînée aux seuils inhospitaliers*
> *Morte—c'est le mépris qui se lève en moi avec le soleil*
> *Franchissant des monceaux informes*
>
> *Un jour peut-être jaillira*
> *La lumière dans la grandeur*
> *Et le front enfin levé de la boue comme un enfant au sein*
> *Tu partiras dans son audace de blancheur immémoriale.*

> They are dead the expanses swept by the stellar trails
> Which grow in the blood-stained shadow
> Of birds—living islets amid the swarming reefs
> Where love was given us as a pledge of eternity
>
> Black youth with glittering eyes has cut the road of prophecy,
> My youth bound to inhospitable thresholds—
> It is contempt that rises in me as the sun
> Moves across formless mounds

One day perhaps the light
Will emerge in grandeur
And raising your head at last from the mud like a suckling babe
You will go forth in the audacity of its immemorial whiteness.

(Où boivent les Loups).

We are reminded of certain rhythms in Rimbaud's lyrical prose. Such similarities are significant. There is in Tzara the impulse of rebellious youth, he is haunted by catastrophe, and his eloquence carries the prophetic accent. Undeniably he is subject to the attraction of "mysterious assonances," undeniably his verse and prose distill a verbal alchemy partly composed of subtle modulations and harsh vocalic or consonantal discords, though it is hard to say how much of this is deliberate.

Nevertheless this poetry, especially if it is considered in its epic aspect, in *L'Homme approximatif*, where it surges and foams like the incoming tide, is characterized by something basically primitive, savage, elemental. It first impresses us as an extraordinary linguistic orgy. "Under each stone," says Tzara, "there is a nest of words, and it is out of their rapid whirling that the substance of the world is formed" (*L'Antitête*). To yield without resistance to this whirl of words—"after losing your self in your inner self which no one dares enter save oblivion"—to let them freely compose and decompose like spinning molecules, is to form the substance of a world, to favor all "the bloody hypotheses of life" in a tragic travail, a dolorous Spring ritual. Diderot liked to look upon Creation as a belated fruit of chance, the outcome of a lucky throw of the dice following an unknown number of failures and vain attempts of dynamic matter to overcome chaos. In *L'Homme approximatif* we are present at such a chaotic dream. And yet, above this seething amorphous mass, lashed by tumultuous forces, there emerge known forms that bear names; fine intelligible verses are wrested free from the anonymous seething of matter:

La terre me tient serré dans son poing d'orageuse angoisse . . .
Et le long des veines chantent des flûtes marines . . .

The earth holds me tight in its fist of stormy anguish . . .
And the flutes of the sea sing through my veins . . .

(L'Homme approximatif)

It is not only isolated lines that break through, soaring as high as existence, but whole epic strophes detach themselves like floating islands. Then, as the poem progresses, an igneous throbbing arises, an element bursts forth—fire, invincible fire:

> *Des tonnes de vent se sont déversés dans la sourde citadelle de la fièvre*
> *Une quille à la merci d'un élan étourdi que suis-je*
> *Un point de départ inconsolé auquel je reviens fumant le mot au coin de*
>   *la bouche*
> *Une fleur battue par la rugueuse fièvre du vent*
> *Et rocailleux dans mes vêtements de schiste j'ai voué mon attente*
> *Au tourment du désert oxydé*
> *Au robuste avénement du feu*

> Tons of wind poured into the deaf citadel of fever
> A ninepin at the mercy of a thoughtless impulsion what am I
> A disconsolate starting point to which I return smoking the word
>   in the corner of my mouth
> A flower lashed by the harsh fever of the wind
> And stony in my garments of schist I dedicated my hope
> To the pangs of the oxydized desert
> To the robust advent of fire.

                                                             (*Ibid.*)

"The word alone suffices to make us see," says Tzara, and in another of the precious avowals that we find in some of his prose poems: "He merged the meaning and the word in a burst of exaggerated gesture" (*L'Antitête*). His purpose is to confer more than a meaning upon words—to give them real existence; words tend to become once more the true "substance of the world." *Nomina, numina,* Hugo often said. And it is of Hugo more than of Rimbaud that we are reminded by these titanic revolutions, these visions of the underside or reverse side of Creation, this region where so many unnamed things scream "in the tarred ravines of death." I am also reminded of Guillaume-Salluste Du Bartas, author of *Les Semaines,* who described the Creation with every object set in its proper place, in the infallible order of the spirit, illumined by an omnipotent and consoling God. Things and life and "approximative" man are mimicked here in their nakedness, restored to their absolute meaninglessness, seized in the movement that leads them from the primal disorder to the order of a raw and impenetrable reality, forever inaccessible to the intellect.

One cannot help being struck by the diversity of the works bearing the surrealist label, even if only those which have received the imprimatur of André Breton are taken into account. It is a long way from the rugged poetry of Tzara to the diaphanous and imponderable crystals of Eluard, or from the oratorical delirium of Desnos to the gratuitous marvels of Breton. "The mental substance common to all men," which the surrealists set out to disclose is decidedly not a uniform possession; each poet has his own destiny, his individuality. And if this great exploration of man, this great enterprise of discovering the "underside of life" fails to produce universally valid results—that is to say, results rationally communicable—there will always remain the poets, those latest descendants of the romanticism of the depths, which had previously given to symbolism its most precious nourishment.

CHAPTER SEVENTEEN

On the Fringe of Surrealism

1.

"A perfect sentence marks the culminating point of the greatest
vital experience." There is no doubt that Pierre-Jean Jouve and
Jules Supervielle would subscribe to this declaration of Fargue.
On the fringe of surrealism, outside the groups and schools, these
men and a few others, including Saint-John Perse, all of them mature
men, represent the true face of post-war poetry. They have renewed
themselves, they have lived intensely, and now, at the end of
passions and adventures, it is their desire to possess themselves, to
discover words that do not betray. There would be little interest in
trying to measure them by a common yardstick. Each of them is
determined to obey his own law, and what brings them together is a
need for selection among the products of their imagination, a need
for a living and personal order in a poetry which at first sight seems
to owe little to the classical and romantic traditions.

At the time when Gide wrote *Paludes* (1895), Léon-Paul Fargue
had already published *Tancrède*:

> *Main charitable qui réchauffe*
> *L'autre main glacée, chastement.*
> *Paille qu'un peu de soleil baise*
> *Devant la porte du mourant.*
> *Femme qu'on tient sans la serrer*
> *Comme l'oiseau ou bien l'épée.*
> *Bouche souriante de loin*
> *Qui veille à ce qu'on meure bien . . .*

> Charitable hand that chastely
> Warms the other, frozen hand.

Straw that a bit of sun kisses
Before the door of a dying man.
A woman held out but not embraced
Like a bird or a sword.
A mouth smiling far off
To make certain that you die well.

There is a secret pathos in these scales and arpeggios, entitled "variants." Fargue's groping, stubborn quest for the one necessary thing has remained unchanged since his earliest works. "One night I found—I think I found—a thing to be happy about." For nothing deserves to be placed above feeling.

Fargue made his debut under the sign of Rimbaud (of the *Chansons*), Verlaine, Laforgue, and Jarry, at a time when symbolism was being humanized and nature was reappearing in a chilly dawn; life, rediscovered by such poets as Paul Fort, Jammes, Henri Bataille, Charles-Louis Philippe, gave forth an atmosphere of languor, nostalgia, and hope. In his prose poems dated 1902, Fargue tries to call upon the resources of music—the music of Debussy's *Préludes*. He conveys the same impressionism in depth, the same fluid arabesques, the same delicate refinement in the expression of uncertain states of mind; the broken impetus of desire falls back like Baudelaire's fountain, and always "the quivering violins behind the hills," and the theme of impossible happiness:

The footlights glow. A keyboard is lighted at the edge of the waves. The noctiluca form a chain. The slow seething and seeping sounds of the sand beasts are heard. . . .

A loaded bark enters the shadow where the glassy mantles of the jelly-fish rise obliquely and come to the surface like the first dreams of the hot night. . . .

Strange passers-by emerge like undersea waves, almost motionless, with an obscure sweetness. Slow forms tear themselves from the ground and move the air like plants with broad palms. The phantoms of an hour of weakness march along this river bank whither music and thought drawn from the remotest ages come to die. Outside the villa, in the black garden once so bright, a familiar step awakens the dead roses. . . .

An old hope unwilling to cease struggling in the light. . . . Memories we would not have dared to snatch from their hiding

> places hail us in a piercing voice.... They make great signs. They
> cry like those sweet white birds with slender golden legs, that
> were running from the foam one day as we walked on the beach....
> (*Poèmes*, 1919)

There persists a minor, slightly flatted elegiac tone. In the same
period Samain, Guérin, and Despax were writing elegies, and
Jammes *Le Deuil des Primevères*. Like Jammes, Fargue has the ability
to vibrate at the least contact of things, at the least recall of the
past. But even then it was almost always in his lost childhood that he
discovered the face of life, and of poetry. As in a dream, his memory
sends him a smell, a cry, the song of a boatman, "the awkwardness of
an ardent soul"—all this with a ring of authenticity. In this respect
Fargue has been likened to Proust; but Fargue never ventures into
exhaustive analyses, he merely juxtaposes synthetic notations that
revive the very substance of the sensation. And these notations
form an inner world which reflects an urbanized nature, cities gray
or reddish in the smoke, a Paris of the people, sadly or tenderly
human. Before the futurists he was attracted by railroad stations,
by the black trains at the hour when the signal lights slowly ripen;
for then the trains move us less with their power than with their
sadness, and behind them in the night there lingers a frightened
complaint:

> When the train is fully loaded, it counts in a low voice and makes
> up its mind with a sigh. The locomotive, with its boxer's nose, its
> tough beard, its somber sternum, its big starfish, its bosom full of
> burning oil, its icons that light up, its lamps in all their niches,
> its men bloodstained with coal, it makes a pretty picture, like an
> illuminated capital. All the signs and letters are at the windows. The
> dining car follows the metaphor. The rear car has its ruby holes, its
> conjunctivitis and its black breath.
>
> A great intake of air full of iron filings. The night collapses like a
> dead dog. He was killed along the tracks. Where is he?
>
> Invisible, you may sit on the enbankment.
>
> Beyond the walls, the windows of the city can now be seen.
> (*D'après Paris*)

Léon-Paul Fargue can be classed among the most recent poets of
Paris, side by side with Jules Romains, Louis Aragon, and Francis
Carco.

But the foregoing passage is from a recent book—it is painting as much as music, a painting on the verge of caricature, a living presence. In Fargue's early poems, the object remained remote; the rediscovered sensations, detached, treated musically, gave it scarcely more existence than a dream. Today, Fargue encompasses the object in a network of metaphors, comparisons, hypotheses; he rushes forward to meet it, pierces it with light, dry, percussive words. The result is certainly not an objective vision, but rather a hallucinatory vision, sparkling and obsessive for the mind and the senses.

At the same time, the poetic transfiguration is governed by a kind of transcendent humor which is at present an integral element of Fargue's nature. He thus preserves an imperceptible and variable distance between the world and himself, a distance sufficient to secure his judgment, to let him resist the temptation of pantheism, and the need of tenderness. It is a way of "swaggering" before the world, by deforming objects, crumpling the images of Creation—and all this out of love. Fargue's former poems were sung, his present ones are spoken. His poetry is now a vital, biological function, exercised by means of words. For he needs all the words there are, the words of Rabelais, of science, of modern technology. Gabriel Bounoure correctly sees in him a kind of *Neveu de Rameau*, "seized by a lucid alienation of the mind," skillfully mimicking the molecular motion of things. The poems collected in *Espaces* emanate a poetry which is both cosmic and burlesque, and shot through with "pataphysical" formulas. One is reminded of Dr. Faustroll and Jarry's Ubuesque madness; but the subject matter is always the great human adventure. At the end of *Vulturne*, the voice of God bursts forth from a loudspeaker, on Judgment Day, for the mental ears of the souls lost in the ether.

This poetry which looks like an improvisation is by no means dependent on the whims of chance. Fargue arranges and harmonizes the disorder. "In his opinion poetry is the only dream in which one must not dream" (*Sous la Lampe*). This is enough to distinguish him from the surrealists. Marvelously sensitive to the universe, he tries to discover spirit through the body and matter. His imagination rushes down the most perilous pathways, but he uproots himself only temporarily; soon he returns to the streets of Paris, a successor to so many sentimental, ironical, intelligent poets, who are Parisians like himself.

Since his first attempts he has been using blank verse:

Voix dans la chambre à côté
Derniers doigts de la musique
Longue et bleue comme une route
Saurez-vous y depister
L'immense larme qui sonne
A l'évent de ma cachette
Et que j'attends chaque jour?

Voice in the adjoining room
Last fingers of the music
Long and blue as a road
Will you be able to track down
The immense tear that rings
At the vent hole of my hiding place
And that I await each day?

(*Espaces*)

He composes free verse "governed by the alexandrine" (and he might add, by the octosyllable), which moves away from the alexandrine or octosyllable as one moves away from a center of gravity to which one regularly returns. But he gravitates toward prose, a prose that is becoming less and less "poetical" in its rhythms and sonorities. His poems written about 1900 were in a prose perhaps excessively charged with music. The prose of *Epaisseurs* and *Vulturne* has a more solid structure, it gathers its strength in order to hurl high its spray of imagery. According to Fargue, the tendency is toward the fantastic tale, the scientific fairy-tale, a composition which may be eminently poetical as to its subject, but which is prose, a sequence of facts and sometimes judgments. Despite the extreme uncertainty prevailing in these matters, one hesitates to call these pieces "prose poems." Because, for the very best reasons, we have set up a distinction between verse (regular or free) and poetry, between the form and the essence, we are no longer able to decide immediately what is and what is not poetry, since the only judge is individual feeling.

There is an element of the fairy tale in Fargue. He sometimes recalls Perrault and Andersen, convokes the nymphs and Vivien, the mushrooms, the fireflies, and the turquoise blue monster in the shade of the garden path (*Poèmes*). Less felicitously, but not without charm, Francis de Miomandre plays with "the whirl of what is and what is not" in *Samsara*. It was perhaps Breton and the surrealists who encouraged him to let his imagination run free. He has a very human tenderness toward plants, beasts, the shapes of clouds, the movements of light in greenish water, the infinite iridescence of appearances. The lianas tangled in his sinuous sentences form complicated designs, but of a somewhat dry clearness of outline, and his gardens are too sunny to be truly mysterious. The Fargue of 1900 reminds one of the Debussy of the *Préludes*; Francis de Miomandre, if only his fantasy were less Banvillesque in its details, would be akin to Ravel.

He elected prose like so many other contemporary poets, like Saint-John-Perse in his *Anabase* and—if we reduce certain typographical arrangements to their just value—in most of his *Eloges*. But the prose of *l'Anabase* is a disciplined cadenced prose, that employs all the resources of rhythm. Like Fargue's free verse, it is "governed," by the alexandrine and the octosyllabic verse; it is these steady meters, so perfectly in accord with the rhythm of thought, which give the work of Saint-John Perse its nobility and eloquence. (Though, unlike Paul Fort, this poet reserves the right to relinquish these rhythmic constants at any moment).

His *Eloges* (written between 1904 and 1908) were born at the meeting point of several crucial influences: Rimbaud, Claudel, Mallarmé, perhaps *Les Nourritures terrestres*, and doubtless the Asiatic lyric poets. But the cardinal virtues which were to give *l'Anabase* its flavor and power were already discernible. There is first of all that singular intimacy with the things of remote lands and seas, concrete, ripe things, secret, tangible, infinitely old and new. The poet sets out to live with them in candid communion; to feel their impeccable grandeur, resurrected each morning at daybreak; or is it perhaps the function of the soul, "that big little girl," to preserve them in their childhood, in a bath of candor, fresh and pale, like the lines of water and verdure in a moist air?

> ... *alors, de se nourrir comme nous de racines, de grandes bêtes taciturnes s'ennoblissaient;*
>
> *et plus longues sur plus d'ombre se levaient les paupières ...*
>
> ... and then, by feeding like us on roots, great taciturn beasts became ennobled;
>
> and the eyes looked longer upon more shadow ...

(Eloges)

In Saint-John Perse there are numerous key words, such as beautiful, great, grave, pure, vast, and favor, sweetness, ease, delight. The salt, thanks to which each thing has its essence, is restored to the universe. And language, too, must make itself a new, diaphanous and succulent flesh. Eternal virginity of words! In the *Eloges* this is achieved by an art subtle to the point of preciosity, by a special manner of inverting the grammatical order, of rejuvenating the abstract, of grouping lively touches as in a Gauguin painting.

L'Anabase reveals a new sobriety, a hard soil, a domed sky limned to the world's measure, wandering tribes, an infinite permanence. The sinuous motions, the roaming sweetness, the lyrical effusions are subordinated to the goal, which is epic. From the very first page, an immense nature is composed with broad strokes, in solitude; a mankind sure of itself is brought to life by means of a discourse that is admirable and laconic in its clarity:

> *Sur trois grandes saisons m'établissant avec honneur, j'augure bien du sol où j'ai fondé ma loi.*
>
> *Les armes au matin sont belles et la mer. A nos chevaux livrée la terre sans amandes*
>
> *Nous vaut ce ciel incorruptible. Et le soleil n'est point nommé mais sa puissance est parmi nous*
>
> *Et la mer au matin comme une présomption de l'esprit.*
>
> *Puissance, tu chantais sur nos routes nocturnes! . . . Aux ides pures du matin que savons-nous du songe, notre aînesse?*
>
> *Pour une années encore parmi vous! Maître du grain, maître du sel, et la chose publique sur des justes balances!*
>
> *Je ne hélerai point les gens d'une autre rive. Je ne tracerai point de grands*
>
> *Quartiers de villes sur les pentes avec le sucre des coraux. Mais j'ai dessein de vivre parmi vous.*
>
> *Au seuil des tentes toutes gloire! ma force parmi vous! et l'idée pure comme un sel tient ses assises dans le jour.*

> I have built myself, with honor and dignity have I built myself upon three great seasons, and it promises well, the soil whereon I have established my Law.
>
> Our burnished arms are fair in the morning and behind us the sea is fair. This husk of earth given over to our horses

Delivers to us this incorruptible sky. The Sun is unmentioned but his
power is amongst us

And the sea at morning like a presumption of the mind.

Power, you sang on our tracks of bivouac and vigil. At the pure ides of
day what know we of our entail of dream?

Yet one more year among you! Master of the Grain, Master of the Salt,
and the commonwealth on an even beam!

I shall not hail the people of another shore. I shall not trace the great

Boroughs of towns on the slopes with powder of coral. But I have the
idea of living among you.

Glory at the thresholds of the tents, and my strength among you, and
the idea pure as salt holds its assize in the light.

(Transl. T. S. Eliot)

I can think of no poems of great scope, written during and after
the first world war, that can be placed on the same level as *l'Anabase*
or *La Jeune Parque*. To bring together these two works of art, which
everything separates, might seem surprising. But the mere fact that
they deserve to be called works of art . . . The taste for perfection
is almost as rare today as perfection itself. Moreover, Valéry and
Saint-John Perse represent two attempts to synthesize symbolism
and classicism—although the results are very different.

2.

Pierre-Jean Jouve's poetry in its highest form reminds one of those
artesian wells that pierce rocks and arid soil, and give forth pure,
delicious water. These two elements, parched volcanic dryness, and
exalted tenderness, perfumed with angelic grace, mutually determine each other, like the antagonistic forces of the dream which
holds the poet's heart in its inexorable fist.

Before the war Jouve was related to the poets of the Abbaye;
during the war he reacted like them, shaking the dust from his shoes,
condemning the war in the name of justice, and setting himself up as
guardian of "two or three divine things" (like J. Romains in *Europe*).
But already a voice was summoning him to a slope that he would
have to climb alone. Refusing to pin his hope on those European
mobs whose "unanimous" awakening Romains demanded, he

advanced on the icy heights of solitude, and silently crossed "the morning globe of the soul" in quest of another flame. Bitter experiences, torn loves which hurled him into the darkest suffering were in store for him—but also the instrument of his deliverance, the premonition of a *vita nuova*. For a moment religious and poetic inspiration merged, and Pierre-Jean Jouve saw in poetry nothing more and nothing less than a spiritual exercise, a possibility of perceiving the world, for the space of a second, under the flashing light of revelation and of acceding to the divine plane of love where contradictions vanish in the inherent vanity of earthly things.

The sequel of this voyage—for there can be no question of an end, of certainty since everything is always on the verge of being won or lost—led Jouve to a kind of mysticism of being, of presence. But he did not enter into any system; there are no pillars in his Temple. God remains hidden behind his cloud, *absconditus*. If he speaks through the mouth of Elohim, one doubts whether it is He who speaks. It is a poetry of the divine, not a poetry of God. Jouve has dedicated himself to "the most unknown, the most humble and trembling religious ideas." Sometimes he is left with no other hope than a dove perched on a naked branch. For the temptation is there; "the sense of the earth with its pleasures," is terribly present.

This poetry is almost entirely dominated by the sense of sin, or by the hope of escaping from it. Sometimes an anguish of shame traverses it as veins furrow a living body. Incapable of "contemplating his body and his heart without disgust," of turning his eyes away from "the face of the world of Sin" (cf. foreword to *Sueur de Sang*), the poet falls under the spell of Freud's universal Eros. In the good, evil shows its wound. In Christian terms, Satan is in Creation as in a fruit, and he wrangles with God for its flesh. Jouve imagines him "on the shore of a strange land, the earth," before the Fall:

> Satan voit s'écrouler la mer longue et laiteuse
> A ses pieds, le rivage grandir, se dénuder
> Comme une tête horriblement perd sa chevelure.
> Un soleil vague rougeoyant devient liquide
> Un autre à l'autre bout du ciel pousse un cri
> De rage froide et de mauvais sort et la nature
> Naissante est trop fatiguée pour gémir.

Un signe velu se produit dans l'éther
Bête ou démon futur
Il couvre ce qui reste ensanglanté de jour
Avec des larmes et avec des pleurs.

Satan beholds the long and milky sea collapse
At his feet, the shore grow large and naked
As a head horribly losing its hair.
A vague reddish sun becomes liquid
Another at the other end of the sky utters a cry
Of cold fury, an evil spell, and nascent
Nature is too tired to moan.
A hairy sign appears in the ether
A beast or future demon,
Covering the blood-drenched remnant of the day
With tears and laments.

(*Le Paradis perdu*)

The climate of sin is the torpor of bright days, when the sun weighs on things, devours our being, exasperates our desires. The realities of love are suddenly bared like a sword:

C'est vrai que je n'ai jamais prié
Dit la femme grande et douce de taille,
Mais donne-lui mon sein, mon ventre et ma jeunesse
Il sera satisfait.

It is true that I have never prayed
Said the tall woman with the gentle body,
But give him my breast, my belly and my youth
He will be satisfied.

(*Oeuvres poétiques*)

And man yields to this need of infamy which is in him. The cure can come only from renunciation, silence, asceticism. We must wrest ourselves free from the body, from the "desert world"; there are too many words, ashes among ashes; thus the tree, the male symbol, denudes itself and dies to be reborn:

Ayant renoncé aux yeux, nuit plus qu'obscure,
Aux mains ces vaines employées du monde, au coeur ce sang
Et à la bouche coupure saignante de la beauté
Et aux mots qui n'ont plus la magie ni l'éternité
L'arbre se sauve en laissant tomber ses feuilles.

> Having renounced his eyes, a night more than dark;
> His hands, those vain employees of the world;
> His heart, but blood,
> And his mouth, bleeding cut of beauty,
> And words which no longer have magic nor eternity,
> The tree saves itself by letting its leaves fall.

> (*Ibid.*)

Purification is the only way. Only when the poet is enduringly blind to "the night more than dark" of external things, will a sense of innocence graze his skill like a breath; "the dew of origins" will moisten his lips and

> *Un monde plus vrai, de dix tons plus brillant*
> *Que le monde . . .*

> A truer world, more brilliant by ten tones
> Than the world . . .

will emerge for him in the dazzling blue—the very world in which we live, and yet different, virgin, essential, infinitely human and divine, a world where the accidents of being have been replaced by Being in itself, where God speaks in the wind and the soul rises with the smoke.

For the genuine mystic, this "truer world" is ineffable. In so far as Jouve is a mystical poet, he must detach himself from images, or at least present them in his works with that delicacy, humility, hesitation—so moving in him—which makes them permeable, transparent, and sometimes foreign, like the words of a translation. This last feature must not be considered a weakness; for his poetry is a translation from the language of the soul into the French language; it aims at evoking something that infinitely transcends our senses, something that has no form. The everyday words that might have led us to ordinary objects and thoughts must be isolated, filtered, exiled, chased by one another, and it is in this process that one can detect the poet's effort to express fittingly the singular presences that dwell in his thoughts. He thus occasionally achieves a remarkable blend of painting and music. These movements of light which are harmonized in the spiritual sky like the songs of birds are animated by grace, in the human and mystical sense of the word. The beginning of the poem entitled "Mozart" will give the reader a glimpse of this sweetness:

A Toi quand j'écoutais ton arc-en-ciel d'été:
Le bonheur y commence à mi-hauteur des airs
Les glaives du chagrin
Sont recouverts par mille effusions de nuages et d'oiseaux,
Une ancolie dans les prairies pour plaire au jour
A été oubliée par la faux,
Nostalgie délivrée tendresse si amère
Connaissez-vous Salzburg a six heures l'été
Frissonnement plaisir le soleil est couché est bu par un nuage.

To You when I was listening to your summer rainbow:
There happiness begins half-way up in the air
The swords of sorrow
Are covered by a thousand effusions of clouds and birds,
A columbine in the meadow was forgotten by the scythe
To please the day,
Nostalgia set free, tenderness so bitter
Do you know Salzburg at six of a summer morning
Shivers pleasure the sun sets is sucked in by a cloud.

For a moment the anguish has been exorcised, in an oasis of greenness and music, the burden has no weight. But the happiness remains precarious. One look is enough to make the blood flow again; once again life sets its glowing iron to man's exposed flesh. In recent years poems such as *Sueur de Sang* or *Matière céleste* gave one ground to fear that the sexual obsession kept alive by the study of Freud was drawing Jouve's poetry into an infernal circle. At best the image of the deer added a slight touch of monotonous whiteness to a long nightmare; the son of God appeared only as the son of the sobbing Mother, crucified, too much loved. To wrest the poet away from this almost incestuous contemplation, it was necessary for history, after a quarter of a century, to awaken, for political developments and the sufferings of men to become sufficiently acute to fertilize the inner drama of Man. Once again, there opened before Man a vast field for the disasters of the universal unconscious, this time unfolding amidst the rattle of machine guns and in the twilight of freedom. Extraordinarily sensitive to the fleshly smell of events, Jouve revived the great prophetic style. His poetry has rediscovered a sky, which is that of the Apocalypse. There we see the White Horse, the Red Horse, the Black Horse ...

Surgit le quatrième cheval le pire
Celui que la parole humaine n'a pas dit
Jaune tu nous éclaires en plein jour
Comment te voir sans être aveugle d'avoir vu
. . . .

Tu es jaune et ta forme coule à ta charpente
Sur le tonneau ajouré de tes côtes
Les lambeaux verts tombent plus transparents
La queue est chauve et le bassin a des béquilles
Pour le stérile va-et-vient de la violence
Et le vent des chimies
Souffle par ta narine et par ton oeil blanchi
Mâle mort! figure le premier péché
En la verdure calme et d'or de l'Histoire.

Now rises the fourth horse, the worst,
The one that human speech has not uttered
You cast a yellow light upon us in full daylight
How look upon you without being blinded from having seen
. . . .

You are yellow and your form is molded to your frame
On the riddled barrel of your ribs
The green shreds fall more transparent
The tail is bald and the pelvis has crutches
For the sterile comings and goings of violence
And the wind of chemistry
Blows from your nostrils and through your whitened eye
Virile death! figures the first sin
In the calm and golden verdure of History.

(*Résurrection des Morts*)

These gusts from heaven or hell, as in William Blake, this alternation of divine relief and demoniacal temptation compose the atmosphere and tissue of this existence. Jouve's poetry is most moving when its flashing lines traced on a background of silence and absolute absence evoke the momentary transports of an utterly crushed or intoxicated soul, torn from its established position, laid open to the inner abyss, to God, or to that "God in reverse" which is the spirit of sin.

The influences to which Jules Supervielle has been subjected, include Laforgue, Claudel, Rimbaud, Whitman, Romains, and

Rilke. His meditations on Rilke, for example, seem to have helped him in making the dividing line between life and death so tenuous and translucid. And yet Supervielle does not resemble any of his masters: he is "irreplaceable" to such a point that even today it is quite apparent how much would be lacking in post-war poetry if he had not existed, and if he had not exerted on our most recent poets, an influence more evident even than that of Eluard, Jouve, or Fargue.

Jules Supervielle is the poet of metempsychosis, of the metamorphoses of man, of the mysterious telepathies through which "the same is the other," through which all things communicate invisibly, exchanging their fluids and messages, so that "in the villages most dedicated to the earth" one can hear "the corals forming on the bottom of the sea" (*Le Forçat innocent*). In the words of Pierre Guéguen, he is the anti-Narcissus eager to break the prison of the self, to escape from the jealous surveillance of the soul; he is "porous to the eternal," porous to the infinite, eager to rediscover himself in the beasts, the waters, the stones, born perhaps from some breeze under the open skies of the pampas, or from the white foam of the South Atlantic under a night crackling with stars. For him, in contrast to the surrealists, the universe is "infinitely innervated." He is obsessed by the hope of fleeing, escaping from himself, but not in order to escape from the earth, from the universe; on the contrary, he needs space and time, the past and the future, life and death, the immense interplanetary vacuum, the first nebulae and all the strange thunderous adventures that go on "behind the silence."

The great animating principle of this poetry is a metaphysical sense of the world and existence—a metaphysical anguish. In Jules Supervielle this does not imply an attitude of pride, a Promethean impulse. The charge of the cuirassiers flung by Hugo against the absolute, the blasphemous gestures of the "ghastly laborer" whose name was Arthur Rimbaud, romantic revolt in all its forms— including that of the surrealists—all this is far removed from his nature. He has in him no Christian fervor, or anti-Christian fury; he does not have to exact vengeance from God. The poet-convict is innocent. He is tender, intimate, insinuating, modest, although when necessary he knows how to question the dead in a loud voice. His totemic animal is the lizard. Like the lizard he lies motionless, waiting for a sign, "and one would say that he thought by the same process as the lizard." If you would overhear secrets, walk stealthily, and listen:

> *Présences, parlez bas,*
> *On pourrait nous entendre*
> *Et me vendre à la mort*
> *Cachez-moi la figure*
> *Derrière la ramure*
> *Et que l'on me confonde*
> *Avec l'ombre du monde.*

> Presences, speak low,
> Someone might hear us
> And sell me to death
> Hide my face
> Behind the branches
> And let me be indistinguishable
> From the shadow of the world.

(Le Forçat innocent)

Supervielle's first poems emanated a virgin feeling for South American and oceanic nature, an air-filled poetry progressing in waves, carrying sea plants and flowers, and dying in long fingers of water on the sand. Even then his work was full of the sea swell that makes ships roll and pitch. Since then Supervielle has never quite reached terra firma; if he raises his eyes, it is to see the zenith reeling "like the top of a mast." The poems in *Gravitations* are no longer geographical but cosmogonic; the motions of the stars and the landscapes of the cosmic void are transposed into mental images; it is a poetry shaken, shattered by permanent fear of the great shipwreck. In the collection entitled *Forçat innocent*, this cosmogonic vision is enriched by a new dimension, and gradually evolves into a metapsychical poetry, which retains the universe as its object. A "human climate" now prevails even on the remotest beaches of the Milky Way, and, most important, there is no longer any death, either of beings or memories. All that we once were, our sensations and desires, follow us, scatter in the ether where they voyage like disembodied forms, abstract and invisible molds, fluids which lave our present lives, orient our thoughts, and speak to us unbeknown to ourselves.

O morts à la démarche dérobée
Que nous confondons toujours avec l'immobilité,
Perdus dans votre sourire comme sous la pluie l'épitaphe
Morts aux postures contraintes et gênés par trop d'espace
. . . .

Vous êtes guéris du sang
De ce sang qui nous assoiffe

Vous etes guéris de voir
La mer, le ciel et les bois.
Vous en avez fini avec les lèvres, leurs raisons et leurs baisers,
Avec nos mains qui nous suivent partout sans nous apaiser . . .

Mais en nous rien n'est plus vrai
Que ce froid qui vous ressemble.

O dead with your stealthy gait
that we always mistake for immobility,
lost in your smile like the epitaph under the rain
dead men with constrained postures, cramped by too much space

You are cured of blood
Of the blood for which we thirst

You are cured of seeing
The sea, the sky, and the woods
You have done with lips, their reasons and their kisses
With our hands which follow us everywhere but cannot appease
    us . . .

But nothing in us is truer
Than this cold which resembles you.

                                                    (*Ibid.*)

Just as Valéry meditated on life and death in the seaside cemetery
where his ancestors were buried, so Supervielle chose Oloron-Sainte-
Marie, the place of his forefathers, where the mountain torrent
flows, "with lowered eyelids, effacing the difference between men
and shadows," there to sing softly his great hesitation between
life and death, and his humble and tender supplication to the "lime-
faced" host deep within him, which secretly desires to be reunited
with the blind skeletons asleep under the ground.

But the somnambulist poet who passes his hand over a candle
flame to convince himself that he is still alive (*Gravitations*) does
not lose the thread of the metamorphoses. Nothing is alien to him—

nothing except his soul which bids him be himself. It is a burden-some servitude ... so intensely does he feel the profound bond of solidarity uniting him with everything that vegetates, stirs, flies, or rolls in the bed of the torrent:

> *Pierre, obscure compagnie,*
> *Sois bonne enfin, sois docile*
> . . . .
>
> *Le jour tu es toute chaude*
> *Toute sereine la nuit*
> *Autour de toi mon coeur rôde ...*

> Stone, obscure companion
> Be good at last, be docile
> . . . .
>
> By day you are all warm
> At night you are all serene,
> Around you my heart wanders

(Le Forçat innocent)

Everything emerged from stone, even the birds that turn about in the evening like thoughts, even the eyes of beasts and men, exchanging their flashes in the unknown space. And no less than he needs the past and present, Supervielle needs the geneses to come.

> *Ce qui sera dans mille et mille ans*
> *Une jeune fille encore somnolente*
> *Amphidontes, carinaires, mes coquillages*
> *Formez-le moi, formez,*
> *Que je colore la naissance*
> *De ses lèvres et de ses yeux.*

> What will be in a thousand and thousand years
> A young girl still slumbering
> Amphidonta, carinaria, my sea shells,
> Shape it for me, shape it,
> That I may color the birth
> Of her lips and of her eyes.

(Gravitations)

He needs stone and beasts, just as he needs men and love, for awareness of his universal homeland, for consolation and reassurance against fear.

In the poem entitled *Sans Dieu*, we can see the anguish of the poet who already *knows* what the other life will be like, the other journey, or at least the beginning and the horrors of that fall into the icy ether with two blind dogs for guides:

> Girafes faméliques
> O lécheuses d'étoiles,
> Dans le trouble de l'herbe
> Boeufs cherchant l'infini,
> Lévriers qui croyez
> L'attraper à la course,
> Racines qui savez
> Qu'il se cache dessous,
> Qu'êtes-vous devenus
> Pour moi qui suis perdu
> Vivant, sans autre appui
> Que les sables nocturnes?

> Famished giraffes,
> Who lick the stars,
> Oxen seeking the infinite,
> In tangled grasses
> Greyhounds who think
> It lies at the end of the race,
> Roots who know
> It is hidden beneath

> What has become of you
> For me who am lost
> Alive, with no support
> But the nocturnal sands

But the earth is far away ...

> Le ciel tout près de moi me tourmente et me ment
> Il m'a pris mes deux chiens gelés restés derrière,
> Et j'entends leur exsangue, immobile aboiement,
> Les étoiles se groupent et me tendent des chaînes.
> Faudra-t-il humblement leur offrir mes poignets?
> Une voix qui voudrait faire croire à l'été
> Décrit un banc de parc à ma fatigue humaine.
> Le ciel est toujours là qui creuse son chemin,
> Voici l'écho des coups de pic dans ma poitrine.
> O ciel, ciel abaissé, je te touche des mains
> Et m'enfonce voûté dans la céleste mine.

The sky so close to me torments me and deceives me
It has taken my two frozen dogs that were left behind,
And I hear their bloodless motionless barking,
The stars stand in groups and hold out chains.
Must I humbly offer them my wrists?
A voice that would make me believe in summer
Describes a park bench to my human weariness.
The sky is always there digging its path,
And now the echo of the pick axe in my breast.
O sky, lowered sky, I touch you with my hands
And stooping I go down into the celestial mine.

Unless God exists.... But even then, it is an unsatisfied, incomplete God, incapable of wielding power over the living and the dead; a God to whom one can pray believing in him, as the poet does at the beginning of *La Fable du Monde* (cf. especially *Prière à l'Inconnu*, and *Tristesse de Dieu*), his latest book. It is the sense of the human, the realization of the threat to man, the fear of the catastrophe that leads him to the rediscovery of the sense of the divine, and to the *need* for the first of the virtues (according to Péguy), Hope—if not to hope itself. For the unknown, the invisible, the undiscoverable God stammers that it is too late, that he can do nothing now; elder brother of man, he too asks to be pitied.

For the last few years Supervielle seems to have been hibernating. That is to say, he distrusts cosmic adventures, he no longer hurls his imagination into oceanic or interstellar spaces. Convinced that everything takes place within himself, he lives hidden between night and day, in the twilight, trying to tame, to auscultate his inner powers, which are forbidden powers, the organs, "beasts deserted in their bloodstained stable" (*La Fable du Monde*) ready to suffer the pressure of the infinite, "rivers burning and gentle" (*Le Forçat innocent*). Here the element of the marvelous bears no resemblance to a fairy tale acted out by a disembodied spirit. On the contrary, Supervielle calls upon us to return into our bodies, into our blood, to merge with our earthly destiny, to become aware of our authentic ties in a spirit of trembling sympathy and secret tragedy.

A poet of ineffable emotions and indefinable atmospheres, his language by a profound necessity becomes ever increasingly bare, direct and simple. He does not attempt to create the miracles of verbal alchemy, to leave the reader breathless and dispossessed of himself. Supervielle's poems seem at first to be hardly more than prose; they move without abruptness, with unequalled gravity, ease and humility; they take form slowly in the twilight, like a gray image in an unsilvered mirror. Our whole life would seem to be reflected in them, and our soul, awakened for a moment from its dispersion, dreams that it has grasped the shadow of its existence in a few unhurried words.

> *Quand les chevaux du temps s'arrêtent à ma porte*
> *J'hésite un peu toujours à les regarder boire*
> *Puisque c'est de mon sang qu'ils étanchent leur soif.*
> *Ils tourent vers ma face un oeil reconnaissant*
> *Pendant que leurs longs traits m'emplissent de faiblesse*
> *Et me laissent si las, si seul et décevant*
> *Qu'une nuit passagère envahit mes paupières*
> *Et qu'il me faut soudain refaire en moi des forces*
> *Pour qu'un jour où viendrait l'attelage assoiffé*
> *Je puisse encore vivre et me désaltérer.*

> When the horses of time stop at my door
> I always hesitate a little to watch them drink
> Since it is with my own blood that they quench their thirst.
> They turn toward me with grateful eyes
> While their long draughts fill me with weakness
> And leave me so weary, so alone and uncertain
> That a passing night invades my eyelids
> And suddenly I feel the need to rebuild my strength
> So that one day when the team comes to drink
> I may live again and slake my thirst.

> (*Les Chevaux du Temps* in *Amis inconnus*)

Fargue, Jouve, Saint-John Perse, and Supervielle "have gone back to the sources of poetic imagination"; they have wrested the mind from appearances to commit it to adventures which reveal its powers as a medium in the great free spaces of the modern fantastic. None among them, however, aims at "writing gratuitously," at surrendering to the need of psychic destruction which characterizes surrealism seen in its aspect of verbal automatism. Even though they have faith in the "lucky find," they do not refuse to adjust and subordinate it to the meaning of their work. Needless to say, Saint-John Perse must be considered separately; his *l'Anabase*, an epic poem impersonal in its design, is obviously calculated in its smallest details. But though all of them let themselves be borne by a spirit which overflows reason, they bring themselves back to a point of lucid awareness. They consent to forget themselves only to rediscover themselves, or at least to catch a glimpse of themselves in a luminous night, and their poetry is at its best when it draws its material from those moments when man has the illusion of belonging to himself, of determining himself.

The Modern Myth of Poetry

Breton by Picasso

After having threatened to submerge the whole of the younger literature, surrealism leaves the impression of a force that did not succeed in finding its path, of a great disappointed hope. Meanwhile things continue in their customary course. Fernand Gregh evinces no desire to be released from his oath of allegiance to the romantics; Armand Godoy abundantly illustrates the "musicist" doctrine advocated by Jean Royère; Noël de la Houssaye still composes Pindaric odes in the style of Ronsard; in his last years Pierre de Nolhac continued to publish verses in the Parnassian humanist manner; Jules Romains' metrics and style retain their appeal for poets as original as Gabriel Audisio or Louis Brauquier; the seeds that Apollinaire sowed in all directions are still maturing; and there are still *fantaisiste* or "whimsical" poets, on the "right" and on the "left. . . ." Let us accept as a principle that all the poets of France, from the sixteenth to the twentieth century must have admirers and disciples, that the most widely differing traditions, as well as the most diverse varieties of revolt and anarchism will be represented in our epoch which is so liberal—for how much longer?—and which permits all ideas and beliefs to coexist and proliferate.

However, if we confine ourselves to the living aspects of recent poetry, there emerges a preliminary distinction that may introduce some order into all this confusion. On the one hand, we have artists who have faith in beauty and strive to produce works of art; at the other extreme, there are those who despise art, convinced like Rimbaud that "the idea of beauty has become stale," who subordinate poetic activity to goals that transcend it. Between these poles, intermediate positions can be conceived, and needless to say, all the "artists" do not worship the same god; but all of them accept "the old game of verse" that Apollinaire claimed to have forgotten, that is to say, convention and constraint, and in this they are clearly opposed to the partisans of freedom of inspiration, who dream of reducing convention to a minimum or of doing away with it altogether.

Among the traditionalists, the most attractive and the most modern no doubt are among the descendants of Romantism (rather than the Romanic school) and of Mallarmeism. The classicists of the twentieth century happen also to be symbolists. Between the aesthetics of the "Précieux" and the theory of pure poetry which came into being with Poe and Baudelaire and was recently defined by Valéry, paths have opened which make it possible to slip from one epoch into another with the greatest ease. Here we witness the triumph of a skillful and refined poetry, which uses an idiom with a strangely imagistic style, archaic in vocabulary and syntax, a kind of timeless nontemporal Κοινή, not far removed in many instances from what André Thérive called a dead language. Here, a very old and noble culture plays with ideas or with their shadows, with feelings and sensations, which it tends to consider less in themselves than in terms of their aesthetic "efficacy," of the "charm" they release. Many, among them Valéry, harbor a certain skepticism regarding their truth and regarding the justification of the conventions and rules of the poetic game. But according to them, without convention everything collapses, society, man, and his universe, and the poem sinks to the level of stammering. Constraints are needed "to resist the permanent dissipation of thoughts."* In referring to these poets as Alexandrians, I am only adopting an epithet that Henri Charpentier suggested by way of owning to an ancestry in which he and his friends take pride.† All of them believe, if not in the omnipotence of thought, at least in its power, in its ability to beget durable forms.

Using a convenient antithesis, we may say that their adversaries humiliate art (technique, deliberate and conscious activity) before nature. This nature is not assimilable to reason, as in the century of Boileau, or to feeling, as in 1830, or even to imagination, but, in the view of the most revolutionary among them, to oneiric, spontaneous thought, prejudged to be "sincere." The "divine goal," as Baudelaire maintained, is still "the infallibility of poetic creation." Only, it is no longer creation in the strict sense of the term that is involved—the only important thing is the sense of an occult presence that eludes definition. In repudiating art as falsification, in scorning man who thinks himself superior to nature, which does its work well, these poets yield to a romantic confidence in the value of the immediate data of consciousness.

*Cf. *Au sujet d'Adonis*, by Valéry.
†Cf. the manifesto in the first issue of *Latinité* (January 1929).

Today we are also witnessing the consequences of the dissociation of two ideas that for a long time were identified: the idea of poetic form and the idea of poetic essence. There was a time when versified speech was poetry; there was also the requirement of ornamentation by a few "bold figures"; then came the reign of the image, and the added contribution of the play of sonorities. . . . In the eyes of the modern critic, the poem is "an ineffable state of mind, which is served and betrayed by certain figures of language" (Jean Paulhan), a state that can be penetrated only at the price of an inner, almost mystic experience. As for poetry, it is regarded as a psychic pheno- menon whose nature is unknown, an x quantity which occurs only in minds that are good conductors; or if you will, a visitation. Con- sequently, poetry cannot reside in any form. It strives to avoid all sorts of condensation in verses, rhythms, images, and it increasingly tends to suggest the impression of a volatile, floating essence impos- sible to apprehend. Every time a convention is rejected, a betrayal is avoided; and some writers have attempted to break with the ultimate and "worst of all conventions," language.

The disadvantage of such a doctrine is that in striving to be com- pletely pure, this poetry tends to scorn cadence, melodious arabes- ques, assonances, and to diverge increasingly from the noble sensuousness which is awakened by perfect eurythmia, by the complex harmony of a poem steered like a ship, sustained by a regular vital breathing, of which one might say—I have in mind certain poems by Valéry, Muselli, Toulet—

> Là, tout n'est qu'ordre et beauté,
> Luxe, calme et volupté.

> There everything is order and beauty,
> Luxury, calm, and sensuousness.

For centuries the poetic incantation has been favored by the recurrence of certain rhythmical elements; it is thus that the magic of verse, *carmina*, operates. Indeed, only a few writers are capable of making a poem progress without any external support, and of actualizing the living law that secretly orders a thought without breaks and dead zones.

Moreover, in order to escape from forms, the poets entrust them- selves to other forms, more uncertain, and broken; it is useless to attempt to liberate oneself from the falsity of words except through other words or through silence. The stubborn effort to liberate the poetic fluid, although such a liberation is always incomplete, involves the risk of losing it in the limitless.

Modern poetry bursts the limits of the books of verse and must be sought in every literary genre, but it would seem that this is not enough. There are some who go so far as to assure us that their only concern is to make it pour from their lives, to live it, after burning all the books.

It is not only for Rimbaud's disciples that poetry is in process of becoming a means of gaining a special, para-scientific kind of knowledge. Even among the greatest skeptics one can sense an instinctive aversion to literature aspiring to be self-sufficient. And what goal can be imagined outside it, what goal transcending its traditional function of diverting or edifying "souls," what object beyond the true and the false can be attributed to it, unless it is that of presaging, and perhaps of apprehending, a reality or its projection in the light and shadow of thought and in certain accidents of language? It is as though this reality were an absolute spirit which absorbs the phenomena of the external world and the inner world (since man is situated in both these worlds, at their very point of intersection), and as though the poet's mission consisted in mastering this dualism, or at least in striving to master it, by cultivating a sense of the metaphysical identity of the inside and the outside, a sense of their "correspondence," of their ultimate resolution in a "dark and profound unity."

In this there is nothing genuinely new. "It is doubtless the essential feature of all art, and not only of poetry," says Jean Paulhan, "both to shake us and to detach us from nature and reality—but in such a way as to make us feel that by surrendering to it we accede to a more authentic, and as it were, more real, reality." But the modern poets have pushed this detachment exceedingly far. In everything that is commonly held to be self-evident and indisputable, they have suddenly come to perceive only the problematic aspect; everything appears to them under the sign of arbitrariness, and of that "more real reality" (of which so many others before them dreamed as a vague "ideal," or in the form of a "spiritual life" or a "beyond," or a lost paradise). And with their everyday existence the modern poets have mingled a mysterious presence, seductive and narcotic as a miracle. For some, poetry has finally become nothing other than a vague sense of this presence, this strange and always unexpected summons to doubt appearances, to question the meaning of the most trivial phenomena and objects, to despise second causes and to make all life enter into an order of magical things spinning above the void.

As to whether this absolute spirit represents an acceptable hypothesis, or whether it is only, as M. Teste supposed, "the radiation of our miserable matter," this is a question that must be left to the philosophers. If, for the sake of argument, we grant the existence of such a spirit, we would still have to discover to what degree it is commensurable with thought, and specifically, with language. Speaking of the nature of things, Henri Poincaré observed that "if some god knew it, he could not find the words to express it." But there are images . . . jarring, mutually destructive images, yielding to every fluctuation of life, following the curves traced by the most ephemeral mirages of thought—could not such images prevent the mind from fixating itself, could they not orient it unswervingly toward that ineffable Being which cannot be formulated? Most mystics have granted such power to images. Some poets are ready to go a step further, to believe that words can be more than symbols, that they can do more than merely participate in essential Being— that the absolute is embodied in the poet's works. Be that as it may, the problem is still with us, still insoluble.

In the world that man has built for his use, where he feels at home, in safety, protected by reason, morality, society, the police, sheltered in cities where the birds of the sky can no longer be seen, in houses, in rooms, in "comfortable" ideas, with the pleasant possibility of roaming a bit along the beaten paths that he calls his freedom, surrounded by conventions which he regards as necessary truths—in this fictitious world that is thought to be real, on this planet hurled into space (but no one suspects it!), a poet makes his appearance. At first it will be difficult for him to be anything other than a sower of disturbances, an instigator of disorder. His primary mission is to disorientate. Gradually he will reveal the original meaninglessness of the world. At a time when science is becoming aware of its anthropomorphic character, when philosophy, at least in

France, would define itself as a science if it had the courage, in order to eliminate a number of problems in advance on the ground that they are imaginary, when an industrial civilization is dreaming of subjecting the mind to the rigorous laws that prevail in physics, the poet's task will be to unsettle man, to make him lose heart in the face of his life and the world, and to put him in permanent contact with the irrational.

"Sometimes I suddenly lose the whole thread of my life; sitting in some corner of the universe, before a cup of steaming black coffee, before polished pieces of metal, in the midst of the coming and going of tall gentle women, I wonder by what path of madness I have finally come to be under this arch, what is the true nature of that bridge which they call the sky. That moment when everything slips away from me, when immense cracks come to light in the palace of the world, I would sacrifice my whole life to it if only it would consent to endure at such a laughable price" (Louis Aragon, *Une Vague de Rêves*).

Such moments when everything seems to be on the brink of dissolution belong to poetry; its obligation is to perpetuate their memory. But in reality it is the whole of life, and *a fortiori* all of poetry, even the poetry that evokes the simplest, most familiar objects—"a handkerchief is enough to arouse the world," said Apollinaire—that is thrown out of joint and gradually drawn into a new gravitational system. The aberrant forms of thought, daydreams, desires, the indistinct pullulation that accompanies our "clear" ideas, all this occasionally assumes such strange colors, and forms a complex mythology so stirring in design that one is tempted to give it a meaning, to take it for a language. It seems, then, that by passively yielding to this chaos one may penetrate into the heart of things, which are reflected in their entirety, "made present" in a mind.

Let us call "metaphysical sensibility" the poet's gift of spontaneously feeling things, not according to their logical relationships, but according to their essence and the spiritual analogies revealed to the imagination; and let us, if we may use the term, call "metaphysic sensibility" his power to apprehend, by means of mysterious antennae, the events woven on the background of the mind, below the threshold of conscious thought and even the more developed forms of affective life. It is only today that the definition of poetry once given by Brunetière has acquired its full meaning—a meta-physics made sensible to the heart, and expressing itself in images.

But it is not sufficient to break the armature that encompasses man, to foment revolt against self-evident truths, to open abysses everywhere. The poet, like the god, must also fill the abyss, exalt man, sow the seeds of a temporary but superhuman quietude. It is an ardent quietude in which all the powers of the soul are strained to the limit, not an inactive and vegetative quietude. The most eminent triumph achieved by the great poets of all times has consisted in wresting the privileged reader from his life, from time, and in keeping him in a suspended state of ecstatic rapture. All genuine poetry suggests a "sacred action." In this respect the situation of the moderns is more difficult, because they are more violent in negating the appearances of reality than in affirming its spiritual, mystical existence. The latest poets even refuse (this they call sincerity!) to seek a calculated effect by combining in a single work elements originating in various states of mind and at various moments in time, for this they regard as falsification. The poet can only wait or work toward the blessed emergence of the exceptional moment in which all the energies of life are polarized around a single focus, and nothing in the world exists except its luminous radiance.

Thus modern poetry is primarily a poetry of fulgurant marvels, brief touches, phantom-images, poetic islets on the blank page, light as foam, as distinct from language as a divine voice can be from all the noise of the earth. It has been called a poetry of the eternal present,[*] whose source begins at the point where man's inner being, having eradicated the stigmata of the individual, adheres to the present which concentrates in its depths all the depths of life. It is perhaps Jouve and (by the use of different means) Eluard, who give us the most adequate idea of this lyricism of the anonymous moment when the mind appears to itself in its solitude, in its resplendent nakedness, angelic or demoniacal.

This fervent peace in which man transcends himself is constantly threatened by life, by the course of events that are stronger than man and draw him into time. I am not referring to the everyday things

[*]Cf. for example, *La Comédie psychologique* by Carlo Suarès (J. Corti, 1932), especially pp. 129 and 130, and Jean Cassou's article on this book in *Les NouvellesLittéraires*.

which form the futile setting of appearances that lulls us to sleep, but to revolutionary events, real forces which are revealed to anyone who has once and for all let himself be disoriented. An epic lyricism will have to espouse these universal rhythms, to become the sonorous echo of the cries of the modern mob demanding bread or a Messiah. However, this is no longer the time for descriptive music, for historical narratives. On the plane of the marvelous, under a light different from that of the days and nights, there will unfold the epic adventures and painful births which alone can perpetuate the world and mankind.

The only feature common to certain works by Claudel, to the work of Romains and his disciples, to *L'Anabase* of Saint-John Perse, to some of the poems of Apollinaire, Salmon, Cendrars, and Fargue, is a certain underlying epic current. Yet in those who are close to the neo-symbolists and even more so in the surrealists, serious obstacles hinder the development of this poetry, prevent it from openly constituting itself as an epic. The attraction of uncertain forms, always on the point of drowning in darkness and returning to the immobility of death, the obsession with dreams, compel the poet to lose interest in the visible world and to remain in the quicksands of the unconscious, apart from the great currents of life. The example of Rimbaud or Lautréamont proves, however, that epic dramas engaging the whole man can take place within the mind. Thus it is from within that must come the impetus, the *élan vital* which will prolong itself in a poetic rhythm, as can be seen in a poem as remote from anecdote and subject matter as Tristan Tzara's *L'Homme approximatif*.

But whether the purpose is to plunge into life or to transcend it, to accept or to negate time, the first requirement is to forget oneself, to break the limits of the self, to advance beyond personal lyricism.

"My poems have the meaning that is given them. . . . To maintain that to each poem there corresponds a true and single meaning, consonant or identical with the author's idea, is an error contrary to the nature of poetry, a fatal error." By this declaration and others of the same kind, Paul Valéry—whether out of coquetry, out of a desire to remain incognito, or to cover his retreat—likes to suggest that his poems are not intended to mean anything. If this is so, the idea of poetry as professed by the latest partisans of art (however skeptical they may sometimes be with regard to the metaphysical or mystical goals of art) is not so very different from the idea of the "seers." The great quarrel between them bears upon the method, the former applying themselves to correcting the data of the mind, the latter submitting to constraints only in order the more surely to achieve the moment of abandon to the hidden forces. For both of them, although in different degrees, the poem tends to become something other than an "expression" more or less faithful to the particular circumstances of a life, an expression susceptible to evaluation on the basis of an inner model imagined by induction. An ideal poem would thus be an *object* existing for itself, without communication with its author, his feelings, or states of mind—an autonomous object, an aerolith come from an unknown planet, "calm stone fallen into this world out of obscure disaster."

Deprived of meaning or at least of any exactly formulable meaning, and capable of arousing ten different poetic reveries in ten different readers, the poem becomes comparable to a spectacle of nature. At first nature, too, seems silent, and speaks to us only if we interpret it, if we span the distance between it and our mind with a network of analogies. Pierre Reverdy, who is a spokesman of the partisans of free inspiration, writes without intending to be paradoxical: "The poet, and this is today an established fact, no longer seeks to stir the reader by a more or less eloquent exposition of an event, but to move him as broadly, as *purely* as he would be moved by a sky all crackling with stars, by a calm, grandiose, tragic sea or a great silent drama played by the clouds under the sun" (*Le Gant de Crin*). The term "purely" in this context means "without specific reference to the poet as an individual," by directly acting upon the reader's affectivity, his hidden treasury of memories and premonitions, outside his intellect. One might almost say "musically," speaking of a music that is immaterial and unsensual, basically ambiguous and polyvalent.

One can foresee the obstacles which the poet will meet in trying to achieve this extra-intellectual purity. Whatever he does, words retain meanings, or at least they drag after them a vague halo of ideas and superstitions. Language has too long been used for the purpose of communicating; André Breton says that this is a "monstrous aberration," but it is an aberration many centuries old. However assiduously the futurist or surrealist may try to trick logic by breaking customary associations, he can seldom entirely prevent the reader from indulging in the perverse game of trying to understand.

Moreover, is it not possible that to expect a poem to affect us in the same way as a sky, a sea, or a cloud, is to misunderstand the specific nature of all literature? A poem has sometimes been defined as an instrument of power; and as such, it constrains us, "holding the reins of our affections, leading us here and there at will," as Du Bellay said. In the face of nature, however resolved we may be to yield to it, we retain greater freedom, we lend it charms that are the reflection of the thoughts in the bottom of our minds, animating and nourishing with our lives the dream which it supplies only with its color. But a poem penetrates us with an explicit force, it unsettles our whole being, and in this adventure even our intellect finds its share.

Even if it is the mission of poetry to suggest the presence of an irrational world by speaking to the very depths of man, even if, in its nobility and purity, poetry derives from the states of "supernaturalist" revery of which Gérard de Nerval speaks, this does not imply that it must cease to move us by means of an intelligible language. The greatest poets have done just this; "a slight shift" in the choice of words enabled them to condense, to attract into the sphere of influence of the words in question infinitely more meanings than analysis can discover in them. A poem absolutely impervious to the world of things and without any islet of consciousness has a disadvantage that it may merely skim over us, like a speech in a completely unfamiliar language. It is demonstrable that the sense of the unknown arises only on the basis of the known, and that the marvelous does not touch us unless we are permitted to observe our own feeling of strangeness.

We are no longer living in the period when Goethe praised the French romantics to Eckermann for not moving away from nature like the German romantics. The symbolists, and especially the surrealists, broke the balance between the inner and the outer worlds in favor of the inner world, and the danger pointed out by Goethe exists today in France. Even though it is true that the sources of all poetry are in the mind, external nature is the surest path by which men who aspire to know themselves through means other than analysis, can approach poetry. Nature is the receptacle of the mind, the locus of all its visible and sensuous symbols, the repertory of all the analogies, as Baudelaire believed. Our dream itself is perhaps only as valuable as our waking hours. Genuine poetry does not spring from sensation, but sensation must water the dark lands of memory. Man's whole being in communication with the whole universe must participate in the elaboration of the poetry that is seemingly most disembodied.

Poetry is equally threatened by the temptation of the inhuman. To be sure, the romantic notion of sentimental lyricism survives itself only with the greatest difficulty, and the need to distinguish poetry from everything that is not poetry corresponds to the recently acquired and infinitely valuable realization of the essential nature of poetry. "For too long a time," says Apollinaire, "the French loved beauty only because it supplied them with information." But it may be feared that a poetry relegated to the unconscious, the dream, the free imagination, or reduced to being born out of a mystical or premystical contemplation like an icy pool reflecting only one flower, will be weakened by the loss of all it has abandoned. The power of poetic genius to transfigure and authenticate the world includes the power to consider man and his life without rejecting any of their elements, to penetrate them to the point where this vile matter is mysteriously transmuted. Proof of this can be found in many passages of Claudel, in Jules Romains' *Odes*, in some poems by Apollinaire and Fargue. Why must the hope of discovering a super-reality as one advances ever farther in the shadow and the silence, be accompanied more often than one might wish by a preliminary resignation of the mind, incapable of directly confronting present reality, of making it transparent and significant?

But perhaps we have reached the moment when man, weary of seeking himself in vain, hopes to rediscover himself in action and thus to palliate all his uncertainties; the crucial moment when our labours and pleasures, even those that are most disinterested, are in need of a renewal, when a movement that has attained the end of its curve aspires to change direction. How can we fail to assume that there is a relation between the freest poetic experiments and the course of events, when we observe that during the last one hundred and fifty years there has been a constant aggravation of the conflict between the modern world and those who reject this world in the hope of replacing it with another, more authentic world, which is like a vague synthesis of their desires, and which might quench for a moment a thirst for the absolute that is sometimes beguiled into strange adventures. . . . As for the latest form of this hope, which is more violent and more conscious than almost any that preceded it, Louis Aragon foresaw its fate as early as 1924: "And once again, no doubt, my friends, are we dropping the substance for the shadow, and no doubt it is in vain that we question the abyss . . . but it is this great failure that is perpetuated" (*Une Vague de Rêves*).

Let us regard this poetry, of which I have traced some essential features (there are others, and the pictures vary according to the light cast upon them), as a myth rather than a historical reality. Many works give us glimpse of it, in none is it positively embodied; it is an airy dream, a mirage, which attracts pilgrims to the horizon. Let us regard it as one of those signs of the times in which men formerly read the fate of their century. Some critics repeat that it has but little influence in our day, that it occupies only a limited place in literature as a whole. To maintain this is to be blind to the obvious fact that since romanticism, and particularly from 1912 to 1927, the poet has often performed the function of the look-out aboard ship. It is true that this poetry has few readers, and that it sometimes discourages readers; nevertheless, it registers the slightest changes in the atmosphere, it makes the gesture that others will imitate and develop (in writings that will be read and rewarded), and it is first to utter the long awaited word.

Select Bibliography

Abbreviations

General
bil.: bilingual: when a translation gives both the French and English texts.
O.C.: Œuvres Complètes.
O.P.(C); Œuvres Poétiques (Complètes).
Tr.: translated.

Publishers
The usual abbreviations for English and American publishers are used, e.g.
O.U.P.: Oxford University Press. Place of publication is not given for books
published in Paris, New York, London and at the main university presses.

French, Belgian and Swiss publishers
La Bac: La Baconnière, Neuchâtel.
C.F.L.: Le Club Français du Livre, Paris.
C.M.L.: Le Club du Meilleur Livre, Paris.
D. de B.: Desclée de Brouwer, Paris.
E.R.: Editions Rencontre, Lausanne.
M. de F.: Mercure de France, Paris.
T.R.: La Table Ronde, Paris.
Minuit: Editions de Minuit, Paris.
P.U.F.: Presses Universitaires de France, Paris.
Renaiss. du L.: La Renaissance du Livre, Bruxelles.

Series of texts
Cl. Garnier: *Classiques Garnier.* Authoritative, scholarly editions, relatively
   inexpensive.
C.L., *N.C.L.*, *C.V.*, *S.L.B.*: *Classiques Larousse, Nouveaux Classiques Larousse,
   Classiques Vaubourdolle, Sélections Littéraires Bordas.* Small volumes, mainly
   selections, with notes and exercises, for school use.
Cluny: *Bibliothèque de Cluny* (A. Colin). Usually has short introduction and
   brief notes.
10 × 18: *Le monde en 10 × 18* (Union Générale d'Editions) Paperback,
   complete texts.
G.F.: *Collection Garnier-Flammarion.* Paperback, complete texts, brief introduction.

P.A.: *Poètes d'Aujourd'hui* (Seghers). Selections, preceded by a long critical essay, full bibliography, etc.

Pléiade: *Bibliothèque de la Pléiade* (Gallimard). Authoritative, scholarly editions, printed on fine paper.

Poés.: *Poésie/Gallimard*. The main paperback poetry series. Mainly 20th century, complete texts, brief introduction in some cases.

Critical series

B.I., P.B.I.: *Bibliothèque Idéale*, being replaced by *Pour une Bibliothèque Idéale* (Gallimard). Critical essay on each writer, analysis of his works, bibliography, etc. *B.I.* also had selections, excluded from *P.B.I.*

Class XX: *Classiques du XXe Siècle* (Editions Universitaires). Paperback. Monographs on writers.

C.Lett.: *Connaissance des Lettres* (Hatier.). Compact academic studies by leading scholars.

C.E.M.W.: *Columbia Essays on Modern Writers*. Paperback. Brief monographs.

E.D.D.: *Ecrivains Devant Dieu* (Desclée de Brouwer). Short studies of spiritual aspects of poets' works.

Idées: *Collection Idées* (Gallimard). Critical and theoretical texts in paperback.

W. and C.: *Writers and Critics* (Oliver and Boyd). General critical studies in paperback.

1 General Anthologies of Modern French Poetry

The anthologies in this section contain the French text only, unless otherwise stated.

Two anthologies are particularly useful:

A. M. Boase, *The Poetry of France* Vol. 3: 1800–1900 Vol. 4: 1900–1965. Methuen, 1967–9. (University Paperback.)

> With critical introduction, and note on reading of French verse. Biographical notes on poets, advice on critical reading and annotations.

C. A. Hackett, *An Anthology of Modern French Poetry from Baudelaire to the Present Day*. Blackwell, 1952. Revised and enlarged edition, 1964.

> Critical introduction. Biographical notes on poets, giving full lists of works with dates of publication, and advice on critical reading. Annotations.

Consult also:

W. Alwyn, *Anthology of Twentieth Century French Poetry*, Chatto, 1969.

> Free verse translations.

M. Arland, *Anthologie de la Poésie Française*, Stock. New edition 1964.

J. L. Bédouin, *La Poésie Surréaliste*, Seghers, 1964.

> Introduction and biographical notes.

S. Burnshaw, *The Poem Itself*, Penguin Books, 1964.

> Translation and analysis of 150 European poems, including several modern French.

G. E. Clancier, *La Poésie Française: Panorama Critique de Chénier à Baudelaire*, Seghers, 1963.

———*La Poésie Française: Panorama Critique de Rimbaud au Surréalisme*, Seghers, 1953.

A. Hartley, *The Penguin Book of French Verse* Vol. 3: The Nineteenth Century. Vol. 4: The Twentieth Century. Penguin Books, 1957.

> Introduction and prose translations.

P. M. Jones, *Modern French Verse, an Anthology of Poems 1850–1920*, M.U.P. 1954.

> Introduction; annotations.

P. M. Jones and G. Richardson, *A Book of French Verse, Lamartine to Eluard*, O.U.P. 1964.

> Introduction includes notes on evolution of French versification. Annotations.

R. Kanters and M. Nadeau, *Anthologie de la Poésie Française.* Le XIXe Siècle: Vols. 8—10; Le XXe Siècle: Vols. 11—12. E.R., 1967.

> The most extensive anthology available.

H. Lemaître, *La Poésie depuis Baudelaire*, Colin (Collection U) New edition 1966.

> Includes minor poets, especially among Symbolists, not represented in other anthologies.

St John Lucas, *The Oxford Book of French Verse.* Second edition revised and edited by P. Mansell Jones. O.U.P., 1957.

> Pp. 436—492. Brief notes and advice on critical reading.

C. F. MacIntyre, *French Symbolist Poetry*, Univ. of Cal. Press, 1961.

> English verse translations.

E. Marks, *French Poetry from Baudelaire to the Present*, Dell, 1962.

> Introduction and prose translations.

J. Matthews, *Anthology of French Surrealist Poetry*, Univ. of London Press, 1966. (Textes Français Classiques et Modernes).

> Introduction; notes on poets, including full lists of works; substantial bibliography.

P. Seghers, *Le Livre d'Or de la Poésie Française (1940—60)*, 2 vols. Marabout Université, 1969.

> Very full selection of contemporary poetry.

2   General Critical Studies on Modern French Poetry

General histories of literature have not been included in this section.

Anna Balakian, *Literary Origins of Surrealism: a new mysticism in French poetry.* New edn.: N.Y. Univ. Press, 1966.

Anna Balakian, *The Symbolist Movement. A Critical Appraisement*, Random House, 1967.

Suzanne Bernard, *Le poème en prose de Baudelaire jusqu'à nos jours*, Nizet, 1959.

G. Brereton, *Introduction to the French Poets*, Methuen, 1956. (University Paperbacks.)

> The second half of the book, approximately, covers poetry from Baudelaire.

J. Chiari, *Contemporary French Poetry*, M.U.P., 1952.

> From Valéry to Michaux.

Y. Duplessis, *Le Surréalisme*. (Que Sais-Je? No. 432.)

H. S. Gershman, *Surrealist Revolution in France*, Univ. of Mich. Press, 1969.

R. Gibson, *Modern French Poets on Poetry*, C.U.P., 1961.
> An anthology of French poetic theory culled from poets' statements, linked by a critical commentary.

P. M. Jones, *The Background of Modern French Poetry*, C.U.P. 1951.

A. G. Lehmann, *The Symbolist Aesthetic in France 1885–1895*. Second edn.: Blackwell, 1968.

P. Martino, *Parnasse et Symbolisme*. New edn.: Colin 1963 (Collection U).

J. H. Matthews, *An Introduction to Surrealism*, Pennsylvania Univ. Press, 1965.

G. Michaud, *Message Poétique du Symbolisme*, Nizet, 1966.
> With an appendix, *La Doctrine Symboliste*, gathering together the main aesthetic pronouncements of the Symbolist poets.

M. Nadeau, *Histoire du Surréalisme* with *Documents Surréalistes*. New edn.: Seuil, 1964.
> Translated by R. Howard *The History of Surrealism*. Introduction by R. Shattuck. Macmillan, 1965.

A. W. Raitt, *Life and Letters in France*. Vol. 3: The Nineteenth Century, Nelson, 1965.
> Chapters on Baudelaire, Verlaine and Mallarmé outline the literary and intellectual background to Symbolism.

J. Rousselot, *Dictionnaire de la poésie française contemporaine*, Larousse, 1968.
Les nouveaux poètes français, panorama critique, Seghers, 1969.

A. M. Schmidt, *La Littérature Symboliste*, P.U.F. 1947. (Que Sais-Je? No. 82.)

E. Wilson, *Axel's Castle: A Study in the imaginative literature of 1870–1930*. Rep. Collins, 1961.

For further reading

F. Alquié, *Philosophie du Surréalisme*, Flammarion, 1955.
———, *The Philosophy of Surrealism*, tr. by B. Waldrop. Univ. of Mich. Press, 1965.

F. Alquié (ed.), *Entretiens sur le Surréalisme*, Mouton, 1968.

S. L. Bédouin, *Vingt ans de surréalisme 1939–59*, Denoël, 1961.

Y. Belaval, *Dictionnaire Abrégé du Surréalisme*. New edn.: Corti, 1969.

A. E. Carter, *The Idea of Decadence in French Literature 1830–1900*, Univ. of Toronto Press, 1958.

J. Chiari, *Symbolism from Poe to Mallarmé. The Growth of a Myth*, Rockliff, 1956.

K. Cornell, *The Symbolist Movement*, Yale U.P., 1951.

K. Cornell, *The Post Symbolist Period. French Poetic Currents 1900–1920*, Yale U.P., 1958.

M. Décaudin, *La Crise des Valeurs symbolistes. Vingt ans de poésie française*, Privat, Toulouse, 1960.

R. Fiser, *Le Symbole Littéraire : essai sur la signification du symbole chez Wagner, Baudelaire, Mallarmé, Bergson et Proust*, Corti, 1942.

W. Fowlie, *Age of Surrealism*. New edn.: Indiana U.P., 1960.

J. R. Lawler, *The Language of French Symbolism*, 1969.

G. Lemaitre, *From Cubism to Surrealism in French Literature*. New edn.: Russell, 1947.

M. Parent (ed.), *Le Vers Français au XXe Siècle*, Klincksieck, 1967.

M. Sanouillet, *Dada à Paris*. Histoire Générale du Mouvement Dada, T. IV., Pauvert, 1965.

B. Weinberg, *The Limits of Symbolism : Studies of Five Modern French Poets*, Univ. of Chicago Press, 1966.

Early Studies on Symbolism

Remy de Gourmont, *Le Livre des Masques* Vols. I and II, M. de F. 1896, 1898.

Arthur Symons, *The Symbolist Movement in Literature*, Heinemann, 1899. New edn.: Dutton, 1958.

Ezra Pound, *Make it New*, Faber, 1934.

With these works, which are still of great interest, might be read:

Ruth Temple, *The Critics alchemy: a study of the introduction of French Symbolism into England*, Twayne, 1953.

The 'new critics' and modern French poetry

Modern French poetry has provided the subject matter for some of the most interesting studies of the so-called "new critics" in France. One of the main tendencies of *la nouvelle critique* is towards a phenomenological and structural study of the creative imagination, an interest which led many of its practitioners to the field of modern poetry. Raymond's *From Baudelaire to Surrealism*, indeed, is often quoted as being one of the early examples of criticism concerned with deeper patterns in poetry rather than with the external facts of literary history. (This is also true of his collection of essays, *Vérité et Poésie, La Bac*, 1964.) Among other studies of the new criticism some of the most important are noted below.

G. Bachalard, *La Psychanalyse du feu*, Gallimard, 1938, and *Idées*.
    Translated by A. Ross: *Psychoanalysis of Fire*, Beacon Press, Boston: Routledge, 1964.
    Lautréamont, Corti, 1939.
    L'Eau et les Rêves, Corti, 1942.
    L'Air et les Songes, Corti, 1943.
    La Terre et les Rêveries du Repos, Corti, 1948.

La Poétique de l'Espace, P.U.F., 1957.
  Translated by M. Lolas: *Poetics of Space*, Orion Press, 1964.
La Poétique de la Rêverie, P.U.F., 1960.
A. Béguin, *L'Ame Romantique et le Rêve*, Corti, 1946.
M. Blanchot, *Lautréamont et Sade*, Minuit, 1949.
  L'Espace Littéraire, Gallimard, 1955.
C. Mauron, *Introduction à la psychanalyse de Mallarmé*, Payot, 1968.
  Translated by W. McLendon and A. Henderson Jr.: *Introduction to the Psychoanalysis of Mallarmé*, Univ. of Calif. Press: C.U.P., 1963.
  Des Métaphores obsédantes au mythe personnel, Corti, 1963.
G. Poulet, *Etudes sur le Temps Humain*, Plon, 1950. Translated by E. Coleman: *Studies in Human Time*, John Hopkins Press: O.U.P. 1956.
  Etudes sur le Temps Humain II: La Distance Intérieure, Plon, 1952. Translated by E. Coleman: *Interior Distance*, John Hopkins Press: O.U.P. 1959.
  Etudes sur le Temps Humain III: Le Point de Départ, Plon, 1964.
  Etudes sur le Temps Humain IV: Mesure de l'Instant, Plon, 1968.
  Les Métamorphoses du Cercle, Plon, 1961. Translated by C. Dawson and E. Coleman: *The Metamorphoses of the Circle*, John Hopkins Press: O.U.P. 1967.
J. P. Richard, *Poésie et Profondeur*, Seuil, 1955.
  L'Univers Imaginaire de Mallarmé, Seuil, 1961.
  Onze études sur la poésie moderne, Seuil, 1964. (Referred to later as *Onze études*.)
J. P. Sartre, *Baudelaire*, Gallimard, 1947, and *Idées*. Tr. by M. Turnell, New Directions, 1950.

For further information on the new criticism consult:
L. Lesage, *The French New Criticism. An Introduction and a Sampler*, Pennsylvania State Univ. Press, 1967.
G. Poulet, (ed.), *Les Chemins actuels de la critique*, Plon, 1967, and *10 × 18*.
S. Doubrovsky, *Pourquoi la nouvelle critique*, M. de F., 1967.

Reviews and learned journals
Among reviews and learned journals which have devoted special numbers to modern French poetry, the following are of particular interest:
Cahiers de L'Association Internationale
  des Etudes Françaises No. 6 (1954): *Symbolique et Symbolisme.*
  No. 12 (1960): *Impressionisme et Symbolisme dans la Littérature et dans les Arts.*
Comparative Literary Studies Nos. 1, 2 (1967): *The Symbolist Movement.*
L'Esprit Créateur, Vol. 6 (1966): *Surrealist Literature.*
Europe Nos. 475–6 (1968): *Le Surréalisme.*

Revue des Sciences Humaines Nos. 77, 78 (1955): *Autour du Symbolisme*.
Romanic Review XLVI No. 3 (1955): *The Poetics of French Symbolism*.
Yale French Studies No. 9 (1952): *Symbol and Symbolism*; No. 31 (1964):
  Surrealism.

3   Individual Poets

This section deals with the main poets discussed by Raymond. The works of
each writer are given in the following way:
(a) the best collected or critical editions where these exist.
(b) useful inexpensive editions, including volumes of selections. Often
     these will be in one of the series listed under Abbreviations.
(c) translations into English, where they exist.
The main critical works on each writer are then listed, subdivided where
appropriate into introductory studies and works for further reading.

Guillaume Apollinaire

O.C. 4 vols. + 4 vols. of documents, ed. Décaudin, Balland et Lecat, 1966.
O.P. ed. Adéma and Décaudin, *Pléiade*, 1959. (Includes theatre.)
Alcools, Calligrammes and other main vols. in *Poés*; selections in *P.A.* and
  N.C.L. (*Alcools* only).

Translations
Selected Writings of Guillaume Apollinaire (bil.), tr. by R. Shattuck, New
Directions: Harvill Press, 1949; *Alcools* (bil.), tr. by A. Hyde Greet, Univ. of
Calif. Press: C.U.P., 1965; tr. by W. Meredith (bil.), Anchor Doubleday;
Selected Poems tr. by O. Bernard, Penguin.

Critical Studies
P. M. Adéma, *Guillaume Apollinaire le Mal Aimé*, rev. edn. La T.R., 1968.
L. C. Breunig, *Apollinaire*, *C.E.M.W.*, 1969.
R. Couffignal, *Apollinaire*, *E.D.D.*, 1966.
Margaret Davies, *Apollinaire*, Oliver and Boyd, 1963: St Martin's Press,
  1964.
Marie-Jeanne Durry, *Guillaume Apollinaire: Alcools*, 3 vols, S.E.D.E.S., 1956–
  65.
P. Pia, *Apollinaire par lui-même*, Seuil, 1954.
R. Shattuck, *The Banquet Years*, new edn.: Harcourt Brace, 1968: Cape Paper-
  back.
F. Steegmuller, *Apollinaire: Poet among the Painters*, Farrer, Strauss: Hart
  Davis, 1963.

Further Reading

S. Bates, *Guillaume Apollinaire*, Twayne, 1967.

C. Bonnefoy, *Apollinaire, Class XX*, 1969.

R. Couffignal, *L'Inspiration Biblique dans l'Œuvre d'Apollinaire*, Minard, 1966.

M. Décaudin, *Le Dossier d' 'Alcools'*, Minard: Droz, 1965.

Jeanine Moulin, *Guillaume Apollinaire: Textes Inédits*, Droz, 1952.
   (Introduction.)

A. Rouveyre, *Amour et Poésie d'Apollinaire*, Seuil, 1955.

P. Renaud, *Lecture d'Apollinaire*, L'Age d'Homme, Geneva, 1969.

The *Revue des Lettres Modernes* (Minard, 1961–) publishes an Apollinaire number annually. There is also an Apollinaire series, appearing irregularly, in the *Archives des Lettres Modernes* (Minard).

Louis Aragon

No collected edition. Main works: *Le Roman Inachevé* in *Poés*; *Les Yeux d'Elsa* and *La Diane Française* in Seghers paperback. See also: *Le Crève-Coeur* (1941); *Le Nouveau Crève-Coeur* (1948); *Le Fou d'Elsa* (1963).
Selections in *P.A.* and *Poésies, anthologie 1917–60*, C.M.L., 1960.

Critical Studies

R. Garaudy, *L'Itinéraire d'Aragon*, Gallimard, 1961.

H. Juin, *Aragon, B.I.*

C. Haroche, *L'Idée de l'amour dans le 'Fou d'Elsa'*, Gallimard, 1966.

G. Raillard, *Aragon, Class. XX*, 1964.

H. Sur, *Aragon, le réalisme de l'amour*, le Centurion, 1966.

See also: *Aragon parle avec Dominique Arban*, Seghers, 1968.
        Entretiens avec Francis Crémieux, Gallimard, 1964.

Jacques Audiberti

Main volumes: *Race des Hommes* in *Poés*; *Rempart* (1953); *Ange aux entrailles* (1964).
See also: *Entretiens avec G. Charbonnier*, Gallimard, 1965.

Critical Studies

A. Deslandes, *Audiberti, B.I.*, 1964.

M. Giroud, *Audiberti, Class XX*, 1967.

Charles Baudelaire

Main editions:

O.C. 19 vols., ed. Crépet, Conard, 1920–53.

O.C. 2 vols., *C.M.L.*, 1955.

Œuvres, ed. Pichois, *Pléiade*, 1966.

Les Fleurs du Mal, ed. Crépet and Blin, Corti, 1942, new edn.: Corti, 1966.

Good smaller editions: *Les Fleurs du Mal* ed. Adam, *Cl. Garnier*; ed. Lemaître, *G.F.*; ed. Starkie, Blackwell. *Petits Poèmes en Prose* ed. Lemaître, *Cl. Garnier*; ed. Kopp, Corti, 1969; ed. Zimmerman, M.U.P. 1968.

Other editions in *Cluny, Poche*, etc. Selections in *P.A., C.L., S.L.P.*

Translations. Among others, see:

Flowers of Evil (bil.) tr. by F. Duke, Univ. Press of Virginia, 1961; tr. by Marthiel and Jackson Mathews, rev. edn.: New Directions, 1962 (bil.); tr. by W. Fowlie, Bantam, 1964 (bil.). *Selected Verse* (bil.) tr. by F. Scarfe, Penguin, 1961. *Poems of Baudelaire*, tr. by R. Campbell, Harvill Press, 1952. *Twenty prose poems*, tr. by M. Hamburger, Cape, 1968.

Critical Studies.

L. J. Austin, *L'Univers Poétique de Baudelaire*, M. de F., 1951.

C. Borgal, *Baudelaire, Class XX*, 1967.

Alison Fairlie, *Baudelaire: 'Les Fleurs du Mal'*, Arnold, 1960.

P. M. Jones, *Baudelaire*, Bowes and Bowes, 1952.

H. Peyre, *Connaissance de Baudelaire*, Corti, 1951. (ed.) *Baudelaire*, Twentieth Century Views, Prentice Hall, 1962.

J. Prévost, *Baudelaire*, M. de F., 1956.

M. Ruff, *Baudelaire, C. Lett.*, new edn. 1966.

J. P. Richard, *Poésie et Profondeur*, Seuil, 1955.

Enid Starkie, *Baudelaire*, Faber, 1957.

M. Turnell, *Baudelaire*, Hamilton, 1953.

R. Vivier, *L'Originalité de Baudelaire*, new edn.: Palais des Académies, Brussels, 1965.

Further Reading.

L. Bopp, *Psychologie des 'Fleurs du Mal'*, 4 vols., Droz: Minard, 1964–9.

R. B. Chérix, *Commentaire des 'Fleurs du Mal'*, Droz: Minard, 1962.

A. Ferran, *L'Esthétique de Baudelaire*, Hachette, 1933.

J. D. Hubert, *L'Esthétique des 'Fleurs du Mal'*, Cailler, 1953.

D. J. Mossop, *Baudelaire's Tragic Hero*, O.U.P., 1961.

J. Pommier, *La Mystique de Baudelaire*, Slatkine Reprints, 1967.

André Breton

Poèmes, Gallimard, 1949.

Clair de Terre and *Signe Ascendant* in *Poés.* contain most of poems in above edition. Selections in *P.A.*

See also: *Manifestes du surréalisme, Idées; Entretiens (1913–1952) avec A. Parinaud*, new edn.: Gallimard, 1969; and three early Surrealist texts, recently republished: *Les Champs Magnétiques* (with Soupault), Gallimard, 1967, *Ralentir Travaux* (with Eluard), Corti, 1968, *L'Immaculée Conception* (with Eluard), Seghers, 1961.

Critical Studies

C. Browder, *André Breton, arbiter of Surrealism*, Droz, 1967.

M. Carrouges, *André Breton et les données fondamentales du Surréalisme, Idées*, 1967.

C. Duits, *André Breton a-t-il dit passe?* Denoël, 1969.

M. Eigeldinger (ed.), *André Breton: Essais et Témoignages*, La Bac, 1950.

J. Gracq, *André Breton: Quelques Aspects de l'Ecrivain*, Corti, 1948.

J. Matthews, *André Breton, C.E.M.W.*, 1967.

Blaise Cendrars

O.C. Denoël, 1963, *C.F.L.*, 1968.
Du Monde Entier au Cœur du Monde, Poésies Complètes 1912–29, 2 vols. in *Poés*. Selections in *P.A.*

Translations
Selected Writings (bil.), tr. by W. Albert, New Directions.

Critical Studies
J.C. Lovey, *Situation de Blaise Cendrars*, La Bac, 1965.
L. Parrot, Introduction to *P.A.*
J. Rousselot, *Blaise Cendrars, Class XX*, 1955.
See also: *Dites-nous, Monsieur Blaise Cendrars, réponse aux enquêtes littéraires 1919–57*, ed. H. Richard, E.R.

René Char

No collected edition. *Fureur et Mystère* and *Les Matinaux suivi de la Parole en Archipel* in *Poés*. See also: *Le Marteau sans maître*, new edn.: Corti, 1963; *L'Age Cassant*, Corti, 1966; *Retour Amont*, Gallimard, 1966.
Important anthologies: *Poèmes et Proses choisis*, Gallimard, 1957; *Commune Présence*, Gallimard, 1964. Selections also in *P.A.*

Translations
Hypnos Waking: poems and prose (bil.), tr. by Jackson Mathews, W. Carlos Williams et al., Random House, 1956.

Critical Studies

P. Guerre, Introduction to *P.A.*, 1961.

Virginia La Charité, *The Poetics and the Poetry of René Char*. Univ. of North Carolina Press, 1968.

R. Ménard, *La condition poétique: cinq essais pour interpréter Char*, Gallimard, 1959.

G. Mounin, *Avez-vous lu Char?* Rep. in *La Communication Poétique*, Gallimard, 1969.

Greta Rau, *Char on la Poésie accrue*, Corti, 1957.

J. P. Richard, *Onze études*.

See also: P. A. Benoit, *Bibliographie des œuvres de René Char de 1928 à 1963*, Minard, 1964.

Paul Claudel

O.P. ed. S. Fumet, *Pléiade*, 1957.

Cinq Grandes Odes and *Poèmes en Prose* in *Poés*. Selections in *P.A.*; *Morceaux Choisis*, Gallimard, 1956.

See also: *Réflexions sur la Poésie, Idées*; *Mémoires Improvisés, Idées*; *Journal*, 2 vols., *Pléiade*, 1968.

Translations

Five great Odes, tr. by E. Lucie-Smith, Rapp and Carroll, 1967.

Critical Studies

G. Antoine, *Les 'Cinq Grandes Odes' de Claudel*, Minard, 1959.

L. Barjon, *P. Claudel, Class XX*, 1953.

L. Chaigne, *Vie de Paul Claudel et genèse de son œuvre*, Maine, Tours, 1961.

W. Fowlie, *P. Claudel*, Bowes and Bowes, 1957.

S. Fumet, *Claudel, P.B.I.*, 1968.

H. Guillemin, *Claudel et son art d'écrire*, Gallimard, 1955.

P. Lesort, *Paul Claudel par lui-même*, Seuil, 1966.

A. Mavrocordato, *L'Ode de Paul Claudel*, Droz, 1955.

R. Griffiths (ed.), *Claudel, a reappraisal*, Rapp and Whiting, 1968.

Further reading

G. Cattaui and J. Madaule (eds.), *Entretiens sur Paul Claudel*, Mouton, 1969.

M.-F. Guyard, *Recherches claudéliennes, autour des 'Cinq Grandes Odes'*, Klincksieck, 1963.

J. Madaule, *Claudel et le langage*, D. de B., 1968.

F. Varillon, Claudel, *E.D.D.*, 1967.

The *Cahiers Paul Claudel*, Gallimard, appearing at irregular intervals, have published some important studies.

Jean Cocteau

O.C. Marguerat, Lausanne, 1948–51. (Poetry: Tomes III and IV); *Poésies 1916–23*, N.R.F., 1924.

Le Cap de Bonne Espérance suivi de Discours du Grand Sommeil in *Poés*; *Opéra suivi de Plain-Chant* in *Poche*. Selections in *P.A.*; *Poèmes 1916–55*, Gallimard, 1955.

See also: *La difficulté d'être, 10 × 18*; *Entretiens avec André Fraigneau, 10 × 18*.

Critical Studies

C. Borgal, *Cocteau, Dieu, la mort, la poésie*, Le Centurion, 1968.

F. Brown, *Impersonation of Angels, a biography of Cocteau.*

J.-J. Kihm, *Cocteau, B.I.*, 1960.

R. Lannes, Introduction to *P.A.*

J.-M. Magnan, *Cocteau, E.D.D.*, 1968.

G. Mourgne, *Cocteau, Class XX*, 1965.

Elizabeth Sprigge and J. J. Kihm, *Jean Cocteau, the Man and the Mirror*, Gollancz, 1968. (There is a similar French edition, T.R., 1968.)

Tristan Corbière

Les Amours Jaunes, with posthumous poems and prose, ed. Y.-G. Le Dantec, Gallimard, 1953.

Other editions in *Poés.* and *Poche-Club*. Selections in *P.A.*

Translations

Selections from Les Amours Jaunes (bil.) tr. by C. F. MacIntyre, Univ. of Calif. Press: C.U.P., 1954.

Critical Studies.

J. Rousselot, Introduction to *P.A.*, 1951.

C. Angelet, *La poétique de Tristan Corbière*, Palais des Académies, Brussels, 1961

A. Sonnenfeld, *L'Œuvre poétique de Tristan Corbière*, P.U.F., 1960.

Robert Desnos

Most of his work is collected in *Corps et Biens* and *Fortune* in *Poés*. Selections in *P.A.*, *Choix de Poèmes*, Minuit, 1946.

Critical Studies

P. Berger, Introduction to *P.A.*, 1949.

Rosa Bachide, *L'évolution poétique de Robert Desnos*, Palais des Académies, Brussels, 1956.

Paul Eluard

O.C. 2 vols. ed. Marcelle Dumas and L. Scheler, *Pléiade*, 1968.

*Capitale de la Douleur suivi de L'Amour, la poésie; La Vie immédiate suivi de
    La Rose Publique, Les Yeux Fertiles*; and *Poésie Ininterrompue* all in *Poés.
    Derniers Poèmes d'Amour* in Seghers paperback.

Selections in *P.A., Choix de Poèmes*, Gallimard 1951.

Translations.

Selected Writings tr. by L. Alexander, New Directions, 1951: Routledge
    1952.

Le dur désir de durer tr. by S. Spender and F. Cornford, Trianon Press,
    1950.

Critical Studies.

M. Carrouges, *Eluard et Claudel*, Seuil, 1945.

L. Decaunes, *Paul Eluard, biographie pour une approche*, Ed. Subervie, Rodez,
    1964.

P. Emmanuel, *Le Je universel chez Paul Eluard*, G.L.M. 1948.

R. Jean, *Paul Eluard par lui-même*, Seuil, 1968.

L. Perche, *Eluard, Class XX*, 1964.

J. P. Richard, *Onze Etudes*.

Further Reading.

Ursula Jucker-Wehrli, *La poésie de Paul Eluard et le thème de la pureté*, Juris-
    Verlag, Zürich, 1965.

A. Kittang, *D'amour de poésie, essai sur l'univers des métamorphoses dans l'œuvre
    surréaliste de Paul Eluard*, Minard, 1969.

Maryvonne Meuraud, *L'image végétale dans la poésie d'Eluard*, Minard, 1966.

Léon-Paul Fargue

No collected edition. *Poésies* in *Poés.* represent his best known work. See
also: *Espaces* (1928); *Sous la Lampe* (1929); *Haute Solitude* (1941).
Selections in *P.A.*

Critical Studies

Claudine Chonez, Introduction to *P.A.*, 1950.

E. de la Rochefoucauld, *Fargue, Class XX*, 1959.

Max Jacob

No collected edition. Main works: *Le Cornet à Dés* in *Poés; Le Cornet a Dés II*,
    Gallimard, 1955; *La Défense de Tartuffe*, new edn.: Gallimard 1964; *Le
    Laboratoire Central*, new edn.: Gallimard, 1960.

Selections in *P.A.* See also *Max Jacob, Lettres 1920—41*, ed. S. J. Collier, Blackwell, 1966.

Translations
Drawings and Poems, tr. by S. J. Collier, Lotus Press, Hull, 1951.

Critical Studies
A. Billy, Introduction to *P.A.*, 1946.
R. G. Cadou, *Esthétique de Max Jacob*, Seghers, 1956.

Alfred Jarry

O.P.C. Gallimard, 1945.
See also *Tout Ubu, Poche*. Selections in *P.A.*, *Choix de Textes*, Nizet, 1946.

Translations
Selected Works tr. by R. Shattuck and S. W. Taylor, Methuen, Cape Paper; Grove, 1965.

Critical Studies
A. Lebois, *Alfred Jarry l'Irremplaçable*, le Cercle du Livre, 1950.
J. H. Levesque, Introduction to *P.A.*
L. Perche, *Alfred Jarry, Class XX*, 1965.
R. Shattuck, *The Banquet Years*, Harcourt Brace, 1968: Cape Paperback.

Pierre Jean Jouve

Poésies I—XI (4 vols.). M. de F., 1962—68.
Les Noces suivi de Sueur de Sang in *Poés*. Selections in *P.A.*

Translations
An idiom of night, tr. by K. Bosley, Rapp and Whiting, 1968.

Critical Studies
Margaret Callendar, *The Poetry of Pierre-Jean Jouve*, M.U.P., 1965.
R. Micha, Introduction to *P.A.*
Starobinski, Alexandre, Eigeldinger, *Pierre-Jean Jouve*, La Bac., 1946.

Jules Laforgue

O.C., vols 1—2, 4—6, ed. G. Jean-Aubry, Mercure de France 1930 — Still incomplete. The poetry is in vols. 1—2.
Derniers Vers ed. M. Collie and J. M. L'Heureux, Univ. of Toronto Press, 1965.
Poésies Complètes in *Poche* and *Poche-Club*. Selections in *P.A.*, *Cluny, N.C.L.*

Translations
Selected Writings, tr. by W. J. Smith, Grove: Calder, 1956.
Poems (bil.) tr. by Patricia Terry, Univ. of Calif. Press, 1958: C.U.P.

Critical Studies
M. Collie, *Laforgue, W. and C.*, 1963.
Marie-Jeanne Durry, Introduction to *P.A.*
L. Guichard, *Jules Laforgue et ses poésies*, P.U.F., 1950.
P. Reboul, *Laforgue, C. Lett.*, 1960.
F. Ruchon, *Jules Laforgue: Sa Vie, Son Œuvre*, Ciana, Geneva, 1924.
W. Ramsay, *Jules Laforgue and the Ironic Inheritance*, O.U.P., 1953.
   (ed.), *Jules Laforgue: essays on a poet's life and work*, Ill. U.P., 1969.

Valéry Larbaud

Œuvres ed. G. Jean-Aubry et R. Mallet, *Pléiade* 1957. Selections in *P.A.*
Les Poésies de A.O. Barnabooth in *Poés.*

Translations
Poems of a multimillionaire, tr. by W. J. Smith, Bonacio and Savil, 1955.

Critical Studies
B. Delvaille, Introduction to *P.A.*
N. R. F. Special No. Sept. 1957: *Hommage à Valery Larbaud*.
Frida Weissman, *L'Exotisme de Valery Larbaud, Nizet, 1966*.

Patrice de la Tour du Pin

Main work collected in *Une Somme de Poésie*, 3 vols., Gallimard, 1947–63.
La Quête de Joie suivie de Petite Somme de Poésie in *Poés.* Selections in *P.A.*

Translations
The dedicated life in poetry (*Une somme de poésie*) tr. by G. S. Fraser, Harvill Press, 1948.

Critical Studies
Eva Kushner, Introduction to *P.A.*

Lautréamont

O.C., Corti, 1961, also in *G.F.* and *Poche*.
Les Chants de Maldoror in *Poche-Club*. Selections in *P.A.*
See also: *Poésies* édition commentée par G. Goldfayn et G. Legrand, Le Terrain Vague, 1960.

Translations
Maldoror, tr. by G. Wernham, New Directions, 1965.

Critical Studies
G. Bachelard, *Lautréamont*, new edn.: Corti, 1956.
M. Blanchot, *Lautréamont et Sade*, new edn.: Minuit, 1963, and *10 × 18*.
M. Jean et A. Mezei, *Les chants de Maldoror: essai sur Lautréamont et son œuvre*, Ed. du Pavois, 1947.
M. Pleynet, *Lautréamont par lui-même*, Seuil, 1967.
L. Pierre-Quint, *Le comte de Lautréamont et Dieu*, new edn.: Fasquelle, 1967.
Ph. Soupault, Introduction to *P.A.*
P. Zweig, *Lautréamont ou les Violences du Narcisse*, Minard, 1967.

Maurice Maeterlinck

Poésies Complètes, la Renaissance du Livre, Brussels, 1965.
Selections in *P.A.*

Critical Studies
J.-M. Andrieu, *Maurice Maeterlinck, Class XX*, 1962.
R. Bodart, Introduction to *P.A.*
W. D. Halls, *Maurice Maeterlinck, a study of his life and thought*, Clarendon P., 1960.
J. Hanse, R. Vivier (ed.), *Maurice Maeterlinck 1862–1962*, la Renaissance du Livre, Brussels, 1963.

Stéphane Mallarmé

O.C. ed. H. Mondor and G. Jean-Aubry, *Pléiade*, 1945.
Poésies in *Poés*; *Vers et prose* in *10 × 18*. Selections in *N.C.L.*, *C.V.*
See also *Correspondance*, 3 vols., ed. H. Mondor and L. J. Austin, Gallimard, 1959–68.

Translations
Selected poems (bil.) tr. by C. F. MacIntyre, Univ. of Calif. Press, 1957: C.U.P.
Poems (bil.) tr. by Roger Fry, New Directions, 1951: Vision Press, 1952.
Selected prose poems tr. by B. Cooke, Johns Hopkins Press: O.U.P., 1956.
Poems tr. by A. Hartly, Penguin, 1965.
Dice Thrown Never Will Annul Chance tr. by B. Coffey, O.U.P., 1965.

Critical Studies
G. Davies, *Mallarmé et le drame solaire*, Corti, 1959.
G. Michaud, *Mallarmé, C. Lett.*, 4th edn.: 1963.
C. Mauron, *Mallarmé par lui-même*, Seuil, 1964.

H. Mondor, *Vie de Mallarmé*, Gallimard, 1941.

E. Noulet, *L'Œuvre poétique de Stéphane Mallarmé*, Droz, 1940.

   Vingt poèmes de Stéphane Mallarmé, Droz: Minard, 1967.

J. P. Richard, *L'univers imaginaire de Mallarmé*, Seuil, 1961.

A. Thibaudet, *La Poésie de Stéphane Mallarmé*, rep. Gallimard, 1960.

P. O. Walzer, *Essai sur Mallarmé*, Seghers, 1963.

Further reading

Suzanne Bernard, *Mallarmé et la musique*, Nizet, 1959.

L. Cellier, *Mallarmé et la morte qui parle*, Univ. de Grenoble, 1959.

C. Chadwick, *Mallarmé, sa pensée dans sa poésie*, Corti, 1962.

C. Chassé, *Les Clefs de Mallarmé*, Aubier, 1954.

A. R. Chisholm, *Mallarmé's Grand Œuvre*, M.U.P., 1962.

R. G. Cohn, *Toward the poems of Mallarmé*, Univ. of Calif. Press: C.U.P., 1965.

G. Delfel, *L'Esthétique de Stéphane Mallarmé*, Flammarion, 1951.

C. Mauron, *Introduction à la psychanalyse de Mallarmé*, new edn.: Payot, 1968.

H. Mondor, *Autres précisions sur Mallarmé*, Gallimard, 1961.

Henri Michaux

No collected edition. *L'Espace du dedans* (rev. edn.: Gallimard, 1966) contains a full selection of his work.

See also *Epreuves, Exorcismes*, 1946; *La Vie dans les Plis*, 1949. *Passages*, 1963. Further selections in *P.A.*

Translations

Barbarian in Asia tr. by Sylvia Beach, New Directions, 1949.

L'Espace du Dedans tr. by R. Ellmann, New Directions, 1951.

Light through Darkness, tr. by H. Chevalier, Orion Press: Bodley Head, 1964.

Selected writing (bil.) tr. by R. Ellmann, New Directions, 1968.

Critical Studies

R. Bellour, *Henri Michaux ou une mesure de l'être*, Gallimard, 1965.

R. Bertelé, Introduction to *P.A.*, new edn.: 1965.

R. Bréchon, *Henri Michaux*, P.B.I., 1969.

A. Gide, *Découvrons Henri Michaux*, Gallimard, 1941.

N. Murat, *Henri Michaux, Class XX*, 1967.

R. Bellow (ed.), Les Cahiers de l'Herne, no. 8, *Henri Michaux*.

Oscar-Venceslas de Lubica-Milosz

O.C., 11 vols., ed. J. Buge, A. Silvaire, 1960–63.

Selection in *Choix de textes*, Silvaire, 1965.

Translations
14 Poems, tr. by K. Rexroth, Peregrine Press, San Francisco, 1952.

Critical Studies
A. Godoy, *Milosz le poète de l'amour*, Silvaire, 1960.
A. Lebois, *L'œuvre de Milosz*, Denoël, 1960.
A. Richter, *Milosz, Class XX*, 1965.

Charles Péguy

O.P.C. ed. M. and P. Péguy, *Pléiade*, 1961.
Les Tapisseries in *Poés*. Selections in *P.A., C.L., C.V.*

Critical Studies
A. Chabanon, *La Poétique de Charles Péguy*, Laffont, 1947.
B. Guyon, *L'Art de Péguy*, Labergerie, 1948.
       Péguy, C. Lett., 1960.
       Péguy, E.D.D., 1968.
J. Roussel, *Péguy, Class XX*, 1963.
The *Cahiers de l'amitié Charles Péguy*, 1952 have published a number of
    substantial studies.

Saint-John Perse

O.P. 2 vols., Gallimard, 1960.
Eloges suivi de la Gloire des Rois, Anabase, Exil; and *Vents suivi de Chronique*
    in *Poés*. Selections in *P.A.*

Translations
Anabasis (bil.) tr. by T. S. Eliot, rev. edn.: Harcourt, 1949; Faber, 1959.
Exile and other poems (bil.) tr. by D. Devlin, second edn.: Princeton U.P.:
    O.U.P. 1954.
Eloges and other poems (bil.) tr. by Louise Varèse, Princeton U.P.: O.U.P., 1956.
Seamarks (bil.) tr. by W. Fowlie, Princeton U.P.; O.U.P., 1958.
Winds (bil.) tr. by H. Chisholm, second edn.: Princeton U.P.; O.U.P., 1962.
Birds (bil.) tr. by R. Fitzgerald, Princeton U.P.; O.U.P., 1966.

Critical Studies
A. Bosquet, Introduction to *P.A.*, new edn.: 1967.
R. Caillois, *Poétique de Saint-John Perse*, M. de F., 1952.
J. Charpier, *Saint-John Perse, B.I.*, 1962.
A. Knodel, *Saint-John Perse, a study of his poetry*, Edin. U.P., 1966.
R. Garaudy, *D'un réalisme sans rivages*, Plon, 1963.
A. Henry, *'Amers' de Saint-John Perse*, La Bac. 1963.

C. Murciaux, *Saint-John Perse, Class XX*, 1961.

Monique Parent, *Saint-John Perse et quelques devanciers, études sur le poème en prose*, Klincksieck, 1960.

J. P. Richard, *Onze études*.

Jacques Prévert

Most of his work is contained in *Paroles* (1947), *Spectacle* (1951), *La Pluie et le Beau Temps* (1953), *Histoire et d'autres Histoires* (1963), all available in *Poche*.

Translation
Selection from 'Paroles' tr. by L. Ferlinghetti, City Lights, San Francisco, 1958: Penguin, 1958.

Critical Studies.
J. Quéval, *Jacques Prévert*, M. de F., 1955.

Pierre Reverdy

Most of his work is collected in *Plupart du Temps*, new edn.; Flammarion, 1967; and *Main d'Œuvre*, M. de F., 1949.
Plupart du Temps also in *Poés.*, 2 vols. Selections in *P.A.*

Translations
Poems tr. by Anne H. Greet, Unicorn Press, 1968.

Critical Studies
R. W. Greene, *The Poetic Theory of Pierre Reverdy*, Univ. of Calif. Press, 1967.
M. Guiney, *La poésie de Pierre Reverdy*, Georg, Geneva, 1966.
G. Picon, *Poétique et poésie de Pierre Reverdy* in *L'Usage de la Lecture 1*, M. de F., 1960.
J. P. Richard, *Onze études*.
J. Rousselot, Introduction to *P.A.*

Arthur Rimbaud

O.C. ed. R. de Renéville and J. Mouquet, *Pléiade*, 1963. *Œuvres*, ed. Suzanne Bernard, *Cl. Garnier*, 1961.
Other useful editions: *Poésies* (1939), *Une Saison en Enfer* (1941), *Illuminations* (1949) all ed. by Bouillane de Lacoste, M. de F.; *Œuvres* ed. by A. Adam, *C.L.M.*, 1957, *Illuminations* ed. A. Py, Droz: Minard, 1967.
Paperback editions of complete poetry in *Cluny*, *G.F.*, *Poche*. Selections in *P.A.*, *C.L.*, *C.V.*

Translations

Complete Works, Selected Letters (bil.) tr. by W. Fowlie, Univ. of Chicago Press, 1966.

A Season in Hell, tr. by T. Cameron, Lehmann, 1950: MacDonald and Co., 1951.

The Drunken Boat (36 poems) tr. by B. Hill, Hart Davis, 1952.

Selected Verse (bil.) tr. by O. Bernard, Penguin.

Critical Studies

Y. Bonnefoy, *Rimbaud par lui-même,* Seuil, 1961.

R. Etiemble and Y. Gauclère, *Rimbaud,* third edn.; Gallimard,1 1966.

W. M. Frohock, *Rimbaud's Poetic Practice,* Harvard U.P.; O.U.P., 1963.

C. A. Hackett, *Rimbaud,* Bowes and Bowes, 1957.
    Rimbaud l'enfant, Corti, 1948.

H. Matarasso and P. Petitfils, *Vie d'Arthur Rimbaud,* Hachette, 1962.

R. Montale, Rimbaud, *Class XX,* 1967.

E. Noulet, *Le premier visage de Rimbaud,* Palais des Académies, Brussels, 1953.

P. Petitfils, *L'Œuvre et le visage de Rimbaud,* Nizet, 1949.

J. P. Richard, *Poésie et profondeur,* Seuil, 1955.

M. A. Ruff, *Rimbaud, C. Lett.,* 1968.

J. Rivière, *Rimbaud,* Kra, 1930.

E. Starkie, *A. Rimbaud,* new edn.; Faber, 1961.

Further reading

C. Chadwick, *Etudes sur Rimbaud,* Nizet, 1960.

C. A. Hackett, *Autour de Rimbaud,* Klincksieck, 1967.

R. Etièmble, *Le Mythe de Rimbaud,* 3 vols., Gallimard, 1952–61.
    Le 'sonnet des voyelles', Gallimard, 1968.

W. Fowlie, *Rimbaud,* Univ. of Chicago Press, 1965.

J. Houston, *The design of Rimbaud's poetry,* Yale U.P., 1963.

Jules Romains

No collected edition. Main volumes *La Vie Ûnanime* (1908); *Odes et Prières* (1913); *L'Homme Blanc* (1936); *Pierres Levées* (1948).
Selections in *P.A.; Choix de Poèmes,* Gallimard, 1948.

Critical Studies

A. Figueras, Introduction to *P.A.,* new edn., 1964.

A. Cuisinier, *Jules Romains et l'unanimisme,* new edn.: Flammarion, 1968.

Madeleine Berry, *J. Romains, Class XX,* 1959.

Jules Supervielle

No collected edition. *Gravitations précédé de Débarcadères*; and *Le Forçat Innocent suivi de Les Amis Inconnus* in *Poés*. See also *La Fable du Monde* (1938), *Oublieuse Mémoire* (1949), *Le Corps Tragique* (1959).
Selections in *P.A.* and *Choix de poèmes*, Gallimard, 1947.

Translations
Selected Writings (bil.), New Directions, 1967.

Critical Studies
Dorothy S. Blair, *Jules Supervielle, a modern fabulist*, Blackwell, 1960.
R. Etiemble, *Supervielle*, *P.B.I.*, 1968.
Tatiana W. Greene, *Jules Supervielle*, Droz, 1958.
J. A. Hiddleston, *L'Univers de Jules Supervielle*, Corti, 1965.

Tristan Tzara

No collected edition. Main works: *L'Homme Approximatif* in *Poés.*; *La deuxième aventure céleste de Monsieur Antipyrine* (1938); *De Mémoire d'Homme* (1949).
See also: *Lampisteries précédées des Sept Manifestes Dada*, Pauvert, 1963.
Selections in *P.A.*; *Morceaux Choisis*, Bordas, 1947.

Critical Studies
R. Lacôte, Introduction to *P.A.*, 1961.

Paul Valéry

Œuvres, Vol. I (*Poésies*) ed. J. Hytier, *Pléiade*, 1957.
Poésies (*Album de vers anciens*, *Charmes*, etc.) in *Poés.*; *Charmes* in *N.C.L.*
Selections in *P.A.*, *C.V.*
See also: *La Jeune Parque*, ed. O. Nadal, C.M.L., 1957.

Translations
The Collected Works of Paul Valéry, 9 vols., ed. Jackson Mathews, Princeton U.P. 1958—
Selected Writings, New Directions, 1950: Peter Owen 1951.

Critical Studies.
M. Bémol, *Paul Valéry*, Les Belles Lettres, 1949.
A. Berne-Joffroy, *Valéry*, *B.I.*
G. Cohen, *Essai d'explication du 'Cimetière Marin'*, Gallimard, 1946.
H. Grubbs, *P. Valéry*, Twayne, 1968.

J. Hytier, *La poétique de Valéry*, Colin, 1954.
J. R. Lawler, *Lecture de Valéry, une étude de 'Charmes'*, P.U.F., 1963.
E. Noulet, *P. Valéry*, La Renaissance du Livre, 1950.
Edmée de la Rochefoucauld, *Valéry, Class XX*, 1954.
F. Scarfe, *The Art of Paul Valéry*, Heinemann, 1954.
Elizabeth Sewell, *Paul Valéry, the mind in the mirror*, Bowes and Bowes, 1952.
A. W. Thomson, *Valéry, W. and C.*, 1965.
P.O. Walzer, *La poésie de Valéry*, Cailler, 1953.

Further Reading
P. Guiraud, *Langage et Versification d'après l'œuvre de Paul Valéry*, Klincksieck, 1953.
W. N. Ince, *The Poetic Theory of Paul Valéry*, Leicester U.P., 1961
L'Esprit Créateur, Vol. 4. No. I (1964): *Valéry*.
E. Noulet (ed.), *Entretiens sur Paul Valéry*, Mouton, 1968

Emile Verhaeren

No collected edition. Main volumes: *Les Campagnes Hallucinées* (1893), *Les Villes Tentaculaires* (1895), *Les Forces Tumultueuses* (1902), *La Multiple Splendeur* (1906).
Selections in *P.A.*, *N.C.L.*

Critical Studies
L. Christophe, *Verhaeren, Class XX*, 1955.
F. Hellens, Introduction to *P.A.*
P. Mansell Jones, *Verhaeren*, Bowes and Bowes, 1957.

Paul Verlaine

O.P.C. ed. Y. G. Le Dantec, *Pléiade*, revised edn. by J. Borel, 1965.
O.C. ed. H. de Bouillane de Lacoste and J. Borel, *C.M.L.*, 1959.

Useful editions
O.P. ed. J. Robichez, *Cl. Garnier*, 1969; *Fêtes Galantes, La Bonne Chanson, Romances sans Paroles*, ed. V. P. Underwood, M.U.P., 1963; *Sagesse* ed. V. P. Underwood, Zwemmer, 1944; *Sagesse* ed. L. Morice, 1948.
Numerous vols. in *Cluny* and *Poche*. Selections in *P.A., C.L., C.V., S.L.B.* and *Selected Poems*, ed. R. C. D. Perman, O.U.P., 1965.

Translations
Selected Poems (bil.) tr. by C. F. MacIntyre, Univ. of Calif. P.: C.U.P., 1949.
Forty poems tr. by R. Gant and C. Apcher, Falcon Press, 1948.
The Sky above the Roof: 56 poems tr. by B. Hill, Hart Davis: Collier, 1962.

Critical Studies

A. Adam, *Verlaine*, C.Lett., new edn., 1966.

J. H. Bornecque, *Etudes Verlainiennes I: les Poèmes Saturniens; II: Lumières sur les Fêtes Galantes*, Nizet, 1952—1959.

   Verlaine par lui-même, Seuil, 1966.

P. Martino, *Verlaine*, new edn.: Boivin, 1951.

O. Nadal, *Verlaine*, M. de F., 1961.

J. P. Richard, *Poésie et profondeur*. Seuil, 1955.

J. Richer, Introduction to *P.A.*, new edn., 1960.

Further Reading.

C. Cuénot, *Le style de Paul Verlaine*, Centre de Documentation Universitaire, 1963

V. P. Underwood, *Verlaine et l'Angleterre*, Nizet, 1956.

G. Zayed, *La Formation Littéraire de Verlaine*, Droz: Minard, 1962.

Eléonore M. Zimmermann, *Magies de Verlaine*, Corti, 1967.

Charles Vildrac

Main works: *Le Livre d'amour suivi des Premiers Vers*, Seghers, 1959; *Chants du Désespéré* (1920). Selections in *P.A.*

Critical Studies

G. Bouquet and P. Menanteau, Introduction to *P.A.*

M. Bidal, *Les écrivains de l'Abbaye*, Boivin, 1938.

Index of names